JULIAN BELL

JULIAN BELL

From Bloomsbury to the Spanish Civil War

Peter Stansky and

William Abrahams

Stanford University Press
Stanford, California

© 2012 Peter Stansky. All rights reserved.

Excerpts from *The Letters of Virginia Woolf, I: 1888–1912; II: 1912–1922; III: 1923–1928; IV: 1929–1931; V: 1932–1935; VI: 1936–1941*, copyright © 1975, 1976, 1978, 1979, 1980 by Quentin Bell and Angelica Garnett, reprinted by permission of Houghton Mifflin Harcourt Publishing Company. Excerpt from *The Diary of Virginia Woolf, I: 1915–1919; II: 1920–1924; III: 1925–1930, IV: 1931–1935, V: 1936–1941*, copyright © 1977, 1978, 1980, 1982, 1984 by Quentin Bell and Angelica Garnett, reprinted by permission of Houghton Mifflin Harcourt Publishing Company.

No part of this book may be reproduced or transmitted in any form or by any means, electronic or mechanical, including photocopying and recording, or in any information storage or retrieval system without the prior written permission of Stanford University Press.

Printed in the United States of America on acid-free, archival-quality paper

Library of Congress Cataloging-in-Publication Data

Stansky, Peter, author.
 Julian Bell : from Bloomsbury to the Spanish Civil War / Peter Stansky and William Abrahams.
     pages cm.
  Includes bibliographical references and index.
  ISBN 978-0-8047-7413-0 (cloth : alk. paper)
  1. Bell, Julian, 1908–1937. 2. Poets, English—20th century—Biography. 3. Bloomsbury group. I. Abrahams, William Miller, author. II. Title.
 PR6003.E434Z855 2012
 821'.912—dc22
                                                                          2011008958

Typeset at Stanford University Press in 10.5/15 Adobe Garamond

CONTENTS

Preface vii

1 *A Bloomsbury Childhood* 1
2 *A Young Apostle* 45
3 *Searching* 117
4 *China* 181
5 *Spain* 254

Notes 289

Acknowledgments and Credits 303

Index 307

ILLUSTRATIONS

Julian and Vanessa, 1910   16
Virginia Woolf and Julian Bell, Blean, near Canterbury   17
A Group of Apostles: Richard Llewellyn-Davies, Hugh Sykes Davies, Alister Watson, Anthony Blunt, Julian Bell, Andrew Cohen   54
Vanessa at Charleston, taken by Helen (Soutar) Morris   85
Julian at Charleston, taken by Helen (Soutar) Morris   86
Julian at Cassis   139
Duncan Grant, Clive Bell, Vanessa Bell, Julian Bell; tea at Charleston, taken by Lettice Ramsey   149
Lettice at Charleston, taken by Vanessa Bell   150
Julian at Charleston, taken by Lettice Ramsey   151
Cambridge, November 11, 1933   157
Julian with Ling Shuhua and Chen Yuan   199
Julian and Richard Rees in Spain, July 1937   277

PREFACE

MORE THAN FORTY YEARS after the original publication of *Journey to the Frontier*—William Abrahams's and my life of both John Cornford and Julian Bell—I decided to return to a reconsideration of the life of Julian Bell. I have observed with admiration that Sir Michael Holroyd has published subsequent versions of his great life of Lytton Strachey. (It originally appeared just after the decriminalization of homosexuality in Britain; hence now all could be told.) So did Noel Annan in the case of his intellectual biography of Sir Leslie Stephen. No doubt others have issued revised and expanded versions of a biography written earlier. But up to now I felt that I shouldn't revise an already published text. Also, if a new version were to be done, it would have to be on my own, as my coauthor had died in 1998. It would still, however, be his book as well.

My attitude towards the question of a new version changed in the summer of 2004. The previous year I had published *Sassoon: The Worlds of Philip and Sybil*. If less literary than some of my previous work, and far less concerned with radical figures, it combined my interests in society, politics, and art with a comparatively new interest in Anglo-Jewry. Now I was at work on quite a different project: the Blitz. While in England in the summer of 2004, doing research on that book, I participated in several events associated with what is considered the one hundredth anniversary of the beginning of Bloomsbury. In 1904 the four Stephen children, all in their twenties, scandalized their elders, after the death of their father, Sir Leslie, by leaving Kensington and taking a house together, without a chaperone, in the respectable but nondescript area of Bloomsbury, hence eventually and inadvertently creating a term in literary history. In *Journey to the Frontier* Billy Abrahams and I had written on what might be considered a late aspect of Bloomsbury, that is, its second generation as represented by Julian Bell, Vanessa Bell's son and Virginia Woolf's nephew. I had also written on my own, many years later, about the very early years of Bloomsbury in *On or About December 1910*. In that study I explored as deeply as I could the Bloomsbury events that lay behind Virginia Woolf's famous and somewhat tongue-in-cheek remark, "on or about December 1910 human character changed."

Julian Bell was on my mind in 2004 as I chaired a session largely concerned with him at the first International Virginia Woolf Conference to be held outside of the United States, at the Senate House of the University of London, appropriately in the Bloomsbury district. Patricia Laurence had just published her *Lily Briscoe's Chinese Eyes* on Bloomsbury and China with much attention to Julian's year and a half teaching at Wuhan University. A novel, *K*, had come out based on Julian's affair there with Ling Shuhua. I also met William Beekman, a prominent Bloomsbury collector who had a particular interest in Julian and who owned many of the surviving letters that Virginia Woolf had written to him. Marking the anniversary was not only the Virginia Woolf conference but associated events, including a day visit to Charleston, most notably marked by a splendid interview with Olivier Bell. The climax of the celebration was a grand dinner at King's College, Cambridge, Julian's College as well as E. M. Forster's, Roger Fry's, and John Maynard Keynes's (and mine, where I did a second bachelor of arts after my American one). There Dadie Rylands had given Virginia Woolf the lunch immortalized in *A Room of One's Own*.

It hadn't yet occurred to me that I might return to the study of Julian myself. There was a reception before the dinner, on the great lawn at the back of the Gibbs building at King's—it was a ravishing summer evening, England at its best—with a view of the Cam, of Clare College, of the building where

Dadie Rylands had his rooms, and of Bodley's, where I had lived my first undergraduate year. There was a small display of photocopies from the King's Archives to be looked at during the reception. Included was a letter from Duncan Grant to Julian saying that of course he must do what he thought best, but pointing out how much pain his participating in the civil war in Spain would cause his mother. And there was a copy of the few notes that Vanessa had jotted down about Julian's life. She never really recovered from his death. These two documents, which had not been available years before, made me realize, as of course I would have known in theory, how much new material was likely to have surfaced in the forty years since Billy Abrahams and I had initially, with the extraordinary cooperation of Quentin and Olivier Bell, looked into Julian's life. It suddenly occurred to me that when I had finished my study of the Blitz, I might well turn or rather return to the life of Julian Bell. I was going back to London by bus after the dinner, but just before hurrying to catch it, I had a message that Olivier would like to speak to me for a moment. She was wondering, in reaction to Patricia Laurence's interest in doing a biography of Julian (some years later she would publish a pamphlet, *The Violent Pacifist*, about him), whether there should be another life of Julian. After all, as she kindly said, there was *Journey to the Frontier*. Pat Laurence had spoken to me earlier about this possibility, and I had urged her, should she so wish, to go ahead. When I had that conversation, it had never occurred to me that I might be interested myself. It was an idea, almost indeed a revelation, that came to me that evening on the lawn at King's. I hurriedly indicated that possibility to Olivier and said that I would write to her about it. Indeed I did, although I knew that it wouldn't be for some time that I would turn to looking again at Julian in any committed way.

But gradually I began to do so. In the spring of 2006 I spent some time in New York, and at the Berg Collection of the New York Public Library I read the small archive of the papers of Ling Shuhua, Julian's Chinese mistress, which Patricia Laurence had used in her work. That summer I spent a few days in the Archives at King's College, read some material, and acquired a sense of how very much had come to light over the years. And then, in 2007, I spent February and March in Cambridge, much enjoying a residency at Wolfson College. I also reread *Journey to the Frontier*. I thought that the book had held up well, and I did wonder, as had Olivier Bell, whether another version was necessary. This does raise a fundamental question. Julian's life was one of promise and beginnings, very sadly cut short five and a half months after his twenty-ninth birthday. What he had accomplished in his short life, in his writings, his poetry, his ideas, was of considerable interest. But he was, no doubt, a minor figure. Nowadays we are interested in such lives, not only the lives of fulfilled accomplishments and importance. And then there was the matter of Bloomsbury. Interest in Bloomsbury can become excessive. There are those who can never get enough about the Bloomsbury figures, and there are others who loathe the very idea and are sick of what is sometimes referred to as the "Bloomsbury industry." Julian himself had somewhat mixed feelings about his situation. He was at the very heart of Bloomsbury: the two sisters, Vanessa and Virginia, and Vanessa's children. Their husbands, Clive Bell and Leonard Woolf, at times felt a sense of exclusion. Clive in fact spent a decreasing amount of time with Vanessa, whose more constant companion was the homosexual Duncan Grant, the father of her third child, Angelica. Julian's closest relationship was with his mother, and in many senses he was a great supporter of Bloomsbury's values. But in other ways he turned against them. He felt that Bloomsbury's politics had to be updated in order to deal with the contemporary situation of the 1930s. He enjoyed being a child of Bloomsbury and the status and advantages that it gave him. But he also wanted to be his own person and be on his own. He felt driven to prove his worth to Virginia and Leonard, and he might not have minded if they had been a little less honest in telling him their views of his writings. Bloomsbury believed in the overriding importance of personal relations. But that did not mean, as some might think, that the obligation was necessarily to be endlessly supportive. Rather it might mean, in the tradition of English moralism, telling one's nearest and dearest what one actually thought about what they were doing and writing (although Leonard did recognize his wife's fragility and was always supportive in reacting to her work, no matter what he might privately have thought).

On rereading *Journey to the Frontier*, I was impressed at how good it is. I feel it is not immodest of me to say this, as I believe the voice of the book is more Billy's than mine. This led me to have doubts and problems about how to proceed with a project of writing a fuller life of Julian Bell. I did not wish to rewrite and destroy the original text. What I have tried to do then is to rewrite, but only to an extent, the original text about Julian, and when appropriate to provide some account of this search for Julian Bell from its beginning until the present, a span of more than fifty years. (I first wrote about him when I was an undergraduate.) But I have also incorporated the extensive and I believe very important new material that has become available. This is to a considerable extent a new book, almost double the original text.

Much of the new material is personal. Bloomsbury has always had an intriguing relationship between the private and the public. As pioneers of the modern, freeing themselves from what they saw as Victorian conventions, its members believed that they should live the lives that they wished. But that was not to say that there were not many personal problems and issues. A willingness and an effort to be "honest" about personal relations does not necessarily lead to personal happiness, particularly as it might involve informing others of your honest opinion about their characters and actions. On the other hand, Bloomsbury was not "postmodern." This has led some to accuse it of hypocrisy. It did not necessarily believe that private life, which in theory (although sometimes not in fact) was to be as free as one might wish, should become public. Angelica Bell felt that she was badly treated in not being told until she was eighteen that Duncan Grant, and not Clive Bell, was her father. Duncan Grant, who led exactly the sexual life that he wished, still felt uneasy even in the post-Wolfenden age, when homosexual activity had been decriminalized, that all should be revealed in Michael Holroyd's pathbreaking life of Lytton Strachey. Members of Bloomsbury were still figures of the upper middle classes who might well feel that those in the know should know and those not in the know should not. Mightn't it be better, as Roy Harrod, Keynes's first biographer, thought, that those who knew had it confirmed that Duncan Grant and Maynard Keynes were lovers through the publication of the photograph of Grant and Keynes looking dolefully at one another rather than through anything more specific? Quentin and Olivier Bell couldn't have been more helpful to us many years ago when we were working on what is now the first version of Julian's life, but they didn't feel it was appropriate to tell us all the ramifications of Julian's love life. And much of the material documenting it and other aspects of his life had not yet come to light. Now Julian's story can be told in much more depth and detail. That is what I have attempted to do.

JULIAN BELL

CHAPTER I

A BLOOMSBURY CHILDHOOD

BLOOMSBURY HAS its international fame. Studious visitors from abroad know it as the area of the British Museum and the University of London. Readers of fiction feel an immediate familiarity with its Georgian squares—each having a fenced-in bit of green park at its center—and streets, lined with well-proportioned, tall-windowed houses, large but not ostentatious, that served as homes for professional and merchant families throughout the nineteenth century. In the twentieth century Bloomsbury had been increasingly vandalized, in part by the destruction of the Second World War, in part by the constructions of the University of London. In 1940 Max Beerbohm was complaining that there seemed to be no limits to the University's "desire for expansion of that bleak, bland, hideous, and already vast whited sepulcher, which bears its name." He was referring to the University's Senate House, the model for the Ministry of Truth in George Orwell's *Nineteen Eighty-Four*. But in 1904, the year of the "birth" of Bloomsbury, the changes that war and the University were to effect had not yet occurred: past and present were still harmoniously conjoined.

Early in that year, and nine years after the death of his second wife, Julia Jackson Duckworth, Sir Leslie Stephen had died of cancer. He was seventy-two years old. In his time he had been the first editor of the *Dictionary of National Biography*, editor of the *Cornhill Magazine*, essayist, literary critic, biographer, religious doubter, and a celebrated mountaineer and Alpinist—he was the first to climb the Schreckhorn. Soon after his death, the four children from his second marriage, Vanessa, Thoby, Virginia, and Adrian Stephen, sufficiently grown up and with sufficient money, settled upon themselves to do as they pleased and moved from the family house in Hyde Park Gate, Kensington, across London to Bloomsbury, where they took a house together in Gordon Square, No. 46. Nevertheless, relatives disapproved; it was considered shocking that four young people should live on their own. The move was an early indication that these four were determined to go their own way and make their own decisions. For them, it was a highly agreeable arrangement, but it had never been thought of as other than provisional, and indeed it was soon altered: first, tragically, in the summer of 1906, by the sudden death of Thoby Stephen from typhoid, contracted while traveling in Greece. Though known by his second name, Thoby, his actual first name was Julian. His death played a central role in the story of Bloomsbury (as did the death of his namesake, Julian Bell, thirty-one years later). Thoby's death was an important factor in precipitating major changes in his sisters' lives. His close Trinity College, Cambridge, friend, Clive Bell, married Vanessa Stephen a year later, in 1907, and in 1912 another close Trinity friend, Leonard Woolf, married Virginia. Indeed, in the correspondence after Thoby's death between Lytton Strachey and Leonard, at the time in the civil service in Ceylon, Lytton argued that Leonard should marry Virginia, whom Leonard knew but far from well. In the new arrangement of things, Virginia and Adrian Stephen moved to a house of their own nearby in Fitzroy Square, and the Bells kept No. 46. It was there, on February 4, 1908, that Julian Heward Bell, their first child, was born: "Julian," after his late uncle, and "Heward," a Bell family name.

Bloomsbury, however, is not merely a place. It has a figurative as well as a physical existence. It stands for an idea, a philosophy, a style. It serves as a word of praise or deprecation. It provides an occasion for disagreement, for nostalgia, for condescension or approval. In all these aspects it would play an important part in Julian Bell's life, from his earliest childhood even to the circumstances leading up to his death—that he went out to Spain as an ambulance driver rather than as a fighter in the International Brigade. Julian was always conscious of Bloomsbury, of its values and standards, from which he knew he was not to be exempted, and conscious also of its high expectations for him: that he was to be not less than its son. Of course, something of this sort would never be said; it would simply be taken for granted. But the pressure was there, the possibility of tension and opposition. And if he were to be a writer, there would be the complicated question of his relationship with his aunt Virginia. She loved him deeply, but as she was fully aware, she could be in a state of rivalry with writers, and at times that might influence her relationship with Julian. There is no question that Julian loved and admired Bloomsbury, and respected it, and even believed in it; yet at the same time, although only rarely explicitly and openly, he was in rebellion against it.

But how is this Bloomsbury, which figures now in literary histories as the "Bloomsbury Group," to be described? Since the shorter telling of Julian's life—*Journey to the Frontier*—was published, in 1966, Bloomsbury has been the subject of ever increasing attention, to a significant degree driven by the intense interest in Virginia Woolf. Almost without number have there been scholarly studies and more popular books, and innumerable biographies. Of the many biographies of Virginia Woolf herself, the two most important are one of the earliest, by her nephew Quentin, Julian's brother, in 1972, and one of the more recent, the magisterial work by Hermione Lee in 1996. Not to be forgotten are the six volumes of her letters and the five volumes of her diary.

There is something rather daunting, or at least cautionary, about the statement by Clive Bell, one of the founding members, that Bloomsbury never really existed, that it was an invention of outsiders. Of course, he did not expect (perhaps not even want) to be believed; still, one does well to go cautiously. To speak of "members" where Bloomsbury is concerned is more than a little misleading, for it never was a formal Group, never issued a manifesto or declaration of principles, was never a movement (Bloomsburyisme) in the style of the Continent, and was not even, as its detractors darkly imagined, a conspiracy for self-advancement or a mutual admiration society. On the whole, one does best to conform to Bloomsbury's own usage and describe it simply as a group (lowercase) of very close friends, many of them living in the same district of London (Bloomsbury), who saw a great deal of one another (in the early days frequently on Thursday evenings after dinner) either there or in the country (usually Sussex), and who gained imposing reputations in the various arts they practiced during the period 1910–1940: painting (Vanessa Bell, Duncan Grant); the novel (Virginia Woolf, and in a sense slightly tangential to the group, E. M. Forster); art criticism (Clive Bell, Roger Fry); political theory (Leonard Woolf); biography (Lytton Strachey); and economics (John Maynard Keynes). Quite a few others would also be close friends, but these were at the group's very center, with the possible exception of Forster, and were the members who achieved the greatest renown. They made extraordinary contributions to the culture of the twentieth century. Yet at the emotional heart of the group were Virginia and Vanessa, the Stephen sisters, and by extension, Vanessa's children, Julian, Quentin, and Angelica.

Let us make a first approach to Bloomsbury—and to Julian—by way of an exchange of letters. It is April 1908. On Wednesday the 22nd, Virginia Stephen, who is on holiday in Cornwall, writes to Lytton Strachey in London. She has taken rooms at Trevose House, Draycot Terrace, St. Ives, a town she knows well as the Stephen family in earlier years had vacationed there frequently. She has been attempting to write a review, for the *Cornhill Magazine*, of a life of John Delane, a famous nineteenth-century editor of the *Times*. But the conditions are not favorable:

> My landlady, though a woman of 50, has nine children, and once had 11; and the youngest is able to cry all day long. When you consider that the family sitting room is next mine, and we are parted by folding doors only—what kind of sentence do you call this?—you will understand that I find it hard to write of Delane "the Man".... I spend most of my time, however, alone with my God, on the moors. I sat for an hour (perhaps it was 10 minutes) on a rock this afternoon, and considered how I should describe the colour of the Atlantic.[1]

On Thursday the 23rd, Strachey replies:

> I went away last Friday, partly to get rid of my cold, to the Green Dragon, on Salisbury Plain, where James [his brother] and Keynes and others were for Easter. Of course it finally destroyed me—the coldest winds you can imagine sweeping over the plain, and inferior food, and not enough comfortable chairs. But on the whole I was amused. The others were Bob Trevy [Trevelyan] ... Moore ... and a young undergraduate called Rupert Brooke—isn't it a romantic name?—with pink cheeks and bright yellow hair—it sounds horrible, but it wasn't. Moore is a colossal being, and he also sings and plays in a wonderful way, so that the evenings passed pleasantly.[2]

This letter leads us to the early years of Bloomsbury, but before we follow it there, let us attend to Virginia's reply, written five days later. It is Tuesday, April 28, and she is still at Trevose House in St. Ives.

> Your letter was a great solace to me. I had begun to doubt my own identity—and imagined I was part of a sea-gull, and dreamt at night of deep pools of blue water, full of eels. However, Adrian came suddenly that very day. . . . Then Nessa and Clive and the Baby [Julian, age three months] and the Nurse all came, and we have been so domestic that I have not read, or wrote. My article upon Delane is left in the middle of a page thus—"But what of the Man?" . . . A child is the very devil calling out, as I believe, all the worst and least explicable passions of the parents—and the Aunts. When we talk of marriage, friendship or prose, we are suddenly held up by Nessa, who has heard a cry, and then we must all distinguish whether it is Julian's cry, or the cry of the 2 year old—the landlady's youngest—who has an abscess, and uses therefore a different scale. . . . We are going to a place called the Gurnard's Head this afternoon—and now I look up and behold it pours! So we shall sit over the fire instead, and I shall say some very sharp things, and Clive and Nessa will treat me like a spoilt monkey, and the Baby will cry. However, I daresay Hampstead is under snow. How is your cold? I got a stiff neck on the rocks—but it went.[3]

A certain acerbity in this need not be taken seriously—in fact Virginia would prove to be the most affectionate of aunts, devoted to her sister's three children, Julian, Quentin, and Angelica, and they were devoted to her. But that is the future, to be looked at as it happens. Now we must go back, a few years at least, to the past, to where Bloomsbury has its origins: to Cambridge. In the autumn of 1899, Lytton Strachey, next-to-youngest son amongst the ten children of Lieutenant-General Sir Richard and Lady Strachey—a family long associated with the administration of India—went up to Trinity College. Very soon there formed about him a circle of young men almost as brilliant as himself. There was Leonard Woolf, from St. Paul's School, the son of a London barrister. There was Clive Bell, from Marlborough, of a Wiltshire "huntin'-shootin'" county family who had got their money a generation back as owners of Welsh coal mines. And there was Julian Thoby Prinsep Stephen. Thoby Stephen died too early to fulfill the promise that his family and friends had recognized in him, but he would be remembered glowingly—especially by his sisters, who had worshipped him, and who looked for him, as it were, in the next generation, in Julian. He was truly a founder of Bloomsbury as a group, for he introduced Clive Bell to his sister Vanessa, and Leonard Woolf to his sister Virginia. The marriages that grew out of these introductions would give the group a center, a coherence, and a strength that came with family interconnection, which it would not otherwise have had. (In all this there is a resemblance between Bloomsbury and the Clapham Sect, that important evangelical group or movement of a hundred years earlier, among whose members had been the great-grandfather of Vanessa and Virginia Stephen, the great-great-grandfather of E. M. Forster, and the great-grandmother of Lytton Strachey.)

Strachey and his friends at Trinity—Bell, Woolf, Thoby Stephen, as well as A. J. Robertson and Saxon Sydney-Turner—were caught up in the prevailing Cambridge passion for "little groups" and formed an informal one of their own, the Midnight Society, which met on Saturdays at midnight in the rooms of Clive Bell. It was dedicated to the reading aloud of plays of a rather formidable character—*The Cenci, Prometheus Unbound, Bartholomew Fair*—but the meetings were not as austere as this may suggest. The members fortified themselves with whisky or punch and meat pies, and when the last speech was spoken—usually at about 5 A.M.—they would sally forth, still exhilarated, to listen to the nightingales and sometimes to chant passages from Swinburne as they perambulated through the cloisters of Neville's Court in Trinity.

There was another "little group," distinguished in lineage and ostensibly secret, to which Strachey and Woolf—but not Clive Bell nor Thoby Stephen—also belonged, and which also met on Saturday evenings but a good deal earlier. (Indeed, the Midnight Society chose the midnight hour not only for its drama but simply to allow others to attend both meetings.) Founded in about 1820 by a future bishop of Gibraltar, this was the Conversazione Society, or the Society, or—to use the name by which it is best known—the Apostles. Over its history, the Apostles had had as members many of the most brilliant Cambridge undergraduates, from Tennyson and Hallam on, and most of them, as it happened, were at Trinity College. In 1899 the form was much as it had been since the beginning of the Society: weekly meetings, at which a paper was delivered by one of the members and discussed (dissected) by the others. Tradition provided that there should be a full and frank response to any question, objection, or speculation that might be raised, even at the risk of hurt feelings. On the whole, Apostolic papers were dedicated to abstract, or metaphysical, or political, or poetical, or ethical problems; the Apostolic aim was to pursue the truth with absolute devotion and personal candor. (On occasion, however, the aim seems to have been simply to amuse, as when Lytton Strachey addressed himself to the question "Ought the Father to Grow a Beard?" Since Victorian fathers were usually bearded, one presumes that the correct, Stracheyan answer would have been no. Strachey himself, in the later years of his life, grew a luxuriant beard, though he never married.) The concerns of the Society had always been more philosophical than literary; now, at the turn of the century, the inclination and professional interests of certain of its older members strengthened the claims of philosophy. At this time the number of undergraduate members was comparatively small: only about six. (Here a latecomer must be mentioned: John Maynard Keynes, who did not arrive in Cambridge as an undergraduate until the autumn of 1902, and who so impressed Strachey and Woolf when they went to call that he was brought into the Society in the winter of his first year.) But the membership as a whole had never been limited to the biblical number of Apostles, and there were still many active members who had already received their degrees. These included not only men still at Cambridge (usually as dons) but a few others—future literary figures in the very early stages of their careers, men like Desmond MacCarthy and E. M. Forster—who might come up from London to attend meetings. In Cambridge the most eminent of the older members, who of course were still young men at the time, were Alfred North Whitehead, Bertrand Russell, G. E. Moore (the Moore mentioned in Strachey's letter to Virginia Woolf), and Goldsworthy Lowes Dickinson. It is hardly surprising then that the bent of the Society should have been philosophical.

The young Apostles of 1900 felt quite consciously the need for a new philosophy for the new century. Strachey had already persuaded his friends to question the Utilitarian pieties of the past, and to hold in high disdain what appeared to be the hypocrisies, deceits, catchwords, cant, and uncertainties of their immediate ancestors, whom he would call those "Eminent Victorians" in his famous 1918 book by that name. One recognizes a familiar pattern: the opposition of fathers and sons, the war of the generations. Sir Leslie Stephen had been an agnostic, and he had resigned his fellowship at Trinity Hall, his College at Cambridge, because of doubts. But he doubted the existence of God with all the passion and soul-searching that his Claphamite ancestors had devoted to affirming God's existence. With equal passion, his descendants and their friends would claim that the problem was not even worth considering. In 1906, after reading a memoir of Henry Sidgwick, an earlier Apostle who had suffered like Sir Leslie from doubts, Keynes commented:

> He never did anything but wonder whether Christianity was true and prove that it wasn't and hope that it was. . . . And then his conscience—incredible. There is no doubt about his moral goodness. And yet it is all so dreadfully depressing—no intimacy, no clear-cut crisp boldness. Oh, I suppose he was intimate but he didn't seem to have anything to be intimate about except his religious doubts. And he really ought to have got over that a little sooner; because he knew that the thing wasn't true perfectly well from the beginning.[4]

The publication of G. E. Moore's *Principia Ethica* in 1903 struck the Midnighters and the Apostles with the force of revelation. A half century later, looking back, Clive Bell testified that Moore was "the dominant influence in all our lives."[5] Lytton Strachey, we are told by E. M. Forster (in his biography of Lowes Dickinson), welcomed *Principia Ethica* with the words "the age of reason has come!"[6] And Keynes summed up its effect upon himself and his friends as "the beginning of a renaissance, the opening of a new heaven on a new earth."[7] Clearly, the future Bloomsburians (or Bloomsberries, as they were called by Molly MacCarthy) had found their Bible.

It should be said at the outset that Moore's was very much a private philosophy—in itself and as interpreted by his disciples, who were not above picking and choosing amongst its elements those they found most congenial. As such, it provided a dramatic contrast, and contradiction, to the public philosophy of the nineteenth century, the Utilitarianism of Bentham, Mill, Spencer, and other thinkers in the Victorian galaxy. The Utilitarian notions of "good" as something fixed, already defined, and as publicly in the world as the memorial to Albert the Good in Hyde Park were firmly rejected. "Good" is an indefinable attribute, Moore explained; the sense of it is instinctive in oneself; one's discriminations, based upon it, lead to evaluations of one's own. One asks questions, and one questions the questions: "What *exactly* do you mean?" That famous, often parodied Bloomsbury remark originates here, in Moore's own conversation—which his younger friends could find intimidating—and in the very first sentence of his preface to *Principia Ethica*: "It appears to me that in Ethics, as in all other philosophical studies, the difficulties and disagreements, of which its history is full, are mainly due to a very simple cause: namely to the attempt to answer questions, without first discovering precisely *what* question it is which you desire to answer."

But Moore contributed more to Bloomsbury than a conversational gambit. The central aspect of his doctrine, as it helped bring about a Bloomsbury "attitude," was his assertion that

> By far the most valuable things, which we know or can imagine, are certain states of consciousness, which may be roughly described as the pleasures of human intercourse and the enjoyment of beautiful objects. No one, probably, who has asked himself the question, has ever doubted that personal affection and the appreciation of what is beautiful in Art or Nature, are good in themselves; nor, if we consider strictly what things are worth having *purely for their own sakes*, does it appear probable that anyone will think that anything else has *nearly* so great a value as the things which are included under these two heads. . . . [This] is the ultimate and fundamental truth of Moral Philosophy. That it is only for the sake of these things—in order that as much of them as possible may at some time exist—that anyone can be justified in performing any public or private duty; that they are the *raison d'être* of virtue; that it is they . . . that form the rational ultimate end of human action and the sole criterion of social progress: these appear to be truths which have been generally overlooked.[8]

Here then was the new Gospel but, unlike the old, arrived at, so its believers thought, with complete rationality. In fact, there was considerably more in *Principia Ethica* than this exaltation of "certain states of consciousness," but Moore's disciples chose not to notice those aspects of it that dealt with the relation of ethics to conduct. "We accepted Moore's religion, so to speak, and discarded his morals," Keynes wrote in 1938. "Indeed, in our opinion, one of the great advantages of his religion, was that it made morals unnecessary—meaning by 'religion' one's attitude towards oneself and the ultimate, and by 'morals' one's attitude towards the outside world and the intermediate." What Keynes and his friends took from Moore's "religion, so to speak" was the belief that "one's prime objects in life were love, the creation and enjoyment of aesthetic experience and the pursuit of knowledge."[9]

Obviously, if one is to practice a religion that gives primacy to "certain states of consciousness," one must be capable of discriminations and subtlety and deep feeling. But there are two preconditions outside oneself that must also be fulfilled: first, a stable society; and second, a measure of financial security. A chaotic or threatened society involves the individual in its concerns; anxieties about money, the mere business of survival, preempt the major areas of consciousness. At the time of which we are writing, both preconditions obtained. In 1903 the world was at peace: no "shadow of a war," such as darkened the 1930s, haunted the imagination of the sensitive. Indeed, as Leonard Woolf recalled, there were events like the vindication of Captain Dreyfus that seemed to justify one's taking an optimistic view of the future: the day of reason was almost at hand. As for financial security, that too, in varying degree, Moore's young disciples had. None was rich—Strachey and Woolf could count on very little money—but all had the assurance, the poise of identity, that was inherent in belonging to a certain class in a certain place at a certain moment in history. None was in the position of poor Leonard Bast in E. M. Forster's *Howards End*. A clerk living on the very fringes of the middle class, Leonard has been educated (at the expense of the state) up to a level of cultural aspiration: he yearns, shall we say, for "certain states of consciousness." But for him they are unattainable, and Forster makes it clear that this is because Leonard lacks money:

> Give people cash, for it is the warp of civilization, whatever the woof may be. The imagination ought to play upon money and realize it vividly, for it's the—the second most important thing in the world. It is so slurred over and hushed up, there is so little clear thinking—oh, political economy of course; but so few of us think clearly about our own private incomes, and admit that independent thoughts are in nine cases out of ten the result of independent means. Money: give Mr Bast money, and don't bother about his ideals. He'll pick up those for himself.[10]

The period in which Forster was writing, in which Bloomsbury was coming into being, was the Edwardian heyday, a time when money was having a golden age. Rarely has it been regarded with such adulation. After all, it was England's main product—money making money—and most of the coupon-clippers, the rentier class, had little sense, and cared less, of what was actually happening in some vague place in the Empire in order to keep them in pounds. Money was to be collected and spent. It was the era of the last great splurge—the fantastic country house weekends devoted to killing as many birds as possible, changing into as many clothes as possible, and eating as much food as possible. In all this, Edward VII, in his liking for bankers and financiers, set the tone of his age. England was more egalitarian than the Continent and would permit the plutocrat "to get ahead in society." But it had never happened at quite the pace that was set in the first fourteen years of the twentieth century.

Ironically, the money-making-money that made possible the endless extravagance of the echt Edwardians also made possible the life of Bloomsbury with its emphasis upon personal relations and aesthetic experience. The money of its Victorian forebears had been wisely invested. Certainly in the Cambridge period, the future members of Bloomsbury did not overly concern themselves with the sources of their income: as Apostles they had made it a point, in the rather austere tradition of the Society and of Cambridge itself, to turn away from worldly values. (Here, perhaps, it should be noticed that Clive Bell, who was not an Apostle, was the one among the group who chose to have a foot, as Desmond MacCarthy, another member of Bloomsbury, observed, in two very different communities within the University. "He seemed to live, half with the rich sporting-set, and half with the intellectuals." And MacCarthy recalled that at their first meeting Bell was "dressed with careless opulence" in a dark fur coat with a deep astrakhan collar.[11] Not, one ventures to think, the ideal of Apostolic costume.) Unconcerned with wealth and power, indifferent to fame and success, these young men tended to regard the world where such things mattered with contempt—although with some pity also for its being so unenlightened. As late as 1906 Keynes was writing to Strachey, not humorously, "How amazing to think that we and only we know the rudiments of a true theory of ethic."[12] This was an abiding characteristic of the Apostles—a certain elitist point of view towards the world—and it was reinforced by Moore's philosophy, which emphasized the importance of individual judgments and discriminations. At the same time, and this too was Apostolic, there was a willingness to enter the world, if one were summoned, and help it along its way. (It seems not unreasonable to suggest that Keynes's attitude towards economics and one basis for his economic theory derive from this cast of mind.)

In fact, when their period at Cambridge ended, Moore's disciples did not, as one might have expected, withdraw into contemplation and a further refining of sensibility. Instead, at their own pace and in their own fashion, they began careers—as writers, artists, editors, publishers, civil servants—and they went into the world. There was, however, remarkably little dispersion. Except for Leonard Woolf, who went out to Ceylon for seven years as a junior colonial officer, carrying in his luggage a set of Voltaire in ninety volumes, they remained a group in London as they had been in Cambridge. Only the setting of the conversation changed: from Neville's Court at Trinity College to Gordon Square in Bloomsbury to the house that the four Stephen children, Thoby, Vanessa, Virginia, and Adrian, had taken on their own. From time to time they added to their number regular visitors: most importantly, in the prewar years, Roger Fry, E. M. Forster, David Garnett, Desmond MacCarthy, and the painter Duncan Grant, who was a cousin of Lytton Strachey and the lover of Maynard Keynes. And they proceeded with their work.

Moore's text speaks of "the enjoyment of beautiful objects." Keynes, in his paraphrase, makes a significant addition: "the creation and enjoyment of aesthetic experience." Indeed, the creation proved formidable in quality, and in quantity. It's worth remembering that Virginia Woolf, for example, despite periods of mental illness when she could do no writing at all, had produced twenty-four books before her suicide, at the age of fifty-nine, in 1941. Vanessa Bell painted almost a thousand pictures. E. M. Forster, who is traditionally regarded as having written very little, has fourteen books to his credit. As a group, its members seem, in retrospect, to have been as industrious as Victorians.

> I stay myself, . . .

These are the opening words of Julian Bell's poem "Autobiography," which appeared in his second and, as it proved, final volume, *Work for the Winter* (1936). The remark is characteristic of his strong sense of individuality: "I stay myself, . . ." Yet at the same time he recognizes that he is also

> . . . the product made
> By several hundred English years,
> Of harried labourers underpaid,
> Of Venns who plied the parson's trade,
> Of regicides, of Clapham sects,
> Of high Victorian intellects,
> Leslie, FitzJames.

This, of course, is the Stephen inheritance. And it is equally characteristic of Julian that he should acknowledge it with a kind of sweeping inclusiveness:

from the missionary austerities of the Clapham Sect to the violence of the regicides. We are dealing here with something very different from "the enlightenment of Bloomsbury." His mother and his aunt might accept as just the praise accorded their father, Sir Leslie; they would be less likely to respond to praise for their uncle, Sir James Fitzjames Stephen, who as a conservative Utilitarian had a decidedly more authoritarian cast of mind. Bloomsbury, with Lytton Strachey in the forefront, had attempted to discredit the immediate past at least, while Julian, one might almost say, revels in it, revels in it all. "I stay myself, the product made . . ." On the one hand, there are "high Victorian intellects"; on the other, "not among such honoured, marble names,

> That cavalry ruffian, Hodson of Hodson's Horse,
> Who helped take Delhi, murdered the Moguls

He was "At least a soldiering brigand," a category for which Julian would always entertain a certain fondness. "There were worse," he goes on to say,

> Who built a country house from iron and coal:
> Hard-bitten capitalists, if on the whole
> They kept the general average of their class.

This, of course, is the Bell inheritance, his father's side, very different from the Stephens and representing a family which had made its money in coal, and at whose large, ugly Victorian country house, at Seend in Wiltshire, the Clive Bells and their children spent some vacations and, with some reluctance, most Christmases. To his indulgent parents, Clive nevertheless appeared to be a wild radical, and a dangerous advocate of a new aestheticism, or so they interpreted the fame he had won as the author of such books as *Art* and *Civilization*; as an exponent of the idea of "significant form"; and as a sponsor—along with their central organizing figure, Roger Fry—of the notorious exhibitions of Postimpressionist painting in 1910 and 1912, which introduced Cézanne, Matisse, and Picasso to England in the years before the First World War. But if he seemed almost a black sheep to his own family, to the Stephen side he seemed almost a little too conventional in his "huntin', shootin', fishin'" interests (quite a bit of which he conveyed to his son) and in his comparatively conservative political views, except in his absolute pacifism in both World Wars. Virginia Woolf, in a memoir of Julian written immediately after his death, felt that Julian owed a great deal to the Bell inheritance, particularly in his yearning for the active rather than the contemplative life. This differentiated him somewhat from her beloved Thoby, whose death in 1906, thirty-one years before Julian's, had had such a profound and lasting effect upon her. Thoby's tragic, early death from typhoid that year helped focus, in reaction, the attention of his great friends on his sisters, and played an important role in bringing the Bloomsbury group into sharper focus. Julian's death, and Virginia's subsequent suicide, as well as the earlier deaths of Lytton Strachey and Roger Fry, were crucial moments in its later stages. Julian's death brought back to Virginia Thoby's. Though Thoby was more worldly than his sisters, and had become a barrister, "in fact Julian was much rougher, more impulsive; more vigorous than Thoby. He had a strong element of the Bell in him. What do I mean? I think I mean that he was practical & caustic & shrewd. . . . He had much higher spirits. He was much more adapted to life. He was much less regularly beautiful to look at. But then he had a warmth, an impetuosity that the Stephens dont have."[13]

This is to give the Bell inheritance its due. But it must be said that Julian's family, in its loyalties and intimacies, almost seemed to exclude the non-Stephen part of it. Clive did not completely fit into the Stephen inheritance of "Clapham sects, / Of high Victorian intellects," nor did Leonard. Clive and Leonard were certainly original progenitors of Bloomsbury, of undoubted importance; nevertheless, one feels the slightest sense of unease in their relationships with their wives, the Stephen sisters, who were the heart of Bloomsbury, whatever its masculine intellectual origins at Cambridge. Both men were perhaps a little too worldly. If Clive was a little too much to the Right in his political thinking, perhaps Leonard went a little too far in his interests in the practice of radical socialism. And if Clive's squire background did not exactly fit with the Stephen inheritance, neither did the London professional and mercantile background of the Woolfs, not to mention that family's being Jewish. In her memoir of Julian, Virginia speaks of "L's family complex wh. made him eager, no, on the alert, to criticise her [Vanessa's] children because he thought I admired them more than his family."[14] But it seems not to have occurred to her that this imputed preference of hers was almost certainly the case and, more importantly, that there was indeed a Stephen "family complex" of mutual affection and admiration that must have been formidable (as well as enviable) to an outsider.

Julian was born on February 4, 1908. The most important person in Julian's life, from its very beginning to its very end, was his mother, the gifted and beautiful Vanessa Bell. Theirs was a relationship without a break and without concealment: in it the full implications of Bloomsbury candor were taken to their limits, and the connection between mother and son never weakened. Vanessa herself made it so evident in her notes about him jotted down in the fullness of her grief in the month of his death, July 1937:

> When I first held him in my arms—the softness of his dark brown silky hair. All pain had become worth while. Confused overwhelming feelings one did not understand. . . . Intense peace & joy. Painting him in his cradle every morning as he lay & kicked. Drawing him as he began to stagger about. . . . Telling the hospital nurse at Seend I would never punish my child. Argument—she became angry & thought me foolish & ignorant. . . . My life changed, invaded by this creature suddenly alive. . . . going away when he was 6 months old—to Italy for a month or so—but I could hardly bear it.

When he was three and a half, she remembered when he "put a handful of gravel and earth all over my head & neck—R[oger Fry].'s astonishment that I did not scold him." In London, during the air raids of the First World War, "he was cross at not being taken out to see them but allowed to sleep."[15]

Although they would become very close, Julian's aunt Virginia's early reaction to him was far less enthusiastic, treating Julian as an object rather than as a person. As she wrote on May 13, 1908, to Violet Dickinson:

> I had a fortnight at St. Ives. Adrian and Nessa and Clive came for the last week. I doubt that I shall ever have a baby. Its voice is too terrible, a senseless scream, like an ill omened cat. Nobody would wish to comfort it, or pretend that it was a human being. Now, thank God, it sleeps with its nurse. Now and then it smiled at Nessa, and it has a very nice back; but the amount of business that has to be got through before you can enjoy it, is dismaying. Clive and I went for some long walks; but I felt that we were deserters, but then I was quite useless, as a nurse, and Clive will not even hold it.[16]

But her attitude towards him changed, and they were eventually very close, as she was with Vanessa's two other children, Quentin, born in 1910, and Angelica, her child by Duncan Grant, born in 1918. Virginia remarked in her diary in 1919, "Do I envy Nessa her overflowing household? Perhaps at moments."[17]

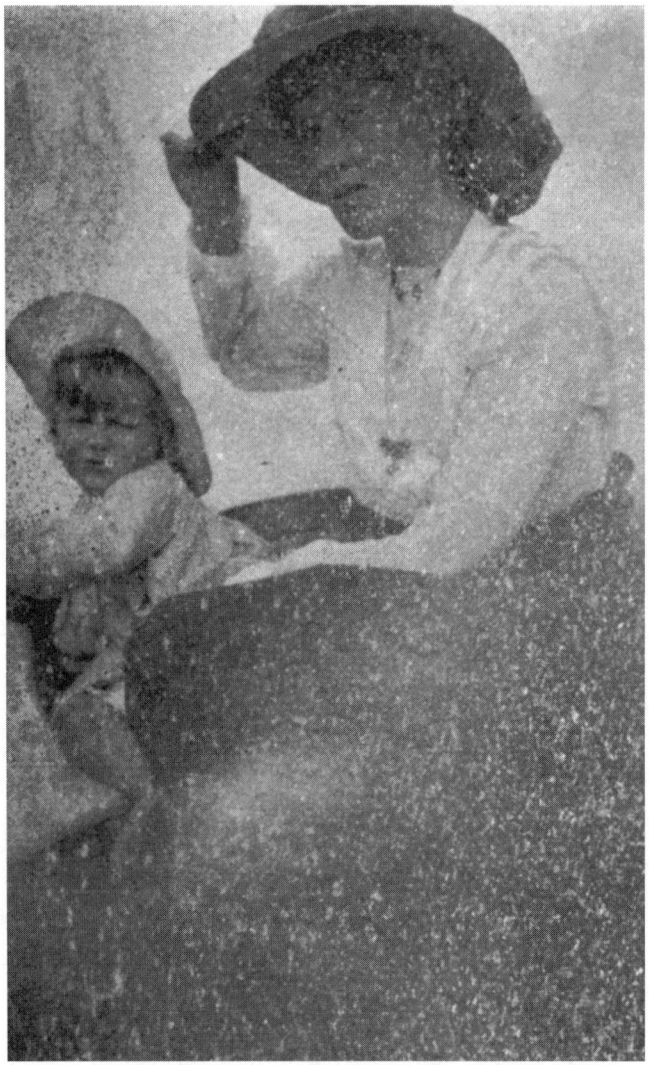

Julian and Vanessa, 1910.

It was an extraordinary rapport that Julian had with his mother, which one cannot but admire, and impressive testimony to Bloomsbury's belief in personal relations. Yet in some ways the relationship was so perfect and intense that it may have truncated others, provided a standard impossible to achieve elsewhere. The possibility will have to be considered in its place, many years later, in the history of Julian's grand and casual passions (should one share one's private life completely with one's mother?). From the first, his mother

Virginia Woolf and Julian Bell, Blean, near Canterbury. Taken by Vanessa Bell, 1910. ©Tate, London, 2010

took great pains with his upbringing, intending it to be as "natural" and undogmatic as possible: he was not to be Victorianized, a miniature grown-up, seen but not heard, in a spotless pinafore. Yet for all their intellectual adventuresomeness, the Bells were still a fairly well-to-do upper-middle-class family in the comfortable years before the First World War. There were maids and a series of governesses—one of whom Julian got rid of by pushing into a ditch. And whatever they might think of religion "upstairs," Julian found it impossible to escape completely the religion of his country "downstairs," although it would leave no permanent mark upon him. In a fragment of autobiography written shortly before going out to Spain, he remarks: "I remember as independent ideas—more or less—a Darwinian argument with Mabel and Flossie—our nurses—which must have been very early—pre-war Gordon Square." In other words, this memory dates from before Julian was six. "Though obdurate I was secretly frightened of Jehovah, and even asked to be taught prayers. (Later, learning the Lord's Prayer, I used it as a magic defence against ghosts, and still do: or as a soporific.)" But religion was hardly very significant in Julian's life. Far more important was the education he received from his mother. He writes of this same prewar time, "The great liberating influence of the period was the reading aloud by Nessa of elementary children's astronomies and geologies." And there was a similar intellectual excitement when she read aloud to him a shortened translation of the *Odyssey*. Before he was able to read himself, he made Flossie read to him a school textbook of history. History, like astronomy, was a passion. "There was also the famous occasion when Roger [Fry] demonstrated a home chemistry box, and brewed coal gas; Mabel was sent out and bought a clay pipe from a pub: it was tamped with plasticine, and, being cooked over the fire, eventually produced a jet of flame." In 1916, when he was eight years old, he had what he called his "first, definite, independent idea. It was a solution of the desire for immortality. I worked out a possible cycle by which a human body would return through grass and sheep, into another human body."[18] But it would be very misleading to give a picture of a male bluestocking pondering his science, classics, and history at a tender age. Rather it would be more accurate to see him as an extremely adventurous, reckless child bounding from activity to activity, his parents anxious to introduce him, through explanations and discussions, to the Bloomsbury dictum of rationality, which held that even irrational behavior should be understood. David Garnett, in a memoir of Julian, describes him as

> a wilful child, swift and erratic in his movements; he looked at one from large eyes and planned devilment. . . . Julian was shrill, sometimes noisy, always rather catlike and quick. My first row with him was when I found him standing,

unconscious of evil-doing, on some vegetable marrow plants that he had trampled to pieces. . . . He had in those days often to be exhorted to reason, often to listen to tedious explanations about the consequences of his violent experiments. He flung newly-hatched ducklings into the pond and after they had raced ashore flung them in again and again until one or two were drowned. He was not punished as a child, but reasoned with: one saw on his face the lovely sulky look of a half-tame creature.[19]

The free-thinking socialist Edward Carpenter, a good friend of Roger Fry's, was still enough of a Victorian that he was shocked while visiting Fry at Durbins, his house in Guildford, that Julian could pour dirt on his mother without being reprimanded.[20] Virginia had a similar memory from about the same time—or when Julian was slightly older: "We were packing up the tea things. He took a bottle of water & smashed it. He stood there in his knickerbockers with long naked legs looking defiant & triumphant. He smashed the bottle completely. The water or milk spread over the path. . . . He stood quite still smiling. I thought, This is the victorious male; now he feels himself the conqueror. It was a determined bold gesture, as tho' he wanted to express his own force & smiled at the consternation of the maids."[21]

One should not make too much either of the enthusiasm of a little boy for astronomy and history, or of his mischief and high spirits, although it is of some interest that Julian himself should have remembered the former, and those of his parents' generation, the latter. Still, it does not seem too fanciful to read into the division the first hints of a theme that was to figure importantly in Julian's life, and in the lives of many of his contemporaries: how to reconcile the conflicting demands of the life of the mind and the life of action.

The Bells made their home in Bloomsbury, but they were often in the country, and Julian, in his attachment to the land, grew up much more a child of the country than of the city—there would always be something equivocal about his feelings for London; certainly they did not go very deep. Whatever the attractiveness of Bloomsbury for the grown-ups, the children found life more exciting and memorable in the country: to a degree at Seend, the house of their Bell grandparents, and at a variety of rented houses—such as Asheham, near Lewes in Sussex, rented by the Woolfs from 1911 to 1918, where Vanessa and her children spent much time, and where Carrington fell in love with Lytton Strachey. After the birth of Julian's brother, Quentin, in 1910, Clive and Vanessa, while remaining on close terms, drifted apart as a couple. She and Roger Fry were lovers from 1911 to 1913, and remained very fond of one another thereafter. Roger would play an extremely important part in Julian's life. But by 1913 her closest male friend was the painter Duncan Grant, and they would live together until her death in 1961, both in London and in the country. Grant was a happy homosexual, beloved by Maynard Keynes, Lytton Strachey, and Adrian Stephen, and enjoyed a series of affairs. In 1918 he and Vanessa had a daughter, Angelica. In a way, it was quite a paradoxical situation for the two Stephen sisters. Bloomsbury was dedicated to sexual freedom. Yet both sisters had a somewhat restricted sexual life. One reason, perhaps, for the intensity of the relationship between Vanessa and her son Julian was that it was to some degree a compensation for the difficulties, devoted as she was to him, of her largely nonsexual relationship with Duncan. So too, apparently, Leonard and Virginia shared a very limited sexual life, and her later affair with Vita Sackville-West, immortalized in *Orlando,* was comparatively brief, although they remained very close friends.

In his poem "Autobiography," Julian recalls "the passage of those country years." England was at war, and his was "a war-time boyhood," as he acknowledges. But apart from this reference, the details he chooses to record (in the poem) are timeless, of

> orchard trees run wild,
> West wind and rain, winters of holding mud,
> Wood fires in blue-bright frost and tingling blood,
> All brought to the sharp senses of a child.

These are the simplicities of a child's (and a poet's) world. For Julian's parents and their friends the war brought a more complex experience: a true crisis of conscience. On the whole, Bloomsburians, as we have earlier suggested, tended to live at a certain aloof distance from the world. (This attitude is not to be mistaken for unworldliness. If they had little desire for luxury, or even the creature comforts, they did not scorn the world in its more amiable, civilized aspect: civilization, as they defined it, meant taking in the pleasures of food and wine and conversation. And Clive Bell was a great believer in *savoir vivre* and *savoir faire*, bearing as he did an English Francophile's conviction that living and doing were done better across the Channel.) Apart from Keynes and Leonard Woolf, they were indifferent to the day-to-day or even the month-to-month practice of politics. The demands of the private life left one no time for that sort of public interest; one lived *au dessus de la mêlée*. The war changed all that—at least for the duration. After 1914 an attitude of aloofness became increasingly difficult to maintain, even untenable.

Maynard Keynes, Bloomsbury's authority on the subject, predicted a short war brought to an end by economic causes. This must have been some consolation in the beginning, for Bloomsbury was opposed to war in general ("the worst of the epidemic diseases which afflict mankind and the great genetrix of many of the others"[22]) and to this war in particular. But Keynes's optimism was confounded by events. The war was prolonged from one year to the next, and it required increasing tough-mindedness to withstand popular pressure to conform to the war enthusiasm. Not unexpectedly, Bloomsbury, with its belief in the importance of the private life and private convictions, proved extremely good at this. But in 1916, for the first time in British history, conscription was introduced, and thereafter the men of Bloomsbury were compelled to make public their consciences; that is, to declare themselves conscientious objectors to military service.

As such they came to public attention. At Trinity College, Cambridge, for example, Bertrand Russell's lectureship was not renewed; his unpopular pacifist opinions had much to do with the College's action. Lytton Strachey, called before the Hampstead Tribunal in London to prove his conscientious objections, made in passing his celebrated reply to the military representative ("What would you do, Mr Strachey, If you saw a German soldier attempting to rape your sister?" "I should try and come between them.")[23] Some days later he had a military physical examination, and the point became moot: he was declared unfit for any military service. Although he was not required to do so, he spent quite a bit of time at Garsington, Philip and Lady Ottoline Morrell's manor house outside Oxford, where friends, such as Clive Bell, were fulfilling their obligations by being farmers. Bell, a pacifist, who had argued in his pamphlet *Peace at Once* (1915) that "the war ought to be brought to an end as quickly as possible by a negotiated peace," was working on the land under the provisions of the Military Service Act. Duncan Grant and David "Bunny"

Garnett (who earlier had been with a Friends' Ambulance Unit in France) went to Wissett Lodge, outside a remote little village in Suffolk, where they meant to become fruit farmers. Duncan's father, Major Grant, was managing the farm and was willing for Duncan and Bunny to work on it, though disapproving of their conscientious objection. That summer (1916) Vanessa, with Julian, Quentin, and the maid Blanche, came down from London to Wissett to keep house for Duncan and Bunny, who were lovers at the time. The lodge was "a little early Victorian house with numerous small, exceptionally dark, rooms,"[24] shadowed by an enormous ilex, which Julian and Quentin called "the safety tree," for there, in its branches, they were safe from the grown-ups. Life went cheerfully at Wissett. Vanessa painted; the men worked hard in the orchard, kept bees, kept fowls—a large flock of white leghorns; there were frequent visitors: Oliver and Lytton Strachey, Saxon Sydney-Turner, Lady Ottoline Morrell. For Julian it was a memorable time: "orchard trees run wild, / West wind and rain." Long afterwards, with astonishing vividness, he recalled his first evening's fishing at Wissett, "when I must have caught a couple of dozen roach. . . . Bunny was fishing also: Clive advised me. They started to bite hard in the evening: that pond had never been fished before. I think my second was a big one—perhaps an eighth of a pound; impressive enough to a child. We filled a bucket, slimy, fishy smelling; there is something extraordinarily sensual and thrilling about a fish's body in one's hand: the cold, the vigour and convulsive thumping, the odd smell, the gasping open mouth you jag the hook out of."

It was at Wissett too that he read Gardiner's *History of England from Henry VIII to the Corn Laws* ("God knows how much I understood"), and it was there that he first developed "a passion for war and war games."[25] The irony of this, a war-minded child in a conscientiously objecting household, needn't be insisted upon: Julian himself saw it as "a reaction." He knew quite soon that his family and their friends were COs; it explained "the isolation, and later, at Charleston, the expectation of hostility." The war game, which grew increasingly complex and took a variety of forms over the years, originated with Quentin, with Julian as an enthusiastic and inventive collaborator. In one version it was played on a board, moving counters about; in another, it was played "life-size." Perhaps its very beginning can be traced back to an afternoon when Bunny Garnett mounted firecrackers on shingles and sailed them across the pond. There was the normal desire of little boys to play soldiers, to reenact historical battles ("the Armada . . . the Roman wall with oak-apple armies"), although out of deference to the household, contemporary history was not drawn upon: the opposing sides were never English and German. What is remarkable about the war game is that the interest in it should have continued well beyond childhood, and that war and military strategy fascinated Julian until the day of his death.

The fruit farming at Wissett proved unsatisfactory: it had been entered upon, at Keynes's suggestion, to ensure the two men exemption from military service. But the Appeals Tribunal, to which their cases were referred, "declared that though the Wissett Lodge holding might qualify as work of national importance, it was out of the question for us"—we are quoting from Garnett—"to be [in effect] our own employers." The solution appeared simple enough: to continue doing work of "national importance," that is, to continue farming, but on someone else's farm. So Wissett was abandoned. It was thought "preferable," Garnett explains, "to go back to the neighbourhood of Asheham, where Leonard and Virginia were living, and where Vanessa had pre-war acquaintances among the Sussex farmers, rather than to seek work in Suffolk."[26]

Thus it was that the Bells came to Charleston. From 1916 on, where Vanessa and her children lived was initially determined by Duncan, shaped by his need to fulfill alternate service during the First World War. Duncan discovered that such was possible in Sussex, and so Charleston, a short distance from Asheham, was rented in the autumn of 1916; it was thereafter their beloved place in the country. Virginia had discovered the house and wrote to her sister about it in May 1916:

> I wish you'd leave Wissett, and take Charleston. Leonard went over it, and says its a most delightful house and strongly advises you to take it. It is about a mile from Firle, on that little path which leads under the downs. It has a charming garden, with a pond, and fruit trees, and vegetables, all now rather run wild, but you could make it lovely. The house is very nice, with large rooms, and one room with big windows fit for a studio. . . . It sounds a most attractive place—and 4 miles from us, so you wouldn't be badgered by us.[27]

The following September she wrote again: "The garden could be made lovely—there are fruit trees, and vegetables, and a most charming walk under trees. The only drawback seemed to be that there is cold water, and no hot, in the bathroom; not a very nice w.c, and a cesspool in the tennis court.... I'm sure, if you get Charleston, you'll end by buying it forever. If you lived there, you could make it absolutely divine."[28] It was owned by Lord Gage of nearby Firle Place and continued to be so until 1981. The house was a considerable challenge, for water needed to be pumped and heated by wood, and there was no electricity until 1933. For Julian, as for his brother, Quentin, two years younger than he, and his sister, Angelica, born in 1918, Charleston was central for their lives.

Charleston was rented by the Bells in the autumn of 1916. Until 1918 they lived there without interruption, having given up Gordon Square; thereafter, they divided their time between Charleston and London. In the late 1920s, they frequently rented a house in France, at Cassis on the Mediterranean. For Vanessa and Duncan, Charleston was their country base until their deaths. For Julian, Charleston came to represent childhood and the long summer holidays from school; it was the place in which he was most happy, the most loved of his homes.

Charleston is a short distance off the main Lewes-Eastbourne road, right beneath the looming green eminence of Firle Beacon, the highest point on the Sussex Downs. At the turn of the century the house had been a simple country hotel, and many of the small, low-ceilinged rooms still retained porcelain number plates on their doors. There was an orchard, a walled garden, and across the patch of lawn from the front door, a small pond (large enough, however, for naval engagements). There was also, fulfilling the immediate needs of the household, a farm nearby, and there the conscientious objectors loyally carried on work of national importance until eleven o'clock in the morning of November 11, 1918.

In the first decade of the postwar period, Charleston became the center of what Quentin Bell called "Bloomsbury-by-the-Sea," a triangular outpost populated by the Charlestonians (the Bells and their frequent visitors), the Tiltonians (Maynard and Lydia Keynes, who took up residence at Tilton on a very short branch off the road leading to Charleston), and the Rodmellians (Leonard and Virginia Woolf, who moved from Asheham to Monk's House at Rodmell, on the other side of Lewes). The house, rambling in its construction and haphazard-seeming in its additions and outbuildings, was full of many oddly placed and sized rooms (not a disadvantage) and provided (apart from the usual bedrooms and sitting rooms, and a dining room with an immense fireplace) a library for Clive Bell, and studios for Vanessa Bell and Duncan Grant, who when not busy painting canvases, were busy painting the walls, bedsteads, cupboards, tables, chairs, plates, and other flat surfaces they could find. The result of their industry was to give the house a color and a magic (in its unexpectedness) that is unlike anything else: one has no sense, nor is one meant to have, of the self-conscious work of art. The children found the house, its grounds, and the surrounding countryside a perfect place for endless activity: for adventures, walks, war games, butterfly hunting, capture of animals—and when they were older, shooting of birds—and noise: so much noise that poor Clive Bell, in desperation, built himself a little study apart from the house, in which he hoped to gain some quiet. In any case, he was frequently not there. Clive was more in London, and would lead something of a separate life, marked by a series of lovers, most notably Mary St. John Hutchinson. His influence on Julian is not to be neglected, however; his love of the outdoor life and his wide-ranging interests were reflected in his writings, which tended to be more broad than deep.

The children, along with the grown-ups, were at the center of life at Charleston: that is its immediately distinguishing quality. They were not put to one side, categorized, or patronized, taken up enthusiastically and unceremoniously let down. That this did not happen is a tribute in part to their own considerable charm, and even more to the character of the grown-ups, who had not only the ability to love children but also, which is rarer, the ability to respect and to sympathize with them, to educate and to entertain them. Of all the grown-ups, it was Vanessa, naturally, who came first in their affections; and after her, Aunt Virginia. Her arrivals "were a signal for rejoicing on the part of Julian and Quentin who had secrets to share with her. Thus she was always led aside and from the corner of the walled garden where they were ensconced came her clear hoot of laughter—like the mellow hoot of an owl—and Julian's loud explosions of merriment, protests and explanations."[29] There were relationships of rare closeness, too, with Clive, Bunny, Duncan, and Roger Fry. (Indeed, all that seems to have been lacking in this childhood was the presence of other children. When the Desmond MacCarthys came to visit, they would bring their daughter Rachel; one hears also, when Julian was eleven, of the daughter of a woman who was at Charleston to help in the house: with the daughter, Julian fenced and wrestled. But such encounters were the exception, not the rule. On the whole, the children depended on each other and on the grown-ups for company.)

Something of the spirit of Charleston can be glimpsed in the family newspaper that Julian, the editor, and Quentin, the illustrator, put out quite regularly throughout the twenties whenever they were in residence, although in its later period it was carried on with more devotion by Quentin than by his elder brother. Such enterprises are not unusual among families; the Stephen children had done the same in the *Hyde Park News*. Only one copy was produced— printed (that is, typewritten) or handwritten—some of the text being in Virginia's hand. In fact, she would write quite a bit for it, most notably in special Christmas issues, again illustrated by Quentin. There were such texts as "Scenes in the Life of Mrs Bell," "Eminent Charlestonians," and "The Messiah," in seventeen parts largely devoted to making fun of Clive. It was handed round for the enjoyment and edification of its readers, usually at the lunch table, generally when the family was in residence at Charleston. There were weather reports, nature notes, news of arrivals and departures ("Today Mr Raymond Mortimer arrived to the great joy of the family"), and accounts of Duncan's difficulties in building an ornamental pool ("Grant's Folly"), Clive's search for peace, and the foibles and adventures of the servants, with particular emphasis on the attraction of Grace, the housekeeper, for most of the male population of Lewes and the surrounding countryside. (Grace Higgens, only five years older than Julian, came to work for Vanessa in 1920 and became a central figure in the Bell household, especially at Charleston but also in London; she went with the family to France, particularly to look after Angelica.) Mortality was not neglected in the publication ("We regret greatly the death of Marmaduke, the perroquet, who expired suddenly through unknown causes this afternoon. We fear he will be much missed"), and daily events were chronicled ("Angelica triumphed again yesterday, she succeeded without difficulty to persuade Nessa to cut her hair short. Afterwards, she danced a triumphal 'black-bottom' to celebrate her victory"). There was even an occasional advertisement:

> The Life and Adventures of J. Bell by
> VIRGINIA WOOLF
> *profusely illustrated by Quentin Bell, Esq.*

Some press notices.
. . . a profound and moving piece of work
. . . psychological insight.
> WESTERN DAILY NEWS

. . . superb illustrations . . . unwavering truth . . . worthy of royal academy
. . . clearly the work of a pupil of Professor Tonks
> ARTIST AND CRAFTSMAN

The paper, which began as the *Charleston Bulletin*, changed its name quite early in its history to the *New Bulletin*. It was very much a holiday publication: during the summer and for the Christmas and Easter vacations. There were in all 188 issues "published" from 1923 to 1927.[30] It did not, however, until a later issue, state its credo: "'The Bulletin' is unique among daily papers in being controlled by no millionaire or political party. It is not perhaps unique in having no principles."

The *New Bulletin*, subsequently *The Bulletin*, did not confine itself to the activities of the residents of Charleston and their visitors but spread its coverage, and the circulation of its single copy, to Tilton and Rodmell: "The local countryside is now menaced by a new peril. Following Nessa's sensational purchase of a Renault the Woolves have purchased a Singer. And the denizens of Tilton are now the proud owners of a secondhand Morris Cowley. Whatever we may think of the problem of pedestrian traffic and the missuse [sic] of motor-cars, we must all agree that the car will be a great asset to the house and a permanent source of instruction and amusement to the rats in the duck shed [which was being used as a garage at Charleston]." Towards Tilton, where the style of life was somewhat grander than at Charleston and Rodmell, the young editor and the illustrator maintained an attitude of amused tolerance: "We learn that Mr and Mrs Keynes are putting their chauffeur in livery. We remind our more absentminded readers that the Keynes arms are as follows: Innumerable £s rampant, numberless $$$ sinister in concentric circles *or*; Field black. Crest St George Killing the Dragon." Keynes was referred to as "the Squire of Tilton." Julian and Quentin were quite aware of Keynes's importance in the world: hence the references to "Economic Consequences" and "Conferences" that are slyly introduced into accounts, not only of the "Squire and his lady" but of the majordomo of the household, Harland, who assumes mythological proportions in the paper as a drunkard, bore, and unsuccessful suitor for the favors of the alluring Grace. In 1925, while at Charleston for Christmas, the brothers recorded a pheasant shoot in Tilton wood: "We have heard from certain sources that Mr Maynard Keynes & some of his business friends formed the party. From the same source we learn that the bag consisted of: 2 pheasants, 4 rabbits, a blackbird, a cow, 7 beaters, 19 members of the party (including leaders, onlookers, etc.) and 1 dog (shot by mistake for a fox)." In the next number, along with the familiar teasing, there is a clear reflection of Keynes's bitter and justified opposition to the return of Britain to the gold standard: "'We learn that the story that the Keynes are at Tilton has now been fully authenticated. The reason they are not flying a flag to indicate that they are in residence (as, we believe, they intend to in future) is that the price of Union Jacks has risen owing to the introduction of the Gold standard, & only red flags are obtainable."

Towards the Rodmellians, Leonard and Virginia Woolf, *The Bulletin* was more benign, although it entertained a somewhat equivocal attitude towards their dog Grizel. (Tiltonian dogs, too, were looked at askance: "A stray mongrel, possibly the property of the Keynes's, appeared in the orchard this evening. If seen again it is to be shot at sight and the remains returned to its presumed owners.") Perhaps Mrs. Woolf appears most memorably in these pages as

THE DISAPPEARING AUNT

On August 15, 1925, *The Bulletin* reported:

> On Sunday the Woolves paid a visit to the Squire. Virginia, unable to face a Tilton tea with Harland in the offing, decided to walk over to Charleston. She was seen on the road by Angelica and Louie [a Bell servant], and her voice is thought to have been heard by Duncan. She failed to appear at tea, however, and did not afterwards return to Tilton. The most widely accredited theory is that she had a sudden inspiration and sat down on the way to compose a new novel.

The next day a sequel was given: "Nessa and the Illustrator visited the Woolves this afternoon and found the disappearing aunt safe and sound. It appears that for some whim she decided to eat her tea under a hay stack instead of in Charleston dining room. The difference, however, is not great, and it is even possible that she mistook the one for the other."[31] In 1927, Julian and Quentin, probably more the latter than the former, in a piece entitled "A Hundred Years After," even commented on the Bloomsbury group itself and how its history would be misremembered. It is a short play with a guide providing, as does indeed happen now, a tour of Charleston:

> This cactus is a shoot of the original cactus brought over by the Soviet parachutist Lopokova. . . . The photos on the wall are pictures by Vanessa Bell. You will observe that many are signed Duncan Grant & this is owing to the illiberal prejudices of the 20th century against women painters. . . . Here were congregated such figures of 20th century British culture as Virginia Sackville West and her husband Sir Clive Bell, the famous sportsman and wit. Bernard Shaw, Galsworthy, Augustus John, Huxley, Sir James Barrie and other members of the so-called Bloomsbury or WC1 group, must have all been constant visitors. . . . It was in this studio that the colossal statue of queen Mary which bestrode the harbour of Sydney Australia was first conceived by the artist who signed himself Grant but whom modern research has shown to be Sir Percy Bates and Lord Kenneth Clark.[32]

That same year *The Bulletin* published a story by Virginia Woolf, "The Widow and the Parrot," a charming children's tale that takes place in Rodmell. Appropriately, in 1982, it was published with illustrations by Julian Bell, Quentin's son and Julian's nephew and namesake.

Let this presentation of the family newspaper stand for what in fact it was: the charming world of the private joke, the private reference, the intimacy and reassurance within a closely knit family, the glorious world of childhood. Let it also stand for the badinage, the chaffing, yet the deep sense of intellectual and emotional community that existed among the Bloomsbury family and friends—most particularly at the very nucleus, Virginia, Vanessa, and the Bell children.

It was in precisely this spirit of playfulness and affection that Virginia, in the splendidly ironic preface to *Orlando* (1928), acknowledged, along with a galaxy of famous names, "the singularly penetrating, if severe, criticism of my nephew Mr Julian Bell . . . my nephew Mr Quentin Bell (an old and valued collaborator in fiction) . . . Miss Angelica Bell, for a service which none but she could have rendered."

But Charleston, pleasant though it was, was not the whole of Julian's childhood and youthful experience. To begin with it was "Baths in the kitchen.

Playing by the pond. Tobogganing on the downs." But there was the matter of his education. There were informal lessons with his mother in astronomy and geology and Greek mythology, and presumably in other subjects as well. The experiment was made of having a little school with some other children with him, but that didn't work at all. There were governesses, such as Miss Edwards. "Pretty, silly, intolerable, bullied by children—sent away in 6 weeks." Then Mrs. Brereton, a friend of Roger Fry's, who found Julian an unruly pupil. Vanessa commented about her, "On the whole not unsuccessful—though a stupid woman."[33] David Garnett, in the years when he was living at Charleston, taught him "a little elementary science: biology, the evolution and principles of heredity in animals and plants, their physiology and anatomy; the elements of physics and astrophysics, the calendar and the weather." As Julian grew older, Clive began to direct his reading; the father proved, in his son's words, to be "a most admirable educator." And of course there was the education to be got from listening to the conversation (which he was permitted to do, and did) of Clive Bell and Roger Fry on matters of aesthetics and philosophy. If at eleven, then, he was officially unschooled, he was not entirely uneducated. But an education at home, unfortunately, in the eyes of the state and of most parents is not judged sufficient, and so Julian was sent to school from the age of eleven on.

Unlike most male children of his class and age (or a year or two younger), he was not sent away to boarding school to be prepared for public school but attended a day grammar school in London. Owen's, the school chosen by the Bells, was one of the best-known City of London schools, founded in 1613 by Dame Alice Owen and administered since that time by the Brewers' Company. Technically, Owen's was a public school, taking boys until they were eighteen; Julian, however, was there for only two years. He entered in September 1919, at the age of eleven and a half; and for a boy for whom childhood had been unusually pleasant, it was his introduction to the darker side of life. He had not been often in the company of other children, except for his brother and sister, and so had little experience or expectation of the cruelty that children en masse are capable of. He did not have even an older brother to warn him, or, more likely, to give him a foretaste of the bullying that is endemic among schoolboys: as the eldest child in his own family he was probably accustomed to being able to subdue Quentin and Angelica. But he seemed to adapt quickly to this aspect of school life. "Owen's," he wrote in his memoir, "after a first day of utter horror, and a bad week or so, grew not intolerable." On that first day he was "mobbed," the inevitable fate of being a new boy, especially one whose hair was thought too long. But his childhood had not been either so gentle or so sheltered that he had not learned to wrestle and box a little, and as he was heavier and taller than his contemporaries, he soon discovered that he could hold his own. Looking back upon the experience some eighteen years later, he wrote: "I was able to beat off individual bullies, and even, on occasion, intimidate mobs. My natural nervousness, very much increased by isolation and unpopularity, is consequently counteracted by a belief in the efficiency of force and the offensive. When things come to the point of violence I find my nerves under control and my spirits rise."[34] This belief in force—so at variance with the rationality of Bloomsbury as to be a bothersome problem to him thereafter—was learned outside the classroom; inside, in the true business of the classroom, he was less demonstrably affected, perhaps because, as the headmaster of the school in the 1960s tactfully suggested, "the special interests of Bloomsbury were not in line with Owen's." Although the school was more progressive than most at that time, it still emphasized "the acquisition of facts above all else."[35] Julian was exposed to them in a wide range of subjects: English, Divinity, Latin, French, Mathematics, History, and Geography. At this point, as well as for the rest of his life—perhaps it was the fault of his earliest education at home—his spelling was terrible and his handwriting pretty lamentable. In her letters to him, his mother, overindulgent as she might have been in general, tried to correct the former, without success. At Owen's he also received instruction in Drawing, Choral Practice, and Woodworking, as well as in Games. But he did not do well. At the end of his first year, he was ranked eighteenth in a class of twenty-three boys; at the end of his second and final year, he was still eighteenth but in a class of thirty-three. His one official distinction was to win one of the Reading Prizes given to the Junior part of the school—about 150 boys. Julian himself was prepared to acknowledge that Owen's "taught me what little arithmetic and algebra I know, and football—soccer," but he thought it "dreary, dingy, and a baddish education," a verdict that must be considered in the light of the phrase that immediately followed: "at home . . . was a refuge."

What institution, one wonders, devoted to the education of prepubescent males could possibly compete for fascination, charm, and intellectual stimulation with a household like the Bells'? That Julian needed to be schooled is not in question; but it seems highly unlikely that any school to which he was sent would have pleased him. Owen's had not, nor would Leighton Park, the public school to which his parents, conforming to the educational pattern of their class, sent him in January 1922. There was no tradition of a particular public school in Bloomsbury, as there was a well-defined tradition of Cambridge, and even within Cambridge, of Trinity and King's. Clive Bell had gone to Marlborough, but there was no compelling reason for Julian to follow him there. The choice made was Leighton Park School near Reading. On paper it must have looked a particularly appropriate choice, as it was, and is, the leading Quaker public school in England, founded in 1890 in succession to the defunct Grove House School, Tottenham. Both schools have their historic interest, for they can be seen to represent, in the earlier instance, the liberalization of English life and, in the later, its increasing class consciousness. Grove House School had been established in 1828 to prepare boys of Quaker families to take advantage of the new University of London (1827), which unlike Oxford and Cambridge was open to Nonconformists. Leighton Park, founded some sixty years later, was clearly intended to be a school for the wealthier Friends, and as such formed a rather late addition to the boom, largely for social reasons, in public school foundations in the second half of the nineteenth century. But the fact of its being Quaker made it somewhat different from other schools: more serious and more "guarded" in its education, more unified in its student body (in the 1920s half the students were Quakers), smaller, less obsessed with sports and games, and in theory at least, more tolerant of the individualist, the nonconformist, who like the Quakers in society itself wishes to go his own way. It was also free from the traditional public school activities of beating and fagging; and one would have had reason to expect, thanks to the Quaker background, a minimum of bloody-mindedness.

There were other, more particular circumstances to predispose the Bells to the school. Although they were not Friends themselves, Vanessa's aunt Caroline, a sister of Sir Leslie Stephen, had become one, and had long been interested in their educational activities. She had become particularly close to Virginia. Roger Fry (quite irreligious himself) was a member of a famous Quaker family and would have known Leighton Park: junior Frys and Cadburys, both families well known for their association with the manufacture of chocolate, were usually in attendance there. But most important was the attitude of conscientious objection to war which the Quakers and Bloomsburians shared, although perhaps not for the same reasons. In 1914 the headmaster, Charles Evans, had resisted pressure to set up an Officer Training Corps at the school (an omission that Julian rather regretted, given his military interests). He did establish an ambulance training scheme, however; and it should be noted here that twenty-five Old Leightonians lost their lives in the First World War. The Bells had had dealings with Evans, on matters having to do with conscientious objection, during the war, and had found him impressive; he was still headmaster in the 1920s. In short, all the omens were favorable.

But as it happened, 1922 was not a particularly good time to go to Leighton Park. The school's official historian regards the period 1920 to 1928, the last eight years of Evans's headmastership, as a period of decline. Evans was an exciting, imaginative man, and the years of moral crisis—particularly for Quakers—during the war had brought out the best in him. But expansion of the school (which became, officially, a public school in 1922) and many of the educational problems that arose after the war needed more of an administrator than Evans was: he tended to let the affairs, and particularly the discipline, of the school get slightly out of hand. At some schools, Eton being a notable example, the years immediately after the First World War were marked by a kind of radicalism on the part of the boys, a demand for greater liberalization and less stodginess. At Leighton Park too the boys were demanding more power and influence than they had previously had, but there the situation took a rather odd turn: the boys appear to have been less liberal than the masters, more philistine and sports-minded, more interested in chaos and rags than intellectual activity. This was particularly true in Grove House (named after the predecessor school), the perennial winner in school athletics, where the tone was aggressively hearty. Unfortunately, it happened to be the house to which Julian was sent.

He came to the school late in the academic year—a bad beginning. Rather than entering in the Michaelmas term of 1921, he was allowed to spend the time, undoubtedly much more enjoyable, with his family at St. Tropez; on his return to England he fell ill with influenza, so he did not enter Leighton Park until January 1922 in mid-Lent term. On the day after Julian left Charleston,

Quentin, age nine, reported in the *New Bulletin*: "Yesterday Julian departed for Layton Park to the great grief of the household. 'The New Bulletin' has suffered greatly by his absence since he is the joint editor of 'The New Bulletin' and founded The 'Charleston Bulletin' this household will never forget the invaluable services he rendered to the anti kitcheners army during the last ware when he held the office of Generall in cheif." On practically his first day there, Julian wrote home, "I am quite happy but things are very odd and strange."[36]

His late arrival put him at an obvious disadvantage: the other new boys would have had a chance to settle in during the first term, and would gang up on him as a logical victim. Then, as part of his recuperation from influenza, he was not supposed to play games or take cold baths—the sine qua non of a public school—and so gained immediately, or felt he had gained, a reputation for dirt and weakness. Then, having been placed in a form too high for him, he did badly even in his studies. But "the chief memory I have of the school is of bullying by the mob."

> Although I sometimes managed to hit back [he wrote in his "Notes for a Memoir"] I was pretty permanently terrorised and cowed. I lived, often for months on end, in a state of misery and nervous tension. It was not only the pure physical suffering: there were also the horrors of expectation and insecurity. I defended myself to some extent by becoming expert in mob psychology and distracting attention with alternative acts of naughtiness or with other victims. I suppose there were periods of peace, but never of much happiness, though when Q. came [in 1924] we could, in summer, escape on bicycles butterfly-collecting. But up to the very last I was always nervous and always subject to attack.[37]

That this should be his "chief memory," and that he should record it so vividly and with such urgency fifteen years later, is highly suggestive. But looked at objectively, the four and a half years that he spent at Leighton Park were not quite as lamentable as one might infer from this fragment of autobiography, nor were his responses during those years as bleakly despairing as he remembered them to have been. In fact, he could hold his own, not only in rugby but also in rags, pranks, and "alternative acts of naughtiness," to which he may have resorted as a way of "distracting attention" from himself, but which he also enjoyed for their own sake. "When things come to the point of violence I find my nerves under control and my spirits rise." He could be a bully himself and participated in the rather anti-Semitic rags against one poor student, Stern, "the German Jew," who as Julian wrote to his mother, "was hanged from the beam of the Junior dormitory with the fire-rope. Unfortunately he did not appreciate it properly."[38] He may, as he thought, have been bullied "to the very last," but there is reason to suspect the worst was over long before then. J. Duncan Wood, who came to Leighton Park two years after Julian, and looked up to him as an older boy, envied him his bulk: "For one thing it protected him against attack." His spirits seem often to have been exhilarated. One evening he conducted a raid on School House (one of the two other boarding houses), passing through the dormitories, overturning beds and creating chaos, then leading his followers down the housemaster's private stairs and out by the front door before there was any possibility of reply. "The whole affair, which cannot have lasted more than ten minutes, was a brilliant piece of strategy and caused School House considerable loss of face."[39]

But for all his skill at ragging, and in spite of the advantage of his large size, he did not intend to conform to the stereotype of the Grove House "tough." In his studies, in his thinking, even in his pranks, he was determined to go his own way, to be markedly individual, even idiosyncratic. This, though he did not say so, may have been a source of unhappiness, for as the official historian points out, "Julian Bell was at school at the wrong time . . . a time when freedom for the unusual boy hardly existed."[40] Yet he managed to survive, more or less on his own terms, and he did not do badly. By December 1923, he was a member of the Junior Literary Historical and Archaeological Society, one of the leading clubs in the school. He attempted, without success, to have Lytton come to the school to give a talk to the Society. Quentin did persuade their mother to accept an invitation from the headmaster to speak to the school, probably in 1925; apparently it was the only lecture she ever gave. Quentin was ill in bed and missed it; Julian was still at the school and presumably heard it, but there is no record of his reaction. Vanessa presented herself as an "idiot and a revolutionary." She emphasized the importance of form and color in art and that it should be parallel to the point of getting beneath the surface her sister had made in her essay, "Mr Bennett and Mrs Brown," of the previous year.[41]

Doubtless, Julian—as he was never afraid of discussion, indeed reveled in it—participated fully in meetings dedicated to topics about which he must have heard a great deal at home. He became a member of the Junior Debating Society his first spring at the school. He had proposed the resolution that

India should cease to be part of the Empire. "We lost by 8 to 24 but I made several friends owing to this debate."[42] There were four meetings of the Debating Society, for example, on the general topic of "Civilization," two given to the question "What Is Wrong with Civilization?," one to "Utopia," and one to a subject that was to be of much greater interest to Julian towards the end of his life: plans and ideas for a model town. He was house librarian. He participated in theatricals. In 1924 he went to a local meeting of the Independent Labour Party to hear Sidney Webb speak: "I was rather disappointed, having hoped that they would be much more riotous and would sing the 'Red Flag.' Still, it was a very good speech, and Mr Webb was most amusing, staring at the ceiling while the choir sang hymns and looking rather like a goat."[43] His greatest accomplishment, which he considered "the best part of my education," came in 1925 when he won Honourable Mention (actually the second prize) in the J. B. Hodgkin Competition in public speaking. Speeches were delivered to an audience of boys and parents, and heckling was encouraged; this meant that to be successful, one needed not only a talent for declamation but a good deal of poise (nerve) and skill in repartee. In Julian's first try in the competition—not a success—his subject was "Socialism," and he declared for a "bloody revolution." (*Shame!*) But he triumphed with a speech extolling the virtues of alcoholic liquor. (*Hear hear!*) This was his reply to a series of temperance talks to which the students had been exposed at regular intervals throughout the term preceding the competition. He secured his honorable mention, the *Leightonian* felt, for his mock-heroic conclusion drawn from Cromwell, which he addressed directly to the temperance fanatics: "In the words of a great brewer, 'I beseech you in the bowels of Christ think it possible you may be mistaken.'" In July 1926, when he played Sneer in Sheridan's *The Critic*, he received a slightly mixed notice from the *Leightonian*: "The perfection of the performance was marred by a kind of laziness. His sarcasm was too amiably delivered . . . he deserved praise for his clear and natural elocution."

On the whole, this is not an uncommon public school history—a diversity of extracurricular activity, a fair performance in the classroom—yet Julian at Leighton Park was truly uncommon, out of the ordinary, a rare bird: a self-declared intellectual with a few intimates ("fellow dims") to whom he taught the war game; very strong likes and dislikes vehemently expressed; holding forth on Postimpressionist theories; writing essays on Wordsworth and the English naturalists, and the Art of War; reading Shaw, Wells, Belloc, Chesterton, Galsworthy, Kipling, and the *Encyclopaedia Britannica*; and after the general election of 1922, converting to socialism. When he was in his last year, he was one of four speakers at a public occasion reported in the *Reading Observer*. He spoke on the present industrial system, announcing that he was "an out and out Socialist. He was nervous and unconvincing and his subject was clearly too difficult for him. There was a good deal of heckling and much laughter. ... 'I am out to destroy the industrial system and not to put another one in its place.' This took away the breath of the audience."[44] In many ways, he was a typical, bright, rather "bolshie" British public school boy, but one can already see many of his interests—as in power and violence, though in the service of some sort of progressive politics.

He was uncommon enough to be remembered. Writing of him more than thirty-five years after he had gone from Leighton Park School, his French master, T. C. Elliott, recalled him as

> Very untidy, careless of his appearance, interested in ideas in a much more evident way than his schoolfellows. I think he did not scruple to indicate that they were not quite up to his level. By this I don't mean that he was a snob, but the Bloomsbury atmosphere was not really the best preparation for the rough & tumble of a boarding school. He certainly came in for a good deal of teasing. He defended himself with a caustic, but not unkindly tongue, and I should think he was not on the whole very happy. I don't think he found many kindred spirits among boys or Staff.[45]

But however much Julian disliked his school, and however much his masters there were aware of it, the truth of the matter, as Elliott suggests, is that he was unprepared for any public school, that somewhat primitive form of life which the English upper-middle and upper classes seem to think essential for their sons. He wrote home that he was counting the days until term was over. Julian himself, in the same memoir in which he wrote of being "pretty permanently terrorised and cowed," admitted that "Leighton Park . . . probably was no worse than most schools," although he regretted not having gone to College at Eton, as many of his friends at Cambridge had done. Such a rigorous mental training, had he been qualified for it, might have served him better. "The actual education was poor tho' I got a smattering of Latin, a taste of sciences from chemistry, and kept my French." Nevertheless, it prepared him for university. He passed his exams at Leighton Park, received a distinction in history, and did well enough that he was excused from the so-called "previous," the preliminary examination at Cambridge. Julian came from so unusual a home that one feels safe in saying no public school would have been satisfactory—unless he had been in revolt against the freedom, unconventionality, and seductive atmosphere of his home environment and longed to become a businessman, a barrister, a colonial administrator, a civil servant—any of the professions for which the public schools serve as a first rung.

In fact, Julian loved his home life with almost an unhealthy adoration. Given that, no school could provide anything to equal the intellectual and artistic stimulation, the sheer pleasure, of continual discussions, serious and frivolous, with Clive and Vanessa Bell, Leonard and Virginia Woolf, Roger Fry, Duncan Grant, and David Garnett. In the alternations between Charleston (and Gordon Square) and Leighton Park, the advantage would always be with the former. Home, for so many budding intellectuals the crucial battlefield of adolescence, for Julian was the great good place, the source of all those ideas that had, as John Lehmann says, "the authority of graven tablets of the law: the tablets of Bloomsbury."[46] There is a measure of irony, then, that he should have been thought more unusual, unpredictable, uncommon, at school than at home, for it seems not to have occurred to the elders of Bloomsbury, themselves usually so alert in such matters, that his, conceivably, was the sensibility of an artist; that he might, one way or another, prove to be an artist himself. Not that he gave evidence of precocity in these respects: "It must have been in my early years at L.P.S. that I dropped my own efforts as a painter encouraged of course by family." And his contributions to the *New Bulletin* were exuberant and charming but in themselves do not count as "first flights." (From a high-handed, affectionate parody of Mrs. Woolf's manner: "But then things were like that, she thought. The children had just run upstairs with the scuffle of a pack of hounds, and her freed mind floated gently, like a goldfish basking in the autumn sunshine, amid the pale, starlike blooms of the waterlilies. The new refrigerator would cost thirty pounds, she thought.") So there was no evident reason to anticipate a burst of creative activity. Yet it seems odd that the possibility should not even have been entertained.

On Saturday, August 2, 1924, at Monk's House, Virginia Woolf, while she was in the midst of writing *Mrs Dalloway*, noted in her diary:

Julian has just been & gone, a tall young man who, inveterately believing myself to be young as I do, seems to me like a younger brother: anyhow we sit and chatter, as easily as can be. It's all so much the same—his school continues Thoby's school. He tells me about boys & masters as Thoby used to. It interests me just in the same way. He's a sensitive, very quick witted, rather combative boy; full of Wells, & discoveries, & the future of the world. And, being of my own blood, easily understood—going to be very tall, and go to the Bar, I daresay.[47]

⁓

Julian was not yet eighteen when he left Leighton Park, and it was decided that he should have another year of preparation before going off to the University. Clive had an ideal of making his son a man of the world, a feat plainly outside the scope of any English public school. A season in Paris was indicated: where better to achieve the result? As a Francophile and man of the world himself, Clive was frequently in Paris, spoke the language perfectly, and had a large number of friends in French literary and artistic circles. Among them was a nephew of the painter Renoir, who was teaching at one of the great lycées of Paris, *Louis le Grand*. Renoir recommended that Julian be sent to his colleague Pinault, who would take one or two young men each year for intensive study. It seemed an ideal solution: accordingly, from the autumn of 1926 until the summer of 1927 he was in Paris, living with the Pinaults in their flat at 96 Boulevard Port Royal (at the corner of Boulevard Montparnasse). It was an interesting place to be, a perfectly respectable boulevard on the Left Bank, near the Observatory and above the Luxembourg Gardens. At the same time, it was close to the Latin Quarter, ideally situated for Julian to venture, experimentally, into *la vie de Bohème* if he had so wished—but he did not, or did not dare; it came to the same thing. Although he went to the Sorbonne as a student, he took no exams, "followed lectures, steadily less attentively, and presently spent much time walking the streets." Apart from this, he did not seem to participate much in Parisian life, nor, according to his own account, did he acquire the social graces that his father expected him to learn in Paris. That was not his style, then or afterwards. He was in many ways a casual country child, and never totally acquired a city polish. His aunt testifies to this: "He was entirely unself conscious: I doubt if he ever looked in the glass, or thought a moment about his clothes, or his appearance. Nessa used to mend his breeches. He was always patched, or in need of patching."[48]

What he enjoyed most in Paris were his discussions and arguments with Pinault ("one of the nicest human beings I ever knew"), from whom he learned a considerable amount about French literature, art, and politics. He had read Corneille, Racine, and Molière; now, along with much else, he added two particular favorites of Pinault's: Voltaire, who destroyed whatever was left of the religiosity of "downstairs" or Leighton Park, and Anatole France. Pinault was a lively, genial, and very charming radical of the old French school. A countryman come to the capital and a onetime German teacher, he was now secretary of *Louis le Grand* but still had time to demonstrate in Left-wing causes and vent his antagonism to the Church in the classic tradition of French anticlerical republicanism. Pinault "called himself a communist," but this seems to have been more a radical stance than an actuality: "there was nothing of the modern party line about him." He had a fondness for the painters Delacroix and Courbet and introduced their work in the Louvre to Julian, who hitherto had only looked at the Impressionists in the Luxembourg. And Pinault reinforced Julian's theoretical socialism, adding to it a more romantic continental idea of revolution than he might have acquired at home in England.

At the same time, Julian was reading a great deal on his own—Rimbaud, Heredia, Mallarmé—"generally discovering Parnassians and symbolists and moderns." He made "first efforts at Proust and Gide." He "developed a passion for Giraudoux." Indeed, his reading among the modern French appears much more adventurous and advanced than anything he had thus far done in English. There, except for the works of Bloomsbury, he had not yet gone beyond the Edwardians. But the crucial influence of that year's reading in Paris was Maupassant, who "provided to a large extent," Julian wrote, "an introduction to 'life'—I had no experience at first hand. But I became familiar with, and instinctively accepted, a Latin-sensual view of *amour* which, though I have modified it, I think I still keep in essentials, and have found works." That, of course, was written a decade later, when theory had been translated into practice. In Paris, as at Charleston, he was still leading a sheltered existence in which anything and everything could be read about and thought about and talked about (those splendid discussions!), but none of the economic realities (he wanted his mother to check with Keynes about what was likely to happen to the franc) or the sexual realities of the world were actually experienced. "Experience" apart, however, it was a time of great intellectual value, in reading and ideas, and left Julian with a command of bad French, which he spoke with great gusto. Matured and enriched, he rejoined his family in the summer; Renoir's recommendation had been well given.

In one respect had Paris fallen short of expectation: even after his prolonged exposure to it, Julian had not been transformed into the man of the world his father would have liked him to be, a man of his own style, so to speak. But it should be emphasized that neither then nor later did Julian wish to be so transformed. There was a duality in Clive that found a parallel in the ambivalence of Julian's feelings towards him. On the one hand, worldliness and suavity of Clive's sort did not seem to Julian particularly admirable or a model to emulate. On the other hand, Clive in his aspect of country squire greatly attracted him. It was there, in the natural world of birds and dogs, fields, woods, streams, and the changing seasons, and in the masculine pursuits of the countryside, shooting, fishing, beagling—all very plain and foursquare—that father and son were closest to each other in spirit. And it was this world that Julian would evoke in his earliest poetry.

In Paris he became a poet.

For all the intellectual excitement and stimulation, the pleasures of discussion and argument with "old Pinault," he was unhappy in Paris and tired of the city—despite his time in London, he felt it was his "first experience of a large town"—and, pining for the country, he reacted to the capital of civilization to which his father had sent him in a way that he characterized as "fiercely naturalist." In his memoir, written ten years later when the poetic impulse had spent itself (or been thwarted), he gave only a sentence to the event, one of the most significant of his life in making him a poet, concluding, "this unhappiness, sending me to watch all the gulls and sparrows of Paris, sent me also to writing my first poems: pure nature descriptions."[49] Perhaps it also helped that he was able to see lots of birds while joining his family in Cassis for two weeks in April.

Does unhappiness, absence from a landscape passionately loved, force a poet into being? Before Julian comes to Paris, there is no mention of poetry—no serious attempts at writing it, not even of reading it. Yet now, in an almost unpremeditated way, he discovers that he is a poet—interestingly enough, something Bloomsbury had not produced before. (T. S. Eliot was a friend of the Bells—Clive admired him most among modern poets—and a close friend also of Virginia and Leonard Woolf who published *The Waste Land* at the Hogarth Press; but he came into their lives, or they into his, at the end of the war, when he was already a "formed" poet. Eliot's connections and affiliations with Bloomsbury were social and literary, rather than spiritual and philosophical, and it would be misleading, even by proximity, to describe him as a Bloomsbury poet.) These first poems of Julian's, his "nature descriptions," are not at all the usual juvenilia of the period, mere Georgian echoes. Nor is the nature he describes in them what he observed in Paris: the flowering parterres and espaliered hedges of the Luxembourg Gardens; the artful wilderness of the Bois. In spite of the titles he affixed to these poems, "Vendémiaire," "Brumaire," "Frimaire," "Pluviose" (the names of months in the French revolutionary calendar), they are descriptions, as exact and truthful, as "fiercely naturalist" as he could make them, of the countryside he knew best and vividly evoked in absence: the Sussex Downs, the landscapes of southeast England. With some trepidation he sent the poems to his mother. "I trust to you to show them to no-one on any account, as I do not want to be laughed at over them."[50]

He recalled how in winter, "wreathing white misty fogs" from off the sea drift across the land, hiding "the pale sun's sky," and how

> On moonless nights, when the whole sky is dark,
> There comes a sudden rush of intense black,
>   Then, terrified, the sheep
>   Break hurdles and escape.
>
> And from the air comes the full cry of hounds,
> Mixed with the rushing noise of a high wind,
>   As, from the coast, the geese
>   Sweep inland, clamourous.
>   —"Brumaire"

In "Frimaire," describing a pheasant shoot in autumn, there is a deliberate absence of emotion, but what the eye sees and the ear hears are set down with impressive conviction.

>   . . . Far-heard the tapping, distant and gentle,
>   Through the wet, quiet wood, of
> The beaters' sticks. A throbbing, whirring rustle,
>   A pheasant high above.

Grey timid rabbits come forward, hop along,
    The beaters' line draws in.
Sudden tumult of pheasants rising strong.
    The thudding guns begin.

Pale, ghostly woodcock, pointed wings wandering
    Through the trees, in and out.
Wild sudden excitement, beaters calling
    And long, random-wild shot.

And the pheasants hit in their rocket flight
    Come awkwardly tumbling down.
Blue-white, bead-green and black on gold-bronze bright,
    Feminine mottled brown.

John Lehmann, who has written with great sensitivity of Julian and his poetry (they were to become friends and fellow-poets at Cambridge) in his volume of autobiography, *The Whispering Gallery*, sees in these early poems "an attempt to let the countryside, the moods of wind and weather and life outside the cultivated human pale, speak for themselves without any interference of the poet's moralizing thoughts."[51] The result, as the quotations we have given bear out, was a highly original and authentic poetry, too quiet-voiced and unassertive ever to call much attention to itself, and closer in its affinities to painting than to other nature poetry. That image in "Frimaire"—"Pale, ghostly woodcock, pointed wings wandering / Through the trees, in and out"—reads like a transmutation into words of a detail from a Chinese painting. And the final stanza's determination to see things exactly as they are, its meticulous notations of color ("Blue-white, bead-green . . . black on gold-bronze"), call to mind similar notations, a comparable purity of vision, in passages within the journal of Delacroix and the letters of van Gogh.

One does not wish to make excessive claims for this poetry, although it is of a sort easier to underrate than to overpraise. The fact is indisputable: during his year in Paris, and his first two years in Cambridge, Julian was truly a poet. Thereafter he was a poet intermittently, at widening intervals, until, towards the end of his life, he wrote very few poems. Among the older generation of Bloomsbury only David Garnett appears to have recognized this quality: "Julian was first of all a poet," he wrote in 1938, "hard thinking never made him a thinker; but his poems are exact, clear, and perfectly expressive.

In his poetry he has escaped from all his turmoil. He is the poet I like best of his generation."[52] There were, also, in his poetry close affinities with his mother's paintings and those of Duncan Grant's. And as we shall see, Virginia had mixed feelings about his poetry. Although to a degree she wished to be supportive, she was also, as she was self-aware, unable to suppress a sense of rivalry. But that was in the future.

CHAPTER 2

A YOUNG APOSTLE

IN THE AUTUMN OF 1927, after his educative year in Paris, Julian Bell went up to King's College, Cambridge. He was eighteen years old, a budding poet, a socialist, a rationalist in matters of life and love about which he may have had a large theoretical knowledge but as far as one knows no experience: Bloomsbury's principles were "inscribed on his banner." Yet in Paris he had been more independent of these enlightened principles than he perhaps realized. The act of writing poetry was his own choice, prompted by his own need, and the poetry itself followed no precedent of idea or form set by his elders. Bloomsbury's prime commitment was to individuals, in the world, in created works and the civilization they represented. In Julian's early poems the primacy is given to nature, and humankind is of no interest. When in "Vendémiaire" a "covey of brown birds" is brought down, the hunter is not even noticed except obliquely, as

> . . . Blue barrel and black dot,
> Thud and thin smoke of double shot.

Then, like an image of dying nature in Courbet, comes the lingering, carefully observed, impersonal center of the poem:

Feathers drift down
Slowly, from breast and wing.
The chestnut horseshoe bodies bleed
At beak and shattered joint, opaque
Drops, shot unsmoothed
Plumage . . .

Whatever its merits or defects, this is poetry in a different tradition (or mode) from Bloomsbury's world, whatever connection it might have with its paintings, and it was written in a time of absence, when Julian was in Paris, away from home territory.

Cambridge, of course, was very much home territory, and King's College particularly so. Although more of the first generation of Bloomsbury had been at Trinity, the connection had not been maintained. Keynes, however, had continued his close association with his undergraduate College, King's—in 1924 he began his spectacular career as its first bursar, so arranging its investments that for the first time the College had an income commensurate with its buildings and pretensions—and gradually, over the years, it had become a kind of Bloomsbury outpost at Cambridge. So there was no question where Julian would go. His first year, when as was customary, he lived not in college but in lodgings, just across the street (12 St. Edward's Passage) off King's Parade, he afterwards summed up as "a failure on the whole." He was rather shy to begin with; he was eager for "intellectual society," never easily come by, even at King's; and of course, one's earliest undergraduate alliances are almost certain to be mistakes: mutual loneliness and unfamiliarity proving the most tenuous of bonds when one is no longer lonely and knows where one is. Yet "failure" seems a relative judgment. In his first year, even though he felt awkward, he was still meeting people. As he wrote to his mother on October 13: "I have made one friend, rather a nice creature called Barger, who knows Morgan and Sidney Waterlow and Roger a little. But I still find people uncomfortable, I mean in the way that I have always been shy and selfconscious and afraid of them." And as he wrote to her the next day, "One runs across a great many people more or less causally, but they usually either bore or frighten me."[1] But it was shortly later in his first year that he formed the closest and most enduring of his friendships—with Eddie Playfair—the only friendship of which he wrote at length in his memoir.

> Eddy I first scraped acquaintance with in Hall, under a misunderstanding. We discovered a common knowledge of, and interest in, French literature, and very rapidly became intimate. During our three years we met every day, and most evenings, and talked on till one and two in the morning. (Our most extreme effort in this direction was once at Charleston, when I expounded my view of ethics to him until we suddenly noticed that it was six.) Eddy was very much the Etonian [he had been in College there], in spite of the miseries of his school life—hardly, if at all, less than mine. Although at first I reacted very much against it. . . . I think he did a great deal to civilise me, and give me whatever social graces I possess.[2]

But Julian did not hesitate to be in touch with the friends of his family; shortly after arriving, he took tea with the charming young English don George "Dadie" Rylands and had lunch with Keynes. Rylands, only six years older than Julian, had just become a Fellow. He had become well known to his family through working for six months at the Hogarth Press. (In his correspondence, Julian consistently slightly misspelled his friends' names, relying on pronunciation. Eddie was Eddy, Dadie was Dedie, and Anthony Blunt, Antony.)

In some sense, Julian was in an odd position in Cambridge. Through Bloomsbury he had special ties, far closer than other undergraduates, to the luminaries of King's, most notably Keynes, as well as Rylands and the classicist John Sheppard, although the College was a notably friendly place, with homosexual overtones. Julian enjoyed being a younger part of Bloomsbury, and had adored growing up at Charleston, but it also could be restrictive, and might be particularly so when one began to live on one's own. Yet the visits of his mother and his aunt could add to the pleasure of existence. Probably the most notable was in October 1928, the beginning of his second year, when Virginia came to deliver the two talks, one at Newnham and the other at Girton, that would become *A Room of One's Own*. Virginia was just back from her trip to Burgundy with Vita Sackville-West, and her "love letter" to her, *Orlando*, had just been published. One of the visit's most famous moments, as recorded in *A Room of One's Own*, was the elegant lunch held in Rylands's rooms on October 20, immortalized in her book (Rylands claimed that Virginia exaggerated). Julian was at the lunch, along with his sister, Angelica, as well as Keynes, Strachey, and Leonard Woolf. Virginia contrasted the occasion with the grim dinner at Newnham, where Strachey's sister Pernal was the Principal. That meal was made even more disastrous than it might have been, as Virginia was an hour late and had brought Leonard along without telling her hosts that she was doing so. The following week she came again to Cambridge, with Vita, to give the second lecture, at Girton. She wrote about the audience in her diary on October 27: "Intelligent, eager, poor; & destined to become school mistresses in shoals. I blandly told them to drink wine & have a room of their own. Why should all the splendour, all the luxury of life, be lavished on the Julians and the Francises [presumably a reference to Francis Birrell, who had been at King's 1908–1911], & none on the Phares and the Thomases."[3] While it was true that quite a few Newnham and Girton students went on to be school mistresses and that no doubt their style of life was less grand than Julian's, the two women she mentioned actually became distinguished figures. Elsie Phare, later Duncan-Jones, a student at Newnham, did better than any other undergraduate, male or female, on her English exams, although, meanly, as a woman, the results were still not official. She was also much involved with the literary scene at Cambridge and went on to become a very well known academic, particularly as an expert on Andrew Marvell. Margaret Ellen Thomas, Virginia's host at Girton, according to Kate Perry of Girton, "read Classics then Moral Sciences at Girton and went on to become a writer. Before leaving Girton, she had formed the idea of gathering together verse written by women in the University, and approached Woolf about the project. She edited (and contributed to) *An Anthology of Cambridge Women's Verse* which was published by the Hogarth Press in 1931. Her other major publication was *A Perch in Paradise* (London 1952). In 1931, she married Sir Edward Bullard, FRS," who became an eminent maritime geophysicist. Kate Perry also sent the comments that Muriel Bradbrook, the famous Shakespeare scholar and ultimately Mistress of Girton, made in 1989. She had been in the audience. In effect, she accused Virginia of being herself too Julian-like: "She looked very elegant, with long earrings. . . . The impression she gave however, was that she was looking at Girton from the angle of King's. She had not got our wavelength, she saw us as painfully deprived creatures from the Midlands preparing to teach those with the same background. . . . We admired Mrs Woolf but we didn't feel attracted."[4]

From the first Julian responded to the diversity and possibility of Cambridge life: he would write poems and plays (but not show them to many or publish them; for his poetry, that was to come later). As he wrote to his mother: "I have been writing a certain amount, and have sent my poems to Virginia. . . . I wish I knew how they had really impressed her."[5] His aunt did write him a few days later: "I consider that any wits you may find in your head (for writing I mean) come solely from me; so I think I have a right to see your works. I may be partial of course; but I like these poems very much."[6] She then went on to give detailed criticism, both negative and positive, and promised not to show them to others. The next month, "I sent Virginia a play, which I've shown to Morgan who didn't much like it. Nor do I. Nor will she. Or anyone else. Still, I suppose one must work off the Stephen itch."[7] He was right about Virginia's reaction:

> I dont think I like it as much as the other things you've shown me. I dont think its exactly dull; but I think its awkward. . . . I hope you will go on, and write and write and write—every sort of thing. I rather hope it wont be a novel. Anything is better than a novel. . . . Write long letters and send them to me. . . . If I criticise your writings, I shall tell you exactly what I think: on condition that you don't mind when I blame, and don't think me being kind if I praise. Your old Aunt V.[8]

He also devoted time to forming friendships, talking until dawn, reading a good deal "in scattered fashion," going out fortnightly with the University Beagles, and speaking at the Union. With all this he even found time for his academic responsibilities. He had decided to read History, a continuing passion since childhood, and he went to tutorials with John Clapham, the distinguished economic historian. He worked hard. One aim of education at Oxford and Cambridge was to train people to be clever as well as knowledgeable, but knowledge worn lightly, with little indication of being a "swot," even though much work may have gone into the essays written for one's supervisor as preparation for the Tripos examinations. So too style might be pursued more than substance in the political organization, the Cambridge Union, and even in the famous discussion group, the Apostles, to which he was to be elected at the beginning of his second year. Quite a few of the essays he wrote for Clapham, with his supervisor's comments, are preserved in his papers, on such topics as "When is rebellion justified?" and "We learn from History that men never learn anything from History." But there were more straightforward subjects as well, such as the Norman Conquest, the Magna Carta, and the open field system of agriculture. In an essay he wrote on Machiavelli one can see his developing idea of the use of force in the modern world. "He [Machiavelli] never fell into the folly of the communists and his disciples, the fascists, of believing in violence as an end, or at least as an essential means. Machiavelli thought violence one of the most useful weapons of a tyrant in establishing and maintaining his power, but he did not hold, with the fascist, that there is something extremely virtuous about knocking political opponents on the head."[9]

He studied History his first two years. In Part I of the Tripos, the series of three-hour examinations which he took in the late spring of 1929, he received a 2:1; that is, the first division of the second class of the honors degree—a mark reflecting ability and work of some distinction, but not enough of either to achieve a First. In his third year and final undergraduate year he made a change, and read English with F. L. Lucas. "Peter" Lucas was a much more congenial, very much a Bloomsburian figure, as Clapham was not. Although of a younger generation, somewhat between Julian's parents and Julian himself, he was a friend of Keynes and the Bells. Trained as a classicist, in 1920 he had been the first Fellow in English elected by the College. His literary sympathies were of admirable breadth, ranging from the Elizabethans to the moderns: he was preparing an edition of Webster; he was an authority on the eighteenth century; he was informed on the French Enlightenment; he was curious about the psychological aspects of literature. Unlike the older generation of Bloomsbury, he had had a military experience of the First World War, about which he would write powerfully in the 1930s. He and Julian got on extremely well, and it was as pleasant a tutorial and personal relation as one could wish for, yet it achieved precisely the same result as the tutorials with Clapham (no doubt for the same reason). In Part II of the English Tripos, Julian earned a 2:1. Nevertheless, he was deemed worthy of support, and he was awarded research studentships in the gift of the College for the years 1930–1931 and 1931–1932. Such, briefly, was his academic career.

For Julian, as for many other undergraduates, the official academic aspect of things was not necessarily a dominating concern. He had his political, philosophical, poetical, emotional, and sensual interests, and Cambridge was prepared to minister to them all in that order. In the Spring of his first year he spent a fair amount of time at the Cambridge Union, a well-established debating society; as at Oxford, it had its own rather grand quarters and was also a training ground for future politicians. His interest in politics was longstanding, going back to his earliest days at Leighton Park; he had called himself a socialist since the general election of 1922 when the Labour Party became the official opposition; he had talked politics with Pinault in Paris and in Bloomsbury with his Uncle Leonard and with Keynes. His success at Leighton Park in the Hodgkin Competition had increased his interest in public speaking; hence the Union. It was a logical starting point for a politically minded young man with a taste for public speaking. But although it produced a place to be heard, and in that sense was not without value, it offered little in the way of a serious confrontation and discussion of political issues. Its motions for debate tended either to be frivolous or, if serious, to be dealt with frivolously—on occasion, debate on an important but nonpolitical issue, such as birth control, might attract a large and presumably attentive house, but generally not. Of course, it was a comparatively slack time in politics in England, despite the brief first Labour government in 1924 and the intensity of the general strike in 1926. From 1924 to 1929 the Conservatives under Baldwin were in smug possession and were making a futile attempt to restore prewar normalcy. As one would expect, that slackness was reflected in the Union. Tories dominated; debates tended towards the apolitical, and the rather bogus, would-be Victorian style the Union affected—which would wilt noticeably under the onslaught of the 1930s—was still in full flower.

What is surprising about Julian's brief career in the Union is that it should have lasted as long as it did. This can hardly have been the "intellectual society" he craved. But it was his first year, and other alternatives did not present themselves. He spoke for the first time about a month after the beginning of term against the motion "That England thinks too much of her athletes and their doings." He argued that sport was a sort of opiate, and was a good thing for keeping a democracy quiet. The reporter for the *Cambridge Review* characterized his speech as "excellent." The motion was carried 207 to 144. Two months later, in January 1928, he spoke against the motion "That the Application of Socialist principles to the National Finances would be disastrous." The *Cambridge Review* reported that "Mr J. H. Bell, looking every inch the Kingsman, was interesting and distinctive." The motion was carried 196 to 118. Later that month he was again on the losing side when he attacked the cult of efficiency as a menace to civilization. In April, however, he argued in favor of machine civilization, and the small house agreed with him. The Summer term—that is, the spring—of his first year was his most active in the Union: he spoke at almost every meeting from the end of April on. At the meeting of May 15 he was the first speaker for the opposition on the motion "That the time has now come for a decent burial of the Savoy Operas." He wrote to his mother about it: "I made my first paper speech at the Union last night—rather a dreary business in a thin house, but I've some hopes that it may lead to my getting on to the committee and getting something amusing next term."[10] Gilbert Harding, then an undergraduate and later a famous radio and television broadcaster, reporting the event for the *Cambridge Review*, described Julian as doing extraordinarily well, particularly considering that before the formal discussion got under way there had been an hour-long debate during which it was decided that women would not be allowed to come to the Union as speakers. "Mr Bell concluded . . . with a plea against the burial of the living, after some literary arguments which were too intelligent for the House to appreciate." Musical arguments seem not to have been adduced—music was never a Bloomsbury specialty. In any case, Julian's side won the debate, in a house much reduced by the discussion of feminist questions, 59 to 11. The next academic year, on October 30, he spoke in favor of the motion "That the sciences are murdering the arts." As reported in the *Review*, he maintained that "The scientist, the inquirer, the interrogator, was innately incapable either of creating or appreciating art. The business man, the waste product of Science, was the immediate murderer." In the middle of November, towards the end of his active participation in the affairs of the Union, he spoke in favor of the motion "That the foreign missions have outlived their justification," arguing that "it was monstrous to use a monopoly of medicine and education in order to secure conversion"—a proper Bloomsbury retort to a Claphamite Sect tradition and, for Julian, a properly iconoclastic note on which to conclude. Even though at the end of that term, and again at the end of the next, he was elected to the Standing Committee of the Union, his interest in it had not extended much past the first term of his second year. By then he had found his alternatives. "Intellectual society" was elsewhere. He spoke just once more in the Union, in April 1929, and then, significantly, in favor of a political motion that genuinely interested him: "That this House condemns the policy of the Conservative Party as contained in the Budget and the Prime Minister's speech on April 18." The motion was not carried.[11]

~

If his first year had been (in his own eyes) "a failure on the whole," his second was an unqualified success. His aunt Virginia wrote about him at the end of his first year: "Julian is a vast fat powerful sweet tempered engaging young man, into whose arms I let myself fall, half sister, half mother, & half (but arithmetic denies this) the mocking stirring contemporary friend. Mercifully Julian has his instincts sane & normal: has a wide forehead & considerable address & competence in the management of life." And then a year later she provided a somewhat more intellectual portrait: "Julian, to me a very satisfactory young man at present; full of ardour, yet clear, precise; & genial too—with all his apostolic fervour & abstractedness a good fellow, warm, kindly; much more apt to see the good than the bad."[12] At the very beginning of his second year occurred what he described as "the most important event of my Cambridge life . . . being elected to the Apostles." In fact (and certainly as he recalled it),

> the whole period was one of great expansion and a feeling of richness and possibilities in the world. I published my first poems, in *The Venture* and *Cambridge Poetry* [actually, in the *Cambridge Review*] that autumn [actually, that winter]: I had a car, and my own rooms [he had moved into College—into Bodley's, overlooking the river, where he would live for the next two years and where Quentin had decorated his sitting room for him], furniture, pictures—all the amenities of Cambridge at its best. There was an extraordinary *douceur de vivre*, a combination of material wealth (part boom, part credit-system), the general ease of college life, a certain relaxation of work [with the academic result we have already noticed] and a great many new friends . . . a steadily widening and varying circle.[13]

Taking Julian at his word, that "the core of this was the Apostles," we shall turn our attention to that aspect of his life. He would, of course, already have been familiar with the Society, officially the Cambridge Conversazione Society, as the great progenitor of Bloomsbury, and he must have approached it with high expectations. He was not to be disappointed. He was elected in November 1928, having been nominated by a fellow undergraduate, later a mathematics don at the College and a figure of the Left, Alister Watson. At

A Group of Apostles. *Left to right:* Richard Llewellyn-Davies, Hugh Sykes Davies, Alister Watson, Anthony Blunt, Julian Bell, Andrew Cohen. From *Julian Bell: Essays, Poems, and Letters*, edited by Quentin Bell (The Hogarth Press, 1938).

the weekly Saturday evenings, Julian was truly in many ways in his element, for there was nothing he loved more than discussion—"at that time . . . the greatest passion of my life"—and was prepared not only to talk but to listen, and even, perhaps too easily, to defer to another opinion. A paper was presented and discussed (dissected)—just as in the past—and there was a traditional form linking the Apostolic generations, from Tennyson and Hallam, to Strachey and G. E. Moore, to Julian and his friends. Those who were Apostles during his time included Anthony Blunt, who was elected just the previous Spring, Andrew Cohen, Guy Burgess, Dennis Proctor, Hugh Sykes Davies, and Richard Llewellyn-Davies. They were the "Brothers," limited to twelve in number. Senior members were "Angels," and those in residence, such as Keynes, G. M. Trevelyan, G. E. Moore himself, and Richard Braithwaite, then a young philosophy don at King's, would frequently attend and even at times give papers. Other Angels might from time to time come up from London for meetings, and there was an annual dinner there, generally in June, for all. As the historian of the Apostles has noted, the Society "gave them a sense of self-confidence, belonging, liberation, and meaningfulness."[14] Its minute books are singularly uninformative: they do not provide even the proper title of the paper presented by the member standing "on the hearthrug." A topic is noted, but it is generally a whimsical derivative of whatever was the subject of the paper. Names are listed as well, presumably of those who were present, and a vote. Each person would comment, in an order determined by lot. Subjects for discussion changed, inevitably, from generation to generation: the Apostles did not live outside time. In the Julian period they discussed "a classic, post-impressionist view of the arts" and "anarchism ... in the mode of Blake and Dostoievsky." These were the 1920s; one is not surprised to be told that "Practical politics were beneath discussion." Yet certain of their discussions were peculiarly Apostolic and timeless, restatements of restatements of the concerns of their predecessors. From what are probably Apostolic essays preserved in Julian's papers one can tell the sort of topics considered: truth, emotive statements, sincere emotions in poetry, religion, mysticism, prophets, romantics, and common sense. The echo of the past is unmistakable, for example, in this surviving fragment of a paper Julian presented to the Society: "Tho' I know only too well that in reality everyone is more or less blinded by prejudices, I do believe that people have only to see clearly in order to know what is good or bad, and the legitimate means of persuasion are enough to show them clearly the nature of any state of mind or life." Did he really believe this innocent simplification, or did he believe he believed it, for the sake of discussion? As an undergraduate Apostle he thought himself a disciple of G. E. Moore, although he hadn't actually read *Principia Ethica*, and when finally he did, it was "in a very critical spirit." But that was not until some years later when he was attempting to construct a philosophy of his own. In his memoir, from which these quotations are taken, he describes the intellectual climate of the Society as "Bloomsbury *un peu passé*"; but if it was chiefly warmed-over Moore that was served up at meetings, there was also a dash of contemporary spice: "the mild troubles," in Julian's phrase, of I. A. Richards and of Freud. Yet one has the sense of the tail end of a tradition. In the 1930s, when events in the world outside had thrust themselves upon the consciousness of Cambridge, and of the Apostles, the Marxist views of certain of its members were set forth too passionately (perhaps because believed in) to allow for a gentlemanly exchange of opinion, and the atmosphere became so intense that the Society was forced almost totally to suspend its activities. In 1937, in China, Julian wrote: "From the beginning I took it very seriously, and still do: I think the bitterest thing about the communist hysteria at Cambridge has been the virtual death of the Society; my hope is that it is only a temporary coma." Virginia commented on this period to Julian in a letter in 1936: "Leonard went to the Society dinner, and was delighted by Moore—the same sublimity he's known these thirty years. . . . It seems doubtful if the Society will pull through the crisis; whether it isnt the relic of too high a civilisation to attract the young who must have politics and real life to gnaw."[15] Indeed, the Society did survive and after a period of barely meeting continued to flourish. Of the importance of the Society in Julian's life there is no question; that its effect upon him was entirely to the good is less certain. It did encourage him in his philosophic bent, it did encourage him to think, but perhaps in a not sufficiently toughminded way and perhaps at some cost to his instinctive gift as a poet.

His first meeting on November 17 had nine in attendance. It was in Anthony Blunt's rooms in Trinity College, with Moore as moderator. Keynes and Frank Ramsey, the brilliant young philosopher, mathematician, and economist, as well as John Sheppard, the classicist, were there as "Angels." The minute books, as noted, are unhelpful in providing information on what happened at the meeting itself as neither the topic being discussed nor what was said about it is recorded. A motion and a vote are given, but one has no sense whether the motion was connected with the actual discussion. For his first meeting the motion allegedly was "Are we would-be Happy Warriors?" Julian wrote some years later: "My first meeting, in Antony Blunt's room was terrifically impressive, with a paper by Moore himself. I really felt I had reached the pinnacles of Cambridge intellectualism: I am still not quite sure how, for the only real member in actuality I knew was Alistair and him not well."[16]

At his second meeting on November 24 the notation was "Books or Characters," and he voted for books. Forster, who at the time had a three-year fellowship at King's as a result of the great success of his Clark lectures, *Aspects of the Novel*, attended, as he was now in Cambridge for six weeks during the year. Julian saw more of him at Cambridge but felt a little uneasy about him. As he wrote to Virginia at the time, "I like Morgan better the more I see of him, but he is so quiet and mousy one never knows if one is boring him."[17]

The most dramatic event of the Apostolic year was the return of Ludwig Wittgenstein to Cambridge and to the Apostles. Without enthusiasm on his part, he had been elected in November 1912. And indeed he remained a member of the Society for only a few months. Then, most unusually, his membership was terminated. He left Cambridge in 1913. On January 18, 1929, he returned, as Keynes wrote to his wife, Lydia Lopokova: "Well, God has arrived. I met him on the 5:15 train."[18] The next day Keynes gave an Apostolic dinner to introduce him to the bright young men of the time, including Julian. Wittgenstein was elected an honorary member, an Angel. (The following April he was absolved of his former excommunication.) But he made hardly any difference to Julian, as he came barely to any meetings and apparently continued to hold the Society in disdain. In fact he collectively condemned the student members as "these Julian Bells."[19]

The Apostles would meet almost every Saturday evening during term. On May 9, 1931, perhaps the real topic and the whimsical one coincided: "Is a knowledge of the Character of an Artist of profit in the proper Appreciation of his work?" with Julian voting yes and Anthony Blunt voting no. He also went quite regularly to the annual London reunion dinner and had to speak at his first, in June 1929. His aunt Virginia recorded the event in her diary, presumably having heard the tale from Leonard. "Julian broke down in his Apostle speech; came dressed as for a ball, & got muddled in his notes & sat down; but with his admirable Stephen solidity did not mind."[20] She had rather mixed feelings about the Society. Of course she belonged to a "Group," but its membership was informal. As she wrote in one of the chronicle letters she sent to Julian some years later when he was in China: "As for your Apostles, much though I respect them singly, I begin to think that these Societies do more harm than good merely by rousing jealousies and vanities. What d'you think? it seems to me a wrong way to live, drawing chalk marks round ones feet, and saying to the Clives [Bell] you can't come in. However that may be private whim of my own; nothing would make me take a feather of any dye to stick in my hat."[21]

Julian himself presented his first paper to the Society on February 23, 1929, the motion being noted as "The Society was unable to propagate by fission," whatever that might mean. The names of seven present were listed but no vote recorded. He spoke on June 8, 1929, "Can we pull faces"; on March 8, 1930, "Marvel or Marvell"; on July 26, 1930, "Should Tomlinson have torn his letter?"; on February 28, 1931, "Should we systematise our Moods?"; on May 30, 1932, "Is every correspondent a communicant?"; and on November 18, 1933, "Is the Moderator Absolutely wrong?" As he continued to live in Cambridge, hoping to become a Fellow of King's, he remained a Brother until November 25, 1933, when he took "wings."[22]

The immediate effect—we are returning now to his second year, when he was elected—was to enlarge his circle of friends or, perhaps it would be more precise to say, to provide a new category of friends, the Apostles, to be added to the politicians and sportsmen of the first year. And soon there would be the poets. Early in that successful second year, Eddie Playfair, still his closest friend and confidant, as he would always be, introduced him to John Lehmann, who had been with Playfair in College at Eton, and who was now at Trinity. (Julian had put up Eddie for election to the Apostles, but Anthony Blunt had blackballed him as not sufficiently intellectual.[23]) Like Julian, Lehmann was an aspiring poet. They met at a time when each was in need of a sympathetic reader of his own age and level of accomplishment, equally able to praise and to criticize; a colleague with whom to discuss problems of craft and theories of art. Thereafter John Lehmann was Julian's chief literary friend, and they carried on, in conversation and correspondence, a remarkable literary dialogue. Lehmann, in his autobiography twenty-five years later, describes the letters that he and Julian "exchanged in such numbers at that time" as "full of the most detailed arguments and theories about couplets, quatrains, blank verse, free verse, caesuras, rhythm and counter-rhythm, realism and romanticism, dialogue in verse and description in verse, clarity, obscurity, ambiguity and all the other subjects that two eager apprentice craftsmen in poetry can find to discuss with one another." Then, with a valedictory sigh that does not seem quite fair either to himself or to Julian, he concludes, "The light has faded from them, the ashes are dead. And yet"—and this is the heart of the matter—"it was the most exciting colloquy in the world: the whole future of poetry, we felt, depended on these arguments; we were remoulding English literature nearer to our own hearts, and even our great differences of approach seemed to promise a spark of fusion out of which the new way of writing, the completely modern poem would be made."[24]

Until now, in Paris and in his first year at Cambridge, Julian had been writing poetry for himself: unhappiness, it will be recalled, had propelled him to write his first poems. He was now writing at Cambridge, not poems of personal unhappiness but of the natural world, as remote as he could make them from the sentimentality and anthropomorphism of the Georgian tradition. Somehow, in spite of the number of his activities and interests and distractions, even in his first year—the beagling and the debates in the Union, the tutorials with Clapham—his poetic production had been remarkably high; so that when the time came to emerge from the cocoon and to publish, at the beginning of his second year, he had a large assemblage of poems, quite uniform in quality, to draw upon. Whatever diffidence he may have felt in the past, preferring to keep the poems out of sight, he felt none now: he wanted to be read. And the question, more theoretical than pertinent, What is the proper age to publish for the first time? never troubled him. His aunt Virginia, in her *Letter to a Young Poet*—written some years later to John Lehmann—would recommend thirty as the minimum allowable age: three years younger than herself when she published *The Voyage Out*, her first novel. But most young poets get their first books into print long before this: Julian's *Winter Movement* was published in 1930, when he was twenty-two. Of course, to publish a lyric or two in an undergraduate periodical is not quite as compromising as to bring out a whole collection of them; one is not yet irredeemably a "writer." But London editors and publishers have a way of keeping their eyes on undergraduate poets, especially at Oxford and Cambridge: so many careers have begun in just such fashion.

As it happened, the late 1920s were an extraordinarily fertile and important time in the literary life of both the Ancient Universities, although in a retrospective view, the activities at Cambridge are less likely to be noticed than the more glamorous poetic ferment at Oxford. W. H. Auden, Stephen Spender, C. Day Lewis, Rex Warner, and Louis MacNeice were at Oxford between 1927 and 1929; all in their turn contributed to the annual volumes of Oxford poetry (Auden and Day Lewis were its editors in 1927; Spender and MacNeice in 1929); all would go on from Oxford to constitute a movement: Thirties Poetry. At Cambridge the most conspicuous and certainly the most influential literary achievement was the revolution in the practice of criticism that was being led by I. A. Richards, a Fellow of Magdalene. Indeed, one could go so far as to call it the birth of modern literary criticism. It was an extremely exciting time for those interested in literature to be in Cambridge, and Julian was at the center of it. The contrast between Oxford and Cambridge at this time would seem to bear out the stereotyped contrast: impassioned, artistic Oxford; detached, scientific Cambridge.

It was at this time that English studies were taking on its modern form. In that, I. A. Richards was the central new figure. He had been recruited as a teacher for the comparatively recent English option. The subject arose out of the more philological traditions of Cambridge and more specifically from the Medieval and Modern Language Tripos. Mansfield Forbes and H. M. Chadwick were teachers of Anglo-Saxon, but nevertheless they were moving in the direction that English should be taught as literature rather than as language. To a degree it might have been a reaction, after the First World War, against the older study of language being associated with a Germanic tradition of scholarship. E.M.W. Tillyard and Arthur Quiller-Couch, the popular professor of English, played important roles in this development. But certainly a crucial, perhaps the most crucial, figure was I. A. Richards. He had read Moral Sciences at Cambridge, taking his degree in 1915. He had returned there in 1918 in order to study medicine and psychology. But he was about to give this up, and was considering becoming a mountain guide, when Forbes asked him to be a lecturer in English, to give courses on the Modern Novel and Principles of Literary Criticism.[25] The late twenties were a golden age in literary studies at Cambridge, particularly associated with Richards and his brilliant undergraduate student William Empson. Richards published three immensely influential books, *The Meaning of Meaning* (1923) with C. K. Ogden, *Principles of Literary Criticism* (1924), and *Practical Criticism* (1929), their emphasis being on the analysis of the text, shorn of its biographical implications. And in 1924, it should not go unmentioned, F. R. Leavis was appointed lecturer, thus beginning his highly influential career. Julian played a role in these developments, along with other undergraduates who would go on to distinguished literary careers. Eventually the Oxonians—Auden, Spender, Day Lewis, MacNeice, Warner (with their Cambridge affiliates Isherwood and Lehmann)—would make the greater creative contribution, but the Cantabrigians, perhaps more in their scientific tradition, would have in the world of criticism the greater impact.

Poets such as Bell and Empson abounded in Cambridge as well, and two new little periodicals came into existence in which they could place their work: *Experiment* and *The Venture*, competing journals. Both were founded in the autumn of 1928, in the first term of Julian's second year. *Experiment* had a board of five editors of whom the most important were Jacob Bronowski, a mathematician at Jesus, and William Empson at Magdalene. The latter began his undergraduate studies as a mathematician before switching to English under the guidance of I. A. Richards. Also on the board were Hugh Sykes Davies, a friend of Julian's and a fellow Apostle, and Humphrey Jennings, the future great documentary filmmaker at this point studying English at Pembroke College (Basil Wright, also a future important documentary filmmaker, was a contributor.) The fifth member of the board was its main financial backer, William Hare, who wouldn't use his courtesy title, Lord Ennismore. (His father had transferred him from Balliol College, Oxford, to Magdalene, Cambridge, in an unsuccessful attempt to curb his socialism. He ended his career as a Labour peer, the Earl of Listowel, and the last secretary of state for India and then governor-general of Ghana.) Judged by the standards of more avant-garde journals of the time, such as *transition*, in which the *Experiment* writers published a thirty-two-page supplement in June 1930, *Experiment* may not have been that experimental, but it legitimately considered itself the chief organ for contemporary writing by undergraduates and young graduates at Cambridge. Particularly in keeping with Jennings's interests, it had a surrealistic edge. *Experiment* also published art works by Cartier-Bresson, Georges Braque, and Max Ernst. Consistent with the traditions of the University, and the thrust of Richards's sort of literary criticism, its name reflected its commitment to the scientific spirit as well as being avant-garde. Although it published, as one would expect, the kind of undergraduate poems that reflect the advanced taste of the period—echoes from *The Waste Land* or *Mauberley*—it also had work by a number of gifted writers, among them Richard Eberhart, T. H. White, and Kathleen Raine. Its most memorable contributor was Empson himself, who on the evidence of these early poems ("To an Old Lady," "It is the pain, it is the pain, endures," "Legal Fiction," and several others) seemed to have created his own extraordinary style at the very beginning of his career.

Experiment lost some of its impetus when Empson was expelled from Cambridge in the summer of 1929 over the ludicrous incident of a college servant reporting that he had condoms in his college bedroom. Richards was away at the time and was unable to prevent this outburst of prurient Puritanism on the part of the Magdalene College authorities. Seven numbers were issued, the last in May 1931. It made clear its commitment to modernism, including among other items a short piece by James Joyce, "Work in Progress," with a commentary by Stuart Gilbert; a story by Malcolm Lowry; and a poem and an essay on W. H. Auden's *Paid on Both Sides* by Empson himself.

Granta, the long-term Cambridge magazine, appraised both *Experiment* and *The Venture* with the cynical, pseudosophisticated facetiousness of youth: "In *Experiment* [there is] a large number of lamentably clever young gentlemen talking clap-trap much more obviously than any congeries of the 'nineties. In *Venture*, which will aggravate them much less, and reveal its ethical inferiority to *Experiment* by doing so, they will find few who are clever at all. If they are content to approach the two journals from this standpoint, which is exaggerated on the side of derogation, they will suffer no great disappointment, and may have the pleasure of fishing out a great deal of real merit."[26]

Its rival, *The Venture*, regarded with some justification as neo-Georgian, was edited for its first three issues by Anthony Blunt, H. Romilly Fedden, and Michael Redgrave. Though associated with the more conservative journal, Redgrave, a Magdalene undergraduate, was very influenced by Richards's approach to literature as well as the less advanced but more theatrically orientated teaching and friendship of Rylands. (Blunt ceased to be an editor for the last three issues.) Julian was very much in *The Venture*'s camp, committing himself to a rather classical take on literature. He had a great affection for the eighteenth century. He took Redgrave to task for not sufficiently holding to an ideology of the "Right" and for publishing his friends John Davenport and Hugh Sykes Davies. On the basis of ideology Julian believed that those two should appear only in *Experiment*. Although he himself was actually quite friendly with Sykes Davies, he objected to appearing in the same journal with him.[27] *Experiment* was very much under the influence of Eliot, in literary if not political terms. Julian was critical of his influence, yet when John Masefield became poet laureate in 1930, Julian thought the post should have gone to Eliot instead. Aesthetically Julian was more traditional than his elders; perhaps that was one form of rebellion. There were six numbers of *The Venture* in all, the last in June 1930. Much more handsomely produced than *Experiment*, it was more conservative in policy, more aesthetic in taste, more sophisticated in its interests. It also cast a wider net than *Experiment* did initially. Its first number was in part local—with poems by Rylands and Eberhart, essays by Blunt and Alister Watson, a woodcut by John Lehmann, and a story by Michael Redgrave—but it also included poems by non-Cambridge writers J. R. Ackerley and Louis MacNeice and, rather improbably, a story by Clemence Dane. In the second issue the journal devoted itself to Cambridge authors, including Jennings and Wright, more associated with *Experiment*. Although most of the pieces were by students, there was a short essay on "Music and the People" by the distinguished Cambridge musicologist Edward J. Dent. The issue included an ad for the Hogarth Press publication *Cambridge Poetry 1929*, which had poems by both camps. There was a piece by Anthony Blunt on Fonthill Abbey, and in the next issue he would write on Bavarian Rococo. The contents of the final number are not unrepresentative: an essay by Anthony Blunt on Cubism; another by Martin Turnell on Donne, T. S. Eliot, and the Symbolists; one by Julian attacking poetic obscurity; then, in a self-conscious gesture to the enemy—it was thought worthy of editorial comment—two of the *Experiment* regulars, Empson (a poem) and Malcolm Lowry (a story). In fact, quite a few of the *Experiment* authors appeared in issues of *The Venture*. If as a table of contents this is not particularly venturesome, neither is it jejune; indeed there are moments when the tone of *The Venture* suggests a premature middle age. From the third number (June 1929): "Founded originally to supply a need in Cambridge, '*The Venture*' has withstood the violence of a too sudden 'Renaissance' [presumably *Experiment*] and will continue for another year as a protest against the more licentious forms of Free Verse, Surréalisme, and Art without Tears!" Julian, who tended to see literary life in terms of controversy, cast his lot with *The Venture*. In retrospect, Empson himself remarked about Julian in 1938 as "a man I undervalued at Cambridge."[28]

Julian first appeared in its pages in February 1929 (the second number) with a poem, "The Moths," and was represented thereafter in each of the four succeeding numbers. In Paris, writing his earliest poems, and afterwards at Cambridge, in his first year, Julian was happily free of literary principles and theories. Since boyhood he had admired the prose of Richard Jefferies, the late Victorian essayist and novelist, and he wanted to achieve a comparable style. He might have written in both magazines. Others did. But this would have been less exhilarating; battle was in the air, and he called the writers who contributed to both "the mercenaries." In fact, his enthusiasm for *The Venture* was not as frivolous as this may suggest: he thought it more sympathetic to the literary principles of clarity and accuracy in verse. The influence of Jefferies is unmistakable. And there is a detachment and absence of sentiment that he might conceivably have learned from the Parnassians he was reading in Paris. But these early poems were not written to conform to a doctrine, whether borrowed or invented: he was still too innocent to be doctrinaire in a stage, as he described it, of "self-conscious virgin naturalism." In the third issue, in June 1929, he published "Winter Movement: A Formal Ode," which later provided the title for his first book of poems. In the next issue the following November there was a short nature poem, "Nivôse." Then, indicating his philosophical interests, in the fifth issue, in February 1930, there was the very long "An EPISTLE on the Subject of the Ethical and Aesthetic Beliefs of HERR LUDWIG WITTGENSTEIN."

Thus, in his second year in Cambridge, the ambience became for him more explicitly and flatteringly intellectual. There were discussions of aesthetic and ethical principles at the Saturday evening meetings of the Society, of metrics and the principles of versification with John Lehmann (like himself a contributor to *The Venture*); at the same time, he was becoming "more and more consciously and conscientiously literary." Rather belatedly, he advanced from the Edwardians to the moderns in terms of his reading, but not in his opinions. He did read Eliot and I. A. Richards, Huxley, and Wyndham Lewis yet persisted in his dislike of Eliot because of his obscurity (in Julian's view the unforgivable sin of modernism). He set about becoming, in literary matters, "a thoroughgoing classicist reactionary."

It was very odd. He was, he thought, a convinced Bloomsburian, yet he diverged sharply from the creative practice of his elders. It was his form of rebellion. Unfortunately, he could never deal with this divergence; it would have been disloyal to single out for criticism the work of anyone who belonged to him—his aunt Virginia's novels, for example. It is doubtful if he was even aware of the contradiction; hence, the almost obsessive nature of his dislike for Eliot, the symbolic enemy, who was made to bear the burden of all the resentments Julian had difficulty in expressing, even to himself. Bloomsbury's practice in the arts was determinedly new. Virginia Woolf was the outstanding experimental novelist in England. Clive Bell wrote admiringly of Eliot and Proust, of Matisse and Picasso. Vanessa Bell and Duncan Grant were modern painters (yet the domesticity of many of their paintings as well as those of Roger Fry's did have strong similarities with Julian's poems). As late as the mid-1930s they were able to shock the bourgeoisie; specifically, the directors of the Cunard Line, who commissioned Bell and Grant to decorate a room on the *Queen Mary* and then, having seen the work, decided nervously that it would not do. The point hardly needs elaborate documentation. Bloomsbury was a part of the modern movement; Julian, its first and only poet, who had grown up in its midst and for whom its ideas and beliefs were "tablets of the law," was setting out at the same time to become "a thoroughgoing classicist reactionary."

As a statement of principles upon which his own poetic practice was based, the essay "A Brief View of Poetic Obscurity" that he wrote towards the end of his third (and last undergraduate) year, and which was published in the final number of *The Venture*, is admirably clear and explicit. Since, in effect, it was the critical credo he would hold to with just a few variations and modifications throughout his life, it deserves an extensive quotation:

> By obscure poetry I mean poetry that the well educated "common reader," who after all is the juryman giving the final verdict of posterity, finds hard or is unable to understand. My argument is that such obscurity is always a defect, though admittedly some poems are great in spite of, and not because of, a certain obscurity. . . . The reductio ad absurdum of obscurity is nonsense, which in its ideal state, towards which our contemporaries are rapidly approaching, consists of a series of totally unconnected words. . . . Though I think that obscurity often results from subtlety of thought, I do not know that this is much of an argument in its favour. Truly, it is an admirable quality to be able to express an exact shade of meaning, neither more nor less. But this is just what obscurity does not do. It is the cardinal merit of a perfectly clear style to express subtleties without confusion, as witness a hundred writers from Herrick and Jane Austen to Racine and La Fontaine. Moreover it has yet to be proved that the subtlest, most curious, most hidden and exquisite thoughts and feelings are in any way the most valuable. Without wishing to compromise myself in any way with the grand simplicities, I should say that the practice of the masters showed that the

best poems had been written clearly and comprehensibly about simple feelings and ideas.[29]

Even earlier, the previous February, in a letter to his brother, who was then in Paris, he made clear the position he was taking:

> I feel that the classical reaction is at length getting under way and the reform of English poetry.... I find the difficulty of achieving classical restraint and serenity is very great, when you are bubbling over with the wildest metaphysical fancies. But I feel very sure of my central thesis—that the only hope is the Golden Mean and good sense—nothing extreme, but a careful, fairly wide selection of important qualities, all used up to a certain reasonable limit, never beyond. Above all, a careful avoidance of intellectual extravagance, and a thoroughgoing intellectualism.... Originality means imbecility for most people. Really, I do believe that most things worth doing have been defined by Aristotle.[30]

The mark of good sense is upon this, the rationalist view of life and art, the plain, sensible Englishman's view: Julian was perhaps more of a Bell than he realized, and his no-nonsense, straightforward attitude had much in common with that of either a nineteenth-century businessman or a country squire. (He himself would have placed it back a century earlier in the good sense of Dr. Johnson and Pope.) But without contradicting the intelligence of Julian's argument, one might observe that life and art include more than "simple feelings and ideas," and that the more passionate the commitment to a dispassionate clarity, the more art and life have to be ruled out. This was precisely Julian's situation by the end of his third year. He had "finally reached the point," John Lehmann tells us, "where he would have liked to blot out the whole of the romantic movement, and the century and a half of poetry that followed it."[31]

The dilemma was only beginning to appear, however, in his second year; he was still able to write those poems of "virgin naturalism" in which his gift is most unmistakable. Between February and June 1929 he published nine poems, two in *The Venture* and seven in the *Cambridge Review*. The technique is increasingly adventurous and far-ranging: new forms, no doubt talked over with Lehmann and put to him as a challenge, are explored, even the ballade (not very deftly, however). But the range of subjects is as circumscribed, by choice, as it has been from the beginning. Except for the "Ballade of the

Dancing Shadows," which is manifestly an exercise ("Princess, if you should complain / I shall put it down to spite"), he is still "fiercely naturalist," an artist who observes

> Into the north the tall black poplars rise,
> Already the straight upper limbs are bare.
> Like easy fishes, out of cold brown skies,
> The dropping redwings glide through ice-bright air.
> Winterstript, black, fine lines austere and spare,
> Colours half gone, and each green mouldered brown,
> Like stalk-grown depths of stagnant water, where
> Dead leaves decay as they come drifting down,
> In the wet winter days autumn's bright colours drown.
> —"The Hedge"

The most ambitious of the nine was "Winter Movement," very close in subject to "The Hedge" but a "formal ode" of almost two hundred lines, wherein Julian moved, not always dexterously, through a variety of stanzaic and metrical forms—"the metre of two stanzas," his prefatory note explains, "imitated from Gerard Manley Hopkins," whom he and John Lehmann had recently discovered. Julian's ear was not really attuned to the peculiarities of sprung rhythm, and the chief effect of the discovery was to encourage a tendency, already latent, to use too many adjectives. And indeed much of the poem is turgid, prolix, even ungainly; it would appear that Julian thought too much about writing it. Somewhere, among the complexities and ingenuities of technique, the true poetic impulse was lost, although there are two passages of great beauty, each describing the song of the thrush in winter. We quote from the first:

> Clear cold,
>   Unfold
> Long liquid note
>   On note,
> Cadence and trill
>   That fill
> A thrush's throat.
>   Black spot
> On neck and breast
> Sienna apricot,

>   Splash'd, shot
> With olive-gold.
>   At rest,
>   Despite
> The storm and night,
>   Unstirred,
> Lets fall the bright
>   Music far-heard.

Yet if "Winter Movement" falls short of being the major poem it was so clearly intended to be, there is no question of the seriousness and dedication it represents. Its publication in *The Venture* at the end of his second year marks a climax in Julian's life. He was now beyond question a poet, accepted as such by himself, by his friends, by Cambridge. In his conversation with friends, poetry might well have been the most important topic. Added to this, he was or had been a figure at the Union; he was an Apostle; he was a sportsman. He had his books and pictures, an old car which he liked to drive as though it were a racing car, and a large number of friends and acquaintances; he had even done well enough academically. Attractive, charming, intelligent, gifted, he was dangerously close to being one of those golden youths—Rupert Brooke is the prototype—whose years at the University are a kind of conquest, splendid but short-lived. One by one he had got from Cambridge the gifts it had to offer—summed up in his phrase "an extraordinary *douceur de vivre*."

He also made his mark as a contributor to the *Cambridge Review*. It was a weekly, rather parallel to those published in London, but obviously, in its interests and contributors, concentrating on the University. Here he served, one might say, an apprenticeship in the lower levels of the republic of letters, writing short essays and reviews of various books, on Surtees, Shakespeare's sonnets, and T. S. Eliot's essays. As he wrote to his mother, he felt that it was "more or less under my control, and I can publish as many articles as I like."[32] As we have already noted, he also published his poems there as well as in *The Venture*. From the point of view of his ideas about poetry his most important publication in the *Cambridge Review*, on March 7, 1930, was on "The Progress of Poetry." Julian was highly conscious of the problem of style. He knew that style was not something to put on and take off like a peruke, but an integral part of the poetic process. He viewed Eliot, perhaps rather paradoxically, as an obscure romantic, and felt that one needed to return to classical models and "to be clear, simple and forcible in expression, plan precise and appropriate in one language, accurate and polished in our metres, and in our working take great care."[33] He had all the dogmatism of youth.

He did get into trouble reviewing, in very much a young man's farouche style, a book of poems, *Whims and Moods* (the title is a bit shy making), by Thomas Thornely, who in his day was a moderately well-known poet, particularly for his limericks, as well as a history don at Trinity Hall. At this point he was seventy-five and an established member of the Cambridge community, who might expect a sympathetic review in the home periodical. Julian would have none of it. While he found in it a great deal of "metrical skill and a surprising fancy," he complained that too many of these poems "are versified letters to *The Times*, an expression of the prejudices of a middle-aged, vaguely mystical reactionary." He concluded that "the trouble is not so much, however, in Mr Thornely's content—after all, a great deal of metaphysical poetry expresses even sillier prejudices and deals with equally trivial subjects. His verses are valueless because, not being a man of genius, he cannot invent a new technique, while what he has inherited is utterly decayed."[34] In subsequent issues, senior figures of the University came to Thornely's defense.

And then, at the end of his second year at Cambridge, he embarked on a far fuller love life. During his first year there, he had written to his brother: "The principal subject of conversation among my friends is love. I've heard it discussed now from all points of view.... But the lack of any practical experience is a dreadful handicap in these conversations.... However my whole mind is full of the French Revolution. I talk about nothing else and bore all my friends. I'm doing a great essay on Barras, and disinterring all kinds of superb scandal about Napoleon and Joséphine.... On the whole, life here's very pleasant."[35] In his "Notes for a Memoir," of some years later Julian wrote, "There seem to have been three main divisions in my life: roughly, sensations, ideas and love-affairs." And at the conclusion of the "Notes" (as published) he wrote: "Perhaps I should go back and pick up the story of my dealings with literature, and had also better make an effort to indicate, in outline at least, my early love-affairs. For it is exceeding hard to separate them from the rest of the story." There is the further difficulty that Julian's sensations, ideas, and love affairs seem to have been less clearly separate divisions in his life than he may have realized. Indeed the affairs are themselves such a tangle of ideas and sensations that they exemplify in yet another form the dilemma, or conflict, or problem of Julian's life. He had come up to Cambridge a convinced theoretical libertarian. In these matters the Bloomsbury attitude (one "tablet of the law" he would never question) was worldly, tolerant, indulgent but considerate, indifferent to convention, and very much a reaction against Victorian hypocrisy and cant. The initiatory experience that one would have thought (as his father surely did) an inevitable part of his season in Paris had not, or so it would seem, occurred; but he had brought away from his reading of Maupassant at that time "a Latin-sensual view of *amour*." The opportunity to translate this idea into action was not immediately evident in Cambridge. Now that he was away from Paris, he rather wished he were back. To Quentin, who was there studying painting, he wrote, "I should be furiously Jealous, if I weren't suffering from a profound melancholia which only a day's good beagling could cure. . . . Three miles of Cambridgeshire fen, thrice weekly, are essential to one's sanity." (On the whole, this is an Anglo-Saxon rather than a Latin notion—brought on perhaps by "profound melancholia.") David Garnett, who lived nearby and attended a meet of the University Beagles, offers a more cheerful glimpse of Julian as he then was: "Far bigger, noisier, and more raggedly dressed than any of his companions. He was bursting with happy excitement, absolutely unconscious of himself or that anyone present was caring about wearing the right clothes or doing the correct thing, and his primitive delight warmed them so they also forgot their fears. . . . Late in the afternoon Julian turned up with his ragged clothes torn to tatters, which flapped about his white thighs. He put on some clothes of mine and lay panting and sighing after the luxurious enjoyment of so much exercise."[36] He had contrived to fill most every moment of his waking life beagling, speaking at the Union, writing poetry, reading at random in literature and purposefully in history, and talking long and late with friends.

There remained only the addition of a love and sexual life to fill out his time at Cambridge. But before he embarked on a full heterosexual existence, which would continue to an intense degree for the rest of his life, his first affair was with a man, his good friend and fellow Apostle, Anthony Blunt. Up to that point, one knows very little about his sexual experience. In the

Bloomsbury tradition, and given his extraordinarily close relationship with his mother, one suspects he would have indicated to her any sexual activities he might have had before coming up to Cambridge. Before his affair with Blunt, he seems to have been infatuated with a woman called Julia, but I haven't been able to discover anything about her. There is so frequently homosexual experimentation at English boarding schools, but perhaps less so at Leighton Park given its Quaker atmosphere. In a letter he wrote in March 1929 to his younger brother, Quentin, who was spending the year in Paris, before he embarked upon his affair with Blunt, it is hard to tell whether he is being worldly or jealous, and whether he is commenting on Quentin going through a homosexual phase. Julian may be exaggerating the "badness" of his reputation. Presumably he knew that Anthony was homosexual (and being raised in Bloomsbury he was much more familiar with homosexuality than most). He wrote to Quentin about a possible meeting between Blunt and Quentin in Paris. "Plain whoring is comprehensible if somewhat repugnant, but this promiscuous and romantic buggery is the devil's own course. To begin with it makes me jealous. . . . Secondly, I shan't dare to send my friend Antony Blunt, who is going to Paris, to see you. You are both far too pretty to be good, whereas I am unfortunately far too good to be pretty. Thirdly, my reputation is quite bad enough already."[37] (This might be a bit of a boast.)

When William Abrahams and I wrote the earlier study, we had no knowledge of the affair with Blunt. All those we talked to, most particularly Julian's brother, Quentin, and Quentin's wife, Olivier, couldn't have been more helpful and welcoming, as was Julian's greatest undergraduate friend, Eddie Playfair, who undoubtedly knew about the affair, as did Quentin. Years later, Quentin wrote, "Anthony did attempt to convert Julian to homosexuality, but failed utterly."[38] Perhaps they felt that there were limits to what we should know. One characteristic of English life is the deft handling of information: those in the know know, and those not in the know don't. Of course, at the time that we were doing the research for the book in the 1960s, quite a few friends of Julian's were alive. It was a failure on our part that we did not try to get in touch with more of his contemporaries at university. We did interview one of his teachers at Leighton Park, but that largely came about because he was the father of an acquaintance of mine, the distinguished historian Sir John Elliott. We knew that Anthony Blunt was a good friend of Julian's, and we should have been in contact with him. Of course he might well have refused to see us. This was in the early and mid-1960s before homosexuality had been decriminalized. There was certainly lots of homosexual life in Britain and known homosexuals, but a certain discretion had to be observed. There was the continual danger of blackmail and arrest, as in the famous cases involving Sir John Gielgud and Lord Montagu. But if we had known about the affair, as we did about Julian's heterosexual ones, we could have, as with them, written about it anonymously. We did meet Blunt just once after the book was published but years before his outing as a spy. I don't remember if he commented on the book, but it was a perfectly cordial meeting in his flat at the top of the Courtauld Institute, then in Portman Square, at which he had done so much to make the center of art history. He was then one of the most famous art historians in Britain, a knight, and the Keeper of the Queen's Pictures.

In the late 1920s, Guy Burgess was an Apostle. It was he who recruited Blunt to be a spy. Julian referred to Burgess in a letter to his mother in 1935 as "a very queer fish of my friends."[39] There is no evidence that he attempted either to seduce or to recruit Julian. Indeed, as the times became more political, Julian did move more to the Left, but he was always strongly critical of the Communists, despite the sympathies and party membership of quite a few of his friends. A further irony is that it was through the Apostles, so to speak, that Blunt was finally revealed as a spy. He had been questioned over the years after his good friend Burgess had fled to Moscow with Donald Maclean, a contemporary who had been an undergraduate at Trinity Hall. Michael Straight, a wealthy American at Trinity, had been recruited by Blunt into two secret organizations: the Apostles and, covertly, the Communists. (William Abrahams and I interviewed Michael Straight in the 1960s about his close friendship with John Cornford, the other figure we wrote about in *Journey to the Frontier*. Needless to say, he told us nothing about his own Communist involvement.) When Straight was being vetted for a government appointment in the United States in 1963, he felt he had no choice but to reveal his past and his connection with Blunt. The British authorities were informed of this by the American ones. Blunt was offered immunity from prosecution in return for a full confession. Years later, because of this event, Blunt was exposed as a spy. By the late 1970s, rumors were flying about that Blunt was the Fourth Man, after Burgess, Maclean, and Philby. Using the American Freedom of

Information Act, Andrew Boyle virtually exposed Blunt as a spy in his 1979 book *The Climate of Treason*, under the pseudonym of Maurice, a deliberate echo of E. M. Forster's posthumously published homosexual novel, *Maurice*. (The Forster echo evoked his excessively quoted remark that if faced with the choice, he would hope that he would have the courage to betray his country rather than his friend.) Then on November 15, 1979, in Parliament, Prime Minister Margaret Thatcher revealed all.

Blunt became increasingly political in the 1930s, some time after he and Julian had been seeing a great deal of one another in Cambridge, with the Apostles, over *The Venture*, and as it turns out, in bed. The story was there to be found in the Charleston papers in the Archives at King's College. When we were doing our research in the early 1960s, most of the manuscript material was still in private hands. We saw much original material, but some was still undiscovered, sitting about in drawers, boxes, attics. As far as I know, the affair first became public knowledge in Miranda Carter's biography of Blunt of 2001. It also is depicted in the controversial television series on the Cambridge Spies. (The series, in many ways very effective television, has Blunt as its central character. Some have regarded it as too sympathetic to the spies, and apparently it is full of inaccuracies.) Though not a spy, Julian plays a significant role in the series, particularly as a friend of Blunt and Burgess. There is a scene, by definition invented, which depicts Julian and Anthony getting undressed before going to bed together for the first time. Julian asks Blunt whether he should take off his socks, which were given to him by his aunt Virginia. Blunt replies, "Pray don't." According to Carter, Blunt was anxious to be as close to Bloomsbury as possible. Having Julian as a lover certainly helped achieve that aim. But she also believes that Julian was the initiator of the affair. Julian had something of a private joke about Blunt trying to identify with Bloomsbury. In a letter to the *Cambridge Review* refuting a claim about the similarities between his father and Blunt in their views of art, he wrote: "Mr [Geoffrey] Rossetti has also taken it upon himself to say that he would have supposed Mr Blunt to be Mr Clive Bell, if he had not known better. May I also assure you, Sir, from a personal and, I may venture to add, intimate acquaintance with both, that there are numerous and profound differences in their characters."[40]

In an important sense, the affair was not validated until he told his mother about it. She already knew that he was very friendly with Blunt. During his first year she felt it was necessary to reassure him about how he was doing socially in Cambridge while Julian was experiencing the natural insecurity of youth in a comparatively new situation, no matter how well connected he was at King's. But by his second year he was feeling much happier, and he might even be telling her that he was in pursuit of Anthony:

> I have just been elected to the cranium club [a dining club in London], which is making me vain. . . . I am feeling very well, and doing a good deal of work. I find, though, that Cambridge, or rather, of course, all my friends in general, and Antony in particular, keep me in a state of nervous tension that has its advantages, but is not so pleasant as living the life of a turnip or a painter at Cassis. I imagine my affair [I believe he means here his pursuit of Blunt] will eventually come right—at any rate, things are even as it is far better than I ever had any right to hope—but the role of patient Griselda is hardly the more suitable to me that might be imagined.[41]

Vanessa wrote to him on May 6 from Cassis:

> Do ask Antony Blunt to come—I should so much like to see him. If he can't come here he must anyhow come to Charleston but I think thered certainly be room for him here. . . . I am very glad everything seems to be going so well with you darling. Perhaps I am not so much surprised as you are, but then I really don't see why people shouldnt like you at least as well as you like them though I known youre always astonished when they do. To me it seems quite natural. I suppose I mustnt make you vain & tell you what praises I have heard lately from Roger, from Peter Lucas, even from Maynard (by way of Virginia).[42]

On May 14, 1929, he wrote to her that the affair had been consummated. He first discussed in his letter the state of his car. He then went on:

> My great news is about Antony. I feel certain you won't be upset or shaked at my telling you that we sleep together—to use the cambridge euphemism [I don't know why Julian thought that this was a special Cambridge term]. It's a great mercy, thinking you aren't a moral and disapproving parent. Still don't let it go any further, or it may get round to Virginia and then one might as well put a notice in the Times. As his parents are strict and proper clergyman of the church of England and a number of his friends highly shockable athletes, we have to take our precautions. So now I am feeling that life, though crowded and distracting enough in all conscience, is a very pleasant business on the whole.[43]

Vanessa reacted quickly, writing to Julian on May 17:

> You are right of course, my dear, in thinking that I shall not be shocked—I am only delighted at anything that makes you happy. Of course I quite understand that one must be discreet, but you can absolutely rely on me. To tell you the truth, I never breathe a word of anything that I think had better not be made public to either Clive or Virginia & I know that its better not to let this get about. Besides relations there is the absurd law of the land—& anyhow there's no point in spreading such things aboard. But I am very glad you have told me as it makes me happy to think how much you must be enjoying life. I only wish I knew Antony. I am sorry he can't come here, but however I shall see him at Charleston I hope. Duncan met him & liked him, otherwise I had hardly heard of him except through you. It is odd that he is the one of your friends I haven't met, but do arrange that he should come to Charleston.[44]

In July 1937, very shortly after Julian's death, Vanessa wrote down a few notes mostly about his childhood. But the last paragraph touched on his love life and her view of the affair with Blunt as transitory; it lasted until the next fall. "Letters from him at Cassis telling me of his first love affair with A.B. Not a very real one—The joy of reading the letter as I walked down the field path & knew he meant to tell me things I had never expected it. I think his feeling for J. [Julia] must have come first—but that had been stopped by her engagement."[45] Carter, in her biography of Blunt, sees the affair as the consummation of Blunt's pursuit of Bloomsbury. (If so, Blunt did not mind participating in making fun of Bloomsbury. Michael Redgrave published in *Granta* a parody of *Orlando* in which there were photographs of Blunt in drag as Verandah.) Vanessa mentions discussions that she had about it with Eddie Playfair and Quentin, which underplay its importance, Quentin even demoting it, quite wrongly, to a one-night stand. He told his version of the affair to Carter: "the story as I had it from Julian himself was that he had one night with Blunt, which involved scaling the walls of Trinity, and he said it really wasn't worth the climb. That sort of thing was really not for him, but he was quite devoted to him."[46] In our very cordial meetings with Eddie Playfair, he, not surprisingly, told us nothing about it, nor did Quentin. In an undocumented statement, presumably from an interview, Carter quoted Eddie: "'It was very strange,' remembered Eddie Playfair. 'Julian was the passive one, and yet it was he who made the going. I don't think Blunt was really interested in

Julian sexually. I may have been the only one who knew about it while it was going on, though Julian was a great one for talking about his affairs. . . . I regarded it as a bit of fashion more than anything else.'"[47] Eddie didn't seem to know that Julian had told his mother, or his brother, at this point or later on; Julian apparently had also confided in "Topsy" Lucas, the wife of his English supervisor. The Lucases lived close to King's, at "The Pavilion" on West Road, where she had gatherings of students, characterized by frank talk. She herself was a prolific novelist at the time, as "E.B.C. Jones," and had an intriguing literary connection as the niece of Robert Ross, Oscar Wilde's first lover and literary executor. Her own marriage was in the process of unraveling. She clearly much enjoyed the role of confidant, as she wrote to Julian in an undated letter: "I hope you know that if you do want to talk about your troubles I shall be very glad—not quâ novelist. . . . I don't want to press you, or very likely you already have confidants of far more use than I—but you have only to mutter [?] if you want to come alone, & I shall arrange it." And as she wrote in two further letters: "You sound unhappy. *Don't* force Anthony's hand. If necessary fly to the wilderness without a scene. . . . Peter and I are incompatible. Of course I have my intimate friends left." "You are naturally absorbed in living Julian Bell's life, and have no energy over to live Eddie's or Topsy's, even for a half an hour. Anthony's perhaps, but its different in love. . . . You see I *didn't* know you liked me best of your Cambs. Friends; & however much one knows that a person likes one, its *always* comforting to be told. Do remember this, its important."[48]

Keynes noticed, as he mentioned in a letter to Vanessa on May 24, how infatuated Julian was with Blunt, although he may not have known that the two had just become lovers. But by the fall it was over. He wrote to his mother in October 1929, tantalizingly mentioning the mysterious Julia: "Antony and I being about equally bored with each other, and Julia having fallen through completely, I was grateful to him. Moreover, I am astonished at the extent of my own equanimity, and have no intention of taking matters seriously. But I see more and more clearly that I shall have to make the acquaintance of young women, which is rather chilling. It may even end in my learning to dance. Good Lord."[49] She replied on October 30: "How fortunate that you & A.B. should be *equally* bored. But of course you must get to know young women, if not to dance. I must get hold of some for you when you come to London.

There's no lack of them here if one looks for them, only intelligent ones are not plentiful. I hope Peter gave you good advice. You must tell me what it was. He seems at any rate to be making you work, for which I suppose I'm enough of a Stephen to be glad. I don't know why I believe in work."[50]

That November, very man-of-the-worldly, he wrote to Quentin that he was "beginning an investigation of Newnham and Girton—purely scientific, for except as bottle snakes they are really not possible." These investigations in the first instance came to nothing, not even a tentative experimental attachment, perhaps because he did not pursue them wholeheartedly, being prompted more by curiosity than by a deep emotional need. Still his now chaste state bothered him, especially as he suspected that Quentin, younger than himself, might already have had more sexual experiences. He brought the question to his aunt Virginia "if I knew whether Q. had actually had a mistress in Paris, or Austria; and I felt that Julian was slightly perturbed, as if he had not yet taken the plunge, and thought that Q. had outdistanced him."[51] She did not know, for Quentin was close-mouthed in these matters, to Julian's annoyance, and unlike Julian himself, who as we shall see, was frank to the point of indiscretion. When he finally caught up, it was not at all as he had imagined it would be.

Julian was about to embark upon a very serious love affair with Helen Soutar that would last two years. This provides one of the extraordinary coincidences for me, personally, of this story. When I went to study at King's College for a second bachelor of arts, my primary supervisor was Christopher Morris, a history don of the College. He was a wonderful and caring teacher who was extraordinarily generous (as was his wife, Helen) towards his students, and I became a good friend, I believe, of both. My parents became friends of the Morrises as well, and they visited one another in England and in the United States. I had brought with me to England a copy of my senior essay in history at Yale about four Englishmen involved in the Spanish Civil War: John Cornford, George Orwell, Stephen Spender, and Julian Bell. I must have mentioned it to the Morrises. Helen expressed an interest in reading it, which she did, commenting that knowing some of the people involved, she thought they had been portrayed accurately. No more was said, and I had no idea at that point that she had been Julian's lover. When some years later William Abrahams and I were embarked on the book that had its origin in the essay, we knew (I can't remember how we discovered this) that Helen in fact had been Julian's lover and that they had had a serious affair. Perhaps we should have tried to talk to her about it, but we had a sense that she didn't wish to, and for whatever reason we never did before publishing *Journey to the Frontier*. But we did not hide the affair, and Helen figures in the story of his life as—we then thought—Julian's first lover, "A" (a nice irony in that his actual first lover was, in fact, A.). We had chosen this convention of a letter from the usage in the memoir published after Julian's death; there his Chinese lover was referred to as K. That number in the alphabet, eleven, may be a quite low estimate of the number of lovers Julian had had up to that point in his life. After the publication of the book, although I saw the Morrises in England and in the United States, it never seemed right to bring up the past. And after all, the book was now out. Meanwhile, their daughter, Ann, had married the distinguished historian John Dizikes, which brought the Morrises quite frequently to the University of California at Santa Cruz, where he taught and where they themselves did some teaching as well. The proximity to Stanford, where I was teaching, meant that we would meet fairly often and also when I visited Cambridge. After Helen's death, Ann, with mixed feelings, deposited Julian's love letters to Helen in the Archives at King's. John Dizikes and I thought that if Helen had not wanted the letters preserved, she would have destroyed them or left instructions that they should be destroyed. Indeed, years before she had written about her feelings about them. After Julian's death, she sent them to Vanessa, who was soliciting his letters for possible inclusion in the published memoir. (In the end, none of his letters to Helen were included. Vanessa thought that parts were well worth quoting, but the decision was taken, urged by David Garnett, that no pre-China letters be published.) Helen had tied her letters into six bundles, but in April 1938 she destroyed two of them, which covered the period towards the beginning of the affair, "because I didn't want anyone else to read them. I then realized that I wanted to keep them after all, and neither read nor destroyed any more."[52] She was willing to share those that remained with Vanessa and, presumably, ultimately with others.

Helen had come to know the Bloomsbury people (I so wish now I had talked to her about them), but it was a complicated relationship. They believed that short of marriage, Julian should do as he wished. But they did not approve of Helen. The rather unfair, brutal, and mean tone that the sisters Vanessa and Virginia took about Helen is found in what they wrote about her after his death. Virginia commented, "He had great sexual attraction & must have lived a great deal on love affairs—one after another—first that heavy beaver like woman Helen Suter [Soutar]: how cd he see anything in her I wonder?" The very last words in Vanessa's few notes about Julian, immediately after mentioning Blunt and the unknown Julia, were: "Then H.S. Meeting her in his rooms—Very nice but oh dear—He had no illusions about her appearance—But they were happy—staying at Charleston—Jealousy on her part. difficulties."[53]

So I believe that Julian's first heterosexual love affair was with Helen Soutar. The daughter of a Scottish architect, Helen was an undergraduate at Girton reading English. Theirs was at first an intensely romantic relationship, very different from the idea of such things he had entertained since Paris. This, the most enduring of his attachments, lasted a little more than two years. It was succeeded by others significantly like it: a pattern had been established. As David Garnett observed, "there was always some woman with her eyes full of him." One affair would end, another would begin, and some might overlap, going on at the same time. Some were of prolonged duration; a few (at least in the early years after Helen) were entered into lightly or promiscuously or without considerable feeling; and almost all of them, from the first to the last, reveal a pattern of intense involvement followed by withdrawal. As he wrote to a later lover, Lettice Ramsey, on December 27, 1935, from China while he was enduring a period of chastity imposed by a period of recovery from a sexual complaint, which he called "his curse":

> I've got so used to fantasy and chastity these months—not even masturbation—only a very rare dream: in the last of these you figured, and as in life, were charming, and, as in dreams—and, alas, too often in life, it wasn't very satisfactory. . . . I quite often turn over my past now, and it often enough takes literary form. The best is my escape from the Lintotts [a Cambridge contemporary] house barefoot unto Ebury Street [in London] but there are quite a lot more. I shall an unjustified historical reputation as a Casanova—or, far better, make myself one while still alive, and then and thus get the reality—'nothing succeeds like success & advertisement.'

Against this must be set his love for his mother, unvarying and in many ways the richest and finest thing in his life. Yet at the same time it might have been a difficult obstacle to his emotional development. He never felt that he could find a woman who compared with her, and starting with that supposition he found that he never could. "Jane Austen's really the only woman except Nessa," he wrote lightly to Playfair, "whom one can have much respect for—I mean of course intellectual respect."[54]

Vanessa Bell was one of the beautiful women of her time; she was sensitive and cool and tranquil and imbued with the intuitive wisdom of the artist. Julian, obedient to an intuitive wisdom of his own, chose women who were very different from her, physically, temperamentally, and in their intellectual style: they would be interested in history or science or politics, which certainly were not Vanessa's interests. (Her indifference to politics was legendary. Once at a dinner party, allegedly, she was seated next to Asquith, the then prime minister. Thinking that he looked familiar, but unable to place him, she began the conversation with "Are you interested in politics?") Then, either by chance or, more likely, by an act of recognition, he was drawn to women, most particularly in his first and his last great affairs, who however cool they might appear at first, would prove to be much more emotional, at least in outward behavior, than his mother. In all his affairs there was an operatic aspect, which Julian thought he disliked but almost certainly unconsciously encouraged. He was attractive to women, more lovable than loving perhaps, and they might fall very much in love with him, more than he wished ultimately, and they asked for more than he was prepared or able to give of himself, and it was necessary to get free. This, with appropriate variations, was the pattern.

His affair with Helen began rather cynically, and he wrote both nicely and meanly about her to his good friend and King's contemporary Harold Barger in December 1929 from London: "Helen is a dear, and writes the most delightful letters in the world, besides being more or less responsive. And I've no doubt whatever that I do want to sleep with her, and that she is a most amusing companion. But she's not calculated to produce much of an effect in public, and I confess I don't like the idea of Clive's and Quentin's comments. I fear I have a great deal of vanity about cutting a good figure in the eyes of the world."[55] In this first attachment with a woman, simply by virtue of its being the first, there was no pattern: everything was new, one discovery after another. Quite quickly he was in love with Helen, as he wrote to Quentin, in "a state of outrageous and to-the-rest-of-the-world-intolerable happiness," yet as much in the world as ever: all the activities and preoccupations of his second year continued unabated in the third. Love, like poetry and philosophy and politics, was simply another aspect of the total idea of himself. Now that it was happening, he could not have been more pleased; but he did not mean to allow this passionate attachment to dominate—that way led to the romantic heresy.

Perhaps it would be appropriate here to consider the two-year course of the affair, which culminated in their almost getting married. Helen had been born in Dundee, on September 3, 1909. After secondary school there, she went to a well-known progressive school, St. Christopher's, in Letchworth Garden City before entering Girton in 1929 to study mathematics. She did not do well in that subject and changed to English, where her examination results were somewhat better, but not distinguished. After taking her degree, she worked briefly as a secretary to an author. She was at the Foreign Office during the war and afterward had a career as a teacher of English literature at Cambridge, heading the English faculty at Homerton College. She wrote a biography of Alexis Soyer, the famous nineteenth-century chef at the Reform Club who had also organized the cooking for the troops during the Crimean War. And she wrote a short book on Elizabethan literature. She married Christopher Morris in 1933, and they had a son and daughter. The Morrises were very much part of the Cambridge scene. For the two years when she was with Julian she was a familiar with the Bloomsbury group.

I don't know how they met. It is apparent that in the course of the academic year 1929–1930, when she was in her first year at Girton, they became lovers. Julian was firmly in love by January 1930. "After all the last years horrors, to be happily in love with Helen—it is so much too good to be true. . . . Dearest Nessa I do wish I knew what you thought of all this nonsense."[56] It's not clear what he meant by the "horrors," in that the conclusion of his affair with Blunt had appeared to be peaceful. Vanessa replied:

> Of course I'm delighted by your happiness. It doesnt seem to me silly—but very wise to realize & enjoy such things when one can. No, luckily, it is not unprecedented but still rare enough to be thankful for & made the most of. I wish I knew Helen—but I shall I hope. Meanwhile I am glad you have Peter

[Lucas] at hand to give you day by day sympathy & you know I think of you & enjoy your happiness here. I am so happy too that you let me know of it. I shall see you soon my dear. Let me know which day you will come. I want to hear about it all from you yourself. Darling I *am so glad*. That is all I want to say now.[57]

His brother Quentin commented on his life at the time, writing in February, "Your life is spent in eating dinners, making love, pulling the legs of poets, apostles, and publishers."[58] The "dinners" probably refers to a plan that he would take up the law, like his namesake, his uncle Thoby, which would require that he eat a certain number of dinners at one of the Law Inns in London. Vanessa and Clive did not think it was a particularly good idea. As she wrote to him while he was at Charleston on his own, cramming for his examinations:

You sound incredibly austere & virtuous. I had a talk with Clive one day about you. Did your ears burn? They might have. But not to repeat compliments I may tell you that Clive, who seems to have grasped the fact more clearly than before that you have inherited *some* qualities of mind & character from one or other of your parents, is beginning to wonder about the Bar—whether you are wise to go to it—whether you want to be wasted at it—but we must discuss such questions one day. I think it ought to be considered. However for the moment you're clearly wise to work 10 hours a day & see what comes of it.[59]

Vanessa was anxious to meet Helen, and on February 7 (noting at the top of the letter that that was the date of her own wedding!) she wrote about a possible visit she and Angelica and perhaps Leonard and Virginia might make to Cambridge to see a production of the Marlowe Society. "But couldn't we arrange a quiet tea or lunch or something just you & me & Helen? I'd be as mild as a lamb! But I don't want to make her feel she's being inspected—indeed I'm quite ready to wait for a natural meeting only if I see her some time it would be much easier to ask her to Charleston later."[60] They did apparently come to Cambridge the next weekend for *King Henry IV*, Part 2, directed by Rylands, with Michael Redgrave playing the prince and Donald Beves, a King's Fellow, playing Falstaff.[61] The lunch party was expanded to include Angelica and Peter Lucas. In early March she urged Julian to bring Helen to lunch in London, and in this and subsequent letters she couldn't repress two motherly concerns: that he should take special care to drive carefully (underlining that statement twice), and that his spelling, notoriously erratic, should be improved. In a later letter, in which she reported that Roger Fry had liked Julian's Helen (knowing that Julian did not like Roger's Helen, Helen Anrep), she also listed his spelling errors. Whatever the intensity of their relationship, she was still a mother, writing him on November 11: "Since you have dropped your family completely I suppose you don't know any of the latest news—wretched creature! Not one letter since I have been away. . . . I really should like to know something about you. Especially if you're dead. . . . How is Helen? Is she enjoying life? & are you?"[62]

In March he and Helen were discussing religion, Julian believing in a more sensual, secular version. "I envy you your religion—a god of any kind to pray to would be a great comfort. . . . [I] day dream of Abbé of Theléme, inhabited mostly by us, but perhaps also by some of our more intelligent and sympathetic friends, in which we should live and love, talk—a great deal—write, read, listen to music, swim and walk, lie about in an orchard."[63] There was the possibility of her coming to be with him at Charleston during the Spring vacation, but there was too the issue that her parents would make a fuss if she went to stay there. In any case, he went to Charleston on his own that spring and worked very hard in preparation for the English Tripos as well as spending three hours a day walking. He very much missed being with her, writing her almost every day. On March 22, "not seeing you is getting slightly intolerable," and then two days later, "I hardly know which terrifies me the more, to begin [?] wanting your mind or your body—perhaps it really comes to much the same thing." And then the next day, "I love you, my dearest, indeed a month's a dreary long time—growing unbearably long." And in another letter, "Do you ever think of us from the outside, as we appear now to our neighbours, and shall in future to historians." In early April he wrote, "I find it still hard to believe that you love me—at least, I do when I think, not of us, but of you and me, distinct separate persons—in different worlds, not two parts of the same world." He hoped that they might stay together in Clive's flat in London: "This is I suppose a very scandalous proposition. Or perhaps you won't think it so—certainly writing to you, it doesn't seem so, but then, now would it."[64] He also mentioned a visit to the Woolves: "I went to Rodmell on Sunday for tea. Clinker made a mess on the carpet, and they seemed a trifle grumpy." What a surprise!

Being apart from Helen led him to despair a bit about working for his exams and to speculate about the future. He wrote to her on April 6:

> I grow more and more stupid and bored every day—my work gets left undone, my family makes too much noise to think, I never feel alive at all. . . . At Cambridge one talks ideas a great deal of the time, which makes everything seem more important. And then, we are all so young we may easily cut a great figure in the world—I always enjoy the thought of them [?] getting all our biographies wrong or will it all come to nothing, and shall we all drift [?] down into nonentities—it's not likely I feel, everything considered, but possible.

The next day he wrote: "I always used to think, before I loved you, (I remember with an effort—it's a curious thought there was such a time) that I was a thorough-going sensualist. Then the shock of those first weeks. I hardly thought I had a body, and yours was only an accessory delight—your most charming possession." Then on the 8th, "When I have written 'I love you' I have said everything and all the rest of these letters is only a gloss on that fact." Julian is writing as if he had had much experience of love already.

> You are infinitely more important to me than anything else in all the world or ever has been. I can hardly think of anything except you now—which must make me poor company. . . . It would be impossible for me to live without you—and if I am ever to feel or enjoy anything again, it would be together with you. . . . I believe I have sometimes in the past despaired of love and lovers, and have suffered for my mistake by doubting the reality of my emotion at all beyond lust and friendship. Indeed, in my blackest moods, I can still doubt love—or anything, except you. But to do so means doubting my own existence, my own reality. . . . A feeling of complete devotion, possession, ecstasy—I have no words. There is nothing in me that does not adore you, that does not long to serve you. I care for you infinitely more now than I do not only for all other human beings, and all that concerns them, but for nature or poetry—the only two things I have ever cared for in the same way. . . . I know that in many things I am vain—as a poet, as a human being, perhaps even at first as your lover. Now I think I have lost all vanity, all good opinion of myself, and only wonder at the grace that allows me to love you.[65]

Later in the year, some sort of semi-subterfuge was worked out for Helen's parents, and she was there with him at Charleston. Vanessa commented: "I don't know at all how safe it is to deceive her family. All I'm anxious about is

Vanessa at Charleston. Taken by Helen (Soutar) Morris.

Julian at Charleston. Taken by Helen (Soutar) Morris.

that they should be deceived."[66] Julian wrote to his father in the late spring: "Helen and I are established at Charleston in a rather Wordsworthian state of rural bliss, recovering from Cambridge and tripos. I'm hoping—if I have only tricked my examiners into giving me a first to get a studentship out of Kings and get Bunny to find a cottage, and stay up next year writing a dissertation on Pope in the hope of getting a fellowship out of Kings—Maynard and Peter are both encouraging."[67] Virginia wrote to him on May 13 asking him to bring Miss "Suter" to dinner in London, but the special nature of the invitation seems to have been somewhat muted in her adding, "Bring anyone." The next day in another letter, to Quentin, she wrote that she had had lunch with Peter Lucas and that he was worried about Julian's exam results. "Peter rather fears that Miss Helen has taken his mind off the poets and he wont cut such a good figure in the exam as he should. They are inseparable and are asked out together, and interlock on every occasion."[68] Despite his hard work, he didn't get a first but rather the next grade, a respectable 2:1. He was awarded a studentship, worth £60. Maynard told Vanessa that he should have received a first but hadn't worked quite hard enough. Considering that Julian thought he had spent considerable time studying, that might have been a bit galling.

Being apart from Helen in the early spring had intensified his feelings, and taken him out of himself into a state of adoration for her. His brother commented to him on his life at the time: "Give my love to Helen. I thought she was charming, could you suggest that she should grow her hair long? It is her main charm and it seems a pity that she should keep it cut short. . . . I think I shall give up women and keep a cow. Their breath is much sweeter and one neednt worry about birth control, and if the worst came to the worst a minotaur would be rather interesting."[69] Helen and Julian were apart again in August, and at this point his tone is much more matter-of-fact, including a complaint that Keynes had stolen the Bells' *Times* at Charleston by waylaying the postman. "No one would ever think these love letters, would they? In fact, they're not, they're the vehicle for expressing all the things in my head too disorderly for print, too intimate for conversation, and that must be expressed somehow. Perhaps that from a masculine point of view, is the raison d'être of women—an outlet for intimate egotism. . . . What a pity Bloomsbury is not a governing class. So many of them would really be better using their minds on practical affairs rather than on love affairs."

The ardent lover of the spring has been replaced, at least temporarily, by a rather cold and unappealing sensualist. To Helen's bemoaning their separation, he replied in an undated letter, probably in August, "It's rather ridiculous to make this fuss about two months of separation." And then in his next letter: "Darling, please, please cheer up. To be frankly selfish I want a mistress I can respect, and I cannot respect people who let emotion overwhelm sense. Also quite frankly, I don't want a mistress who's a nervous wreck, but someone healthy and strong and fresh . . . who will walk over the downs all day, and make love half the night. So cheer up, sweetheart, and be careful of yourself." Separated from Helen while he was at Charleston in September, he wrote to her that it was hard to remain chaste. "But if you think this means that my feeling is purely physical, you will be wrong. . . . I'm quite certain that if we had been sleeping together, say, twice every week, I could have escaped half the glooms and depressions, and the restless laziness of the summer. . . . It only fair that I should try to explain the truth to you, and not cover everything with romantic figleaves. I'm sorry, dear, to preach to you like this." He was even more cynical in a letter to Eddie Playfair on September 6: "Helen has, typically, picked a quarrel, proclaimed a separation and then changed her mind and made it up. It's no good pretending I'm still romantically in love tho' I'm very fond of her and should be sorry to lose her as a mistress. But I don't really think two people so different as we are can go on much longer on such very intimate terms."[70] He returned to Cambridge later in the month, no longer an undergraduate. He was now living in a country cottage, St. Martin's Farm in Elsworth outside of Cambridge, working on a dissertation on Pope to submit in the hopes of becoming a Fellow of the College. Helen was still an undergraduate at Girton. He wrote to his mother at the time, "Helen seems quite happy at Girton—we see less of each other than we did, which is perhaps as well if we are ever to do any work."[71] He was very busy, not only with Pope but also preparing his book of poems, *Winter Movement*, for publication. As the affair continued, it became somewhat routine, but not without some moments of intensity. In September 1930 he wrote, "The reasonable confidence that in a short time I shall be in bed with you does a great deal to save me from the worst bitterness." But it seemed to be now just part of his life. As he wrote to her: "In my moments of vanity and ambition I know that I've got talents and the many things I want to do are really important. Consequently, one must face the extreme difficulty of carrying on one's life, and the demands it makes on a naturally weak and indolent character." A few days later, on September 19, he wrote, "I don't think anyone would call this a love letter—but none the less the writer is in love with you." And on September 29, he is both the cool and the passionate lover: "Up to the time of writing, and to the best of my knowledge and belief, I'm still your lover, and your [sic] still my mistress. Altogether, things could be far worse—at one moment, they nearly were. I still have cold shivers down my back at the idea of how near I came to losing you. The truth is I'm most unreasonably in love. . . . Two years ago, to think of you in my arms. I believe it will be infinitely more exciting than it ever has been before—which is saying a great deal." Indeed, that fall, intensity appeared to have returned to their relationship. But it became more and more of a roller coaster, with arguments and reconciliations, and a very real possibility of their getting married—while being aware of problems in doing so. In an undated letter, probably from September, he wrote: "We must be about as opposed in character as two lovers well can be. And tho' that suits lovers well enough, it would be very difficult for us to live together for years without quarrelling desperately." And there is a quite extraordinary, undated letter about this time, in which Julian stated, "I shall not send you this letter." Yet the letter is with those Helen kept.

> I wish you would realise that you are as much my master emotionally as I am yours intellectually. I have neither strength, patience or courage enough to withstand you. . . . It is not possible if we are to be lovers to be dishonest. . . . As you have told me, I am too complete an egotist ever to understand your, or anyone else's, feelings. I know that nearly all my emotions about human beings are shallow and superficial. About you, about Nessa and about Angelica they are not, at least as far as I know. . . . You managed to hurt me inexpressibly this afternoon by talking of our shared feelings in a way that was not far from sneering. I very much wish I had obeyed my instinct and hit you in the mouth, instead of trying to use your own weapons of emotion to hurt you. I think you must have by now a great deal to forgive from me. . . . Dear, this is mostly nonsense, and anyhow the whole incident is rather ridiculous, particularly [as] you will not see this letter. . . . I love you completely and unalterably. I cannot believe that this will be the end. Perhaps we shall only go on loving and hurting each other. . . . If the quarrel is irreparable then I don't know what will happen. . . . Whether, as you have suggested, I try to find another mistress or not, I shall

have lost one important part of my life, for there is no possibility of feeling certain things with anyone but you. Perhaps I shall find life possible without loving. If not, even my conceit does not make me think myself very valuable to others. Perhaps I shall just go on and have one affair after another, growing slowly older. . . . I know what a wretched fool I've been, but at least I know that if I lose you I shall lose the most valuable thing in the world.

It would seem that during this year they were both on the verge of breaking up, or of getting married.

The sexual aspect of his life would appear to have become more of a necessity. As he wrote to his close friend and contemporary Harold Barger at about this time:

> Oh what a plague is love. Well, at least it wont go on like this all one's life. For my part, Helens last letter has made me feel that after all there's something to be said for it. Lechery, lechery so early in the day. I shall be two and twenty in February, and I do think that at that age chastity, my brother, chastity especially with a brother like mine, can be carried too far. After a night with Helen, a saner and a wiser man I'd rise the morrow morn. . . . If you were here I should certainly insist on going to bed with you.[72]

In his correspondence with his greatest friend, Eddie Playfair, he presented himself very much as the cynical sensualist. On October 1, he wrote to him that "that unmitigated idiot Helen is descending tomorrow by the same train as Julia. Can you imagine a more embarrassing situation for a quiet man. . . . Helen I know will be jealous and emotional and sulky and altogether impossible. . . . The one excuse for buggery is that it is almost impossible to find a woman with a grain of common sense. If only one could. Really I'd go to bed with Betty Wiskemann if I thought she would refrain from behaving like a child of four. . . . How I loathe violent emotions." (Here again is the mysterious Julia: as indicated earlier, Vanessa mentioned her as someone Julian had been interested in before Helen but who became engaged to someone else. Elizabeth Wiskemann, nine years older than Julian, was nevertheless very much part of the interlocking circles of the time. She was quite infatuated with Bloomsbury and was having, at the time, an affair with the much younger and bisexual William Empson. Wiskemann went on to become a distinguished historian of Europe.) Some days later Julian wrote to Eddie (now a civil servant in London) that Helen had only made two scenes—once, in bed, yesterday afternoon, when I wanted her so, and she suddenly took it into her head that she was being treated as a convenience for lust. However now that I'm not so desperately in love, I can make myself do the right thing—sit quiet and wait. It's effective in the end. Besides, one learns how to manage bodies—and that goes a long way. . . . I have moments of envying the married. . . . It would be so pleasant if instead of Mrs Desborough coming in to look after the house, and Helen coming over every two or three days one person could combine both activities. Alas, tho, it's impossible as I couldn't possibly work with Helen in the room, at least not to any effect.[73]

Helen and Julian were having intense conversations about their future at the time, with marriage or suicide being possible options. It is hard to believe that the latter was a serious consideration. Julian wrote to Eddie:

We are disputing the academic question of suicide-marriage with the most quixotic high mindedness. At one point, we agreed to be secretly married tomorrow, but now that's off, I think, tho' I'm not sure. I can see your gasp [?] of horror. But really, you know, it wouldn't be too impractical, since we probably shan't want to marry anyone else for another ten years, by which time there should be more than enough evidence for a divorce. As things stand, I have had to threaten (a) to tell Helen's parents all in the event of a suicide (b) to follow suit. These threats have some effect, but she is idiotically romantic about marriage "loved, and love only" for her, and so there's a deadlock, and we've each swore not to go to bed with the other except on our own terms, and both want to go to bed, and are both determined to use any means to seduce the other. Could Moliére have invented a more comic situation? Well, we'll see what happens tomorrow. I've just finished a pastoral-satire on love, with the moral "as good fish in the sea as ever came out" which if I can polish it up to decency [?] I shall dedicate to you.

They did make an appointment to be married at the local registry on November 24. But they changed their minds. William Elson, the superintendent registrar of the Chesterton Union wrote to Julian, "I am in receipt of your letter of the 24th instant and note that your wedding is cancelled."

After these dramas, their affair continued in a somewhat calmer and more relaxed way. Julian wrote in a cynical way to Eddie in December: "One advantage of a mistress on the premises is that one doesn't have these horrible feelings of all kinds. It seems to be one of the few beneficent arrangements of providence that physical satisfaction restores one's equilibrium—one's head grows clear and one's heart grows cold—the only tolerable state of affairs. Only, of course, a decently comfortable person wouldnt think so with such violence as I find myself doing. A passion for the intellect is a sign of other passions unsatisfied."[74] Yet, he wrote to Helen at Christmastime in 1930 when as usual, the Bells submitted to the tedium of spending the holidays with Clive's family at Seend House in Wiltshire. "I don't think I've ever been happier in my life in anything concerning a human being. If I analyze my feelings I found that that they were partly, but not wholly altruistic. Certainly, the fact that you experienced intense physical pleasure was one of the chief causes of my happiness. I was also proud of myself for having accomplished what had seemed very difficult, and there was the allied satisfaction of completing perfectly what feels like a work of art—the clarinet quintet, shall we say." (And to Quentin in January: "Cambridge appears to be getting drunker and slightly more heterosexual—I've almost reformed Kings. . . . I shant give you details of my private life, as I never have any of yours."[75]) Despite these pleasures, this academic year was a hard time for Helen. She had been swept up into a rather grand world of well-known figures with whom Julian had grown up. It was not the best preparation for the final examinations she was about to take as the culmination of her Cambridge undergraduate career. Julian was concerned about her as she had been ill and he felt that the situation was not good for either of them.

Despite the drama, he summed up his life in a letter to his brother a few days after his twenty-third birthday in 1931 as follows: "1 dog, 1 car, 1 published work not to speak of various other excursions into print, 1 mistress, 1 lunatic brother, 2 uncles who were the last man off the Gallipoli peninsular, 1 aunt of whom the less said the better, 1 sister with whom we shall most probably fall in love, 1 cottage, innumerable brilliant, intelligent sharing [?] friends."[76]

∽

Let us return to his life as a poet. His primary literary contribution, as suggested in his piece on "The Progress of Poetry," was being a poet, one might say the poet of Bloomsbury, a position that no other member of the group occupied. Julian had spent his vacation alone in the spring of 1929 at the house Vanessa and Duncan rented in Cassis, outside the town in a vineyard. In a letter to John Lehmann, he wrote of "the most incredibly romantic views, with hills, pines, sea, sunsets and distant mountains. Yet the whole affair done in the best grave, sober, French classical style, laid out by Cezanne, with the ghost of Racine at his elbow. So I get the best of both worlds, to say nothing of first-rate French cooking and red wine."[77] He was still at a time of his life when he really did believe he could have the best of both worlds, indeed of all worlds: everything was delicately in balance. Then, almost at once, the scales were heavily weighted in favor of the classic disciplines. The romantic, "the non-rational intuitive side of his nature" (John Lehmann's phrase), was to be controlled, suppressed, denied expression until almost the very end of his life. The process begins in his poetry (afterwards in his affairs), and there is a concatenation of themes and circumstances that must be kept in mind if one is to understand how it came about: the dislike of modernism; the disapproval of obscurity; the commitment, but in a different way, to the rationalism of his elders; the Apostolic preference for abstract ideas; the shift, at the end of his second year, from history to literature. Bloomsbury (especially Strachey) had always had a fondness for the eighteenth century, yet ironically Strachey felt that in the late 1920s and early 1930s Julian's generation was too interested in aesthetics and not sufficiently interested in politics. That would change. At this point, Julian went a giant step further and became, somewhat in violation of eighteenth-century values, an ardent enthusiast, ready to wage war. His premises were simple: twentieth-century modernism originated in, or resulted in, obscurity; nineteenth-century romanticism exalted the impalpable and irrational; eighteenth-century classicism was clear, precise, and disciplined, its enlightenment a forerunner of Bloomsbury and its technique a model to emulate. Romanticism was the enemy. "Above all, we ought to clear our minds of all poeticality," he wrote to Lehmann in the summer of 1929. "Julia's petticoat or the Rape of the Lock are better subjects at the present day than the grand simplicities, Love and Birth and Death, Heaven and the giant wars and all the rest of that old curiosity shop. Down with the romantics, both deluded and disillusioned."[78] Thus he argued, and there perhaps he ought to have stopped. But his admiration for the eighteenth century led him to believe that the heroic couplet, that neat pair of ten-syllable lines joined by a rhyme, was still the ideal vehicle for the expression of ideas in verse, as it had been for Dryden and Pope, encouraging one to be apothegmatic, antithetical, allegorical, and transparent. This notion began to shape his practice as a poet in his own place and time. Lehmann grew alarmed. "I think there is something to be said for taking certain 18th century writers as models, as a counterbalance to Romantic licence and exaggeration. But it would be disastrous I think to *imitate* them."[79] Julian, however, was too caught up in his enthusiasm to be dissuaded.

> Timid, I venture on a doubtful field,
> The heaviest weapon in our verse to wield;
> Presume with Dryden's couplet to engage
> The wild philosophers in all their rage.

These are the opening lines of his first published exercise in the "new" style: an eight-page assemblage of heroic couplets, which appeared, as we've seen, in *The Venture* in February 1930. "AN EPISTLE On the Subject of the Ethical and Aesthetic Beliefs of HERR LUDWIG WITGENSTEIN (Doctor of Philosophy) to RICHARD BRAITHEWAITE ESQ., M.A. (Fellow of King's College)" contains rather more ideas than poetry—the couplets are not so elegantly managed as to justify their revival. It is at its best as comic invective, at its weakest when Julian opposes to the notions of the philosopher some notions of his own. Predictably, he declares his allegiance to

> Good Sense and Reason; for the rest I hope
> Voltaire had owned them, and adorned them Pope:
> The rational Common Sense, the easy rule,
> That marked for centuries the Cambridge school.

Perhaps the most disheartening moment comes somewhat later in the poem when Bloomsbury's cardinal philosophical principle is translated and trivialized in the diction and style of the eighteenth century:

> If further you should ask, I take my stand
> On an old creed, that all can understand.
> Well knowing we this truth shall certain find
> "Value resides alone in States of Mind."

As clever undergraduate mimicry, this is creditable enough; as the new style of a young poet of authentic talent, it is downright ominous. But I. A. Richards adored the poem, writing years later to T. E. B. Howarth and commenting on the book Howarth was writing about Cambridge: "I write while my reading of Julian Bell's daring and astonishing poem is still warm—indeed glowing.

... The best couplets have a fine shocking impact. ... I would think that to make Wittgenstein a key figure in *Cambridge Between the Wars* would be both historically and tactically right. He was, for philosophy, the dazzling disaster and the damage is not by a long chalk yet cleaned up."[80]

Nevertheless, this fortunately did not represent an abiding way of writing, and he was already increasingly prominent as a new young poet in Cambridge and beyond. In the previous autumn he had been represented by two poems in his old manner—descriptive nature pieces—in *Cambridge Poetry 1929*. (This was to have been the first appearance of an annual collection of undergraduate poets, Experimenters and Venturers alike, offered as a counterpart to *Oxford Poetry*, but it proved to be less durable: only one further number appeared, in 1930. The publishers were Leonard and Virginia Woolf at the Hogarth Press.) Here, and in similar enterprises in the future, it was Julian's misfortune not to stand out among the company. His two poems have admirable passages, but they are lesser works; and F. R. Leavis, in a favorable review of the volume in the *Cambridge Review*, quite rightly reserved his warmest praise for Empson and Eberhart.[81] To discover Julian at his best one must read him in his first book, *Winter Movement*, which Chatto and Windus published the next autumn, a few months after the close of his undergraduate career. Since all the poems it contains were written by the end of the first term of his third year—that is, before the publication of "An Epistle"—and since it includes some of the earliest attempts in the "new" style, it seems proper to describe its contents here, and to defer until somewhat later an account of its reception. The book, with its dedicatory stanzas "To Richard Jefferies" ("You are our master . . ."), consists of twenty-seven poems, some very early but the major portion written in Paris and during his first two years at Cambridge, among them "Brumaire," "Vendémaire," "Frimaire," "The Hedge," and "Winter Movement." The intention, as described in the dedicatory poem, is

> To catch those instants in a net
>   Of words; those minutes, crystal clear,
> Which the mind can never forget
>   When all the world stood bright and near.

And indeed, in all but the latest of these poems there is brightness and nearness, a remarkable clarity of seeing and hearing—the consequence, it would seem, of Julian's determination not to allow sentiment or conceit or preconception to distort what he describes. There is "The Goldfinch in the Orchard":

> In the top branches of the dying pear,
> Almost invisible, despite the bar
> Of yellow gold across his wings,
> And his bright crimson crest,
> The long, sweet whistle carrying far,
> High perched, he sings . . .

There are "The Moths," glimpsed in an autumn twilight:

> Among the flowers, soft blurs of misty white
> Poised steady on their slow, vibrating flight . . .
>
> The darkness deepens still. Clouds hide the sky.
> And on the pond the moorhens splash and cry
> With their wild voices of an unknown world.
> Crunching the flints, a shepherd passes by.
>
> The smoking lantern throws its moving rays
> Across the orchard, and the warm light plays
> On all the silver undersides of leaves
> Of pear and apple trees beside the ways.
>
> The lantern closes, leaves an instant's dark
> Then lights the brown beads on the pear tree's bark
> And the drugged moths, with softly quivering wings
> Or drowsy, like some lichened knot or mark . . .

Even when he comes indoors, which he does only once, in "Still Life," there is the same clarity and detachment. Presumably it is the kitchen at Charleston, that house of painters, that is being described as though it were itself a painting, indicating his closeness to his mother's and Duncan's art:

> Plain, scrub-grained, angular, bare deal,
> Littered with Wednesday's groceries
> And meat, stands the kitchen table.
>
> Enamel basin, sink, brass tap,
> Dish-cloth, white plates, circling small flies.
> The kitchen tap leaks, drip, drip, drip.

> A warm grey afternoon. Upon
> The window-sill drowned wasps in jars.
> Black range and grate are cold as stone.
>
> Poured from the basket they were in,
> Straw criss-cross, bellying, handle tied
> With string, dark shadow powdered green,
>
> The apples piled, one rolled astray,
> The others mass, wet light, round shade,
> Where in a heap confused they lie.
>
> A prism's angles curved and squeezed
> In an indented globe. The round
> Sides black bright red to white-green washed.
>
> In white glazed dish, a square cup flat,
> Five eggs before, below them stand,
> Cool, heavy, porous, brown and white.

In many ways the most remarkable poem in the book is "Marsh Birds Pass over London." An "irregular ode" of more than a hundred lines, it is very consciously an attempt to get beyond the limitations of the descriptive poems Julian had until now been writing. Unlike them, it is a poem based on an idea suggested to him by an episode in Jefferies's novel *After London*. It is meant to express an idea; but the idea was not at odds with Julian's poetic imagination and sensibility. It was oddly consonant with the "non-rational intuitive side of his nature," and it could be bodied forth in a true poem. (These poems are so good, it makes one deeply regret that he so soon abandoned in large part his commitment to poetry.) In its opposition of the world of man and the world of nature, the one transient, the other enduring, the idea takes its place among the "grand simplicities." Yet it is translated into a prophetic vision of remarkable intensity.

> High over London—
> So far and high
> That none can see them, few can catch and know
> Their wailing cry

—fly the wild birds of the marshes: Curlew, Whimbrel, Grey and Golden Plover, Lapwing and Dotterel. Their cry is a prophecy of fear:

The Seven Whistlers, as they fly,
Tell of who follows presently.
Loud warning all that they beware
Of armies hastening in the air,
That sweep in with a droning flight,
Continually, by day and night.
All through the night great houses flare,
The tattered walls that the bombs tear
Seem broken tins and jars left bare
In muddy sewers, when the sea
Ebbs from the tide-swept estuary.

There follows a lament for the ruined city:

> Fallen, fallen and fallen,
>   The city fallen and gone.
> The marsh birds' desolate calling
>   Comes menacing from the sky,
> The city is falling, falling.

A final apocalyptic vision shows

>   Grey clouds from the north-east,
> Where the river mouth is wide;
>   The waters piled in a tattered hill
>   Sweep in on the spring tide . . .
> Each ruined bridge comes tumbling down,
>   The waves pour through each gap
> That bombs have torn in great stone dykes,
>   Steadily rise and lap
> Against what doors and window-panes
>   Men had the time to close,
> Cascades down every flight of steps,
>   And still the flooding grows . . .
> The tides sweep in and out again,
>   Fret and grind at the walls
> Already shattered: splashing
> In the spreading marsh each falls.
> A muddy island, small and low,
> Where purples, tall sea asters grow
>   On the columns of St. Paul's . . .

Whether read as darkly romantic prophecy or as a fable of human experience, "Marsh Birds Pass over London" is a considerable achievement; and in its fusion of nature and nightmare it is a reminder that "the black blood of the Stephens" was not only part of Julian's inheritance but an essential element in his poetic gift. Yet it was precisely against this element that he steeled himself. In the summer of 1929 he had written to Lehmann, "Clarity, precision and above all common sense are the real virtues of poetry." Yet he failed to recognize that the qualities he admired were already present in the poems he had been writing. Dissatisfied with merely descriptive poems ("If one means to do anything more than describe—I am sure one ought to"), he left unexplored the very real possibilities for development from a poem like "Marsh Birds Pass over London." Instead, beguiled by the notion of a countermodernist offensive conducted in classical style, he began a program of eighteenth-century imitations. Its early results comprise the final pages of *Winter Movement*. Only one example, "Winter Trees," need be given here:

> Gay-decked with flowers the trees arose,
> Fair maidens, from their sheets of snows,
> The blossoms' ribband, and green leaves' light lace,
> Flung bashfully, in spring, round each sweet face.
> Then, as the sun hotter and higher grew,
> Changed airy robes for staider fashions new,
> Full-leaved in summer, dully green,
> Wore a Victorian crinoline.
> This, too, cast off, startle whoe'er beholds
> With gleaming panoply of reds and golds:
> Their autumn fashion-plates ablaze
> With warmer colours for cold days.
> Now, in the winter naked, they're most fair,
> Most loved, like other nymphs, when they stand bare.

The antithesis of his earlier poems—which, as John Lehmann has said, created "a new kind of poetic 'stuff,' the precipitate of an unusual and difficult, but exciting way of experiencing the objective world"—this trivial and sentimental verbal conceit is evidence enough of the extent of his misapprehension.

Yet was there a lack of connection between his poetic ideas and his personal life? The attachment to Helen was rather more romantic than neoclassic. When Julian, in midwinter, wrote to Quentin that "I find the difficulty of achieving classical restraint and serenity is very great, when you are bubbling over with the wildest metaphysical fancies," he was referring to his literary dilemma. The remark might have applied equally well to the conduct of his emotions, especially when he added, "I feel very sure of my central thesis that the only hope is the Golden Mean and good sense." What this meant, in a practical way, was that one fell in love but not to the point of irrevocable commitment. Yet in this early stage of the relationship with Helen, he was, as we've seen, outrageously happy. And Helen herself had seemed to have been sensible enough and understanding enough—that is, she understood Julian—not to press for what she knew he was not prepared to give. Thus the Golden Mean was maintained.

In June of that year, 1930, he received his bachelor of arts. A period in his life, perhaps the happiest, was at an end. What was he to do next? He had almost too many pursuits to choose from—from poetry to philosophy, from academia to journalism, from politics to criticism—and this very richness of possibilities, a reflection of the successes of his undergraduate career, would dog the rest of his life. He seemed unable to commit himself definitely and wholeheartedly to one particular pursuit, and would move along various paths, either not finding them satisfactory or for some reason or other being deflected from them. In the autumn of 1930 his first book of poems was to be published, but not even then did he choose to think of himself as a poet, or *only* a poet: there was so much else to be. Chatto & Windus had accepted the book in June 1930—it was a coup for any young man to have a book of poetry published—and as it wasn't by the Hogarth Press there wouldn't be any whiff of nepotism. But what, in particular, was he to do next? More or less for want of something better, he decided to continue on at Cambridge, pursuing his interest in Pope and having received a research studentship from King's. The solution, though temporary, had much to recommend it: it meant, for one thing, that his romantic attachment could be continued on approximately the same terms as before. He himself, in a position now to satisfy his passion for the countryside, took a cottage in Elsworth, some miles distant from the turmoil of the University. The prospect was pleasing. Yet inevitably there was a sense of anticlimax: the golden undergraduate years were finished; the friends were dispersing. In September, from Charleston, he wrote to John Lehmann, who was travelling abroad:

The fifth symphony is going on, much against Clive's will, but really just now Beethoven is the only musician I can endure, for I'm suffering from—not melancholy but black blood, the black blood of the Stephens, I suppose, that Virginia talks of, and only hardness, strength, tragedy are endurable. In fact I've had an overdose of romance and beauty. Cures: Beethoven and ten mile walks in big boots, and the slaughter of innocent birds. . . . I've got to save my soul if it's possible. I've just woken up to the fact that effectively I've done nothing except indulge in erotic emotion this last two years. The last really respectable piece of work I did was Winter Movement—Wittgenstein ["An Epistle"] was all right in its way, but not good enough. The trouble is partly that one—I, I mean—needs friends, or at least fairly intimate acquaintances to talk to, and a mistress to sleep with—the latter I find it impossible to do without now. I spend far too much time thinking about the subject. But both take a fearful lot of time and energy, and leave one incapable of writing well. One's friends—mine, at least—are worth the expenditure of energy. But also, they can be dropped and recovered to a certain extent. One can see them—particularly when one feels at all at ease—and yet go on writing. But a mistress involves—at least Helen involves—the devil of a lot of energy, besides taking up time with her presence, and being a constant preoccupation away. And really, a great deal of the summer, I was going about in a dream, without attending to anything properly, which is a wretched state of mind, for which I'm still suffering. In the end, I think I shall have to give up being romantic about love, and turn into a common sense sensualist. Deplorably like my poor father, perhaps, but then I should try not to be civilised and sentimental about it all. "Minds and bodies are best naked, whereas hearts should be carefully wrapped up in flannel."[82]

But a month later, writing to Lehmann again, this time from the cottage at Elsworth, he was in his more usual high spirits: "Then there's Helen, two or three days a week—a very happy relationship now. Cambridge and conversation when I feel inclined. And work. . . . I contemplate a satire Cambridge 1930—but that's dubious. . . . Dedie [sic] has been made dean—he'll be made vice-provost before long. Shades of the combination room about the golden lad," and so on, very gaily. Yet, towards the end, an equivocal note is sounded: "Here am I, solidly attached to monogamous Helen, ready to start affairs, if I were free, with half-a-dozen young women. Not of course, that they'd be successful, but at least I shouldn't languish in despair. . . . Perhaps it's only that success and security make one feel that all adventures are worth trying."[83] The first, "romantic period" of the relationship, when he had been in a state of outrageous happiness, had given way to a quasi-domesticity, which he truly enjoyed—but only for two or three days a week. Here, as in other parts of his life, there were strings and reservations (fantasies, it would seem, that made him "languish in despair"), a reluctance or an inability to commit himself wholeheartedly—to Helen now, and to others afterwards.

Rather surprisingly, he made no mention to Lehmann of an event that must have been much upon his mind at this time: the approaching publication of *Winter Movement*. The book was dedicated to the three most important women in his life: Vanessa, Angelica, and Helen. It was his finest moment as a poet, and one again regrets that he didn't go on. In his papers are many drafts of poems and also a group of unpublished poems that Helen had in her possession. Perhaps his period of greatest poetic inspiration was in fact associated with this love affair. The unpublished poems that she preserved deal with love in a rather lighthearted manner, as in "Song from a Masque":

> I do not trust, I do not lie,
> Nor drive my lovers to despair,
> No one for me shall pine or die,
> No swordsman kill, no poet sigh,
> I am as free as summer's air.
>
> And I shall walk as Flora fair,
> And gather roses on the green,
> I drive no lovers to despair,
> No one through me shall meet black care,
> I dance as free as summer's air,
> With country Flora on the green.

And then there is in the group a poem he wrote, clearly for Helen, on St. Valentine's Day, February 14, 1930, which included the following lines:

> Since we are lovers and are young,
> Grant us some peace and safety, oh kind saint;
> Through the world's uproar we have caught the faint
> Tune that the happier poets dead have sung.
>   Show us the path by which one may
>   Teach us the secret we must learn. . . .
> Oh saint, some refuge to your pilgrims give
> Some quiet world where we may love and live. . . .

> I who have seen Heaven
> In Helen's face
> A land of summer afternoon
> And evening peace.[84]

He may have decided to appear unconcerned about the publication of his book—one possible strategy for a young writer—and thus appear undisturbed if the book should fail. But there is evidence to suggest that these were weeks of anxiety. He wrote to Lehmann in a letter that has its ironies in light of his later ideas and his ultimate trip to Spain: "For the first time in my life, I fainted on getting up out of a chair. Curious, and unpleasant. I shall never make a man of action—I live too much on my nerves. Or at least, not a great one. I daresay I could lead a cavalry charge, or fly an aeroplane, but I couldn't sit still for days under fire. . . . I see that my fate is to [be] an inferior but slightly gayer, Crabbe. He's very sympathetic, despite his heavy Christianity."[85]

At last the day came. It came and went in silence. Then the letters began to trickle in, rather fewer than he might have expected. Edmund Blunden wrote a praising letter to thank him for a copy. There was a brief notice in a Sunday paper. One of the first letters he received was from Lehmann, who had just returned from Paris:

> Here I am, immensely glad to be back, in time to see the last act of an English Autumn. And in time to see the publication of *Winter Movement*. I have seen a copy, and I think it looks admirable—Chatto have not failed you. I re-read the first twenty six pages—to which I am deeply devoted—on the spot. You must let me know what reviews there are—keep them for me. I have not seen anything myself yet, but the Lords of Reviewdom take their time about poetry—if they condescend to notice it at all. I must say I think in some ways Keats was rather lucky to have so many important pages of abuse devoted to him.[86]

Julian answered at once. His letter was very odd in the circumstances. The larger part of it was a thoughtful and straightforward restatement of his poetic beliefs. Without pausing to invoke the example of the eighteenth century, or to prescribe the use of the heroic couplet, he set forth a view of poetry that prefigured much of the work that would be written in the 1930s, although he himself would play only a peripheral role in the coming movement:

> I do believe that poetry must interest the common reader by talking about human beings and about events that he is acquainted with, or of a kind similar to those he is acquainted with. I believe we must abandon everything fantastic, distant and other-worldly . . . and concentrate on the natural and the reasonable. Equally, I begin to believe that poetic beauty must never be pursued for itself, or sought anywhere but in the natural life and events of our subject matter. I mean, we must not strain after beautiful effects, and be for ever opening magic casements and journeying to Xanadu, but discover beauty accidentally.

Only at the end of the letter, and then with an offhandedness that failed to conceal his true feelings, did he mention his book: "Winter M. had a little puff in the Observer—all so far. Peter [Lucas] will do it for the Review, [James] Reeves, I think, for the Granta. Blunden wrote me a charming letter, and so did Morgan Forster and Angelica. I've sold 44 copies—more than I expected."[87]

Lehmann, of course, was right: reviewers do take their time about poetry, especially about first collections, and *Winter Movement* over the next several months would be occasionally noticed, temperately on the whole, but at least not unfavorably. In February 1932 there was a belated act of recognition. Michael Roberts, in his "Notes on English Poets" written for *Poetry* (Chicago), linked *Winter Movement* with Auden's *Poems* as "the outstanding achievement of the younger men in 1930." But this was too long after the event, and at too great a distance from it—who in England would have seen the tribute?—to mean as much to Julian as it would have earlier: by then his expectations had cooled. At home, from the quarter where praise (one feels) would have been most welcome, there was rather less than he might have expected. Those who adhere to the theory of Bloomsbury as a conspiracy dedicated to self-advancement will find no support in this instance. His elders were admirably restrained: there was no hint of a public or subterranean campaign to bring on the next generation. One has the feeling that, dote on Julian though they did, they were not quite prepared (except for David Garnett) to take him as seriously as a poet as he deserved. After his death, Virginia wrote, "it is the one thing I regret in our relationship: that I ought have encouraged him more as a writer."

Since childhood Julian had always been vulnerable to the opinions of others. Lacking the single-mindedness of vocation so evident, for example, in the young Stephen Spender, he could easily persuade himself that there were other, more important things for him than poetry, and strike out in new directions. Encouragement from his elders might conceivably have determined him to continue in his original course; yet it is quite possible that he had already gone as far in that course as he was able to go. *Winter Movement* is not one of those first books of verse that are more exciting in their promise than in their accomplishment: it is admirable in itself, a self-contained achievement. Michael Roberts, having declared, quite justly, that "Mr Bell infuses a new vigour into English pastoral poetry. . . . He can make poetry where the Edwardians made dull verse," concluded, "[his] technique is so appropriate to his chosen subject that probably he is too careful a craftsman to fail in any field he may attempt, but his strict application makes it impossible to forecast his development."

In the summer of 1929, writing to Lehmann, Julian had prescribed "a settled and orderly life in which certainty and precision rule." In that tranquil summer, which might be compared to the summer of 1914 as the end of a period—thereafter one would live and think differently—a life such as the one Julian prescribed was, if one wanted it, still available. Eliot might see the postwar world as a wasteland, but it depended on one's point of view: the 1920s could be an exceedingly pleasant time to live, especially if one had come of age in that careless decade and was not haunted (as one's elders were) by all that had followed upon the summer of 1914. Although he himself thought he was expressing a "thoroughly 18th century point of view," Julian was in fact being very much a young man of the late 1920s when he told Lehmann that there were "plenty of interesting and pleasant things left to do and write about without the Romantics' illusions. They might learn with Candide to cultivate the garden of Epicurus." Then, with an assurance that recalls Keynes writing to Strachey in 1906, he concluded: "Our elders, whose romantic illusions were smashed for them by the war, have an excuse for writing like Tom Eliot and Huxley. But we, who have never believed falsehoods, have no need to be shocked at truth."[88]

That was in the late 1920s. In the 1930s one began to live and think differently. Even if one had wanted "a settled and orderly life in which certainty and precision rule," it would have seemed, as an ideal, an anachronism; and as a reality, difficult to obtain. A famous poem of the period by Stephen

Spender—which appeared in the anthology *New Signatures*—begins:

> Oh young men oh young comrades
> It is too late now to stay in those houses
> your fathers built

and John Lehmann's poem "Travel Bureau," which was published in *Cambridge Poetry 1929*, concludes:

> No track returns through time to what has been
> No wagon-lit is scheduled to the place
> Where twigs begin to cloud with whorls of green
> And purple flags are bursting from their case.

On the whole, it was a time, figuratively speaking, when one was more likely to stand at the barricades (Spender: "advance to rebel") than to cultivate the garden of Epicurus. Julian, like Spender and Lehmann a contributor to *New Signatures*, objected to what he considered the "romanticism" of their position, yet he was himself in many ways a man of the 1930s: his life, almost until its end, was unsettled and disorderly, uncertain and imprecise.

One sees him in this period between 1930 and 1935 trying on, as it were, a variety of roles. Given his interest in poetry and his growing interest in politics, and his ability to practice both, he might have played an important role in the literary life of the decade if he had wished to. With *Winter Movement* he had achieved a small but firm reputation, more than firm enough for a first step; he might have gone much further. But he did not know precisely what it was he wanted yet, and he refused to commit himself to a position just because he might have it. He remained in Cambridge, writing poetry and preparing to write about Pope for his fellowship dissertation, on the fringes rather than at the center of literary life. Lehmann, whom he may have regarded as a disciple and certainly as an ally in their own Cambridge-based "movement," became more and more himself a literary figure, and in part the literary figure that Julian might have become. Towards the end of 1930, Lehmann had submitted his first book of poems, *A Garden Revisited*, to Leonard and Virginia Woolf at the Hogarth Press, and not only did Julian's aunt and uncle want the book, but they wanted John as well—to come work for the press as an apprentice-editor-partner. "I expect you know substantially what the offer of the Woolves was going to be," he wrote to Julian. "I was surprised when they made it to me—on Friday, at tea, when I met them both for the first time, and thought them most charming, Virginia very beautiful."[89] Thus it was that Lehmann, in his own right, entered Julian's world of Bloomsbury; and he brought with him some of the despised Oxford poets—most particularly Stephen Spender, who became a great friend of Virginia's.

The first significant meeting between Oxford and Cambridge poetry occurred during the Christmas holidays of 1930, when Lehmann's sister Rosamond brought Spender to Fieldhead (the Lehmann family home on the Thames). The two young poets walked by the river, and Spender talked with the utmost candor about life and poetry; Lehmann listened and was a good deal more impressed than he thought it diplomatic to admit to Julian. To him he wrote, "A homo-Romantic of the wildest sort I have ever met (you would have ground your teeth, I fancy)."[90] In fact, with that flair for "new writing" that was to make him a commanding figure on the English literary scene over the next three decades, he had recognized an authentic poet.

Appropriately enough, Lehmann, as a Cambridge man who had established a connection with the Oxford group, was instrumental in presenting the new young poets to the world. Soon after the publication of *A Garden Revisited*, as he tells us in his autobiography, he received a letter "from someone I had never heard of before, called Michael Roberts." (Roberts, himself an interesting figure of the 1930s as a critic and poet, had been a poor boy who finally managed to go to Trinity College, Cambridge, in the mid-1920s; at the time of his meeting with Lehmann, he was a mathematics master at a London grammar school.) "He wrote that he admired the poems, had been watching my work for some time, and asked if I would care to come in to see him in his flat one evening to discuss them. An irresistibly flattering call for a young author: a few days later, after dinner, I knocked at his door."

> We plunged into talk about modern poetry at once, and I discovered that he had read all my contemporaries, and what was more had an idea that they belonged together more closely, in spite of the wide apparent differences, than I, in the middle of the *mêlée* that Julian made so dramatic, had detected. The more he talked, the more flattered I felt at the thought of belonging to a revolutionary movement in the arts, and the more my fresh publishing ardour was inflamed by the possibility, which began to grow in my mind, of presenting all of us in some way as a *front*, so that the public, notoriously sluggish in its appreciation of individual poets, should be obliged to sit up and take notice.... During the next

few days I talked it over with Leonard and Virginia, proposed an anthology of poetry of all the young writers whose names had been mentioned that evening, got their sympathy and provisional support, and then wrote to Michael Roberts and suggested he should edit it for us and write an Introduction. The project that was eventually to take shape as *New Signatures* was on.[91]

The book would be a new departure, and the question was whether Julian would join the train or remain behind in the garden of Epicurus (or Charleston). He was, of course, one of the young writers who had been mentioned that night at Michael Roberts's—the others were Auden, Spender, and Day Lewis from Oxford; Empson, Eberhart, and Lehmann from Cambridge; and two poets Lehmann had met since coming to London, A.S.J. Tessimond and William Plomer. Julian was not likely to be happy about joining any group that was not of his own making, and Lehmann, when he wrote to him about the anthology—"We want to know at once whether you'll contribute"—made a point of saying, "it will definitely be a flag for 'us' to rally round." Unfortunately, he greatly weakened the point (as far as Julian was concerned) by adding, "Spender, Auden, Day Lewis will be asked among others."[92] This was not at all an "us" Julian would recognize: he wrote Lehmann "a long growling letter" about what they had stood for hitherto and "the danger of condoning the heresies of Spender and Auden." Lehmann was understandably irritated, and on Christmas Eve he replied: "Thank you for your damned intransigent and intractable letter. I enclose a copy of the blurb for the book which will show you how deeply you will commit yourself if you offer any poems to it. The net is meant to be wide, and naturally the poets are not expected to form a *School*—an idea totally ludicrous. Are we to expunge your name from that provisional list? I hope not—but your letter in tone might have been that of a French General arriving in the Ruhr, 1923."[93] The blurb read: "These new poems and satires by W. H. Auden, Julian Bell, Cecil Day Lewis, Stephen Spender, A. S. J. Tessimond, and others, are a challenge to the pessimism and intellectual aloofness which has marked the best poetry of recent years. These young poets rebel only against those things which they believe can and must be changed in the postwar world, and their work in consequence has a vigour and width of appeal which has long seemed lacking from English poetry."[94] This seemed inoffensive enough, and Julian prepared to capitulate. First, though, he was determined to make his own position absolutely clear.

He wrote to Lehmann, and enclosed a letter to Michael Roberts for Lehmann to read and hand on:

To Lehmann: . . . I don't know Roberts, and I want to be fairly sure of escaping a nonsense blurb of a preface. I don't quite like the look of things from the list you showed me. . . . I believe in facts and logic and in nothing else, and about poetry I believe most firmly that what is needed is the most extreme 18th century domination of the intellect over the emotions—and about life and politics too [and so forth]

To Roberts: . . . as to the anthology, I have no lyrics that I want to publish, but I have two satires. . . . But I should like, before committing myself, to know what line the Editor intends to take in his preface, and what poets are to be included. . . . I believe in common-sense, wit and clarity. But all the rest of your group seem to accept a fundamentally romantic view of poetry in Auden's case perhaps with a Lawrentian tinge. . . . Empson would probably agree with me in thinking Pope a better poet than Keats, but would the rest of your group if they were being sincere?

Lehmann was too loyal and discreet a friend to hand on this challenge to Roberts, who as an outsider might have been less ready than he to indulge or understand the "French General" tone. In any event, Julian, having stated a point, felt that he had gained it: he allowed himself to be published in the book and so became, albeit with much reluctance, a member of the *New Signatures* group.

The slim blue volume (No. 24 in the Hogarth Living Poets Series), which had caused so much fuss to assemble, came out in the spring of 1932, created a mild sensation, and has since been taken to mark the beginning, the formal opening, of the poetic movement of the 1930s. In a sense it was merely a continuation, a sort of joint issue, of *Oxford Poetry* and *Cambridge Poetry*, for only two of the nine contributors, Plomer and Tessimond, had not attended one or other of the Ancient Universities. Several had already published books of verse—Lehmann, Day Lewis (*Transitional Poem* and *From Feathers to Iron*), and Plomer, each in the Hogarth Series. Auden's *Poems* had come out in 1930 (from Faber & Faber, where T. S. Eliot reigned and where he played, like the Woolfs, an important part in sponsoring the new movement) and had had "an overwhelming effect." In that year too came *Winter Movement*, admired but not to be an influence; and Spender's *Twenty Poems*, his first "public edition"—the important *Poems* would not be brought out by Faber until 1933.

And all the contributors, even those whose first books were still two or three years in the future, had published in periodicals: *The Listener, Adelphi, This Quarter,* and *The Criterion* (edited by Eliot). In short, they were not entirely unknown and unrecognized, nor was *New Signatures* quite the succession of discoveries that its legend credits it with being. But Lehmann was entirely right in his intuition that the public, "sluggish in its appreciation of individual poets," might be "obliged to sit up and take notice" if they were presented as "*a front.*"

> The reviewers were impressed [Lehmann sums up], the public bought it and there was a general feeling in the air that Something had happened in poetry. We even had to print a second impression within a few weeks. Several of the poets were already known individually; but the little book was like a searchlight suddenly switched on to reveal that, without anyone noticing it, a group of skirmishers had been creeping up in a concerted movement of attack. Some of us were, perhaps, as surprised as the public to find that we formed part of a secret foray . . . however, an impression had been made . . . that no amount of reservations or protestations on the part of individual contributors could efface, and from that moment we were all lumped together as the "*New Signatures* poets."[95]

It would be convenient to adopt a "revisionist" stance and describe *New Signatures* as simply a collection of verse, some of it remarkably fine, by nine talented young poets of the 1930s. Here are Auden's "Though aware of our rank and alert to obey orders" and "Doom is dark and deeper than any sea-dingle"; and Empson's "You were amused to find you too could fear / 'The eternal silence of the infinite spaces'" and his "Camping Out" ("And now she cleans her teeth into the lake"); and Spender's "The Express" ("After the first powerful plain manifesto") and "I think continually of those who were truly great." Can one find a "group theory" that will really account for them? How, as a "group," do these poets of the 1930s differ from the poets of the previous decade? Roberts, as we have seen, was aiming beyond a mere sampling of excellence: he did have an idea of the sort of poetry he wanted for his anthology, and of the direction he felt poetry ought to take in the coming decade. But his preface is too veiled and generalized to provide satisfactory answers to either question. He begins by saying: "new knowledge and new circumstances have compelled us to think and feel in ways not expressible in the old language at all. The poet who, using an obsolete technique, attempts to express his whole conception is compelled to be partly insincere or be content with slovenly thought and sentimental feeling" (compare this with Julian in the *Cambridge Review*: "he cannot invent a new technique, while what he has inherited is utterly decayed"). Roberts continues, "A poet cannot expect to write well ... unless he is abreast of his own times, honest with himself, and uses a technique sufficiently flexible to express precisely those subtleties of thought and feeling in which he differs from his predecessors." This is so inarguable as to be platitudinous, and as appropriate to the poetry of the 1920s as to that of the 1930s. Roberts is more "thirtyish" when he advances the notion of the poet as a "leader": to lead, he must be understood; therefore "a poem must first be comprehensible.... The poems in this book represent a clear reaction against esoteric poetry in which it is necessary for the reader to catch each recondite allusion" (compare with Julian at any and all points). And he is "thirtyish" too in his concern for a "popular poetry." But his major emphases are given to matters of technique: he notices (correctly) that the poets of *New Signatures* are returning to the older forms and disciplines, turning from the irregular cadence of free verse to explore "the possibilities of counterpointed rhythm." He also claims, with a fine disregard for the achievements of the 1920s, that *his* poets have solved a "major problem": how "to use the material presented by modern civilization.... Mr Auden's *Poems* and Mr Day Lewis's *From Feathers to Iron* were, I think, the first books in which imagery taken from contemporary life consistently appeared as the natural and spontaneous expression of the poet's thought and feeling."[96] Yet it is hard to believe that Eliot, writing

> At the violet hour, when the eyes and back
> Turn upward from the desk, when the human engine waits
> Like a taxi throbbing waiting

is not as "natural and spontaneous" and as "contemporary" as any thirties poet. Roberts's difficulty, one feels, is that he is attempting to define differences in terms of technique rather than content. In this, perhaps, he is too "twentyish," for the crucial point of difference between the writers of the 1930s and their immediate predecessors has more to do with history (content) than with literature (technique). "Perhaps, after all," Spender decided some twenty years later, in his autobiography, *World Within World,*

Perhaps, after all, the qualities which distinguished us from the writers of the previous decade lay not in ourselves but in the events to which we reacted. These were unemployment, economic crisis, nascent fascism, approaching war. . . . The older writers were reacting in the 'twenties to the exhaustion and hopelessness of a Europe in which the old régimes were falling to pieces. We were a "new generation," but it took me some time to appreciate the meaning of this phrase. It amounted to meaning that we had begun to write in circumstances strikingly different from those of our immediate predecessors and that a consciousness of this was shown in our writing. . . . We were the 1930's.[97]

Julian had contributed to *New Signatures* with the greatest reluctance: "I don't quite like the look of things." Preoccupied with technique (rather like Roberts himself), he drew a firm line between himself and the other contributors, but as much as they he was a member of the "new generation," reacting to events of the new decade: "unemployment, economic crisis . . . approaching war." The manner, however, was very much his own; or rather, his own as he had appropriated it from the eighteenth century. Roberts, not having seen the inflammatory note ("I have no lyrics that I want to publish"), assumed that Julian would be sending pieces like those in *Winter Movement*, and wrote his preface accordingly: "[Julian Bell writes] of the English countryside in rhythms which show that for him it means no week-end cottage or funkhole from the town: his clear-cut delineations of landscape express neither jingoism nor sentimental affectation but a feeling for the land itself; a sentiment which, though local in its origins, leads to sympathy with that same feeling in others, and to a love of the earth irrespective of place which is the opposite of militant nationalism."[98] In fact, none of the three poems Julian submitted fits the description. The first, "Still Life," a glimpse of an empty room at night and the landscape outside it, is cast, to its disadvantage, in couplets: it is minor work, less impressive, because more conventional in detail and in phrasing, than the poem of the same title which had appeared in *Winter Movement*. The second of the three, "Tranquility Recollected," is in his earlier manner—Mediterranean landscape evoked with a wealth of sensuous detail—and grew out of a happy visit he and Helen had paid to the Charles Maurons in St. Rémy. His most ambitious contribution to *New Signatures* was the satire "Arms and the Man," a fully fledged example of Julian's later manner, embodying all of his notions of what a poem ought to be, and as such a kind of test case for them. Like his poem about Wittgenstein, it is written in Pope's (or Dryden's) couplets, but more dexterously than before, and the pace is unflagging throughout the poem's four hundred lines. (It occupies twelve pages, more than a tenth of the anthology. Julian's was the largest representation, fifteen pages in all; ten for Auden; nine for Spender; seven for Empson. Impact, however, did not prove commensurate with length.) The interest of the poem, it must be said, lies principally in its ideas, which proved to be more representative of the period than its technique. Its epigraph—Dr. Johnson's "Patriotism is the last refuge of a scoundrel"—then, "Arms and the Man I sing," would appeal to the cynicism of a generation that had watched Ramsay MacDonald become prime minister in the new National government. But Julian's tone thereafter is more Shavian than Virgilian.

The satire is wide-ranging: hardly a branch of the Establishment—"Empire, and State, and Church"—is allowed to escape. After a look at "Britain's glory,"

> Whatever happens, we shall muddle through:
> We muddle out, when we have muddled in,
> And, if a war lasts long enough, we win . . .

he asks, "But what's the use of war?". . .

> See, in reply, Lord Northcliffe's ghost appear,
> Deny mere facts, and tell us undismay'd
> "What is the good of war? It's good for trade."

Trade; and Prestige ("the helpful second cause /Of our prosperity, and fleet, and wars.") and Security:

> By armaments alone we sleep secure,
> Unless all nations are for war prepared,
> Within an instant, war will be declared . . .
> For, as two mot'rists, insolently rich,
> Race side by side, to die in the last ditch,
> So, scarce one nation in the world will dare
> To face the risk of anything but war:
> Courage or common sense we vainly seek,
> All to disarm too stupid or too weak . . .
> Death's the essential: life and all its cares
> Are less important than our future wars,
> "Economy" employs each Press Lord's breath,
> And what economy so great as death?

The realities of the Depression haunt the poem and call upon Julian's otherwise unused descriptive powers for its central passage:

> Down the black streets, dark with unwanted coal
> The harassed miners wait the grudging dole;
> The sinking furnaces, their fires damped down,
> Depress to poverty the hopeless town . . .
> On every hand the stagnant ruin spreads,
> And closed are shops and fact'ries, mines and sheds.
> As, one by one, the farmers break and fail,
> And barns are emptied at the bankrupt's sale,
> Mark from some hill, across the fertile weald,
> The arable retreating field by field,
> The waste advancing as the corn recedes
> Where the lean bullocks chew the fallow weeds.
> See rotting gates hang by the rusted catch,
> The unstopped hedges, and the mouldered thatch,
> The mildewed hay beneath the August rain,
> The fly-pock'd turnips, and the shredded grain.
> Thistles and brambles choke the sinking tracks,
> And deep corruption rots the tumbling stacks.
> Here, in a language all can understand,
> See plainly told the history of our land.
> In war or famine some could still grow fat,
> The capit'list then prospered, and the rat:
> But that great age is done: now comes the day
> When, for their fathers' sins, the children pay;
> Yet, not content with paying for the past,
> We seek another war to match the last.

As Julian approaches his conclusion, he seems almost to be answering a question asked by Spender at the opening of one of his poems in *New Signatures*:

> Who live under the shadow of a war
> What can I do that matters?

Not long before this, Julian had written to Lehmann, "I sometimes think we may have to take a hand in the politicians' dogfight"; now, in "Arms and the Man," he advises:

> Strike then, and swiftly; if the end must come
> May war, like charity, begin at home:
> Do what we can, and use what power we have,
> Confront the ruin, if we cannot save;
> Nor leave the politicians to their trade,
> To spread the idiot tangle they have made.

This is, as it were, the next-to-last word: the declaration of a believer in facts and logic, in the domination of the intellect over the emotions, in life, politics, and poetry. Surely rational men must see the stupidity of war? Yet at the very end of the poem (and how characteristic this is of Julian) there is an irruption of romantic fantasy, an apocalyptic vision of the future:

> When war shall break across the world once more,
> And force the ancient wilderness restore,
> The arches crumble, and the column fall,
> Through the high places the rough satyr call,
> Empire, and State, and Church their turmoil cease,
> And marsh and forest reassume their peace.

Julian, in a sort of filial or perhaps grand-filial gesture, had intended to dedicate "Arms and the Man" to Goldsworthy Lowes Dickinson, the political thinker, Apostle, and friend to Bloomsbury, who had been a prime mover behind the idea of the League of Nations, and whose books, such as *The International Anarchy* (1926), helped to shape the antiwar thinking of the war generation itself, and that of the 1920s. One might presume that he would have welcomed this gesture of affiliation from the younger generation; in fact, it made him uneasy. "Arms and the Man" seems to have been much too forceful for gentle Goldie. Pleased though he was to discover "that there is at least one young man who hates war," he wrote to Julian:

> I feel that your poem will be nothing but provocative and offensive to every kind of man that reads it. You will reply that you mean it to be. Yes, but I am thinking of the main thing, what will tend to change opinion about war. . . . I regret now every escape of irritation satire and rage which I have let escape, and, to be honest, I feel that, if I accept this dedication from you, I shall be supposed to endorse your methods. Will you understand and forgive my dear, and perhaps reconsider the whole poem? For I feel it in my bones that if you publish it you may regret it later.[99]

Reading this letter, so tepid and so temporizing, one can understand the burst of irritation that prompted Virginia Woolf to note in her diary, "what a thin whistle of hot air Goldie lets out through his front teeth."[100] And perhaps it was just as well that Dickinson declined the dedication, and so kept the youth of *New Signatures* uncontaminated by connection with the older generation. When the collection appeared, Julian, despite all his earlier reservations and protests, was wholly approving. To Lehmann he wrote: "I thought *New Signatures* put up a very substantial show indeed—it's a real, definite achievement for the Press. I hope we shall get reviewed by the political, as well as the literary, papers."[101] But the reviewers paid no particular attention to "Arms and the Man"; it stirred up none of the controversy that Julian would have welcomed and that Dickinson had feared. Empson, in his poem "This Last Pain," suggested that one must "learn a style from a despair." But this was precisely what Julian had chosen not to do: he had grafted his very contemporary subject onto the style of the eighteenth century. The hybrid result might have a good deal of intelligence, wit, clarity, and common sense, yet it had failed to quicken beyond verse into poetry.

CHAPTER 3

SEARCHING

JULIAN IN THE EARLY 1930S: a charming, intelligent, and discontented young man. He still kept a good deal of the boyish quality that made David Garnett regard him as something of a puppy—high spirited, alert, and affectionate—and he had never got away from the almost compulsive untidiness of his childhood: his clothes were always in need of repair; he could rarely be bothered to comb his hair, or button his collar or shirt buttons. In scale, in goldenness of aspect, he suggested a disheveled Greek god, Charles Mauron thought, with his generous laughter, large bright eyes, and great height.[1]

Yet even a Greek god from the Olympus of Bloomsbury must do something with his time; in fact, Julian meant to do a great deal, perhaps too much in too many directions, although his only formal commitment in these years was to the University and the academic community. He had achieved a respectable result in the Tripos, and he was judged worthy of a research studentship by King's. In the autumn of 1930 he returned to Cambridge. As a research student he would register with the English faculty as a possible doctoral candidate; more importantly, he would be at work on a dissertation which he hoped would lead to his appointment as a Fellow of his College.

In July, Lehmann had written: "Hooray for the studentship; I felt sure you would get it. Have you settled anything about a house? A fine lonely spot to write masterpieces in, during the intervals of Pope."[2] His expectation of creative and scholarly activity was shared by Julian: one could easily do both, Pope and poetry. Also, if one wanted, politics and criticism.

Thus, he began with a commitment to the academic community that was hedged about with unstated restrictions and ironies. Keynes was in favor of his securing a Fellowship. Even though Keynes himself was both a man of the world and an academic, there was really no strong Bloomsbury tradition of formal scholarship to urge Julian forward. Most of Bloomsbury's own sporadic forays into the groves of academe had not been notable. Strachey had tried to obtain a Fellowship at Trinity (with a dissertation on Warren Hastings) and had failed. Roger Fry had been put up for the Slade Professorship of Fine Arts at both Oxford and Cambridge, but it was not until 1933, the year before his death, that he finally became Slade Professor at Cambridge. Of course there was the extraordinary example of Keynes, who managed to be equally at home in Cambridge and the world beyond, but even as he was himself regarded with the very faintest condescension by the rest of Bloomsbury, so he treated most of his academic brethren with a certain sense of distance, particularly as they were likely to act upon his stock market tips with lamentable timing. It followed, then, that if Julian were to become any sort of academic, it would have to be in a special hybrid category—no shades of the combination room about that golden lad—with strong connections to literary and political London, and the most flexible commitment to the disciplines of formal scholarship. (The category is not unfamiliar among the dons of Oxford and Cambridge—especially the former—who often move out and up into the world after having established a place in the University; it is one recognized road to eminence.) At the end of his scholarly endeavors, when perhaps he felt more bitter about it than when he began, Julian gave vent to a diatribe against the method of the academy, although it is hard to believe that he had not held the same views from the first:

> There are few human activities more painful to contemplate than scholarship. A parody of the scientific method in its parade of exactitude and vigour, scholarship has neither the excitement nor the justification of scientific research. The additions to human knowledge made by those who meticulously collate,

annotate, and demolish their predecessors, are seldom of the slightest importance or interest to anyone. And when the scholars turn from the works of the unreadable obscure . . . to attempt the works of greater writers, the result of their labours is too often a dense sediment of footnotes encumbering the text and a bored suspicion in the reader: the poets are concealed from us by crusty, insensitive and priggish old gentlemen.[3]

He came back to Cambridge in high spirits. "Pope fascinates and terrifies," he wrote to Lehmann. "I must read so much, yet there does seem a real chance of doing something and producing some real criticism."[4] He settled down in a version of "a fine lonely spot to write masterpieces in": a small and pleasant cottage, Martin's Farm, in Elsworth, a little village about ten miles from the University towards Huntingdon, in sparse, green, slightly rolling country. He had the advantage of being near enough to Cambridge to participate as much as he might like in the literary controversies he had become fond of, to continue to attend meetings of the Apostles, take some part in national political questions as they were felt at the University, and be a rather reluctant treasurer of the Heretics, the lively Cambridge organization for somewhat subversive talks—yet he was still far enough away to be able to work without distraction for days at a time, and to live in close touch with the country and natural life that meant so much to him.[5] Elsworth also had the advantage of being comparatively close to the house of his good friend David Garnett, at Hilton, near Huntingdon. Garnett was in a way almost a bridge figure for Bloomsbury, younger than Julian's mother and aunt, yet older than Julian himself. "He liked to come round," Garnett recalls, "and we would rehearse, always with fresh appreciation, some of the comic saga of the past"—that is, "the old anecdotes recording the foibles of his family and their friends." And at Elsworth he could be with Helen in perhaps the most satisfying period of their relationship, when he still set the terms and she appeared to accept them.

It was an existence very much to his liking: the cottage and Cambridge, and driving recklessly back and forth between them. (Garnett is only one of many who remember him as "rash and dangerous driving a car." He adds, "he had either no sense of fear or else, as I suspect, he liked the sensation, but he was slapdash and easily flustered as well as quick and always quite sure every other driver on the road was in the wrong."[6]) He was at the splendid, untested time of youth, before experience bears down, just having finished his formal education, and therefore believing, since no one was telling him what to do, that he could do everything. He reveled in possibility. Even after a year of work, his enthusiasm was uncurbed. To Lehmann, in October 1931 (shortly before the inception of *New Signatures*), he wrote: "My plans, at present, besides Pope, who sticks, include translating one play each of Corneille, Racine, Moliere and Marivaux, a play to finish, another [play], a novel to write, a set of essays, and a second book of poems of which I seem to have the essentials. Enough for a year or two anyway."[7]

His most serious endeavor was working on the text that he hoped would secure him a Fellowship at King's. What exactly, as a member of Bloomsbury might say, Julian was doing about Pope ("who sticks") is unclear. He was firmly opposed, as we have seen, to academic scholarship of the collating, annotating, and footnoting sort; at the same time, he had great faith in his own critical judgment—very much in the English tradition of the golden amateur—and it appears that this, "some real criticism," is what he intended rather than a historical or biographical study. He took issue (in a review published in the *New Statesman and Nation* in December 1934) with two celebrated views of Pope put forth in the 1920s: "Miss Sitwell's view of Pope as a romantic over-sensitive and invalid member of the Sitwell family, has always been most dubious. Strachey's 'fiendishly clever and spiteful monkey,' though more plausible, was based on the Victorian view of the facts of Pope's life." Yet ultimately, he supported Strachey's view of Pope. His own interest was centered on the work itself. As he wrote to John Lehmann in an undated letter, "it has the qualities of great poetry . . . produced not by a genius for taking infinite pains—only charlatans and bores take infinite pains—but by a tried and practised genius."[8] In another letter to Lehmann he wrote, "Lytton's description of Pope always seems to me far and away the best—an appearance of formality on top of the most violent emotions."[9]

~

Part of Julian's dilemma, one feels, was his unwillingness to take infinite pains, as if somehow they would prove him a bore. He wanted to do everything, and in the academic line that included a critical study of Pope, at which he worked hard through the early 1930s; but he was constantly being distracted from it by other things that he wanted to do, and he was never able to give it the single-minded concentration that was necessary to bring it to a successful conclusion. As he wrote to Lettice Ramsey, his second great love (of whom more later), in February 1932, "I see I shall soon have to be pulling myself together about old Pope—except that I seem to be almost equally good at most of the things I'm interested in—which makes it difficult to stick to any one of them."[10] A month later he wrote: "I've turned out my old work on Pope—I must have several bushels of paper and started with squared paper and a dictionary, which seems a silly—and slow—way of analyzing poetry. Still, it's quite fun." But what had plagued him from the inception of the project continued to do so. It was fun to invent interpretations for the poems, to work out explications de texte, and have brilliant ideas and theories (as though one were at a meeting of the Apostles), but it was boring (as though one were a charlatan) to set them all down on paper, to find out whether other people had anticipated one's discoveries, and to do historical research; that is, all the journeyman scholarship that he deplored. "The trouble," he confessed to Lettice in that spring—the Pope period—"now seems to be that I'm much too ingenious at thinking of explanations, and too lazy to work out strict tests of them." Yet his interest did not dwindle: six months later he was writing, "There's such a lot to say about every single line of it." More and more the project began to take shape in his mind as an edition of the poetry, although obviously that would not secure him a Fellowship at his College. Again one is not certain of what exactly he intended: presumably not a variorum for scholars but perhaps a faithful text, with commentary, for lovers of poetry. In 1934 there was some talk of sending a text, presumably his critical work, to Chatto & Windus, who having published his poems, held an option on his next book. When it came to the point, however, he decided more work must be done, and nothing came into print (except for several book reviews) about Pope from this interest, really an obsession, of his in the 1930s. He did, nevertheless, finish an edition of Pope's poems consisting of 680 pages of text, 15 of general commentary and 90 of notes on the poems. The Nonesuch Press was to publish this in a series of British poets announced for 1934. Julian protested about what he considered a meager advance of £65 and managed to have it increased to £75, having remarked in the discussion of terms to the head of the press, Francis Meynell: "I shall wait to reply to your opening sentence until I can find something more effective in the way of an insult. What a pity you're not dealing direct with Pope." It was tactless of him to be difficult, as David Garnett was a very close friend of Meynell's, a partner in the press, and no doubt had been instrumental in arranging the publication. The increased check, however, was sent to him when he was in China in 1937, but the book was held up at this point because of the complications of George Macy and the Limited Editions Club of New York acquiring the press. It was reannounced for publication as late as 1949; fourteen poets were published in the series but sadly never Julian's edition of Pope.[11]

Thus, the work on Pope, which had been begun as a dissertation topic, became eventually an important, though quite inconclusive, intellectual pursuit. The dissertation itself, which he submitted at the end of 1931, was based on his preliminary researches, and it was not a success; that is, it did not result in his being made a Fellow of King's. Lehmann wrote to console him:

> I hope [not getting the Fellowship] wasn't a big disappointment: as far as I'd been able to gather from what you'd said, you hadn't expected it this year at all—I hope this was true. . . . I never thought a don's life was the life for you, you're far too interested in what's going on, and I don't think it's going to give you wide enough scope. . . . I've felt sometimes since leaving Cambridge that one ought to get half a world away from it—physically and spiritually—for a while, unless one's one of those rare people who are simply made for dondom. But I see the working for it gives one a raison d'etre—a line that's thinly held to keep the enemy quiet while the main force concentrates elsewhere.[12]

His mother wrote him a similarly consoling letter. Although on the part of both Lehmann and herself it was an obvious point to say that it wasn't the life for him, there was also a fair amount of truth in that appraisal. "I am afraid from the Times that you haven't got your fellowship & that it will be a disappointment to you. Darling, I *am* so sorry—but don't be depressed. I cannot, whatever happens, think you are altogether meant to be a don—Your interests are too wide & I feel that some day you may be glad not to be have been temporarily buried in Cambridge, however attractive the prospect of the moment."[13]

But Julian was determined to make another try. A Fellowship at King's would give him a firm base in the community and an agreeable life while he considered whether to enter into an academic career. The work on Pope remained his prime interest—he was not in the least disheartened by the unfavorable response to his dissertation, and in time came to agree with it: "Rereading my 18 months old dissertation gives me the cold blush all over my sunburn—what idiotic things I did say and think, to be sure."[14] But meanwhile it was necessary to find another topic, and he decided he would do something not in literature, his avowed subject, but along a philosophical line. It was a choice consistent with his ideal of the eighteenth-century gentleman, accomplished in everything, who would do nothing for gain and was untouched by the professionalism of the marketplace. Really, he had only to decide on a philosophical line—ethics, aesthetics, the psychology of creativity—and proceed. The year before, he had considered submitting to the English Board (for the doctorate) a topic on Wittgenstein. But George Rylands had dissuaded him, pointing out that to offer such a topic to the English faculty would be much the same as sending Swinburne's *Dolores* to Queen Victoria as a birthday ode.[15] So that was abandoned, and he eventually gave up the whole idea, if he had ever entertained it seriously, of working for an advanced degree. What mattered was to win a Fellowship, and for that purpose a dissertation of one or two hundred pages might do. Here he allowed himself to be misled by Apostolic practice. It was an occupational hazard of the Society that one might come to believe that any problem could be dealt with without too much difficulty and with no special qualification beyond the fact of being an Apostle: merely apply the clarity and rationality which a member had by definition—why else was he elected?—and the result was bound to be good. Julian loved the Society; he continued to regard it as the pinnacle of Cambridge intellectualism, and he came in from Elsworth for its Saturday-night gatherings. Over the past three years he had delivered many papers on philosophical themes, and he had had the benefit of rich, full discussion. The thought was inevitable, and irresistible: why should he not take some of his old papers and rework them into a dissertation, or at least make use of some of the ideas that had inspired them? He realized that the competition for the Fellowship would be intense, but he seemed unwilling to acknowledge that more scholarly attainments might weigh with the electors of the College. No doubt there was a strong degree of wishful thinking: the Fellowship more and more appeared as an answer to the question of what he was to do. He needed it; therefore he must have it. He did not intend to commit himself permanently to the academic life, of course, but it would allow him time to discover some viable alternative. The range of possibilities was narrowing. The publication of *New Signatures* had not materially altered his somewhat equivocal position as a poet. It had brought Auden and Spender conspicuously to the front of a movement to which Julian only tenuously belonged: he was, in the phrase of a later critic, "in but not of."[16] So, in the circumstances, the idea of the Fellowship was more attractive than it might otherwise have been. But he was determined to win it on his own terms, which in effect was to lose it on theirs.

Much of his energies for the next year and a half were given to the new dissertation. His working title was "The Good and All That," and it disguised a long essay dedicated to the sort of problems the Apostles haggled about over their anchovy paste and toast. It was also influenced by his increasing involvement, appropriate as the 1930s developed, with political questions. When he finished writing in the autumn of 1933, he began to think of it not only as a dissertation to win him a Fellowship but also as a book. To Lettice he wrote, "I've decided to send in 'The Good' as a dissertation—as it may shock a few of the older electors—and I shall have it finished and typed by Christmas, and ready to try on publishers." Early the next year it was in the hands of the College's electors.

The first pages of a carbon of the dissertation to be found in Julian's papers at King's gives the flavor of the enterprise (it may be a version of the dissertation he prepared to be submitted to a publisher):

GOOD AND ALL THAT
An essay on a provisional theory of ethics
By JULIAN BELL

An essay submitted as a dissertation to the Fellowship Electors of King's College, Cambridge, and originally called "Some general considerations on ethical theory, with their application to aesthetics and politics."

Dedicated to Alister Watson to whom in reality I owe everything

Chapters: An Apology, Metaphysics, Right and Wrong, Naturalism, Pleasant, Desired and Balanced Good and Bad, A Working Hypothesis, Choice: A Digression Rational Behaviour, Aesthetics, Politics, A Weltanschaung

Out of deference to the feelings of the electors, Julian had substituted for "The Good and All That" the more decorous title "Some general considerations on ethical theory, with their application to aesthetics and politics." But the title was almost the only conventionally academic aspect of the dissertation. Julian did not pretend to be a professional or trained philosopher. He operated on the assumption that the electors would prefer to see the quality of mind rather than a display of expertise. He was wrong. He must have known that the dissertation, and the Fellowship it might win, were designed to further scholarly activity, as well as to provide a new member of the College staff. But of course he had no patience with the appearance of scholarship, and declared in his prefatory note: "I have made use of no authorities beyond those mentioned in the text: I have stolen ideas wherever I came across them, usually in conversation, and used them without acknowledgement, since I cannot trace their authors. I am writing first and foremost for those amateurs of philosophy who like myself are more concerned with practice than with refinements of theory. I hope what I have said is true: I am fairly sure it is useful." Again, as though to make certain that there shall be no doubt of his academic disqualification, he reiterates his amateur status: "I am not a professional philosopher. . . . My claim to be, interested in the theory of ethics is that, in a small way, I am a practising poet and politician. As such, I am commonly confronted with ridiculous arguments based on ethical assertions." Given the vigor and forthrightness of his style, one might wish that Julian had attempted a new Candide, or a new Gulliver. As he himself was quick to declare, he hadn't the qualification to write a systematic critique; hence, the somewhat disorganized, arbitrary, and improvisational character of much of the dissertation. His aim is to distinguish between ideas of Good and Bad (or in fact, good and bad ideas) in Art and Life, Politics, Religion, War, Peace—the spectrum of human behavior. In the working out, he allowed himself the pleasure of expounding, in a very lively style, many of his favorite prejudices; Christianity, for example: "Most of the human misery not due to capitalism is due to Christianity, either directly, or through the religious muddle about means and ends. The Christian religion, or the traces of it that remain in the minds of politicians, old gentlemen and the great British public, holds that certain specific actions—for instance, making love to a married woman, or the direct removal of coal from a pit to a miner's fireplace—are sins." Yet for all the entertaining hodgepodge of the whole, a dominant theme does emerge. More perhaps than he himself realized, Julian was in full revolt against his Bloomsbury philosophical background and its static conception "of states of mind" as values in themselves, without regard to the effects, or actions, or consequences that might ensue from them. He thought of himself as modernizing a deeply cherished set of values; in fact, he was calling them into question.

In a chapter devoted largely to the ideas of G. E. Moore, he wrote:

> Professor Moore is, in a sense, my spiritual grandparent, though I fear he might question my legitimacy. For I was born into, and grew up in a world very largely of his making, the world of "Old Bloomsbury." And the hard, vigorous lucidity of mind, the orderly beauty of that view of the universe, seems to me to have been very much the reflection in life of the teaching of "Principia Ethica." And perhaps the society of painters, in particular, may have made familiar and congenial to me the habit of relying, in the last resort, on direct intuitive judgments, and on their apparent application to real, tangibly and indubitably existing entities. Equally, I am familiar with the self-reliant judgment asserted without the faintest regard to the opinions of any but a minute group of friends, or the collected judgments of centuries, if even of those.

Consequently I feel at home with a theory which asserts that there exist certain "states of mind" intrinsically and universally good, good in themselves, good simply, undefinably, self-evidently; which asserts that we perceive states of mind to be good as if we perceived apples to be red, and as if they were good with no more ado about the matter. To anyone of a contemplative turn of mind, averse to moralities of action and strenuous right-doing, to anyone more concerned to enjoy the good life than to reform the bad, to anyone to whom the arts are of the first importance, such a theory naturally recommends itself.

But, alas . . . the belief in universal and absolute good is only too often the second line of defence in priests and tyrants. It is apt to lead to intolerance, interference, misery and error in personal relations, to mistakes, at least, in discussions of aesthetic theory, to Fascism, tyranny and reaction in politics. Julian could not have made any clearer his break with his parents, with the generation of Apostles who had gathered together before the First World War and thought they were discovering values far superior to the didactic moralizations of their Victorian forebears. For a young man of the 1930s, what he might view as the simultaneous authoritarianism and comparative quietism of Bloomsbury philosophy were suspect and unsatisfactory. How in any absolute sense could one be certain of the rightness of one's values? As a thoroughgoing relativist, he asked why choose this particular set of values, and answered, "Because I choose to choose it," which, in effect, is a restatement of what he had written in an earlier chapter: "the only 'ideal' I feel I am supporting against others is that of the toleration of all 'ideals.'" And yet, "The victory is to whoever shouts loudest and, ultimately, I suppose to whoever shoots straightest." Here he is caught in a classic paradox of English middle-class liberalism: all have the right to believe as they please, yet it is the enlightened liberal who knows what is best for them to believe. The Victorians had not hesitated to resolve the paradox in favor of "strenuous right-doing" in the public world; Bloomsbury, serenely in possession of its own private values, which were perhaps too rare and special for the commonality, had no wish to proselytize, except, as it were, incidentally, by example. In the end, Julian plumps for the "good" in action: it is better to do something than to do nothing. Writing in a time of "unemployment, economic crisis, nascent fascism, and approaching war," he rejects the quietism of Bloomsbury for the activism of the 1930s:

> We should cultivate all those valued states of mind that are produced by action. . . . For one thing, it is obviously prudent to dive in of your own accord rather than wait to be pushed. For another, action is the most potent of drugs, and battlefields and revolutions are usually fairly good at curing romantic despairs—and other diseases incident to life. For another, intellectuals often turn out to be good men of action, and would probably do so more often if they could keep their minds clear—could become intellectuals rather than emotionals—and if they acquired a hard enough outer shell of cynicism and practical commonsense. . . . What I shall mean by ethics is the study of what are possible arguments about politics, the arts and human behaviour in general.[17]

One of the readers, as it happened, was Roger Fry, the newly appointed Slade Professor at Cambridge. In February he told Julian that he was reading the dissertation and liked it, with reservations. It does seem a bit dubious that someone so close to Julian should be reading the work, but his reading was far from a total endorsement. At the same time, Julian's uncle, Leonard Woolf, was reading it as a publisher. He disapproved strongly of the sort of philosophizing it contained, and turned it down.

As a compendium or anthology or grab bag of Julian's thought in the early 1930s, or even as a period document, "The Good and All That" has considerable interest. But it was clearly not a success, nor did it deserve to be, as an academic dissertation intended to demonstrate its author's worthiness to receive a College Fellowship. The system at King's was for the electors to refer the dissertation to two qualified readers, who would make a recommendation which the electors might or might not follow: the final decision was theirs. Julian saw the comments of his readers. Keynes sent him the mimeographed copies of their reports, noting that he had received their permission to do so. One of them, as has already been mentioned, was Roger Fry, a great friend of all the Bells (and all Bloomsbury), and a formative influence upon Julian's mind. He began his remarks with a disclaimer rather like Julian's own: "I have not read recent works and I gather from his frank avowal that Mr Bell is in the same state of ignorance." He did not allow friendship to inhibit criticism. He found that his pupil had not really learned the great Bloomsbury lesson of clarity, particularly in regard to the definition of terms, and he objected to the unsubstantiated attack on Christianity. But in spite of these and other objections, he was more favorable than not, and concluded with an enthusiastic recommendation:

> The subject is beset by many difficulties arising out of the vagueness of the terms in common use and I do not think that Mr. Bell has been able to clear them up. . . . In spite of these confusions I think it contains a great deal that is of real value both in the destructive criticism of theories of valuation and in his constructive work. . . . His disposal of Hedonism seems to me one of the best I have ever seen and is to me convincing and I should say the same of his acute criticism of Dr. Moore's absolutism. . . . On the whole in spite of the defects which I have pointed out I think this is a very praiseworthy and courageous attempt to think out some of the most difficult problems of life. Mr. Bell shows a keen desire to arrive at the truth regardless of his preconceptions and a much more balanced judgment than some of his rather reckless outbursts might suggest. It is eminently the work of a very young mind but one that should develop rapidly. I cannot help thinking that if Mr. Bell were to become a resident Fellow his influence in stimulating and guiding younger men would be of real value to the College.

The other reader, the distinguished philosopher C. D. Broad, a Fellow of Trinity, was not as kind. Like Fry, he too commented on the rather hasty dismissal of Christianity, "a religion for which [Mr. Bell] expresses a contempt which would not appear to be bred from any great familiarity with its doctrines." Unlike Fry, who had written quite briefly, he provided an exhaustive five-page summary of the thesis and did it the justice, which it could hardly bear, of treating it as a serious piece of philosophical writing. After pointing out a succession of errors, omissions, and inconsistencies, he concluded:

> Mr. Bell considers that the work of Dr. Richards and Mr. Empson is a promising beginning of a genuine Aesthetics. (He should learn to spell the name of his fellow-poet, the Kennedy Professor of Latin [A. E. Housman], whom he always loads with a redundant "e.") . . . He thinks that, in England, there is a good enough chance of securing the blessings of socialism without the evils of civil war to make it worth while to attempt the introduction of socialism by peaceful means. . . . He infers from his principles that existing laws against blasphemy, homosexual practices, and incest should be repealed. . . . He ends by considering rather elaborately the laws against cruelty to animals. . . . Mr. Bell refers with great respect to Prof. Moore, whom he calls his "spiritual grandfather." It is therefore all the more regrettable that he seems to have wholly ignored the *Principle of Organic Unities*, which is a most important part of Moore's ethical theories. . . . Mr. Bell's theory appears to be supported by faulty arguments and to be very doubtful. . . . Mr. Bell seems to assume that the value or disvalue of an experience will be determined entirely by its qualities and not at all by its relational properties. This seems to me very unlikely. . . . The question of Socialism and Capitalism is not worth discussing so long as those two extremely vague terms remain completely undefined, as they do in Mr. Bell's dissertation. . . . I have no clear views about the question of cruelty to animals, but I have some very strong prejudices in the opposite direction [Julian was rather brutal about animals in the dissertation] to Mr. Bell's. . . . It is by no means easy to pass a fair judgment on such a dissertation as this, since it is liable to fall between two stools. Plainly, it must not be judged simply as a contribution to the theory of ethics, and it must not be judged simply as a contribution to aesthetics and current politics. On either ground, taken separately, I should say that it falls definitely below the standard required of a fellowship dissertation. It does not follow that it may not be up to that standard when these two factors are taken jointly into consideration.

It appears to me that Mr. Bell inherits from his father the power of writing an absolutely first-rate political pamphlet, addressed to intelligent men, and moving at a far higher intellectual level than, e.g., the average leading articles in the most "high-brow" weekly reviews, such as the *New Statesman*. . . . I have tried to show that the ethical analysis is very inadequate; but, so far as it goes, it is clear, consistent, and well argued. . . . Plainly the dissertation cannot claim to be an important original contribution to knowledge. I have tried to explain to the Electors that it is a very intelligent, lively, and well-written politico-ethical pamphlet of a rather special kind. It is for them to decide whether they consider this the kind of dissertation on which they are willing to award a fellowship at King's.

Broad would have been happier to recommend Julian to the editor of the *New Statesman* than to the electors of the College. Even Roger Fry, recommending that he be given the Fellowship, did not claim high marks for the dissertation itself. Julian, shortly after submitting it, wrote to Lettice, "I've begun, I must confess, to have a quite mad hope—for it will surely be disappointed—that I shall after all get a fellowship." A mad hope it proved to be: the electors decided against him. His association with Cambridge was at an end. What he had written to Playfair in December 1931 still held true in the spring of 1934: "I must make up my mind what I'm going to do, failing a fellowship or I shall be in the soup." There was some talk of publishing the dissertation as a book on its own, if he could revise to his uncle Leonard's satisfaction, but nothing came of that.

~

He had been leading a poetic, academic, literary-critical, philosophic, political, and romantic existence. It was all very crowded, everything contemporaneous and exciting for that reason, but for the same reason not entirely satisfactory in any of its aspects. He was so talented in so many areas, but almost because of that, he could not make a sufficiently strong mark in one. From the time he began his research studentship until his final rejection by King's—from 1930 to 1934—he was publishing poetry and book reviews, working on a study and edition of Pope, participating in politics in Sussex and Cambridge, writing his dissertation on ethics, and conducting a full-scale social life, with a generous allotment of time to family, friends, and love affairs. He was capable of being in love and in literature and in politics, simultaneously and passionately yet inconclusively. Whichever direction he turned, there are disquieting similarities; his involvement with women and his involvement with politics seem different aspects of the same experience.

We have already described the rare emotional fulfillment that he found within his family circle; school and university had done very little to disengage him from his family; Pinault was a surrogate father; in a sense, Cambridge was his family writ large. His deepest attachment, unchanged throughout his life, was to his mother: it meant that it was very difficult for him to commit himself fully to other women. To a degree, a kind of emotional reluctance marks all his romantic involvements. He found his mother a perfect confidante. "I told Nessa all about it [whatever it might be] last night," he wrote; "somehow I find it very consoling to confide in her. Perhaps because she never does anything to shatter my self-confidence or vanity."[18] He particularly enjoyed talking to her or writing to her about his love affairs and other sexual matters, which he did with astonishing frankness. It was almost as though the happenings of his life were authenticated, became real and manageable, only when reported to his mother, who was certainly the only woman, and at times the only person, for whom he had full and absolute respect, and love. He never changed in this regard.

Nor did he change in his need to confide. The pleasure of self-disclosure was very real to him, and his list of confidants, headed by his mother and Eddie Playfair, was not a short one. He did not expect a return of disclosures comparable to his own, although he did rather resent Quentin's reluctance to tell him exactly what he was doing and with whom. "It's a ridiculous state of affairs," he wrote to him in 1931, "when you come to think [and plainly, he wanted Quentin to think as he did] that money and sex, the two most interesting and important subjects, are the things people are shyest about, particularly parents and children."[19] Of course these subjects were not at all taboo between Julian and his parents, whatever might be the situation between himself and Quentin: Julian discussed sex with his mother and money with his father. Clive Bell was convinced that the Crash of 1929 would ruin them all, but although there may have been somewhat less money immediately available to spend, there seemed to be enough for everything to go on as before, and it was assumed, as it had always been assumed, that Julian would have the advantage of a small private income. Clive continued to complain and worry; Julian, however, did not take seriously his contention that the family's economic difficulties would force him, Julian, to become an advertising-man or a schoolmaster. In his letter to Quentin he was ready to talk not only about sex ("The Apostles and Dr Freud are going into the whole matter of sexual life in the modern world") but also about money (a brisk discussion of the expectations of the young Bells, based upon what he had been told by their mother). He was determined to be honest about those "two most interesting and important subjects."

And indeed, given his temperament, it was easy enough to be honest, or at least forthright, in letters to his mother and friends. What was really much more difficult was to be honest with himself. It is unlikely that Julian ever achieved this ideal state. When it came to the experience of women, then he found that he could not do without them; at the same time, a part of his mind was sufficiently detached to resent the time they demanded, and he felt that his work, his writing, his various intellectual pursuits suffered as a result. He was in many ways, as John Lehmann suspected, a romantic who did his best to conceal the fact from himself and others. He liked to think of himself as cold and hard and calm; actually he was gentle but passionate, and full of a simmering violence. But this was an aspect of himself he feared and disliked and was determined to curb. Set in this context, his admiration for the eighteenth century comes to seem less a literary eccentricity than the expression of psychological unease. When he first fell in love with Helen, he could think of nothing else: he was outrageously happy. That summer, away from her, he was wretched. He was shocked at his vulnerability. As a Bloomsbury intellectual he tended to look askance at the heart, which in a community of talkers, he regarded as a rather "inarticulate beast."

The same division of thought continued throughout his life. He wanted to discipline himself against emotionalism and felt that writing in neoclassical couplets helped him to do this; later he recognized that the miseries and storms that entered into his affairs were necessary to arouse the dormant creative impulse. As quoted earlier, he wrote to Eddie Playfair that "It seems to be one of the few beneficent arrangements of providence that physical satisfaction restores one's equilibrium—one's head grows clear and one's heart grows cold—the only tolerable state of affairs." Yet the ideal of clear head and cold heart was in contradiction to the basic elements of his character. Julian thought he loathed violent emotions, but in everything, in politics and in love, he could not avoid them. The relationship with Helen was very happy in its middle phase, less romantic than it had been, less tempestuous than it was to become. There were a few weeks, a few months, when he was first at Elsworth, of the desired "Golden Mean": he would have been content—as what young man would not?—to have had it indefinitely prolonged. But he recognized that Helen was becoming concerned about the future. While he hesitated and temporized, she grew demanding, difficult, distrustful. She scrutinized his poems for allusions to herself. There were scenes, storms, quarrels, reconciliations. By the spring of 1931 it was clear to them both that they could not go on as they had been: they must either marry or put an end to the relationship. Twice Julian obtained a marriage license, but he went no further.

In a letter postmarked May 2, 1931, he wrote to his mother that he tried to spend most of his week at work on his Fellowship dissertation but that "I devote one day entirely to Helen, the weekend to Cambridge. . . . Helen is in a very bad way. She's not at all recovered from her illness yet, which makes her very weak, she can't sleep or eat, she's overworking for her tripos, and she's very worried about her future." She might return home to Dundee.

> The possibility of being separated has led me to consider the idea of our marrying. I wish you would let me know what you think. I should be in some way trapped. . . . I shall very probably want to marry someone else later. On the other hand, perhaps it's foolish, when one's as much in love as the one [sic], not to take such a risk. The real trouble, I think, is how we should get on together. Certainly there are the most appalling possibilities. We differ and disagree about endless things, and we've each got the power of driving the other frantic with rage. . . . I know that I am still very violently in love, though perhaps not very romantically. . . . In a great many ways I should very much like to be married. It would put an end to all the nervous strain of the life I lead, and judging from the past I think we should probably be very happy. On the other hand, I hate losing my freedom. . . . So give me some good advice. You know much better what I'm like than anyone else does, and you've seen a good deal of Helen.[20]

Eddie wrote to him in no uncertain terms about marriage: "It is my firm belief that a marriage with Helen would be fatal to both of you. . . . You must keep yourself free till you are really grown up."[21]

Vanessa replied to him at length on May 5 from Rome, where she, Duncan, Quentin, and Angelica had gone for an extended visit.

> Well, in this case I think you really dont quite know what you want to do yourself so possibly you may be more ready to listen to my notions than is generally the case. . . . Of course I want you to be happy & I want Helen to be & one tries to do a most difficult thing which is to imagine you both as you'll be in a few years time & how you'd affect each other & so on. Naturally I have thought a great deal about all this for some time, as you know for we

talked about it a little in the winter & I tried very hard to understand clearly her character & temperament from what little I've seen of her. So perhaps what I feel at any rate has the advantage of a good deal of conversation, for I felt in spite of your telling me then that you definitely didnt want to marry was that the question would inevitably arise before long. But before telling you as far as I can what I feel about that I think one thing is quite clear—you must whatever happens both get into a normal calm healthy state. . . . Even if this present way of life is unsatisfactory you will get all right as soon as you give it up. . . . Meanwhile why not see a doctor? . . . I really think you had better see someone my dear if you're having headaches. It's absurd not to. As for Helen, surely unless she can do the work for her exams without getting ill its nonsense to go in for it. . . . I'm sure she thinks far too much of the importance of work & exams. What do they matter? It's far more important to keep well. . . . Now as to the marriage question. You know my reputation for being against marriage. But I am not against it always & certainly not against it for you. . . . I quite expect you will find it much the happiest way of life for yourself to marry & have children & live rather a domestic existence. What I am not so sure about is that Helen is the right person for you to marry. I think too that one has to take risks—life would be very dull if one didn't—& as for the practical part of marriage I suppose that could quite well be arranged. Its the other part, the emotional part that worries me. You see, it seems to me that you, who are only 23, which is really you know still *very* young, are not a very precocious person. I think that you may & ought to change & grow & develop enormously in the next 5 or 6 years. I think you ought to see life, get to know different kinds of people, be free to change & expand. You have a great deal of Stephen in you & I think are like them in being rather late in developing. You met Helen when you were very young & I suppose rather sore & hurt in your feelings & she gave you what you wanted & still does to a large extent. But I think there can be very little doubt that you will some day fall in love perhaps in rather a different sort of way. If you marry Helen now you will certainly give up doing many things & getting to know many things & people that you might otherwise, because you will be tied to her & will have to lead a much quieter & less adventurous (in every way) existence. This may seem to you an advantage at the moment but I don't think it would if you were in a perfectly well & normal state. . . . I see that you cannot now bear the idea of making Helen unhappy & I think some way must be arranged by which she wont be. That can be considered & perhaps I can help to suggest something. But my dear if you marry her aren't you running a risk, too great a one, of making her much more unhappy later? . . . You will perhaps fall in love—& you will quite certainly be fallen in love with. . . . You might at first both find it a relief to be married, not to have to consider proprieties & all the other horrors of your present way of life. . . . My dearest, I hope I'm not being too outspoken & that you wont think I am in any way against Helen. I think she has a quite remarkably nice character & perhaps is in many ways one of the most charming & delightful people you may ever meet. . . . If I say that she does not seem to me to be certainly the right person for you to marry its not so much criticism of her as simply a perception of what seems to me incompatibility. . . . Fundamentally she has a very strong romantic view of marriage & looks on it as a kind of holy state. In fact it is partly my feeling that she would be so much upset if later you took any other view of it that makes me feel uneasy at the idea. . . . But of course I may be wrong about this. I do not really know. . . . If you were both older & had had experience of other people & knew that you wanted each more than you could want any one else then, given her temperament, it might be all right, but as things are I should be very much afraid of that sort of difficulty. I feel I am doing what is always a foolish thing to do, telling you freely what I think & giving advice which cannot be altogether very welcome. But I shant be hurt if you tell me so. Meanwhile whatever you think of what I say, there is no actual hurry. This term must I suppose be got through. . . . If Helen can stay up a fourth year it will I suppose help matters. If she cant I think we must consider what can be done so that she shant be miserable. . . . I suppose mothers always say they only want their children's good—it sounds familiar—but indeed I dont think its so much that I want your good exactly as that I do terribly want you to be yourself—to have freedom to grow & be whatever you have it in you to be. The one terrible thing seems to me not so much unhappiness—which is inevitable, as being thwarted—stunted, to miss opportunities & not live fully & completely as far as one can. I think if you tie yourself to someone to whom marriage would be a tie, when youre still very young, that may happen. If you do it later it may mean unhappiness, but at least you have had a chance to find things out for yourself & to become yourself. . . . Goodbye my dear—please write to me & tell me if you think there's any sense in all this or not—& do please do see Ellie or some other doctor & get rid of headaches & general tiredness. . . . Your loving Nessa.

Then a few days later, on May 11, she wrote again:

Since writing to you it has occurred to me that perhaps Helen may feel uneasy if she knows I have written lest I may be in some sense plotting against her—not that she would really think that, but I dont want there to be any suggestion of it. I have talked to her about you & her—some time ago at Charleston I think last summer—& I really said then very much what I say now but it may be as well to

> repeat it. I've therefore written her the enclosed letter, which I leave open for you to read, but if she doesnt know I have written to you on the subject you neednt give it to her. . . . I'm not even sure from your letter whether you have talked to her herself about the question of marriage or whether you have only been considering it yourself.

And then on May 18:

> Its such a relief to have letters from you both. . . . I am so glad my dear to know that my letter was a help & not a hindrance—I am sometimes so terrified of giving advice—not perhaps that I did actually give much—but it seems such a responsibility to influence other people in any way. . . . Helen says you are seeing a doctor. Do do so. Its not long now till the end of term. If Helen really doesnt take her exam to heart surely theres no need for her to make herself ill. Once you get away I feel sure everything will calm down & get rational again. . . . I think you & Helen ought to have a calm time together so that you neednt feel hurried & driven, but I'm not sure its not a good thing not to have a little other companionship too, as long as its tactful & sympathetic. . . . Please give Helen my love & thank her very much indeed for writing & tell her I count upon her to be really sensible & not get ill. . . . Do both vegetate a little, emotionally, for a few weeks.[22]

Vanessa was calm and reasonable to Julian, but in fact there was a lot more activity involving her, Quentin, and Eddie Playfair about the possibility of marriage. They all felt it would be a great mistake. Virginia too seemed to be anxious that the connection should end. On April 24, 1931, she wrote to Quentin that "I must scrape Julian free from his Great Barnacle," and then a month later she reported to Vanessa that Lytton "had seen Julian and Helen he said, and deplores the Cambridge infection, as I do—but whats to be done? He's bound to get a Fellowship, and there Helen will sit forever, talking. Lytton said, minute provincialities about exams; and Cambridge parties."[23] On May 16, Quentin wrote to Eddie from Rome: "As usual you emerge from the diplomatic mêlée with flying colours and the gratitude of the entire Bell family. . . . I should like to know how exactly you got round Helen, getting round Helen seems to be your forte, personally I should have found her far too sticky and lumpy an obstacle for any kind of mobility." It is not clear what Eddie wrote to Julian to dissuade him from marriage. He also wrote to Helen directly, as he reported to Vanessa on May 16, viewing the possible marriage as "quite disastrous. . . . I really hope that absurd couple will give up all such wild plans now. I wrote to Helen too, so as not to seem to be doing things behind her back & told her openly I thought marriage out of the question. . . . I wonder whether Helen will stick to her project of bringing the affair to an end after the summer. I can't help feeling a little doubtful."[24] In any case, a marriage did not take place. Helen wrote a letter to Vanessa on May 15, confirming the end of the crisis. "We shall both become sane again, I hope, in France and laugh at all the alarms and excursions now—though they had been wretchedly real and hurting while they lasted. . . . I, with vanity and rather to Julian's scorn, have ceased to both bother about anything except the dress in which I shall go to the King's Ball—with long gloves, a rather exciting addition."[25] Her plan now was to go to London after her examinations, about which she claimed she didn't care how she did, to take a secretarial course. Even so, Julian was still very worried about her, and wrote to his mother on May 18, "She's become absolutely unmanageable, and I think it's rather a matter of chance whether or not she breaks down before the end of the term."[26]

After all this, they were still together, and in the summer they went to Charleston. The situation didn't sound too good, as Julian wrote to his mother: "Helen and I thought we might possibly ask some one else down to Charleston while we are staying there as a sort of buffer state."[27] They then went to France to visit Charles and Marie Mauron in St. Rémy in Provence, as Julian wished to work on his French. A gifted critic and the translator of E. M. Forster, Mauron and his wife, Marie, were great friends of both the older and younger generations of Bloomsbury, particularly of Roger Fry's. Mauron was a well-known critic and aesthetician, particularly interested in a psychoanalytical approach to literature. He and Fry were engaged in translating Mallarmé, about whom Mauron wrote quite extensively; Julian would become involved with this project. The Maurons had the peculiar merit, in Julian's case, of taking him seriously on his own terms, something that did not always happen on home territory. The visit presented some problems. The Maurons were concerned about what the community would think. Roger Fry had told Mauron that Julian and Helen were in a serious relationship. Living in a small French town, Mauron was worried about scandal, the attacks from the *"parti religieux qui est puissant."* He proposed two possible solutions: one, that Julian passed his girlfriend off as Mrs. Bell, even though the mail she would receive would have to be addressed accordingly; second, that he say she was just a friend and she slept in her own room. Mauron thought that the latter strategy was the best option.[28] They then went on to the Bloomsbury outpost in Cassis, and Quentin wrote to Eddie about their visit: "J and H seem amicable and apathetic, it seems to me that will be almost certain discovered sometime soon. . . . Then there will be devil to pay. No doubt Julian will be called on to make an honest woman of Helen, an impossible feat to one who is not a psychoanalyist, but perhaps various Sotars [sic] will attempt to horsewhip Julian. . . . Helen will go stark staring mad and jump off the Cap-canaille (1305 ft). And we shall all live happily ever after."[29] The affair was still continuing, but in fact it was on the verge of ending.

That fall, Helen did go forward with her plan to take a secretarial course in London. Julian remained in Cambridge, and this apparently meant the end of their affair. John Lehmann, now in London himself as the manager of the Hogarth Press, wrote to Julian: "I saw Helen one night, and had a long talk with her. It worried me a lot. I don't believe it's really any good that you should see much of one another *for a while*. I think it certainly upsets her, and clearly it must be a final break for both your sakes."[30] Julian felt it took him a year to recover, but whatever regrets he might have felt, they did not prevent him from continuing his amorous life. He wrote to Lettice Ramsey in early 1933 that "I've had a reconciliation with Helen, which is highly comic and rather interesting historically." He took an almost excessive interest in her marriage to Christopher Morris, a fellow Kingsman, which he thought he had helped bring about. He even looked out for a house in which they might live. Two years older than Julian, Morris had become a Fellow of the College in History in 1930. They knew one another, as the College was a fairly small community, but weren't particularly close. Keynes told Julian about the announcement of the engagement in the *Times* in December 1933. Joking on the College's reputation for homosexuality, Julian commented in a letter to Lettice Ramsey that "King's will begin to get rather bothered if all its fellows go on like this." Much later, in a letter to Peter Lucas in 1936, he remarked: "I think he's [Christopher is] happy. . . . I hope so, having done such a blatant match-make. Still though I did try my best to bring them together, I'm not responsible for their marrying. And in the state that Helen was in, I should do the same again. Actually, I think they get on well. . . . He's a v. nice character."[31]

Julian at Cassis.

So the break with Helen had taken place; for the next few months he was unattached, which proved more trying than he had anticipated. Then, in the autumn of 1931, he began a relationship with Lettice Ramsey. She was older than both Julian and Helen, and a good deal more worldly: on the face of it he could look forward, in theory if not in practice, to a calm, stable, undemanding love such as he imagined he wanted. It was understood that they would love within limits and without expectations: that was the "Golden Mean." In a sense he was now introduced into a more mature world than his undergraduate circle. And although Lettice's friends perhaps were not as self-conscious about their sexual freedom (and Vanessa and Virginia in actual practice led rather circumscribed lives), they appeared to be more committed to "free love" than the Bloomsbury group. Julian, perhaps a libertine in theory, in fact became rather jealous of Lettice's practice of sexual freedom. As time passed, he had relationships with some of Lettice's friends, the one with Antoinette Pirie being quite serious. Lettice Baker, born in 1898, had gone to the well-known progressive public school Bedales and then to Newnham College, where she studied psychology. She worked for a while in London in vocational guidance before returning to Cambridge for a job at the Psychological Library. In 1925 she married Frank Ramsey, a Fellow of King's, five years her junior (Julian would be ten years younger than she). It was a rather whirlwind romance. She and Frank had met in November 1924, first seeing one another, appropriately, at a talk on philosophy in G. E. Moore's rooms in Trinity. Frank had just embarked upon his sexual life, having lost his virginity a few months before to a prostitute in Vienna. At their first dinner together, Frank asked Lettice to go to bed with him; she declined as being too soon, but the next week they did enthusiastically. They felt they were in love by December. She also had another lover at the time, whom she continued to see until Frank proposed to her. They married at the St. Pancras Registry office in London on August 25, 1925.[32]

Frank was a brilliant mathematician, philosopher, and economist, a Trinity undergraduate and only the second non-Kingsman to be made a Fellow of the College. He was both an influence upon and influenced by Wittgenstein. He was born into a Cambridge academic family, his father a Fellow of Magdalene. His younger brother, Michael, would go on to be Archbishop of Canterbury, although Frank himself as well as Lettice were firm atheists and were rather scornful of Michael's religiosity. They had an open marriage, and their correspondence suggests the sort of ambiance that Julian would enter some years later with Lettice. But for all his sophistication, Frank found "free love" a little more difficult to handle than he expected. Among his papers at King's are the extraordinary letters the Ramseys sent to one another in 1927 and 1928. In a letter of August 1, 1927, he wrote in detail about an affair he was having, yet "I feel ours is fundamentally such a stable, calm, and happy relationship. I believe someday I shall be able to achieve calm happiness with E. too, but at the moment it is so exhausting. . . . You wrote her the most charming letter, darling. . . . I think of you a lot, darling, with great affection. . . . I feel I love you very much so I do E. but it doesn't destroy my love for you." But despite their protestations of love for one another, one suspects that the affair she started with the Irish writer Liam O'Flaherty, a few years older than she, while visiting her family in Dublin was some sort of revenge. She reported to Frank that although they had only met eight days before, they had already been to bed together three times. "Darling, do these accounts pain you? I long to get a letter from you. You've not the least cause for real worry, love." Her affair in fact deeply bothered Frank, as Julian too would be disturbed by her behavior later, although he unlike Frank wouldn't become obsessed over the question of who might be the father of a child. (The Ramseys already had two daughters.) On January 10, 1928, she wrote to him: "It does not seem to me that a light affair which brings a lot of temporary happiness is wrong or in any way permanently upsetting to *us*—you & me. Do you remember that I always said that if your affair with E. had been *less* serious I should not have found it so hard to bear? . . . Our life together is the most important."[33]

She was writing to Julian in December 1931 in a similar way, though they were probably not lovers yet, in this case about the young King's College philosophy don Richard Braithwaite, with whom she was having an affair. He had married in 1925, but his wife had died in 1928. He would marry again—not Lettice—in 1932.

> He is very jealous physically—though he is *really* far more unfaithful than I am only in a different form. However, its all *too* complicated, Julian dear, to write about. . . . I suppose what I want—if I am not married to Richard—is to remain on intimate terms with him but to do as *I* like without hurting him—consequently upsetting myself. Richard hurt can be a most dangerous animal &

Richard jealous & *disliking* himself for being so is worse. . . . Could we spend weekend of Jan 1st together? . . . I think I really believe I have decided not to go to bed with you. . . . [Yet she wrote,] My dear, I think it would be a splendid arrangement for me to have an affair with you while R. had one with Moya & then both to end simultaneously & for R. & me to settle down to a quiet married life."[34]

Through King's, Julian and Lettice may well have met before the tragically young death of Frank Ramsey in 1930—although wives, with exceptions such as Topsy Lucas and later Helen Morris, might not have seen that much of the undergraduates in their husbands' colleges (even if, as in *Jacob's Room*, they had them to Sunday lunch). In fact, Julian originally had planned to dedicate his poem about Wittgenstein to Ramsey rather than to Braithwaite. He would have known both quite well, as they were Fellows of King's and fellow Apostles. It would appear that shortly after this letter Julian and Lettice became lovers. He wrote to her on the following January 12 that she had left her purse behind when she had visited him. "I feel a little tempted to invent pretty speeches about your leaving your purse with me and I my heart, etc in the manner of Mr Pope. . . . I've never spent a happier two days." Yet the next month she returned to the question of whether she should marry Richard. She wrote on February 14:

> What a fool I was not to be perfectly content with being happy with you—which I am so eternally, darling. . . . I felt very obsessed by R. Now I feel much happier in a complicated sort of way. . . . Yesterday R. changed his mind about not wanting to go to bed with me and did. The effect on me is a kind of release. I think I can be more fatalistic & not worry about R. I see myself approaching a relation of friendship only with him with much more equanimity. . . . I may not have explained myself at all—the danger of undressing on paper & partial nakedness is often worse than complete undress. . . . I do like being in love with you & it will be Thursday fairly soon.

On March 25 she wrote to him:

> I felt rather bad about Wednesday evening but I felt it was time I saw Richard (did you have an amicable dinner—yes?) I was delighted that you took it so calmly (But I have to confess that my worse nature was a *little* peaked [sic] that you weren't a *bit* jealous!) So tiresome is my nature that I to some extent always want what I have not got e.g. I should like to be an intellectual & interested in

abstract ideas. I should like to be a good talker. I should like to be married to Richard. When I am with him part of me wants to be with you. I'd like to roll you both into one. But then probably what I like best about both of you would be incompatible! Or go wrong somehow.

As seemed to be usual with Julian, the antiromantic vied with the romantic, as he wrote to her on August 5: "My dear, I've thought and dreamt a great deal about you lately, tho' I've not written. Having been so determinedly anti-romantic, I didn't realise until we parted how thoroughly I cared for you. Also how much I remember of your look and taste and touch." He generally now signed his letters, "Your lover Julian." Apparently, Richard and Lettice ceased being lovers, as Julian wrote to John Lehmann in an undated letter: "Thank God Richard Braithwaite has more or less made up his mind and Lettice and I are to be allowed to have our affair in peace."

That same year, in 1932, Lettice embarked on her own distinguished career as a photographer, particularly of portraits. She established a firm, Ramsey & Muspratt, with Helen Muspratt, who had had a successful photography practice in Swanage but had now moved to Cambridge. Lettice had the contacts, and Muspratt, the know-how. Quite quickly, the firm became renowned for its portraits of the Cambridge elite. (In 1937 they opened an office in Oxford, when Muspratt moved there.) In April 1932 Lettice was hoping to photograph all the Fellows of King's, as Julian remarked to his mother, "in an album—what a collection."[35]

In March 1932 he had written to Lettice, "Nessa congratulated us on having such a satisfactory relationship." Lettice might have welcomed a rather less considered, more spendthrift passion than he was prepared to give. She was determined to preserve her own freedom of action. He was working a good deal of the time in the cottage in Elsworth as well as at Charleston, and he wrote to her often in Cambridge. His letters tended to be more bulletins than romantic missives. When she complained gently, he replied, "My dear, whatever you say, I really cant break out on paper." That was the point of danger, of course—to break out. A few months later he wrote to her, "I as far as I am reasonable, am consciously trying to keep my balance in a torrent—fortunately of conflicting emotions." He found it odd that she was not afraid, as he was, of losing control: "you seem both imperious to and respectful of romanticism—which I dread as a vice." In fact, he had fallen deeply in love again, and the "Golden Mean" or the "Latin-sensual view of *amour*" did not make any provision for this. The conflict of emotions was essentially what it had been in his relationship with Helen: on the one hand, a commitment to love; on the other, a determination to remain free. The next year, away from Cambridge a good deal, spending more time in London and at Charleston, he was prey to fits of jealousy and depression. The virtue of his relationship with Lettice as he had envisioned it was the measure of freedom it allowed them both. But it had been *his* freedom, not hers, that he had been principally concerned with. Lettice, now, was sufficiently impervious to romanticism to insist on terms of her own; ironically, she had adopted his original position. She offered him a love that was not completely demanding, and asked of him confidence and affection which he could have given, albeit with a certain lack of grace. Theoretically, he ought to have found this perfect, but he did not. For all his rationality, Julian could not accept the idea that Lettice should be as free as he wished to be himself. Nor was he untrammeled enough to offer her a full alternative commitment. Early on in their relationship, it was clear that she would feel herself to be sexually free, as she had asserted in her marriage and in her involvement with Richard Braithwaite.

> It's a great pity [he wrote quite late in their relationship, in January 1934] we should be the sort of people we are—able to feel seriously, but with our feelings so arranged that we make each other miserable. I sometimes think we reflect the world at large—the way in which it seems that all that is needed is a small, simple change, but really all the devils of the abysses have to be let loose to make it, and suffering and destruction which seem out of all proportion to the cause. I can't think why I shouldn't give in, knowing what I do about your feeling for me and mine for you. But I couldn't make myself do it—I should break something inside if I did. The worst of being a rather easy-going character is that if you do get your mind made up you can't change it back again. No doubt it comes of taking too external and dramatic a view of oneself, and of my military fixation. So that I see everything in terms of a struggle and victory and defeat, and get an obstinate "no surrender" feeling. But there it is—I'm like that, and now it's too late for me to change.

A month later, when he was waiting for word about his Fellowship, he concocted a fantasy in which, he wrote to her on February 10, he would "come back to Cambridge with a definite life that could be shared with you, and sane enough and settled enough in my own mind not to be jealous or suspicious, but to value you properly for being the sort of person you are, without having to think about myself." Two days before, he had written:

> For one reason or another, life seems to improve a bit. I'm not as happy as I have been, principally because I'm not living with you and my life has grown more involved with you than I had thought. It's not so much that I've ceased to be self-sufficient as that I've grown to need a particular atmosphere of sanity and happiness that you make, and that I've come to depend enormously on having you to talk to about things as they happen. But I feel that we've managed to build something sufficiently permanent to stand a separation of this kind—after all its not so frightfully long before I shall see you again. But I've begun, I must confess, to have a quite mad hope—for it will surely be disappointed—that I shall after all get a fellowship and come back and live where I can see you as often as I want to. With a great deal of love my dearest your Julian.

And he wrote a few days later:

> I shall only say that now looking back I think the two years we lived together [something of an exaggeration] were as near perfect happiness as human beings could expect. . . . [Yet] I feel that if I could have some very mild affair with someone I just rather liked I should stop being bothered about my prestige and all that and we could reconstruct a better relation. For clearly you will sooner or later want something better than a lover you see every other week-end. Of course, as you said, my day-dream now is to come back to Cambridge, because I don't feel in the least if things had ended between us (by which I mean not everything, but anything) or would end in any foreseeable future: I feel as if we had just begun to learn how really to lead a good life together, and as if we ought to go on with its future developments—not a gradual drifting and dying away, but taking on new things and developing new possibilities. . . . with a very great deal of love Julian.

As he grew older—but it must be remembered that he was only twenty-one to twenty-six in the years that are being considered here—he thought that he was becoming increasingly dispassionate about love in his life, and he more nearly achieved the "Latin-sensual view" he had aimed at from the beginning. Yet he rather regretted the romantic excitements of the past. "I should like to be eighteen again," he wrote to Lettice some time later, when he was twenty-six, "and feel I had everything to learn and everything mattered. . . . You say I was deliberately unromantic and so on, but I find it difficult to remember unromantically. But then I suppose one always improves the past."

To a degree he deceived himself, and he was profoundly upset, despite his claim to understand, by Lettice's involvements and desire to go to bed with others. At a later point she was sleeping with an undergraduate of whom she was very fond. She felt that she was more in love with him than he with her; for him it was just a very pleasant experience. She wrote a revealing letter to Julian about this episode.

> I can only *wish* that I thought friendship was better than love. It would be more convenient, if one were willing to be satisfied with friendship, but I must be in love & if you are *in love* with someone who values your friendship & *is* a good friend but not in love, it is often painful & frustrating. My John I find a most satisfactory & interesting person but he is not in love with me, alas. He is going to be my lodger next term. I've got myself licensed for university lodgings which I think is rather good! Now *don't* write to your friends saying "Ha! Ha! Have you heard L is to be a lodging house keeper!" because I don't want any general gossip about it. It's quite a good joke but keep it to yourself!

And in early 1934, Julian was not best pleased when she took up with the poet Harry Kemp, even though he was in London. Three years younger than Julian, Kemp had been educated at the new public school, Stowe, and had been an undergraduate at Clare. At this point he was (briefly) a member of the Communist Party. Kemp is now best remembered for his association with Laura (Riding) Jackson, the American poet and sometime lover of Robert Graves. In February Julian was having dreams about the affair, as he wrote to Lettice:

> I suddenly noticed that he [Harry] was almost in tears. I felt suddenly sorry for him. . . . I heard him say something like "we must get this settled." I turned round and saw him and Lettice standing up clasped in each others arms. I came back and said something like "Yes, you must now make a definite choice." . . . Then Lettice said, I think smiling, and in a plain, commonsense voice "I choose Clive." This I assumed to be myself. Then I suddenly realised how miserable Harry must be, if he had been feeling depressed before, and I put my hands over my face and began to sob a little, and to consider if I could tolerate their affair. But I could not make up my mind to this, and then the dream changed, or I woke or half-woke.

She wrote to him on April 13: "What you are, in fact, asking me to do is to stop seeing Harry, start again with you—not necessarily as lovers—while you in the mean time are in love with Tony [Antoinette Pirie, to be introduced shortly]. . . . You don't seem to find it incompatible to be fond of us both. Nor is it incompatible for me to be *exceedingly* fond of you & want your company very much & at the same time wish to go to bed with Harry occasionally." He replied on April 18:

> I don't really think there's any point in my seeing you until your affair with Kemp—at any rate—is finally done with and over. To be perfectly brutal and frank, I don't think your offer—intimate friendship—good enough. Certainly its not worth my while as long as I am upset and made miserable by you. As far as I am concerned friendship means something calm, stable and reliable. Well, six months beating on a stone wall isn't a very good preparation. How can I help it if you have made me feel more hostile than intimate? You haven't given me a great deal of intimacy since last summer. Besides, friendship's not our thing at all. If I want intimacy and friendship its easier for me to get it from Kathleen [Raine]or Phyllis [Lintott] or Barbara [Rothschild]—or Eddy or Quentin or Nessa—who don't hurt me and who do try and understand and who will give something back. No, if we are going to see each other at all, we've got to construct more than a friendship. Quite apart from not liking playing second fiddle to anyone (and certainly not to Kemp) I don't much want simply another friend. It's much simpler for me to go free, as I've done with a good many old friends. You see, I dont feel simply friendly. I feel either hostile or a good deal more. I havent just died down and died down—I still care about you in some of the ways I have cared in the past. But I'm utterly sick of being the one who feels most, the one who cares and fusses and bothers. So as far as I'm concerned if you mean by "intimate friendship" the sort of thing I mean the best and simplest thing is to break for good.
>
> So you see it now depends very much on you what happens. If, when you're done with Kemp, you still care enough about our affair to want to reconstruct it as some sort of love affair (By which I dont mean necessarily copulation but [some] sort of serious and valuable emotion) then I think we shall still succeed both in saving a great deal that has been very good, and in starting something new growing. . . . And since I've started being brutal, do take some advice. You're probably getting on badly with Harry out of bed for rather the same reason that you got on badly with me in bed, that you don't try to understand other people and you wont take the initiative and control your behaviour. You expect things to happen right, and they dont you just accept it that they dont. When I'm feeling angry with you, I think that you expect to have everything your own way without giving anything. I know you'll say that you gave me far more than

I had any right to expect. But you see you made sacrifices without even trying to take advantage of them. Certainly last September, possibly last January, you could have reconstructed our affair by an effort of will. Instead of which, you left me to beat on that stone wall of yours. I think you did something of the sort with Richard. And I can't help believing that unless Harry's an unusually unpleasant young man you're spoiling things now for rather the same reason. Which is perhaps a pity, tho' I daresay you'd better either stick to casual affairs or marry. Anyway, don't get involved again with anyone sensitive who has serious emotions, unless you don't mind causing a devil of a lot of misery. I hope you will go on writing to me—if you feel theres any hope or point in doing so.

In his next letter he wrote:

Wish you hadn't stonewalled so successfully these last six months. . . . The situation is simply this. At present you can still hurt and upset me, and I waste time and energy resenting you and the past. This is a state of mind of which I've had enough. . . . As soon as I stop feeling hostile, jealous, injured in my vanity and so on—and consequently stop wanting to hurt you—I hope we shall be able to start seeing each other again. I really think this is sense. I know its also selfish, but I intend to be selfish. When shall I stop feeling hostile? I dont know. Two or three months, a year—I got over Helen in about a year.

As to Harry—if you hadn't been able to begin again with him, I should have felt definitely guilty and responsible. But since you have, and since you seem to think it may go on indefinitely, I can't help feeling that you're asking an unreasonable amount when you say you want us both. After all, you've got a generally very satisfactory life—in most ways much better than mine. You have your job, the [Communist] party, your friends, your children, your lover. Surely you wont be as depressed when term starts and Harry is back in Cambridge. . . . I had no chance to try and persuade you against going to bed with Harry, or to tell you that it would make me miserable. However—that's spilt milk now. And as soon as I stop minding it we can see what we can make of a new affair (or friendship, or whatever you care to call it)—if you still want to and if I do.

And then a final letter in this series:

I'm very sorry indeed about the last two letters I wrote to you. I think they will have made you miserable and I've seen that fundamentally that's not what I want. I'll give you anything I can give and you take: any sort of friendship, intimacy, love if possible that we can feel for each other. I expect I shall go on having my bad moments about you, but that's no reason really why you should be unhappy. So enjoy yourself with Harry as much as you can, and good luck to you. . . . I've changed my mind in this way partly because I find London with a hell of lot of work a pretty effective drug, partly because I'm very happy myself—more than I've ever been before—and I feel it's too mean and spiteful to nurse a grievance. . . . I don't want to think of you as being miserable over me. . . . So, my dear, if you will treat me as your most intimate friend (and pull down your stonewall, even if it hurts me) that's what I want to be and what I think I am.

Let us return to the early 1930s when Julian was becoming increasingly involved with politics. In the autumn of 1931 he was alone at Charleston, intending to "rush through" his dissertation on Pope. But the coming general election absorbed the greater part of his attention: he set enthusiastically to work to help create some sort of Labour organization in his area of Sussex. As the 1930s moved forward, it is not surprising that he became increasingly involved with politics, particularly as those close to him, such as Lettice and John Lehmann, moved more to the Left. "My life's absorbed by politics now," he wrote to John Lehmann. "I spent about 14 hours yesterday canvassing, and drove 200 miles, which has left me pretty tired. . . . Most of the Labour work-

Duncan Grant, Clive Bell, Vanessa Bell, Julian Bell. Tea at Charleston. Taken by Lettice Ramsey. By permission of her daughter, Jane Burch.

Lettice Ramsay, Charleston. Taken by Vanessa Bell. ©Tate, London, 2010.

ers—a lot of my fellow-canvassers are unemployed dockers—are thoroughly sensible, intelligent, very nice. . . . I believe if one troubled one could get a strong pacifist party, or even get men to strike against a threatened war." Unemployment; opposition to war: these were dominant political themes of the early 1930s, and Julian's interest in them was shared by his fellow poets. Poli-

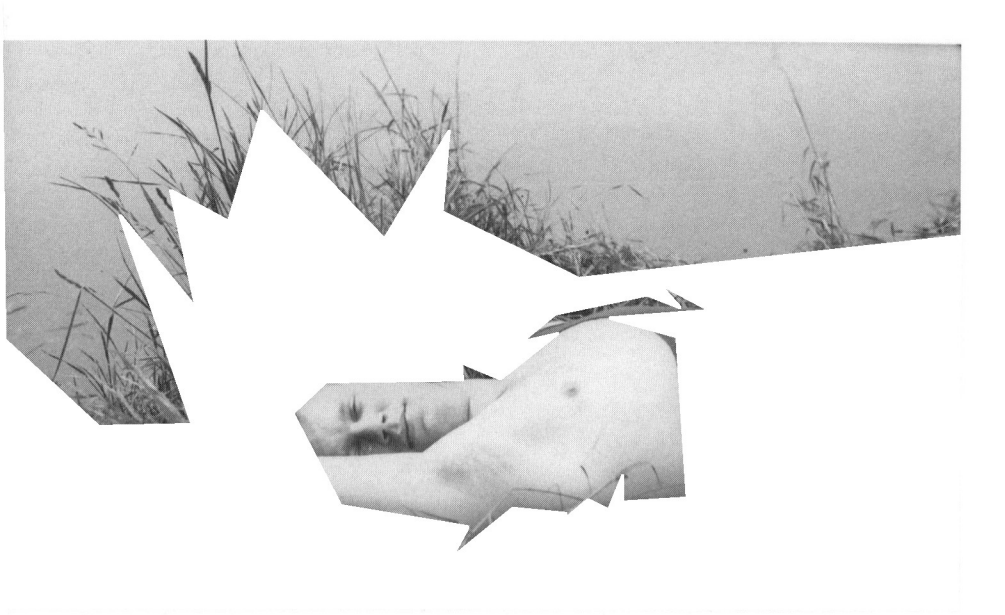

Julian at Charleston. Taken by Lettice Ramsey. By permission of her daughter, Jane Burch.

tics was even reflected in an undated poem of the time, entitled "Nonsense." Its last lines read: "Starve and grow cold without, / And ask the reason why / The guns are in the garden, / And battle's in the sky."[36] But the closer he came to practical politics, the more impatient he became with poetry. "The only thing I'm sure of," he told Lehmann in another letter, "gift and talent aren't enough to save us. . . . We may have to take a hand in the politicians' dogfight if we're to have enough leisure and freedom to work at all." In the first burst of enthusiasm, he was tempted to turn to politics altogether. "There's action and excitement. I seem to get on well with people and say the right sort of thing. I've a notion I could get at a country village meeting rather more effectively than most of these people. They keep on missing the point through not seeing how countrymen feel, and not knowing what conditions really are. (This may be just my imagination.) I suspect a Cambridge education . . . has its uses."

Working even at the village level of politics in a general election campaign was exhilarating, and Julian allowed his enthusiasm to delude him that Labour would not do too badly: in fact, in the general election the number of Labour MPs in the south of England went down from thirty-five to five. "What a state the world has got itself into," he wrote to Lehmann, "general elections, financial crisis. . . . I feel we should all go out into the streets and agitate for a 75% cut, at least, in armaments expenditure." Lehmann took a bleak view of the aftermath of the election. "I'm all for you being more political," he told Julian, "if you've found you have some gifts that way, whether you do it by articles or by talking. Some of us must make a stand against the old gang and shake off the clutch of the drowning before they pull us down." Julian was less pessimistic. Although he shared the disgust and disillusionment felt by the intelligent young of the Labour Party when Ramsey MacDonald, prime minister of the Labour government, chose to remain as prime minister of the National government, he believed that the party would survive the "betrayal of 1931," and in the next few months he spent much of his time in attempts to rebuild the local organization.

His first political activism had been local when in 1930 he was involved in organizing a branch of the Labour Party in Firle, and he planned to be active on behalf of the party in the nearby villages. He found it unexpectedly difficult to recruit new members from among the farm laborers. They were terrified of losing their jobs and therefore reluctant to declare themselves openly. This was not so unreasonable a fear in the 1930s, a time when jobs were scarce, poverty widespread, and landowners for the most part Tories, although Julian felt that it was not based on "anything more than a general nervousness—I've not yet been told of anything specific." In 1932, he made the center of his operations the little village of Glynde, a few miles from Charleston. (It was to come into international prominence in the summer of 1934 on the inauguration of an annual season of opera at the nearby country house, Glyndebourne.) In February, at a meeting in Glynde at which eight people were present, he was made secretary of the local Labour organization. "The people are nice," he wrote to Lettice, "and seem ready to treat me as an ordinary human being—tho I'm still horribly shy of them." Four days later he was able to report that he had succeeded in winning over the local publican, which was a great coup. He also got into a fight with the greatest landlord of the area, Lord Gage, who was also the owner of Charleston, from whom Julian's mother rented. In a letter to Lettice postmarked January 20, 1932, he wrote: "It's been a most exciting day, for local politics have been getting almost too much for me. My notion of writing to Lord Gage has produced a muddled, but quite satisfactory, letter from him, but also a visit to my friend Swain the shepherd, which has frightened him out of his wits, and scared me a good deal for it would be too bloody to get him turned out of his job." He entered into a correspondence with Lord Gage, accusing him of victimizing his tenants because of their political beliefs, an accusation that his Lordship vehemently denied.[37] He continued to pursue his local organizing. In March he reported that the "meeting was a great success—the membership increased. Everyone seeming very friendly and cheerful." Yet enthusiasm for politics on this level was difficult to sustain: "I'm rather 'on the shrink' over my various commitments to an active life," he reported, and "Local politics have been getting almost too much for me."

His strongest commitments continued to be given to an intellectual life—although he was "thoroughly distrustful" of his abilities to lead one—to Cambridge, to Pope, to poetry, to philosophy, to political theory. The experience of practical politics, canvassing, gingering up the small Labour group in Glynde, would not issue any practical result: it was fairly clear that he hadn't time or temperament to become a figure in local politics, or to get himself adopted as a candidate for Parliament in a constituency. But it had been instructive: "I shall anyway be able to feel practical and effectively revolutionary at Cambridge," he wrote to Lettice. His satire "Arms and the Man" was published in *New Signatures* that winter. We have already described it at some length in a literary context: here we would note only how directly it deals with poverty and unemployment, with disarmament and pacifism; in short, with the significant political themes of the 1930s. The problem of poverty was a more or less obligatory and formal concern for him. He would never respond to it with the intellectual excitement and imaginative identification that he brought to the problem of war. From the war games of early childhood until his death in the battle of Brunete, war was in many ways the abiding concern of his life, suppressed as it might have been at times. In the early 1930s he adopted a strongly antiwar position: the folly of 1914–1918 must not be allowed to recur. In this he was at one with his generation. Then, as the threat of Hitler became increasingly serious, his attitude changed, and was crystallized with the outbreak of the Spanish Civil War. Again he was like many of his generation. This was a crucial moment in the history of the 1930s, when young men on the Left abandoned their antiwar position, and some among them crossed the frontier into Spain. In the late 1920s, when Julian had been an undergraduate, "no one" at the universities had seemed to care very much about politics; then, as it were overnight, with the coming of the new decade, the situation was reversed, and "everyone" was political, arranged on a spectrum from Left of center to furthest Left. On February 9, 1933, when the Oxford Union passed a resolution "That this House in no circumstances will fight for King and Country," it was expressing largely a political rather than a pacifist objection to war. The members of the Union had not gone over in a body to conscientious objection. But the resolution was dramatic enough to attract national and even international notice, and it suggested that Oxford was seething with political activity and disaffection. In fact, this was more the case at Cambridge. Student leaders like John Cornford went about their political business very seriously. The old "extraordinary *douceur de vivre*" of a few years back was quite gone, and Julian felt at times that he was the only non-Communist remaining in Cambridge, so quickly and completely had the atmosphere changed. Of course, there were still plenty of "ordinary" Cambridge undergraduates as well as "hearties" on the Right, but it was those on the Left who set the dominant tone. Conflicting political beliefs too intensely adhered to almost brought about the cessation of the Apostles, some of whom had gone communist—either publicly or in cases such as Anthony Blunt and Guy Burgess, close friends of Julian's, secretly. Quite a few of the leading intellectual lights at Cambridge belonged to the Communist Party. Julian particularly regretted this; so too did Keynes, whose biographer records: "He could not but observe the tendency towards Communism among the young at Cambridge, and most markedly among the choice spirits, those whom thirty years before he would have wished to consider for membership in 'the Society.' He attributed it to a recrudescence of the strain of Puritanism in our blood, the zest to adopt a painful solution because of its painfulness. But he found it depressing."[38] Politics came first, and social life, from the rarefied level of Apostolic Saturday evenings to the more ordinary level of the sherry or dinner party, disintegrated. Julian regretted the lost *douceur de vivre*; at the same time, he approved of the change in the political temperature. Although he never committed himself very far in a Marxist, and certainly not in a communist direction, he did participate to some extent in Left-wing activities in Cambridge itself, most particularly in 1933, the last year when he would be there with any regularity and when the course of political thought, spurred on by the advent of Hitler, was veering leftwards almost at a dizzying rate, as reflected in a letter to Lettice postmarked September 23:

> I've really changed a good deal in your direction since I knew you—for instance, I'm becoming a good deal more sympathetic to science and scientists than I used to be which is certainly a thoroughly good thing. I supposed its considering communism that has brought home to me the way in which you are reasonable by instinct. . . . The odd way in which you seem both impervious to and respectful of romanticism—which I dread as a vice. For instance, I believe you really are most [word missing] about things like intimacy and affection (and copulation; I'm talking about love now). As far as I know you've never fallen helplessly in love with someone you don't know, or hardly know—as I have done, and suppose shall do.

November saw the climax of these activities, and if one were in search of a date to establish when many of the younger people at Cambridge turned Left, a good choice would be Saturday, November 11, 1933. On that day, under the leadership of John Cornford and his friends, a variety of organizations ranging from pacifists to Communists joined forces, in a manner that suggests the later Popular Front, and staged a massive antiwar demonstration in Cambridge. Julian was enthusiastically in the midst of it. His attitude in these matters reveals a fine, parochial inconsistency: he was willing to support causes in Cambridge that he would not support nationally; he would repudiate the activities of the extreme Left in the world at large at the same time that he was participating in its activities at his University. (In this respect he was not untypical.)

For instance, at the beginning of 1933, a friend in London asked him to support the British Anti-War Council: "We hope very much that you'll be able to give your name." Julian refused; he felt that the organization was dominated by Communists. His friend replied tartly, "I rather suspected that for party reasons you'd be unable to oppose war." Yet he was not at all reluctant to work for Cambridge organizations that had precisely the same aims, and with no fewer Communists at their head. He and Lettice were active in arranging a "No More War" exhibit, which was put on display in Cambridge early in November. It was an assemblage of photographs, documents, and posters that followed the preparations leading to the First World War. It contrasted the idealizations of propaganda with the realities of battle, touched on the disillusionment of the war's aftermath, and concluded with a prophetic look at preparations for the next war. Concurrently, a jingoist film, *Our Fighting Navy*, was scheduled for a local cinema, and Julian and Lettice were part of an antiwar group who went to protest against the showing. A crowd of "hearties," out to get those they considered effete and cowardly, gathered in the street to "rag the cads," and there was a brawl. "Quite a decent amount of fighting," Julian reported to his brother, and although the antiwar group got the worst of it, "the reactionaries smashed up some of the cinema, and the management lost their nerve and took the film off," so the protest had achieved its purpose. But the climactic event was the great antiwar demonstration of November 11. Armistice Day itself, since the inauguration of Earl Haig's Poppy Fund, had become the occasion of pranks and parades intended to raise money for the fund. The Socialist Society and the Student Christian Movement joined forces to make the day more meaningful. There was to be a three-mile march through the town to the Cambridge war memorial, where a wreath would be placed bearing the inscription, "To the victims of the Great War, from those who are determined to prevent similar crimes of imperialism." The words "of imperialism" were removed by order of the police, who felt "they were not conducive to maintaining the public peace." Even so, the day was tumultuous. Hundreds of students joined the procession through the town; among them, rather more conspicuous than most, was Julian. Nothing would please him more than to be a soldier for peace, and he had prepared for the demonstration with military efficiency. His beaten-up Morris car, in which he had terrified his friends and deeply worried his mother as he drove it along the roads of Cambridgeshire, he now attempted to transform into a military vehicle. "I tried to use the Morris as an armoured car (stript of everything breakable)," he wrote to Quentin. The armor of the car was mattresses, and his navigator was Guy Burgess, at that point a research student at Trinity. They entered the line of march, and as they moved slowly and conspicuously along, they were a tempting target for tomatoes, and got well pelted. But they made a couple of good charges at the enemy—"hearties" again, attempting to break up the parade—before they were ordered out by the police. Julian merely changed his tactics, driving round through a circuitous route and rejoining the march towards its head. His letter to Quentin concludes: "There was one good fight, which I missed, when they stole our banner and gave a man a concession [sic], until the police used their batons. However, we managed to beat them in the

Cambridge, November 11, 1933.

end, and get our wreath on the War Memorial. Now we're having newspaper news [?] all round and doing leaflets and pamphlets and so on.... There's no real fascism here yet—only toughs and Tories. I'm going to learn ju-jitsu.... The whole world, private and public, seems to be upside down. I feel rather like going Bolshy."[39]

He also coauthored a pamphlet about the antiwar movement in Cambridge with, of all people, Harry Kemp, no matter what his feelings were about him as a fellow lover of Lettice's. The text was written on behalf of various organizations, "the Student Christian Movement and other Christian groups, the League of Nations Union, Radicals, members of the Labour Party, the I.L.P. [Independent Labour Party] and the Communists . . . an united front against war." It pointed out that "The fight of students in England must be directed against the war plans of the National Government, against war preparations in the universities, against the banning of free criticism of the O.T.C. [Officer Training Corp], and the suppression of the October Club by the authorities in Oxford, against the victimisation of individual students."[40]

All this was tremendously exciting, and Julian loved being in the thick of things. It appealed to the romantic and violent aspect of his character—how much fun it was to be using the Morris as a sort of battering ram—and he exulted quite unthinkingly in what he felt. But almost at once the curb was applied: it was not enough to feel; one must also think, clearly and rationally; one must understand. Thus, it was an effort as much at clarification for himself as to communicate to others that he wrote, less than a month after the excitements of Armistice Day, a remarkable letter to the *New Statesman and Nation*, in which he described the political situation at Cambridge:

> In the Cambridge that I first knew, in 1929 and 1930, the central subject of ordinary intelligent conversation was poetry. As far as I can remember we hardly ever talked or thought about politics. For one thing, we almost all of us had implicit confidence in Maynard Keynes's rosy prophecies of continually increasing capitalist prosperity. Only the secondary problems, such as birth control, seemed to need the intervention of intellectuals. By the end of 1933, we have arrived at a situation in which almost the only subject of discussion is contemporary politics, and in which a very large majority of the more intelligent undergraduates are Communists, or almost Communists. As far as an interest in literature continues it has very largely changed its character, and become an ally of Communism under the influence of Mr Auden's Oxford Group. Indeed, it might, with some plausibility, be argued that Communism in England is at present very largely a literary phenomenon—an attempt of a second "post-war generation" to escape from the Waste Land.
>
> Certainly it would be a mistake to take it too seriously, or to neglect the very large element of rather neurotic personal Salvationism in our brand of Communism. It is only too easy to point to the remarkable resemblances between Communism and Buchmanism, the way in which both are used to satisfy the need of some individuals for communion with a group, and the need for some outlet for enthusiasm. Our generation seems to be repeating the experience of Rupert Brooke's, the appearance of a need for "the moral equivalent of war" among a large number of the members of the leisured and educated classes. And Communism provides the activity, the sense of common effort, and something of the hysteria of war.
>
> But this is only one side of the picture. If Communism makes many of its converts among the "emotionals," it appeals almost as strongly to minds a great deal harder. It is not so much that we are all Socialists now as that we are all Marxists now. The burning questions for us are questions of tactics and method, and of our own place in a Socialist State and a Socialist revolution. It would be difficult to find anyone of any intellectual pretensions who would not accept the general Marxist analysis of the present crises. There is a general feeling, which

> perhaps has something to do with the prevalent hysterical enthusiasm, that we are personally and individually involved in the crisis, and that our business is rather to find the least evil course of action that will solve our immediate problems than to argue about rival Utopias.[41]

The enthusiasm he felt in November waned quickly. What Julian thrived on was a mixture of high principles and the conversation of intimate friends—the Apostolic formula—and he found not enough of either in any particular political movement. The following January he attended a conference of Socialist Societies in London. "A thoroughly bad show," he wrote Lettice,

> all details and reports, no real debate on principles and too large for effective discussion. I dare say I shall go and hunger-march as an unemployed student—more likely not. It made me ill and livid and depressed—the sillier sort of communists, particularly the rather scrawny, provincial university ones, are not over-sympathetic. I can't get clearly fixed in my own attitude—I don't like either side, but probably one's got to choose sides. . . . I'm coming to believe that there is just a possibility of a civil war, and without its being too destructive—tho' its bound to be pretty beastly, and all the things one has cared for in the world will get smashed in the process. I do get annoyed with optimists and enthusiasts and people who get mystical about "the workers" as if having a simple situation and a beastly life were really any advantage.

His feelings about communism were compounded of admiration and suspicion. While he was ready to declare "We are all Marxists now," he considered communism a "dismal religion" and did not enjoy reading *Das Kapital*, if indeed he ever got through it—not that not reading it was any bar to being a good communist. But he felt the Marxian analysis to be scientific, and clear, and rational: values he had been trained to rate highly. A Cambridge graduate wrote to the *New Statesman* after Julian's letter was published there to ask in what sense it was accurate to describe undergraduates as "all Marxists now." He answered that they accepted the Marxist explanation for the appalling state in which the world found itself, bankrupt and threatened by war; that the financial slump had resulted, not from the machinations of wicked bankers and financiers but from the nature of capitalism itself; and that the major cause of war was the contest for new markets between rival imperialisms. "It's really cheering," a friend on the far Left wrote to him after reading these public letters, "to see you coming out in a shirt dyed a deeper tint of red at last. I'd been expecting it for a long time: ever since, in fact, you said to me that you saw no point in being a Social-Democrat outside one's own country." But Julian was not likely to become a communicant of the "dismal religion." He was prepared to accept the Marxist analysis; it did not follow that he must accept the communist solution. He was extremely distrustful of commitment for the wrong reason—that is, to become a communist romantically, in a swirl of emotion and muddled thought. Analysis proved that his own way of life, the Bloomsbury way, which he valued dearly and which was based on capitalism, was doomed to disappear. Yet he had no wish to accelerate its disappearance. His position was rather like St. Augustine's before conversion: "Make me chaste, Lord, but not yet." Keynesian theories and the pragmatic experiments of Roosevelt's New Deal might temporarily patch up the fabric. "It looks as if capitalism was going to weather this slump," he wrote to Lehmann, "even if the Americans do get themselves socialized by mistake. Personally, I shan't be sorry to have a few more years on an independent income of sorts—largely consisting of gambling gains on the New York stock exchange at present. At least until I finish Pope and get a job." This was the candid, unromantic, hardheaded side of himself that he enjoyed exhibiting; at the same time, he was troubled by his lack of involvement: "I feel envious of groups and communities and horrified at the isolation of human beings." When black moods of this sort came upon him, he was unquestionably drawn to the Communist Party, and in a set of prose reflections that he wrote at about this time (but never published)—"To My Bourgeois Friends in the Communist Party"—he conceded: "No doubt there are emotional satisfactions; the beloved group; fools gold and ignis fatuus of enthusiasm and flags, and the satisfactions of war—a war of attrition under second-rate generals. And no doubt there is an argument—even apart from Marx there is an argument—and no doubt there is righteous indignation against poverty. And finally, and most importantly, you are in an infernal tangle: you can't deal with your own emotions nor with the world outside you." But he also recognized that the bourgeois communist, unless capable of an absolute commitment, would "always be out of the beloved group, rather suspect and irretrievably different"; so the search for an alternative position of his own to which he could commit himself without reservation continued—but inconclusively. "I *can't, can't* get clear about politics," he wrote to Lehmann in the spring of 1934. "Again, there's an emotional contradiction, or set of contradictions. I'm Left by tradition, and I'm an intellectual of the governing classes by tradition, and I can neither quite make up my mind to trying to get an economically intelligent Roosevelt 'Social Fascism,' nor give way to 'the Party' with its fanatical war mentality."[42]

He had had an interesting exchange with John Cornford, the leading young Communist in Cambridge, who would also die in Spain. Younger than Julian, he was very much the next generation, the political activist rather than of the sort, such as Julian, who moved to an extent from aestheticism to activism. The exchange appeared in *Student Vanguard*, a Communist publication founded by students at the London School of Economics, where John had studied before coming to Trinity College, Cambridge. In the December 1933 issue he wrote a sweeping attack on modern writers—Yeats, Pound, Lawrence, Eliot, Proust, Rilke, Mann—for not being sufficiently willing to be renegades against their class, for not recognizing that it is impossible for the artist to be impartial. In the next issue, of January 1934, Julian replied, disagreeing that those attacked by Cornford are "static" writers in contrast to "dynamic" writers who have committed themselves to revolution, such as Ernest Toller and Louis Aragon. For Julian, "dynamic" is a term that could just as much be applied to fascist writers. He accuses Cornford of demanding that artists, whether a bourgeois like Auden or a proletarian like Lawrence, extract themselves from the "historical process." He questions whether one can be both an artist and a revolutionary, although he also reveals how he himself is moving to the Left.

> It is certainly desirable that anyone with abilities for doing so should take part in the revolutionary movement, but it is highly improbable that anyone who does so will have time and energy enough to carry out a literary revolution at the same moment. For if poetry and imaginative literature are to be directly used in the struggle, and there is no very good reason that they should be—the most far-reaching reforms are necessary—reforms which practically amount to a return to classicism and the development of a new plain style. . . . What is needed at the moment is clear thinking and the clearing away of muddles—an intellectual counter-attack by the scientifically-minded on the mistakes and deceits of fascism and reaction. An appeal to emotion and "dynamic" revolutionary feelings is simply opening the way to intellectual fascism.

Cornford replied to "Comrade Bell," a salutation that probably didn't particularly please Julian. He points out that he did not use the term "static."

He does, however, somewhat misstate Julian's argument. He does not deny that artists are shaped by their class, and he does feel that their writing might form part of the class struggle. Where they disagree is that for Julian that participation is coincidental, not central to art, while for Cornford it is the essential point, and to take an active role in the struggle writers must break from their old ways. In his view, the only solution is a working-class literature. He sees some young poets (unnamed) as groping towards this development. "The inherent contradiction of this position of a revolutionary literature written for the bourgeois intelligentsia daily hastens the process of differentiation between two literatures, the disintegrating tradition of the bourgeoisie, or the gathering strength of revolutionary art."[43]

Julian was very much at loose ends at this time, not having found a real career, living in London and loving in Cambridge. There was some talk of going into advertising, or perhaps something connected with the League of Nations that would involve making speeches against war. In a way, it was a crisis in his life; it was quite unclear what direction he would take. Three years before, he thought that he would never live in London. He wrote to his good friend and King's contemporary Harold Barger at the end of 1929 while visiting his family in Gordon Square:

> I shall do my very best not to be in London again until next winter, if not for the rest of my life. . . . The truth of the matter is, I'm a complete exile and outsider here & don't fit into the life. I'm bad at doing everything from dressing to dancing. I'm made slightly ill and very miserable by lack of exercise, and become so wretched I take no trouble to put matters right. I don't in the least know what I shall do when I have to make a living here. I suppose in rooms of ones own, with a properly organized life, people to see and someone to sleep with it might be just endurable. After all, I remind myself, Cambridge was pretty bloody to begin with. Still, it was never so ghastly as this, and matters did seem to improve there.[44]

Despite his doubts and perhaps as he couldn't think of an alternative, by the end of 1933 he had taken a room in Taviton Street in Bloomsbury. So rather reluctantly that was now his base, as in a rather desultory fashion he looked for some sort of employment, perhaps in advertising, films, or teaching in a girls' school. He also was considering learning how to fly, preferably a military airplane. And then, as we shall see, he concentrated on the possibility of teaching abroad, most likely in the Far East, a not unfamiliar pattern for literary Englishmen of his sort. As he mentioned to Quentin at this time, which perhaps brought the idea to his attention, "The present professor of English at Canton has been found at Hong Kong, without his head, but in a trunk. So there may be a vacancy. I hope not too soon, for I want to try out London first."[45] He was writing, becoming in some sense a journeyman of letters, some projects being achieved, others not. He was twenty-six; he had no definite place in life, in society, and he was not at all sure, now that he had not been made a Fellow of King's, of what he wanted to do. He felt his poetic commitment was not strong enough for him to be a poet; he now saw himself, sadly, as someone who merely happened to write poems. In a letter to his mother, in which he remarked that at the moment all his young women seemed to have left him, he added that it was not this that was making him unhappy but "the trouble of finding some serious occupation. I don't seem able to write poetry—that's obviously not going to be a reliable thing for me; I seem to have been able to at moments only, not all through my life."

John Lehmann, who had given up his job with the Hogarth Press to write, and was spending much of his time in Vienna, suggested: "Why not travel for a bit, or do something entirely different—a foreign correspondent say—before you make up your mind?" But in Julian's present irresolute state he was not capable of the decisiveness such a gesture would have required, even if it had appealed to him. His family was in London, as were many of his close friends—Eddie Playfair was a civil servant in the Treasury—and he had no reason to linger in Cambridge. A new thought was that he might try to become a lecturer at the University of London: "It sounds a heavenly job," he wrote to Lettice, "decently short hours and amusing work. Unfortunately I've no notion of their having a vacancy." Nor is there any indication that he ever pursued such a position. He found that the various odd bits of journalism that came his way were enough, with his small private income, to support him and allow him to lead, if not a satisfactory life at least an interesting one.

He did reviews for the *New Statesman*; he worked on his proposed edition of Pope, and also an edition of Mallarmé in translation, continuing the work that Roger Fry had started with Charles Mauron and that Julian had helped finish after Fry's death in 1934. He had already, with Mauron, published a translation of Rimbaud's *Le Bateau ivre* in the *Cambridge Review*.[46] Fry's translations of twenty-five poems by Mallarmé, with the commentaries by Mauron, including the French texts, finally appeared in June 1936, when Julian was already in China. It had a very brief editorial note by Mauron and Julian; he had translated nine of the twenty-seven commentaries, while the others had been translated previously by Fry. The project had taken a very long time to finish. Fry had written most of his translations by 1920 but continued to tinker with them until 1933, when devastatingly, his suitcase containing the manuscript was stolen in a Paris railroad station. Shortly thereafter with Mauron he reconstructed many of the translations and also incorporated commentaries that Mauron had written. After Fry's death, Mauron wrote to Julian suggesting that Julian work with him to complete the project: "You know that the Mallarmé planned by Roger and me was almost finished. The translation of the poems is almost completed and we finished it with the help of your suggestions. . . . I would be very happy if you agreed to help me finish this book. It seems that Roger has worked so much on the poems that he would be very happy to see them finally published."[47] Mallarmé is notoriously difficult to translate, and Fry's tended too much towards the literal. Mauron mentions in his introduction that Fry had told him that Julian in fact had made suggestions of certain turns of phrase.[48] Julian had volunteered to see the project through, but actually getting the book published required complicated correspondence with Margery Fry, Roger's eminent sister, who eventually subsidized its printing. For months, Julian doggedly and loyally pursued publishers: Faber & Faber, the Cresset Press, Cambridge University Press, the Nonesuch (which suggested Hogarth—a logical choice, but somehow it wasn't part of the loop). It was finally published by Chatto & Windus.

He wrote poems, and drafts of essays. But all this activity, though it kept him occupied and distracted, was too marginal and haphazard to satisfy him that he had embarked on a career. His discontent deepened: the important work of the generation was being done by others. One of the poems he wrote in this period is the lightly ironic "Cambridge Revisited":

> Down by the bridge the lovers walk,
> Above the leaves there rolls the talk
> Of lighted rooms. Across the lawn
> Clare's greyness prophesies the dawn.

> River and grass and classic weight,
> As if the Fellows meditate
> Socratically, the masculine
> Beauty of th' athletic line,
> Squared brow or pediment, and look
> For Greek ghosts out of Rupert Brooke.
> Grey stone, slow river, heavy trees,
> I once had my share of these;
> But now, within the central wood,
> I neglect the wise and good:
> And London smoke, and middle age,
> Open on a grimier page.

The irony is double-edged, turned as much against Julian in his nostalgic "middle age" as against the meditative dons. But there is no comic overemphasis in the final line: "a grimier page" does go directly to the point of what Julian felt about London. He wrote to Lehmann, "I'm being more or less miserable here: poverty & chastity and the other horrors of large towns."[49] The first complaint, poverty, needn't be taken too seriously; the second was somewhat realer now that he was living in London. As he wrote to his brother in early 1934: "I hate chastity, and I only see Lettice at weekends. I wish I had your or Clive's techniques and accomplishments."[50]

Although he was now spending more time in London, his emotional life was still Cambridge-based. He was becoming increasingly involved with Lettice's friends, the Marxist/scientific circle centered on the great crystallographer J. D. Bernal. Bernal's own personal life was famously complicated, and he lived both with his wife, Eileen, who became very close to Julian, as well as Margaret Gardiner, with whom he had a son, Martin. Another close friend of Lettice's was the biologist Antoinette Pirie, who became very well known for her work on the biochemistry of the eye. She was Julian's fourth serious affair, but he was also sleeping with others. (Their correspondence hasn't, as far as I know, survived.) Born in 1905, she had been to Newnham as an undergraduate and had a doctorate as well. She was married to an equally distinguished biologist, Norman "Bill" Pirie, with whom she had two children. Domesticity did not seem to preclude a complicated love life for these liberated young women, not that they were exempt from emotional travails. Writing to Lettice from China in May 1936, Julian remarked: "I hear from

Tony that you, she and Eileen are spending the summer holiday together. I shall be amused to hear how you get on. Very well, I expect, but it is a slightly comic situation somehow. The nuns of Medenham, so to speak. I suppose you'll end up by having your young men down." The previous May he was writing to his mother about Tony: "She's much happier and less nervous now, and no longer gets into panics about her husband which is the greatest relief. Indeed, things have never gone so well—if only I would see rather more of her." In his next letter, he remarked about her, "If there's ever any danger of your being presented with a daughter-in-law I shall send you a long letter by air mail before doing anything."[51] Over the next two years, she replaced Lettice as the most important woman in his life, but even then his commitment had its limitations. On the boat to China he wrote to his mother, on October 13, 1935, "I've found I'm far more in love with Tony than I had supposed." But three days later, while wondering whether he would find a Chinese mistress, he remarked: "Do you really like Tony? She's the best of my young women so far, but I don't know that she's your daughter-in-law. . . . They [his young women] have been an odd lot. But then Bloomsbury doesn't produce enough daughters, so what's one to do?"[52]

Lettice was still extremely important to him, it would appear, as a sometime lover but also very much as a confidant. In the letters he wrote to her one has a picture of his life in the summer and fall of 1934 in its personal dimension. The first of the series is postmarked June 19, 1934, and it begins with his statement about taking a teaching job in China. "Still, it might be just as well, if it weren't for Tony, who I think I keep reasonably happy, and who perhaps doesn't care unduly—at least I feel I probably care at least as much as she does, and that there's no particular disaster impending there." Some months later, on October 19, 1934, Lettice wrote to him:

> I wish I agreed with you that friendship is better than love. I *want* to be in love with someone & unfortunately it seems to matter whether that person is in love with me. Being in love with someone who is not in love with you is bad for one's pride—I suppose that is why it hurts. John Burton [the undergraduate photographer living in her house] is very friendly & we get on extremely well & he is good company & I like going to bed with him but, alas, he is not in love with me, & I am with him. This does not make the situation intolerable but difficult at times.

Despite the frankness of their letters, Julian's apparently still have some reticences. He wrote in November: "Would you do something perfectly angelic for me—steal some French letters—only a few—from the clinic. At least, I say steal, but I think I could to send a cheque to the Cambridge clinic for services rendered. But I do dislike the business of buying the things, and every now and then there are situations in which they are essential. And talking of such matters, I'll give you five—ten—twenty guesses as to who I've been to bed with recently. Someone you know, but I feel sure wont guess. But this is really for you *alone*." He kept reporting to Lettice on his relations with Tony. In March 1935 he wrote to her: "God only knows how it will end—divorce and marriage as like as not. If I were braver, or stupider, that's what I should try for. Certainly Tony's very much the sort of person I want to marry—but I dont want to marry anyone, really. . . . I'm pretty bored with neat sex— I should like some war for a change. Of course, human beings—you, and Tony—are quite another matter, and infinitely preferable to all other attractions." In April he and Tony went to France together. "It seems to have made Tony far happier and less nerve-racked and more generally sensible." The idea of marrying Tony was still in the air. He wrote to Lettice in June:

> She's obviously going to stay married to Bill. . . . We get on admirably together— I've never known anyone quite so honest, so ready to put all her cards on the table. She's interesting to talk to as well—perhaps I've still a rather exaggerated respect for the intelligence of anyone who does an experimental science, but at least she has both the curiosity about the world and the sort of directness of mind one hopes for in a scientist. Altogether I suppose I'm rather more serious about her myself than I should be. Particularly since she's physically entrancing. If only I were younger—as young as I was with Helen. But unfortunately I'm not. So that I begin to get a little bored by the minor details of a very amusing life. . . . There's no longer the same world-shattering importance about romantic love and romantic passions that there used to be nor indeed about most emotions and experiences. . . . So, I should like to be eighteen again, I think, and feel I had everything to learn and everything mattered."

This was very much a between period in his love life, in his professional life, and in his life in London, in view of his comparative discomfort there. The "horrors of large towns" were real to him: he had been unhappy in Paris, and he was unhappy in London; in both cases unhappiness sent him to writing poems. There was some talk that he might succeed David Garnett as literary editor of the *New Statesman* should Garnett leave, but Garnett didn't think he would get on with the editor, Kingsley Martin.[53] Leonard raised the possibility of his doing some writing for the New Fabian Research Bureau, but nothing seemed to come of that. He went to some meetings of socialist students at Marx House on Clerkenwell Green in London and found them very boring. Nevertheless, he appeared as cheerful and as exuberant as ever. That was one side of it. The depression came out in the poetry—which, for the first time, was autobiographical and personal and pervasively melancholy—and sometimes in moody, confessional letters. These tended to be exaggerated, as he himself saw: once, having written in a black mood to Lettice, he drew back and concluded, "Really I lead, I suppose, an unusually sheltered and happy life, and all my miseries are vicarious." But that also was an exaggeration.

One poem concludes:

The world will slowly make us tame,
And events as they pass provide
Some object to the game.

These lines might serve as the epigraph for the period in Julian's life which we are now describing: from the winter, when he came to London, to the summer of 1935, when he went out to China. He allowed himself to appear tamed: he did his various odd jobs, talked politics with friends, alternated between London and Charleston and Cassis, had affairs, and published a few poems and book reviews. That was the surface. His interior life of ideas and feelings was much more turbulent and eventful. Unable to commit himself to his own satisfaction to poetry, or to politics, or to love, he engaged in a kind of strategic retreat, a withdrawal to regather his forces, while he waited for events to provide "Some object to the game."

In politics—indeed, in all aspects of his life—he became a party of one. He wanted to be, as his grandfather Sir Leslie Stephen had proposed a young man should be, "a partisan of the ideas struggling to remould the ancient order and raise the aspirations of mankind,"[54] but he would have to be so in his own fashion. "For my own part," he wrote, "I am proposing to turn myself into a man of action, cultivate my tastes for war and intrigue, conceivably even for town-planning and machines, and, generally for organizing things and running the world. As for poetry, I shall write it more for my own satisfaction, to please my friends or flatter a mistress, and not bother about 'the public.'" The quotation is taken from "To My Friends in the Communist Party," one of several essays he wrote during his London period but never published. Titles of this sort were very fashionable. The sequel to *New Signatures*, *New Country* (1933), in which Julian did not appear—nor Empson nor Eberhart—included "Letter to a Young Revolutionary" by Day Lewis; "Letter to the Intelligentsia" by Charles Madge; and Auden's "A Communist to Others." Julian had earlier written "To My Bourgeois Friends in the Communist Party." It was the great age of the open letter and the manifesto. But the most remarkable example was Auden's "Letter to a Wound" in *The Orators*.

In the autumn of 1933 he had been resolutely antiwar; now his attitude underwent a series of significant modifications. David Garnett, looking about for things for him to do, had arranged for him to edit a book of memoirs by British conscientious objectors during the First World War. Cobden-Sanderson, the publisher, would pay him £20 and a 5 percent royalty after the expenses were met. The book, *We Did Not Fight*, published in 1935, consisted of eighteen short autobiographical essays; a poem by Siegfried Sassoon; a foreword by Canon "Dick" Sheppard, the leader of the Peace Pledge Union; and an introduction by the editor. Among the contributors were Garnett himself; Bertrand Russell; Julian's uncle, Adrian Stephen; Sir Norman Angell; Harry Pollitt, the foremost British Communist; and James Maxton, the leader of the Independent Labour Party. The discordant note in the collection was Julian's introduction, which dealt with questions of war and peace in a paradoxical way that must have given his elders to pause. He imagined himself to be modernizing pacifism; actually, he was making one of the first steps towards resolving a crucial dilemma of the 1930s: how to oppose both war and Hitler. He was aware of the immense pacifist sentiment abroad at the time he was writing—1934—and he cited the evidence of the Oxford Resolution and the Peace Pledge Union, maintaining that the sixteen thousand conscientious objectors of 1914–1918 had now become the twelve million signers of the Peace Ballot of 1934. But he added quite sensibly that when it came to the test, probably very few of those twelve million would prove to be absolute pacifists—nor did he think this regrettable. While he had only praise for the courage of being conscientious objectors during the First World War and commended pacifists for the independence of their thought, he doubted whether absolute pacifism was appropriate to the situation of the 1930s: "I do not think there is likely to be much chance of the absolutist conscientious objector again becoming an important figure in a campaign of war resistance." From his stance of the unsentimental realist, he looked coldly at the individual gesture, no matter how sincerely inspired, that gained no practical result. He felt that the modern pacifist who genuinely wished to oppose war must do so actively rather than in the traditional passive style. The solution was not as in the past to opt out of a society committed to war—that contest of rival imperialisms—but to try to change society. "The most active and ardent war resisters—at least among my own generation, those of military age—are more likely to take the line of revolutionary action than conscientious objection." By a kind of semantic sleight of hand he blurred the distinctions between war resistance and pacifism, conjuring up a movement that conformed to his own prescription: practical, potentially revolutionary, determined "to bring down, by hook or by crook, any government and any governing class that dares to make war." In the last sentence of the introduction he completed his modernization of pacifism with a militant paradox that reveals how far he had traveled from the attitudes of his parents and their friends: "I believe that the war resistance movements of my generation will in the end succeed in putting down war," he declared "—by force if necessary."[55]

This was relatively restrained. As the editor of a collection of memoirs by pacifists of the older generation, he had had to proceed diplomatically. But in an unpublished paper which he wrote at this time, "The Labour Party and War," he took a much stronger antipacifist line: "It is not any more virtuous to hate being killed than to wish to die on the field of battle. . . . It needs courage to say 'I am a Socialist, and I am willing to fight for the peace of Europe.'" He felt certain that the conjunction of German nationalism and English pacifism was leading to war. Accordingly, he objected to the propacifist policies of the Labour Party. "So long as the English people remain content to support either Beaverbrook or the Pacifist in the policy of irresponsible isolation there can be no lasting peace. . . . The [Labour] party must once and for all discard negative Pacifism and preach the Positive Pacifism of Pooled Security, Disarmament, and the National control and International inspection of armament firms."

He was writing in Taviton Street, ostensibly to the Labour Party, or to his Bourgeois Communist Friends, but actually to himself. It was a time of withdrawal, while he waited for events, whatever they might be: manuscripts piled up but were not sent out; he made no effort to translate his ideas into action. In February of that year Leonard Woolf arranged for him to talk with an official of the Labour Party, and the notion was put forward that Julian might have a half-time job drafting party propaganda leaflets; but nothing came of it.

Though he argued for peace and proposed a variety of practical ways to maintain it, war was what fascinated him: civil war, that is, the revolution for socialism; and international war, the struggle against fascism. In 1934 he believed in the possibility of one or the other, or both; in the event of either it would be impossible to stand aside as his elders had done. He had already declared his intention of turning himself into "a man of action." The difficulty was that he was also an intellectual, a poet and a son of Bloomsbury. He could not deceive himself that war was a "good": however much it might fascinate him, scruples, doubts, and hesitations intervened.

> I'm getting rather obsessed about war [he wrote to Lehmann], with a very ambivalent attitude. All my instincts make me want to be a soldier; all my intelligence is against it. I have rather nightmares of "the masses" trying a rising or a civil war and getting beaten—being wasted on impossible attacks by civilian enthusiasts, or crowds being machine-gunned by aeroplanes in the streets. . . . No doubt it's better for one's soul to fight than surrender, but otherwise— . . . One feels that a battlefield's a nicer place to die than a torture chamber, but probably there's not really so much difference, and at least fewer people suffer from the terror than would in a war. Oh, I don't know—personally I'd be for war every time, however hopeless. But that's only a personal feeling.[56]

In spite of his ambivalent attitude, he allowed his fascination with war to go unchecked, and it was characteristic of him that having admitted the possibility, or rather inevitability, of war, he should next address himself to the problem of how it ought to be conducted. It was as though the "war game" which had begun when he was a child at Wissett was now to be played with the utmost calculation, sophistication, and inventiveness. It was a game for one player, however: as in other aspects of his life at this time, here he was a party of one.

Although he did a few reviews of military books for the *New Statesman* in the early months of 1935, his most ambitious efforts, two long essays, "Military Considerations of Socialist Policy" and a study of Michael Collins's guerrilla tactics in the Irish rebellion, were not published. He was very taken with the idea of trying to think out a successful guerilla war. Ironically, considering what was to come, he proposed to Quentin in February 1935 that they might visit Spain, which he saw as a likely locale for such a war.

> I've written an article for Left Review on Collins, as a trial balloon for my plan of campaign. Shouldn't think the oafs will take it tho': too sensible for them. What a world. The capitalists can't pay one dividends, and the communists can't win wars. . . . I have a good mind to visit [Spain] this autumn or summer if I can finish my books and find people to meet. Would there be any chance of your going? I might put in a walk with a mistress first, and then we could see some bulls and see if we couldn't get into touch with some active and reasonable socialists. After all, it's a big country, with a shaky govt, guerilla traditions, violent habits—anyway I suppose this is pure fantasy.[57]

The reviews, written to be read by the public at large, are more straightforward and less venturesome than the essays, yet they are not without point. Perhaps the most interesting review is of the volume devoted to the German March Offensive of 1918 in *The Official History of the War*. Critical of the stalemate strategy that kept the armies in the trenches, he remarked that "the generals were quite right in thinking that they could avoid losing a decisive battle, but it was, of course, a peculiarly clumsy way of winning a war." And he went on to advance a favorite theory, that "the only leaders who showed any obvious brilliance were the civilian soldiers, untrained in classic doctrine, acting in open theatres, and unprovided with limitless reserves: Lawrence, Trotsky and Collins." His conclusion has precisely the note of calculation and sophistication indigenous to the war game: "It will be interesting to see if the present British and German armies, apparently small, highly trained and reasonably mobile, are capable of revising the classic tradition sufficiently to avoid another disastrous and uninteresting deadlock. No doubt it will not be too long before we are allowed to make the experiment."[58]

He had an almost obsessive interest in Michael Collins, and for a time even considered writing his biography. But chiefly he wished to discover what could be learned from his career: how a guerrilla war might best be waged in England, if it had to be waged, to achieve some sort of socialist government. It was a goal that mattered to him, albeit in a rather abstract way; but it is hard to resist the impression that he was most deeply engaged by the phenomenon of guerrilla war in itself, about which his ideas were well in advance of most military thinking of the time. A long sketch, in very rough form, survives of some lessons that Julian felt could be gleaned from the campaigns of Collins, beginning with the creation of a private army—in this case socialist, to be led (secretly) by heads of the Labour Party and staffed by middle-class intellectuals and a few token workers. The effect, for all its air of practicality, is oddly surrealistic, as in much of the writing of the period: a wealth of realistic detail is called upon to substantiate a romantic fantasy. It is the tone of Auden's "Leave for Cape Wrath tonight!" Similarly, there is a period fascination with violence: "Prisoners could be mutilated to prevent further active service: this should be made to appear a reprisal." And again, "Prisoners are an important source of information: it may be necessary to use torture to extract it"—though he felt constrained to add, "The revolutionaries will on the whole profit by a humane war." Events taking place at the time that he was writing appeared to confirm his hypotheses. The February fighting in Vienna, the attack on the working-class tenement the Karl Marx House, proved (to his mind) the need for a private army if there was to be any kind of effective socialist resistance. He did not waver from this position: a year later he was writing to Lehmann, who was in Vienna, to ask if he knew of any socialist paper, "legal or illegal," that might consider publishing his article on Collins. He was convinced that the workers could learn from it "certain military methods and principles which would make all the difference" if they were going to fight again, and he hoped that they would. In his poem "Vienna" he deplored "The useless firing and the weary ends / Of comrades . . . / Who fought well, but too late." And he asked,

> Can we, from that fate
> Wring to some foresight,
> Or will the same lost fight
> Mark too our ends?

He answered by indirection:

> War is a game for the whole mind,
> An art of will and eye . . .

> A hard art of foreseeing,
> Of not too much caring;
> A game for their playing
> Who fall in love with death,
> Doubt, and seeping fear

There is an admirable candor about this: it was easy enough, given his long-standing fascination with war, to describe it as "a game for the whole mind"; it was more difficult to acknowledge that it was also "A game for their playing / Who fall in love with death." The self-confidence and zest with which he recommended the formation of a private army and, in the event of an international war, the resisting of towns, industries, and communications, are somewhat misleading. One gets a more accurate picture of his state of mind from a long letter he wrote to Lehmann at precisely this time:

> I don't mind war as killing, nor as pain, nor utterly as destruction. But it means turning our minds and feelings downwards, growing hard (well, no harm, perhaps) but also savage and stupid and revengeful. You know, the Russians haven't escaped: spies and suspicion and tyranny, and no jobs if your "class origins" aren't above suspicion. That's war—far more than the battlefields, even, tho' I think I shall live to see the people who talk about "the masses" in peace using those same masses like Haig and Wilson [another First World War British general], until you've knocked the heart out of them. For it's clear that "revolution" is a dream of the nineteenth century: now we shall just have civil war, to the last dregs of modern invention. . . . I want to . . . leave the human race free to sit down to think for a bit. It's just another "trahison des clercs" to go into the struggle, whipping up enthusiasm and leading it to war. . . . If there must be violence, there must. But let's be thoroughly cold-blooded and unenthusiastic about it. . . . As you'll see, I'm not yet clear, and pretty near despair either way. I believe one of the differences in our points of view comes from the circumstances of our private lives. I don't know at all, but I fancy you don't hit back when you're hurt. I do. When one has seen the extent of human beastliness in oneself as well as outside one hesitates to let loose devils. There's nothing in the world fouler than enthusiasm, the enthusiasm of a fighting group, not even jealousy or suspicion, not even open-eyed causing of misery.[59]

He was getting himself into a state of some ambiguity about how far Left he was willing to go. He was evolving his own ideas about the current political situation, and their possible solution by some sort of military action, although he recognized its dangers. He had a rather odd mix of ideas, a combination of an almost adolescent fascination with war, reflecting his love of war games, with a steely cast of mind, quite realistic but not totally attractive. He was divided between his older, more liberal ideas and the new sort of realism represented by the communists, particularly as so many of those he knew were moving further to the Left or actually joining the party. But as someone steeped in Bloomsbury sophistication, the enthusiasms of the far Left were deeply uncongenial. On August 10, 1933, he had written to John Lehmann with some exaggeration about the situation in Cambridge: "Everyone except Antony B. and myself is a communist here [of course, in retrospect this was deeply ironic, as Blunt was more communist than anyone else he knew, except for Burgess and Maclean!]. Even Lettice is going to Russia this summer. Not me . . . looking round factories isn't my idea of a holiday, and I find most communists pretty tiresome." And in December he wrote again to John, "I'm sorely tempted to join the party, but really it's too silly and too bad at its job." Yet later in the year he wrote to his brother, "I find it may be difficult not to be carried away by my feelings and join the communists—all my friends seem to have."[60] He went to Anti-War and Socialist League meetings in London, yet found them dispiriting and ineffectual. And yet his views were changing, if slowly, under his growing interest in military questions. Quite some time later, in February 1935, he wrote to Lettice: "Nothing has ever really cured me of my militarist daydreams, and I hope I shall spend at least a part of my life—even the last part—on battlefields." His growing interest in military matters is vividly indicated in a review of two books by the two leading British military thinkers of the day, General Fuller and Captain Liddell Hart. The review, however, is primarily devoted to his own ideas about the military, the importance of tank forces and intelligent soldiers to run them.[61]

He had been disappointed by the reception of *Winter Movement*; he had not been one of the conspicuously admired contributors to *New Signatures*. Judged by his own extremely high expectations for himself—one must be distinguished, as were one's father and mother, aunt and uncle, and their friends—he saw himself as a failure as a poet. (And of course just at this time he had failed at Cambridge.) His solution was to be a poet "at moments only" and to withdraw from the literary game. When *New Country* appeared, to which he had not contributed, he wrote to John Lehmann, who had, "'I hear dreadful things of *New Country*, which I've asked Bunny for to review." Lehmann's reply was ironic and diplomatic, but quite inaccurate in its prophetic aspect: "Amusing that you've got *New Country* to review. Yes, it's a pretty good mess, & a tombstone for us all, I should think. Don't be too nasty, I quail, I quake." But Garnett had already given the book to someone else to review, and so Julian was unable to put an end publicly to his involvement—however tenuous it had been—with Thirties Poetry. Paradoxically, once he had committed himself to being a poet "at moments only," the poetic impulse revived. He wrote a good deal: from the work of this period he eventually selected thirty-three poems from a larger number for his second book, *Work for the Winter*. It was published by the Hogarth Press in the spring of 1936, when he had been in China almost a year and was truly "out" of the literary game. The poems are markedly different from those he had written in the past. The campaign for the heroic couplet has been abandoned—neither the "Epistle to Braithwaite" nor "Arms and the Man" are reprinted—and there is no attempt to maintain the impersonality of the early nature-descriptive pieces.

There is, as Lehmann wrote to him, a "new directness and simplicity." Almost without exception, the poems are drawn from his own experience; they reflect the uncertainties and regrets of his time in London—which is at once their virtue and defect. They have less poetic than autobiographical interest. (Perhaps it should be said that Julian's claims as a poet are based most firmly upon his early poems. In spite of its occasional successes, *Work for the Winter* is the traditional disappointing second book: tentative, pointing towards a new direction not yet firmly discerned. But it is not at all a dead end.) Uncertainties and regrets: the elegiac tone prevails throughout.

> Shall we not often remember
> That summer, flowers, garden,
> Shock and flock of white blossoms
> —How white snow will thicken the branches—
> Dotted and golden in green, in deep green
>   dancing and burning . . .
>
> But now take stronger tools,
> Axe, fire, plough.
> Metal sheathed in despairs, winter is fast
>   come on us.

This is from the title poem, "Work for the Winter," included in the section "Political Poems." It is followed by a section of "London Poems":

> So I shall never in verse put down
> The wringing horror of this town,
> A vision hard to repeat
> Of a long unhappy street . . .
>
> No help now: this town could do
> With some poison gas and a bomb or two.
>   —"London I"
>
> I want—I don't want—the not wanting
> Leaves the need, but stops the acting,
> Nothing worth the winning or saving,
> And the narrow life contracting.
>   —"London II"

Then a section of nine "Love Poems." The collection was dedicated to "A.P.," Antoinette Pirie, the woman he was most in love with when he was putting together the collection.

> Regret, shake hands, and the dry kiss
> Grating too sharply at the past
> Snaps short what yet remains of this,
> Briefly acknowledged for our last.
>   —"Coming to an End"
>
> Is this an end
> Or is there yet
> Waste time to spend,
> More to forget?
>
> Is this an end
> Of the facile rhyme;
> Mistress and friend
> How runs the time?
>
> Is this an end
> Or must I still
> Spiral descend
> The westward hill?
>   —"Finale"

From the section called "Constructions":

Drive on, sharp wings, and cry above
Not contemplating life or love,
Or war or death: a winter flight
Impartial to our human plight . . .

What useless dream, a hope to wring
Comfort from a migrant wing:
Human or beast, between us set
The incommunicable net.

Parallel, yet separate,
The languages we mistranslate,
And knowledge seems no less absurd
If of a mistress, or a bird.
 —"The Redshanks"

His poem "Autobiography" is one of the most impressive examples of his new directness and simplicity. It is an intensely personal poem based upon a crucial conflict in his life that he would never satisfactorily resolve: his emotional commitment to the past against his intellectual commitment to the future, which would almost certainly mean, he thought, the end of all that he valued most. For all his pride in the poem as a poem, he also knew that it was a document, and it was only after he had left Taviton Street, left London, left Charleston, that he was able to make it public. He was reluctant to show the poem even to his mother. It had been written by early 1934, and submitted rashly to Lehmann that spring, and reclaimed, unpublished, in September. More than a year later, on October 13, 1935, from China, he wrote to his mother: "Also, dearest, I've found out how much our relationship matters to me. And we both know it. I feel about it rather like Donne going religious after his profane mistresses, except that I can love you without having to believe nonsense. I've tried to say a little about you—and about you and Roger [Fry] together—in one of my new poems, the 'Autobiography.' It's not enough nearly, but it's the only time I've come at all near putting it down."

AUTOBIOGRAPHY

I stay myself—the product made
 By several hundred English years,
 Of harried labourers underpaid,

Of Venns who plied the parson's trade,
    Of regicides, of Clapham sects,
    Of high Victorian intellects,
    Leslie, FitzJames:

And, not among such honoured, marbled, names,
That cavalry ruffian, Hodson of Hodson's Horse,
Who helped take Delhi, murdered the Moguls;
At least a soldiering brigand: there were worse,
Who built a country house from iron and coal:
Hard-bitten capitalists, if on the whole
They kept the general average of their class.

And then, not breeding but environment,
Leisure without great wealth; people intent
To follow mind, feeling and sense
Where they might lead, and, for the world, content
To let it run along its toppling course.
Humane, just, sensible; with no pretence
To fame, success, or meddling with that world.

And one, my best, with such a calm of mind,
And, I have thought, with clear experience
Of what is felt of waste, confusion, pain,
Faced with a strong good sense, stubborn and plain;
Patient and sensitive, cynic and kind.

The sensuous mind within preoccupied
By lucid vision of form and colour and space,
The careful hand and eye, and where resides
An intellectual landscape's living face,
Oh certitude of mind and sense, and where
Native I love, and feel accustomed air.

And then the passage of those country years,
A war-time boyhood; orchard trees run wild,
West wind and rain, winters of holding mud,
Wood fires in blue-bright frost and tingling blood,
All brought to the sharp senses of a child.

Whatever comes since then, that life appears
Central and certain and undoubted good,
As the known qualities of clay or wood

Live in the finger's ends, as tool or gun
Come easily to hand as they have done.

Whatever games there now remain to play
Of love or war, of ruin or revolt,
I cannot quite admit that world's decay
Or undespairing wish it on its way.

For here was good, built though it was, no doubt,
On poverty I could not live without,
Yet none the less, good certain and secure,
And even though I see it not endure,
And though it sinks within the rising tide,
What can for me replace it good or sure?

CHAPTER 4

CHINA

BY THE WINTER OF 1935 Julian Bell seemed to have come to the end of a line in London: until now his life had fallen far short of the great expectations he and others had entertained for it. The thought occurred, perhaps if he made some break with life in England, he might get away from his dissatisfactions; striking out on his own, he could loosen himself from the environment and heritage that meant so much to him and had done so much to shape him, and perhaps restrict him. For some time he had been attracted by the possibility of teaching in a foreign university, preferably in the Far East. It was fairly common for a bright young man with some academic qualities to look for such a position. It would be a way to cut through the various unsatisfactory choices that were facing him. As he wrote to his brother in 1934: "I've begun the very first steps towards China—probably they'll have no result for years. . . . I've almost dropped politics—they're too much of a job here, and I'm not at all sure of my own mind. . . . I should rather like to go back to Cambridge for a bit and try to clear my head about things. I don't know if I can stand London indefinitely—certainly I cant without a job of sorts. . . . Probably I shall have to write another book about something—which would be a business. I've some thoughts tho' at trying to become a socialist even this late in life."[1] As early as May 1934 he was interested in teaching positions in the Far East and was in touch with the Cambridge Appointments Board. As he wrote to Lettice that month: "I've applied for a job in Siam of all places. There can't be many people wanting to go there. So perhaps I shall get it. I'm going to ask for one or two in China that should be going." He even put in (unsuccessfully) for a post in Japan for which a Methodist was preferred. He was anxious to move, to achieve an aim which was not at all clear in his own mind.

Sometimes he thought that he wanted to go away in search of excitement, to a place where the Communist Party might really be interesting—China perhaps, where a small-scale war could test his military theories. At other times he felt that he must leave England because he had achieved, without too much effort, an agreeable second-generation Bloomsbury existence: poems, women, good conversation. Yet his successes were not important nor significant enough to satisfy him. In this mood, going to China might seem an escape. "My own feeling about China," he wrote to Lettice in June 1934, "is that it's about all I'm fit for now: a genteel form of suicide. Getting most of what I wanted has been bad for my morale, I think. Either I must have stability, or misery, if I'm to get much done."

On July 16, 1935, the job he had applied for a year earlier, professor of English at the National University of Wuhan in China, suddenly materialized. It was to be a two-year appointment according to his contract, the first year being probationary. He was to teach two courses, one on Literary Criticism and the other on selected modern British texts. John Sheppard wrote a testimonial on his behalf, as did Maynard Keynes, in which he stated: "Mr Bell has grown up in a circle of British life which has made it possible for him to know intimately those in this country who have in the recent past perhaps done most to mould the direction of taste and accomplishment both in literature and art. . . . This upbringing and these surroundings would, I think, prove of some real importance in his ability to convey to Chinese pupils the current thought and feeling of England."[2] Margery Fry, Roger's sister, who had played a major role in the publication of the Mallarmé translations and was deeply involved with Chinese education, had supported his application. He wrote on the same day to his mother, who was in Rome. Quite rightly, his greatest concern was that she would be very upset at his going so far away for so long. It came as rather a bolt from the blue. He had just been on a trip to Ireland, and in a letter of

June 30 Vanessa had commented on his attitude towards travel. "Your rather tipsy sounding travelling letter amused us very much & gave the impression you were enjoying it all in spite of prospects of sea sickness & all the horrors of travel which you dislike so much." She had no expectation of such a dramatic development. And now he was going far away probably for one or more years.

He wrote to her on July 16.

> Dearest Nessa
>
> I hope this letter wont be upsetting to you. No, I've not got married. But I have accepted a job in China—the English professorship I tried for last year. It happened completely unexpectedly—I went for an interview this morning, expecting nothing, came away without having taken it seriously—and heard this afternoon I'd got the job. It sounds amusing enough—as a job: £800 a year, one year certain, 3 probable: it could be renewed after that, but I don't want to spend my life away from you. The bore is that I have to be there at latest by the end of September: this means sailing at latest by August 20. I should like to leave from Marseilles and visit you at Cassis for as long as possible: you can imagine I've a busy month ahead. I shall know in a day or two more about dates, sailings, etc., and will let you know.
>
> I might have foreseen things happening like this: one's preparations of a couple of years ago taking effect at last. It felt rather appalling at the moment of hearing—since then I've stopped being sharply conscious of it all: it just stays a daydream. I shall have to go on making arrangements like anything—the confusion will be frightful in an already busy life. I'm appalled at the thought of leaving you all for three years—it seems a terrific slice out of life. I shall be thirty then—1938. Angelica and Quentin settled down. It's the most drastic step I've ever taken, I think, after getting born. I'm sure that its a good thing to do—what I wanted to do also, somewhere. I knew that for the time I'd got most of what I wanted from London. When I come back I should have got straight internally, and also have seen enough of the world to be pretty clear about that. . . . And somehow I'm convinced that it will produce a kind of peace of mind I now want above all things.[3]

Vanessa was determined to see him in England before he left. She replied to him on July 19 from Rome.

> My own darling Julian—I have just got your letter. My dear—of course I couldnt help being a good deal upset when I heard that you might be going away almost at once for such a long time. But I have had a long talk with Duncan—which has helped me to take a reasonable view. In fact I think I am

au fond reasonable darling & much as I mind your going I am really glad you should have this chance. I think it would be a great mistake not to take it & that it will give you just what you really need—experience of a kind most people cant get & self confidence & the power to make your life what you want it to be. But I cant write these things—my dear—I *must* see you. . . . Thank you dearest for your letter which made me very happy as well as upsetting me for I feel we have an intimacy that nothing can spoil.

He was full of excitement. As John Lehmann wrote to him, his going to China might turn out to be "a thing . . . absolutely decisive in your life." Leighton Park School, Cambridge, working for a Fellowship at King's, living to a degree the London literary life, had all been more or less foreordained and what many a bright young man might do: what a Bloomsbury young man was almost bound to do. But to teach in China—that was something different and comparatively adventurous, a step of his own. It is tempting to think that the final poem of the London section in *Work for the Winter* was written after Julian had heard that he was going to China; it very much has the feeling of a new direction taken:

> Resurrect, resurrect,
> The senses and the intellect,
> Swing and stride and march again
> In thundering charges down the plain.
> Carry the dry logs to the fire,
> Relight pride, resurge desire,
> And spin the dead leaves down the wind,
> And let in winter on the mind.
>
> Out with old banners, let them fly,
> Nor care a hang for symbolry:
> I am I, and close to hand
> My world to shape or understand.
> Life goes on, once more I live,
> Once more the open skies can give
> Some native force, some natural power,
> And flaming triumph through an hour.

It was all rather sudden. He had been given the job on July 16; he was to sail no later than August 20. He proposed going out to Cassis to see his mother: it might be the last time for them to be together for some years. She replied that she was cutting short her vacation and returning to England, and of course he was delighted: "I've wanted you very much this last week." His departure was in fact delayed until August 29. From on board ship he wrote to Lettice, on September 2, about their parting: "Nessa and I both have about the same notion of how to behave, but it isn't easy. As it happened, it was her giving me some money as a present that broke me down." Then a bright, cheerful, grim little drive into Lewes and Newhaven to take the boat to France to pick up his ship in Marseilles. "You know, I'm almost the only person I know who has an adult relationship with their mother. It's about the most satisfactory human relationship I have, perhaps because it's the only one where I've deep emotions uncomplicated by power-sadist feelings." He took with him an oil portrait of Vanessa by Duncan, painted around 1933.

The day after he left, Vanessa wrote him the first of many long letters, telling him what she was doing to his room at Charleston:

> It is still difficult to believe that youre on your way & that by the time you get this you will actually be in China—I dont suppose it will become real to me till I get letters from you.... I drove back yesterday in a kind of dream, but it wasnt an unhappy one.... It was rather hard to come into the house with you not here—but Duncan was very nice to me & I don't mind showing my feelings to him which is a great relief—and it seems a shame to do so to Q. & A. Though I think they know very well what I feel.... My instincts are so much the opposite to those of Queen Victoria [keeping Albert's rooms exactly as they were after his death] that I immediately set about changing the state of your room—which while you are away must not be a relic of you but take on another life & become Angelica's room. It will keep quite enough of you but must go on being alive.

She continued the letter on September 3 from London, ending, "Take care of yourself. Want you to be happy & remember I love you & think of you constantly—I looked at you standing on the boat after I had left you when you thought I had gone—you were looking down at your tickets etc. & I can still see you so clearly."[4]

The psychological reasons which impelled him to China seem to be very clear: intense dissatisfaction with his life in the present, the hope of making a fresh start in the future. There were practical reasons too. He imagined that life at a Chinese university would be stable and uneventful enough for him to get a great deal of work accomplished: he intended to write a series of long essays which would clarify his position vis-à-vis his generation and perhaps allow him to play a more central role in the life of England when he returned. Also, there was the attractiveness of the salary he was offered. He did have small private means from family investments, which were beginning to improve in 1935 as the effects of the Depression lessened, but he welcomed the money from a regular job, at a good wage and in a place where living expenses would be low. But in the end one comes back to his situation in London, where he no longer wished to be. The moment was opportune. Wuhan University had wanted an English professor of English; Julian had wanted such a job. At the end of August he sailed from Marseilles on a Japanese ship, the *Fushimi Marui*.

Wuhan University was not, as one might perhaps expect in the circumstances, a missionary institution with official ties to the West, but a creation of the state, one of fifteen National Universities scattered about China. Somewhat removed and out of the way, at a considerable distance from the great coastal cities, Wuhan is on the Yangtze River about four hundred miles upriver from Nanking. Even before the 1911 revolution it had been a center of education, but in very much the provincial sense. It was a worthy rather than a sophisticated milieu, and as such not particularly to Julian's style. In 1895 a Government School of Mines was opened in Wuhan; the reforming viceroy, Chang Chih-tung, inaugurated the system of which Julian was a part: the regular importation of professors from the West. The revolution which overthrew the Manchu dynasty actually began at Wuhan in October 1911; two years later, a National University was founded there, with departments of Chinese Language and Literature, Russian Language and Literature, History, Philosophy, Physics, Chemistry, Biology, Law, and Library Science. By the 1930s it had become one of the more prominent universities in China, but it was still very small and provincial. Chinese higher education in this period was neither adventurous, ambitious—the bachelor of arts was the only degree awarded—nor widespread. Altogether, as of 1931, there were fifty-nine universities with an enrollment of thirty-four thousand students. Most of the twenty-seven private universities were missionary-sponsored and, though comparatively free of government interference, might be inhibited by the doctrinal principles of their sponsors. Even so, they were believed to offer the best education and attracted almost half the entire undergraduate enrollment. The rest was divided among the government's Provincial and National Universities.

State education was of doubtful merit and badly hampered—or so a League of Nations investigating team decided in the early 1930s—because of its hierarchical structure, as everything depended on the whims of the Central Ministry and its politically appointed head. Students and faculty alike might find themselves thrown out for the most trivial political reasons; faculty members were jeopardized by every change in administration. (Professors from abroad, like Julian, would be somewhat removed from this sort of pressure.) Teaching was primarily done by lectures—students might be attending as many as twenty a week—but there were also a few smaller classes and supervisions. (Julian was to do some of these, as well as lecture.)

The National University of Wuhan—there was also a private university in the town—consisted of approximately 700 students and 150 teachers. Most of the students came from the local area, as the University, except perhaps in Library Science, had no particular cachet that would attract anyone to it from a great distance. It was divided into a School of Letters, a School of Law (which included politics and economics), a School of Science, and a School of Technology; and in all but the last, women as well as men were allowed to register. Almost all studied English and English Literature, which was particularly emphasized in the School of Letters. There were the expected courses in Shakespeare, Shelley, and Keats as well as a survey of the novel—it was to teach these courses that Julian had been hired. The University was dowdy-to-respectable rather than distinguished-to-brilliant: it must have regarded Professor Bell as quite a catch. He himself had been somewhat diffident about his chances, particularly as for one reason or another his various efforts to leave England for a teaching post abroad had failed. But he had done well enough at Cambridge; he was the nephew of Virginia Woolf; he was au courant in London; he was supported by Margery Fry, who had Chinese connections. Who better to bring Western culture to the Chinese?

The voyage out was long, leisurely, uneventful, and entirely enjoyable, even though he was not in the best health from an unspecified sexual complaint, which prevented him from pursuing any available ladies who might be on the ship. He was on board the *Fushimi Marui* for almost six weeks, with brief stopovers at a number of outposts of Empire. Along the way he wrote his mother very lively, long, colorful, gossipy "traveler's letters" about his fellow passengers (the inevitable "charming tea planter from Assam" whom Julian summed up, just as inevitably, as "pure Somerset Maugham") and places seen ("We're in Singapore for the night. . . . We came in this afternoon through archipelagoes and palms and sampans and junks: mangrove swamps growing out into the sea: single trees sticking out of the water a hundred yards from the bank") and shipboard happenings ("It's said the laundryman who was ill in the Red Sea and then recovered has gone mad and jumped overboard. However, I don't feel at all concerned about that, since any of us might easily go mad"). The tone is unfailingly exuberant and oddly boyish—a schoolboy let out of school for an unexpected holiday. In Colombo he was entertained by a friend of Leonard Woolf's, who at the moment was acting-governor. "I got a lot of fun out of the grandeurs," he reported. "Sentries to present arms. Two sets of uniformed servants, upstairs and down. . . . And, which really pleased me immensely, I was lent an enormous Humber saloon, with chauffeur (native, extremely competent) and royal arms on a flag on the bonnet! It was terrific fun." Phrases of this sort abound: "I feel a good deal excited and fascinated." In Singapore he went ashore with a fellow passenger and wandered around the amusement parks: "It was fascinating beyond words." Hong Kong "was great fun: a lovely mountain town with a long fjord of a harbour alive with fascinating junks. I was given lunch at the Government House and taken round the town in a car, thanks to Leonard's introduction." In Shanghai occurred his "first real adventure," reported in a letter to his mother on October 1, a classic encounter with a pimp—"'Russian girl, yes?' 'No, no, no time'"—who attempted to extort payment for services not rendered:

> "Go the devil" (I really did say that.) Then, to rickshaw man, "North Station." Rickshaw man hesitates. Pimp: "I shoot, I kill you." "Don't be a damned fool." So far very heroic. But then, fool myself, I got out, and saying to rickshaw man, with vague honesty, "You come," started to walk out. (Thank God for good visual memory and sense of direction.) Attack by pimp, vaguely and weakly supported by rickshaw man. First dive for my balls got home, and I fell, dropping papers carried. However, attack not pressed, and I got up. Second attack, attempt to dislocate my jaw, painful but unsuccessful; another ball dive, some vague hitting by me, and they drew off. I turned and walked out. One picked up a stone, but it never came. I walked back, a long-seeming way, marked a sikh policeman at traffic lights, asked for taxis place, found one, took a taxi to the station, found my American Express man waiting, and a hard sleeper, drank queer-tasting mineral water, and sat down to write to you.

Finally, on the 1st of October, suffering from a mild attack of dysentery, he arrived in Nanking. He found the town "fascinating" and was pleased with the minister of education—"a nice little man who wore national dress: I mistook him for a coolie at first when he came into the room"—who told him that he would receive £700 a year rather than the £800 he had expected, but that he would have to teach only nine to ten hours a week. It turned out that that figure was an underestimate. But the salary would allow him to live perfectly comfortably.

The next day he left for Wuhan, a three-day journey up the Yangtze, on the river steamer *Tuk-mo*. He found the countryside quite beautiful. His fellow passengers were two American women, a Yorkshire businessman and his sister, and an Irish missionary. He particularly approved of the missionary, who it turned out shared his admiration for Michael Collins. But he was in a euphoric mood and took a benevolent view of them all: "The business man amiable. The Americans american, but tolerable. Eddy wouldn't know me now, I've grown so good at tolerating people, and seeing the good in everyman."

He arrived in Wuhan on Sunday morning, October 5. That afternoon he met the dean of the School of Letters, Professor Chen Yuan, his wife, and their six-year-old daughter, "who fell for me." (When I met her years later in London, her memory of Julian was much less benign. She remembers being terrified when his idea of how to teach her to swim was to throw her into the lake.) He described the Chens in his first letter to his mother from China as "angels of light." They were to be his neighbors. From Professor Chen he learned that he was expected to start teaching courses in Shakespeare, Modern Literature, and Composition two days later. His rejection by the electors of King's seems to have strengthened him in his desire to teach, but he had never had any practical experience. Until that Sunday, he had not been told what precisely he was to do at Wuhan; accordingly, he had not been able to prepare. The prospect was intimidating. There was the further difficulty that a bad tooth had worsened, and he was now somewhat ill, though not ill enough he felt to justify taking to his bed and canceling classes. His sexual disorder hadn't gone away, but so far he did not anticipate launching an affair. He had no choice at the beginning but to improvise lectures, and he suspected that his students had some difficulty in following his English. Still, "we're getting on," he wrote to his mother. "I'm not frightened—the fortunate part of being ill is that one grows impervious to the world: I could make myself do anything all last week."

As his health began to improve, he entered into the job with great relish. He found the place beautiful, the library "superb," the staff extremely pleasant. Even the considerable problems of settling down in a strange country did not bother him: he coped with a house that was almost bare of furniture and equipment when he took possession, and with servants (Yang, "a wretched, shifty, rather dishonest creature," and a coolie to help him). His contract with the University called for nine to twelve hours of work a week; having no experience of teaching, he imagined that this would be literally the case and felt that he was being overpaid—"I shall try to do a bit more to salve my conscience." (He didn't realize that the figure represented actual class time, but not the necessary hours of preparation.) Actually he had very little free time. Lectures and supervisions came to sixteen hours a week; he spent three hours a week studying Chinese; he gave a good deal of time to the preparation of lectures. And he found that social life was conducted in a fairly casual and time-consuming way.

His first reactions to China were warmly appreciative: he delighted in its strangeness, and he delighted in its unexpected familiarity. Shanghai had reminded him of Marseilles; a village on the Yangtze was "pure Provence"; on his first day at the University he described it as a "mediterranean Cambridge." Professor Chang was "a friend of Goldie's"; his wife was a painter (Chinese style) a writer of short stories and the editor of a literary page in one of the big Chinese Hankow papers. "I gather she is sometimes called the Chinese Katherine Mansfield." He summed them up for John Lehmann as "very much a Chinese Bloomsbury." He found the University people "extraordinarily like Cambridge, very friendly, informal and social: we all live in houses scattered about the hillside, and there is a great deal of dropping in in a casual Cambridge fashion." His own house looked "like a Cambridge don's house, only smaller . . . built of the local grey brick, and set on a steep hillside, near the top. The kitchen and servants' quarters [were] back, set into the hill." He was constantly struck by resemblances in the landscape: "Now in the dusk"—sailing up the Yangtze—"very soft and damp as an English October—we have come to Cambridgeshire and the fens."

There are passages in the letters that read like notations for unwritten poems in *Winter Movement*: "the trees are turning colour—a small poplar with very light round leaves individually flecked with orange-purpled reds. And a red-hot sky, then moon—I walked in the dark, stumbling through deep grass graves, like peat-bogs almost. There was a clouded moon and wild geese flying." Life had its Charlestonian aspects too. A certain aesthetic impracticality in the Chinese was not unreminiscent; and there were episodes in the countryside beyond Wuhan that might have been chronicled in the *New Bulletin*. "A most Charlestonian scene as I walked this evening," he wrote to his mother in November. "A bull water-buffalo gone wild, with half a dozen dogs chasing, and vague people whacking, halloing. Round and about—graves, fields." It was as though he had come halfway round the world to find himself reminded at every turn of what he had started from and had chosen to leave. He wrote to John Lehmann, "It's all like ten years or more ago," and to Eddie Playfair: "What a world. The lives one leads. Really so alike." Yet at first, as he wrote on October 13, there were moments of "appalling homesickness when I want frightfully to be with you again and in a safe, familiar, friendly world." He now felt that his chief love interest was Tony, but he also so missed Vanessa and liked to think that they were only a fortnight away. "Also, dearest, I've found out more than ever here how much our relationship matters to me. And we both know it." The moments of homesickness occurred at widening intervals. He was really very happy in China; the conditions of his life there were more favorable to his being happy than they had been in the immediate past and as he feared they would prove to be in the future in "an England of nervous tension, towns and politics." At Wuhan he could roam through the open countryside, and he quite soon worked it out so that he could shoot and sail. He had a boat built for himself in Hankow; it was ready by spring, and thereafter he spent a good deal of time on the lake. Many evenings, between five and seven, he would go out with a gun and look for duck or snipe: it was an activity that identified him with the sahib rather than the missionary element in Wuhan, which did not displease him. It also marked him off from the confirmed academics: "It's essential I should shoot, or I may become a don." These were the simple, familiar outdoor pleasures that counted for a great deal with Julian, indeed were indispensable to his well-being, that he had experienced in the past and whose absence he had lamented in London.

But the pleasures (and difficulties) of being a don were new to him; they composed an important part of his experience in China. He had come out to teach at a provincial Chinese university because he felt he must have the stability it offered him. "The truth of the matter," he wrote to a friend, "is that I want to enjoy life: I'm in a better position for doing so than usual." Even his view of the world crisis lightened: "Can one believe it's even conceivable there'll be a stable status quo? Yes, I can, here, teaching literature. But could one in England?" Teaching exhilarated him; he entered into his duties at Wuhan with enthusiasm and dedication. But by the end of his first month he was becoming restive. He had never attached much importance to the conventional methods of scholarship; he was much more agile at a discussion, pursuing various fascinating hares of argument—as "The Good and All That" had demonstrated—than at systematically organizing his material. A course in "composition," by its very nature, lends itself to improvisation and tricks of personality, and there he did well from the start. But his courses in Modern Literature and Shakespeare were more taxing. "It's fun talking to people," he wrote to Lehmann, "but I haven't yet got very much response. They understand me decently. But God knows I'm really unfit for the job: I have to learn it by doing it." His classes were small, about ten, but nevertheless he ran them as lectures rather than as discussion groups. His ambitions were grandiose: he intended to read not only the books he assigned to his students—"I make up lectures on Macbeth in the process of reading"—but also "endless books on China, on philosophy and criticism, on every manner of subject. . . . It's all incomparably odd." To his mother he admitted, "Really, I'm exceedingly ill-trained for anything, and certainly for University teaching work. If I succeed it will be a tribute to my brilliance,—charm and determined character rather than anything else."

The solution he arrived at fell short of his ambitions but was a good deal more realistic. For the Shakespeare course he depended on the Arden edition with its copious footnotes—and his own ingenuity. For the Modern Literature course he chose to deal principally with the writers he knew best. In effect he brought Bloomsbury and the Bloomsbury canon to China. He divided modern writing into two periods, 1890–1914 and 1914–1936, and began with the earlier, about which he knew less. Gissing, Henry James, and Arnold Bennett were omitted from the syllabus; Samuel Butler, Wilde, and Conrad were included. Robert Bridges he found "empty." Rupert Brooke seemed better than he had believed, but he finally decided that "he wasn't a poet—much but the most remarkable human being I've ever heard of. Of course I feel a certain sympathy with some of his letters from foreign parts, and there is far too much of an analogy—King's, Apostles, etc. I suppose I should have liked immensely to have all his gifts—looks and a fellowship and worldly successes. Not that I've done badly, but it would have been superb to have had that sort of 'brilliant career.'" In November, looking forward to the next term when he would be dealing with the writers who mattered to him most, he wrote to his aunt Virginia that he planned to use one of her novels, but he was not sure which. "I think they must do you, Tom and Yeats." In February, grown secure in his idiosyncratic method, he was venturing afield, trying "to push Proust down their throats," the result, as he put it, of "a recent conversion." Before this, he had not been one of the enthusiasts for the great French novelist—unlike his father, whose *Proust* was one of the first appreciations in English—but he would make annual efforts to read *À la recherche du temps perdu*. Convinced that part of his job was to "try and jog and stir the mind," he also attempted to expound Freud to his students. Here his ambition overcame his judgment, and with characteristic frankness he told Playfair, "it's too difficult for an ignoramus like self to explain." He wanted to familiarize them with the basis of Bloomsbury, the philosophical theories and critical principles, as well as its creative practice. "They'll get 'Cambridge School'—[Clive] Bell to [Frank] Ramsey. Not either principle in detail, though I shall explain Moore to them, I think." And they were to analyze prose passages in the manner of I. A. Richards's *Practical Criticism*. By March, lectures on the "family" were in full cry. He wrote to his aunt: "I get a good deal of quiet fun, too, out of lecturing on all of you: Goldie, Maynard, Bertie [Russell] I've done so far: Clive and Roger for next week." Then would come an occasional foray into the badlands to consider writers like T. E. Hulme and Wyndham Lewis; but soon he would be back in familiar territory: "I am wondering if they can be allowed to read Peter [F. L. Lucas], or will his damned charm corrupt them?" Bloomsbury was the center from which he operated: minor works in the school of Bloomsbury would receive as much if not more attention than major works outside it. Lawrence and Joyce, two writers whom Bloomsbury could neither comfortably accept nor dismiss, were ignored at first in his lectures, but later he felt he had to pay some attention to them. But of course he had no desire to be professional about his job, or to go systematically through a conventional syllabus. He did not consider himself a born teacher or scholar but rather an expositor, so to speak, of the family business and a firm believer in the family creed. "Really education is a lot of nonsense; it only happens once in a way as a personal relation—which is why you get it from your contemporaries, family, or friends, or at Cambridge." After his death, George Osborn, a Methodist missionary in China and a somewhat older Kingsman, who had seen Julian there, wrote to his mother: "At first they [his students] found him quite unintelligible then they grew to respect and love him. No one ever had made them read so much but no one had ever made English so interesting, alive and exciting for them before."[5]

Julian felt that his time teaching had demonstrated he had "some gifts as an educator," and he continued to believe that King's had made a mistake in not giving him a Fellowship. He was enjoying himself; the teaching was going well; and with shooting and sailing he had the sort of life outdoors he relished. He was also having an active social life. Unfortunately, the style at Wuhan did not allow for a closeness between pupil and teacher—without personal relations how much could one teach, or learn? As a consequence, he could never finally settle in his own mind what he thought of the Chinese young. His first reaction had been positive. Although he found them perhaps slightly over-romantic and sentimental, timid and conventional, he was impressed by their sensitivity, intuition, taste, and intelligence: they were educable. Familiarity altered his opinion; he began to feel that the Chinese must be toughened up intellectually: "If I had my way I'd forbid them any English prose that wasn't hard, dry, knobbly, masculine: bring them up on Swift and Defoe, switch them over to Bertie Russell and hard-boiled Americans—somehow get them off this infernal gilt-gingerbread elegance." A month later (again to his mother) he wrote, "They're almost like primitives in the way they can be corrupted by sentimentality, romanticism and nonsense." And he reported to his aunt: "I'm conducting an anti-sentiment and fine writing campaign, which they badly need. . . . So much second-rate stuff has been pushed off on them. Stevenson and Lamb and Ruskin and that sort of water intoxicant." He became so impatient with the Chinese that he even felt it necessary to attack their most ardent admirer on the fringe of Bloomsbury, Goldsworthy Lowes Dickinson, whose

Letters from John Chinaman in 1901 was a forerunner of Bloomsbury's abiding interest in the East. Although Julian felt that "softness" was a particular intellectual vice of the Chinese, more widespread among them than among the English, he was also attacking the quality itself. It was a way to continue his war against romanticism and vague sentimental thinking. These were all the more to be regretted when he detected them in the immediate ancestry of his beloved Bloomsbury. "I can't really see," he wrote to his aunt, "why Goldie was so enthusiastic about them [the Chinese]—except indeed for niceness and charm. And perhaps he didn't mind sentimentality as much as his youngers do." He then went on to deprecate Dickinson in general. He disliked his softness. Perhaps he felt this particularly deeply because he suspected that there might be a streak of softness, of gentility, in Bloomsbury, and himself. Would they prove hard enough to cope with a threatened world? "He was really, you know, a little soft—that was what made him so much less impressive than Roger. One saw him the whole time wanting to give way to his feelings, but knowing he mustn't. It was charming enough to meet someone so gentle and saintly and generally admirable, and it's charming enough to read him. But I suppose it was something to do with his being repressed and disappointed that made him—'wistful' is almost the word. Whereas old Roger, having had all the women, and so on, he wanted, never seemed to weaken in any way." Against this must be set a passage from a letter to Lehmann written soon after Julian had arrived at Wuhan and was still suffering from the debilitating and depressing effects of his illness: "I want to have the untroubled bourgeois holiday again. I suppose I shan't get it for long, ever. You know, I'm not going to be really very good at the new world. I am soft, frightfully—above all when I'm unwell, or rather convalescent. And the detail of life can be a horror, though the essentials are worse. Sometimes I sit miserable in a corner and realise them. I shall one day write down the truth about life—and it will look as sentimental as my poems."

With only one of his students was he able to establish a personal relationship. This was a talented young man in his composition course, C. C. Yeh, his brightest and friendliest student. He had already written a novel in Esperanto. Only six years older than Yeh, Julian found him intelligent and sensitive, full of vitality and courage, and very promising. Eager to help him in his career, he recommended him to John Lehmann, who agreed with Julian's estimate and introduced his work in *New Writing*. Later on, he accompanied Auden and Isherwood on part of their trip to China, preserved in their *Journey to a War* (1939). He became quite a well-known writer, living in England and Denmark, including time at King's, from 1945 to 1948. He returned to China to participate in the revolution, was stripped of his positions at the time of the cultural revolution, and was embarrassed at being obligated to disown his Western contacts. He was eventually rehabilitated and died in 1998.

It was Yeh's case in particular that convinced Julian that the education practiced in China was not totally acceptable. "I'm in a fine rage with the Chinese university system," he wrote to Playfair. "My favourite pupil, a very nice, intelligent youth, a promising writer, and with guts enough to treat me as an equal such a relief—is on the verge of a nervous breakdown plus insomnia; he has 28 hours lectures a week plus 1 hour's supervision (mine) and about 20 hours of it involves preparing texts." This was a far cry from the *douceur de vivre* of Cambridge, where education was a personal relation and where there was time for thinking about a subject rather than mere rote learning. "I suspect the whole country needs a good shake up," he wrote indignantly. "You see the sahib? But as you know I can get just as cross with the French or the English."[6]

He would always be intolerant of what he considered to be stupidity, and anxious to correct it—"by force if necessary." Faced with an unfamiliar, infinitely complex, and somewhat bewildering culture, he responded in a rather more simplistic way than he might have in the West; but essentially it was the same feeling of intense irritation at other people's stupidities. Soon after his arrival, when he was still living in a state of enforced chastity, which always made him irritable and which perhaps gave to his fantasies a more sexual coloration than they might ordinarily have had, he decided that the Chinese men were an inferior race but the women were beautiful. What was needed he felt was a new and intelligent Tamerlane, who would come along and castrate the men and breed the women to northern European stock.

Writing to his mother a week after his arrival at Wuhan, Julian had told her: "All sorts of details of life are fascinating and curious and sometimes very lovely. And above all there's the real friendliness of the Chengs [sic] and the Wangs [the president of the University]—and I think I shall find other people whom I can have real and intimate relationships with." Inevitably, this proved to be the case, with only a slight modification—"other people" became one person. Abroad, as at home, Julian could not keep out of love's way, and he was soon to embark upon what was perhaps the most remarkable and certainly the most documented of all his affairs. It was a quirk of his character, already noticed, that when in love he adored publicity, and nothing made him happier than to discuss the progress of his affairs, down to the most intimate details with his mother and certain of his friends. The older generation of Bloomsbury, in rebellion against the taboos of their Victorian forebears, believed, at least in theory, in clear, candid, truthful, and rational personal relationships, and accordingly saw no reason to be reticent in matters of sex. But there is a quality in Julian's revelations that is very different from the candor of his elders, and suggests that he was involved not so much in a relationship as in a performance.

In his first weeks in Wuhan he felt still too ill from his sexual complaint to look about energetically for the indispensable mistress; also, presumably, he felt that he must first grow familiar with his new environment. But at no point did he intend that his teaching position, or whatever may have been his commitments in England, should prevent him from living the same sort of life as he had in the past. Everything conspired to make him a libertine: he saw no reason not to continue to uphold a "Latin-sensual view of *amour*." And as frequently is the case, perhaps more often at a foreign university, where the number of women with whom one can talk and make love in one's own language is so few, the possibility of a "real and intimate relationship" appeared in the person of a faculty wife. In a "casual Cambridge fashion" there was a "great deal of dropping-in" and a great deal of party-giving and party-going among the faculty at Wuhan. This was very much to Julian's taste. He went out often and gave small dinners of his own, once his cook had proved himself moderately accomplished. "I think we can just manage six," he reported to his mother, "which is enough: perhaps later I shall give a big dinner-party, Chinese style: it's more definite, and consequently easier. But you know how I enjoy entertaining, and now it seems I shall really be able to indulge my favourite vice." Late in November, returning home after a party, he wrote to her:

> Your letter answering my first from Wuhan came tonight, and I can't tell you how happy I am. I've fifty things to say to you, and I'm very drunk—alas, solemn, solitary drunk, sobering up on tonic water, only 9 o'clock in the evening. But then Chinese parties are like that—one has dinner 6.30—heavenly

food, and drinking of healths across and around—tonight they produced the famous Tiger's Marrow spirit, which is devastating stuff. . . . Anyway, I'm wildly happy—I've had two letters of yours in two days. And now I really feel we begin communication again. And life here is the greatest fun wildly social now—I either entertain or go out five evenings a week: Chinese, missionaries—2 pretty wives, so they're fun.

And then he began to be more closely involved with Mrs. Chen, or as she rapidly became, Shuhua—or Sue, the way he referred to her most frequently in his letters. In our earlier telling of Julian's life, more than forty years ago, her identify, as those of Julian's other lovers, all of whom were still alive, appeared in our book under a pseudonym, in her case as K., who was presented as someone other than Mrs. Chen, the wife of the dean. This usage was following that of the memorial book itself published after Julian's death. There is no indication of why that particular letter was chosen. Many years have now passed, and the affair has become public knowledge. Some guessed the truth of the matter from our earlier book, including her daughter who had not known about it before. Members of Julian's family and some others knew about it already, particularly as he had written so openly about the affair to his correspondents. And the letters from Julian to Sue are now available, as they have been acquired by the Berg Collection in the New York Public Library. The relationship has been extensively discussed in Patricia Laurence's *Lily Briscoe's Chinese Eyes: Bloomsbury, Modernism and China* (2003). She is also one of the two central figures in *A Thousand Miles of Dreams: The Journeys of Two Chinese Sisters* (2006) written by her great-niece Sasha Su-Ling Welland about her and her sister, Welland's grandmother. They were children of a high Chinese official in Peking who also served at one point as mayor of the city. She is the central figure in an erotic novel about their affair: *K: The Art of Love: Based on a True Story* (2002) by Hong Ying. There is also a quite extensive critical literature about her as a writer.

As Julian settled in, Mrs. Chen helped him, finding crockery and other essentials for his house. She appeared in a letter to his mother on October 16 in a somewhat sexualized context. "Shall I ever find a Chinese mistress, I wonder? Lots of them are attractive, but I doubt there's much doing. The Chens grow nicer and nicer the more I see of them—friendly, sensible, intelligent—the sort of people we should all be devoted to. So far, we've not been able to get

Julian with Shuhua Chen and Chen Yuan. Reproduced with permission from Wuhan University Archives, Wuhan University, People's Republic of China.

an English intimacy, because of our background differences, and the fact that we have only known each other for so short a time; we can hardly talk sex or politics." And then he wrote to his mother on October 23: "I have my angelic Chens as a support and help: she, Shuhua, is an intelligent and sensitive angel. Fortunately she's only reasonably nice-looking, so I'm not yet in love with her. But I can't tell you how nice it is to have someone of the sort as a neighbour. Can you imagine someone quite unaffected, very sensitive, extremely good and kind, with a sense of humour and a firm hand with life: she's a darling, she comes to my Shakespeare and Modern lectures." She was some years older than Julian, though not the ten years he had thought. In the same letter he asked Vanessa to send him a drawing that he might give to her. By October 31, the atmosphere had become a little more intense. All the omens seemed favorable for a possible affair; the casual social arrangements at Wuhan conspired to bring them together often; he was recovering from his illness, although it was still an obstacle. He was clearly tempted, although he appreciated that it might well be a mistake. He wrote to Vanessa: "She's very charming . . . and we meet most days, usually alone. And by now we can talk about anything in the world, including the relations of the sexes. We had one very emotional conversation driving back together in a car from shopping, which made me very uneasy. . . . She's the nicest person I've met here, and one of the nicest I've ever met—well, you see that one changes skies not hearts or lives."[7] The very next day, he wrote to Eddie: "I'm getting into a most complexly delicate situation with the nicest woman I've ever met, Hsu Hua, [sic] my dean's wife. She's as sensitive as Virginia, intelligent, as nice or nicer than anyone I know, not pretty but attracts me, a Chinese Bloomsburian. The whole atmosphere is exactly like Cambridge."[8] He was uncertain of the wishes of the lady, and he was uncertain, too, of how deeply he wanted to be involved. By November 15 he wrote to Virginia that Shuhua was China's leading woman writer and he was "*platonically* in love, more or less."[9] But it clearly was not going to stop there. Love had become a necessity and a habit, yet at the same time he did not savor it as much as he had in the past: he had grown disillusioned. Some months later, when the affair was in full progress, he wrote to a friend:

> It's so hard to get a disinterested emotion out of it [love]. I have, sometimes, got something very valuable, but to be quite honest I don't think it's ever been as good as the peculiar pure thrill I can get from nature: it's much more extensive,

no doubt, one's affected in more ways, more violently, but I only know two, very momentary, emotions I can get from love which seem to me comparable with the other: one's the pleasure of suddenly realizing your lover's physical beauty—the sort of flash of seeing it which hardly lasts a specious present. The other's the perfect intellectual calm and clarity of satisfied lust, when you've gone beyond the bounds of reason and moderation and even pleasure—rather like sleeping on the rack.

But this is to anticipate. At first he and Mrs. Chen were no more than good friends, and he told his mother, "I think we're going to stay that. But it's a ticklish, interesting situation." It remained so a bit longer. But they continued to see each other. She was his guide, helping him with the business of living in China. The likelihood of an affair increased. But for all the sophistication of his attitude—especially as it is made to appear in his letters—he was falling in love. By mid-November he was bothered if he couldn't see her every day. A week later he wrote to his mother: "I've just realised how deeply I'm involved. Oh Nessa dear, you will have to meet her one of these days. She's the most charming creature I've ever met, and the only woman I know who would be a possible daughter in law to you (she isnt, being married with a charming child and 10 years too old!) But she is really in our world."[10] In early December there was a "period of storm": she had come upon an unfinished letter of Julian's to his mother, telling of the "affair—it's almost that," and threatened to break off. But things had already gone too far between them for either of them to take the threat seriously. She was in love with Julian, and Julian wrote to his mother that she was "definitely the most serious, important, and adult person I've ever been in love with—also the most complicated and serious. And one of the nicest and most charming."[11]

Ling Shuhua, her proper name, was an established literary figure in China, a member of the informal literary group the Crescent Moon Society, which was inspired by the title of a book of poems by Rabindranath Tagore. Most of its members had studied in Britain or the United States. It is somewhat ironic that she should be known as the Chinese Katherine Mansfield, considering that his aunt Virginia had somewhat ambivalent feelings about that writer. But it was accurate in that to a degree she modeled her work on Mansfield. She was born March 25, 1900, in Guangdon to the fourth of her father's six wives or concubines. He was a prominent scholar in Peking, where she was brought up. She also spent some early years in Japan, where her father had been ambassador. She was trained as a painter in secondary school and continued to paint throughout her life, in later years having several exhibitions in London and at a museum in Paris. She attended the Sino-American Yanjing University in Peking, graduating in 1924. While a student, she was involved in political protest against Japan's role in China. Her first story appeared in a journal edited by Chen Yuan, then a professor of English at Peking University, who would become her husband some years later. Between 1928 and 1935 she published a novel and three volumes of short stories. At Wuhan, where her husband took up an academic position, she became the literary editor of the *Wuhan Daily*. Many of her stories dwelt on the position of women, concentrating on women weakened by the conventions of society. Recently, her work has received a fair amount of critical attention and has been published in quite a few anthologies, as well as being collected in two volumes in Chinese in 1998, eight years after her death. Julian became involved in her literary life, working on translations of two of her stories, which appeared in China in 1936 and 1937 in an English-language journal the *T'ien Hsia Monthly*, which also had printed seven of his poems. (He wrote several other pieces for English-language publications while in China.) Julian sent three of her stories, which he had translated with her, to David Garnett. Garnett passed them on to Vanessa, who tried, unsuccessfully, to have them published in the *London Mercury*. In the letter conveying them, Julian gave a succinct if perhaps rather romantic summation of her early life. "Her autobiography . . . should be a fascinating work—her mother was the third concubine of an imperial official of the old regime, an absolutely charming man who sounds in some ways a bit like Clive. . . . He was an eminent calligrapher, a connoisseur of painting and poetry, remarkably competent administrator—and he smoked opium, had concubines, courtesans and boys."[12] The Hogarth Press eventually published her story of her early life, *Ancient Melodies* (1953), with her illustrations and an introduction by Vita Sackville-West, who had suggested the title. It was dedicated to Vita and Virginia. After Julian's death, Vanessa, Virginia, Leonard, and Vita did their best to assist her career, particularly after she came to England in 1947. She held exhibitions of her own work and of the art she owned, and in 1967 the Arts Council published *A Chinese Painter's Choice*, selections from her collection. One feels that she might have been a bit of a burden on Julian's connections as a somewhat self-dramatizing woman. She was prone to talk, as she had frequently to Julian, of committing suicide. Vanessa in particular was very kind to her, in Julian's memory, writing her loving letters after his death. On September 16, 1938: "I think Julian has made something between you & me possible by his death that perhaps we could not have had if he were alive—So let us make the most of it, dear Sue. . . . I think it must be easier for me than for you for I feel that Quentin & Angelica depend to some extent on my being cheerful. . . . Julian seems nearer here [Charleston] than anywhere else—everything is associated with him. Even now I could so easily expect to hear his voice and find him sitting on the lawn." And on December 5, 1939: "I still love you & if my love can be of any use to you you know you have it. . . . Please be as happy as you can manage to be in spite of all—I know Julian would have told you the same." And then in 1940 on Julian's birthday, February 4, she wrote, "a day on which I find it very hard not to be overcome by thoughts of him & longing for him." The following August 25, when the war was going badly, she wrote: "The English are a strange people—I don't believe they can really be beaten. . . . I often wonder what Julian would have done—sometimes I am almost glad he isn't here for I know he would have been in danger all of the time. . . . But also he would have been so much interested & would have helped to make things better after the war."[13]

But to return to Wuhan: in an undated letter in December 1935 he wrote to his mother:

> It's been a week of crisis all round: above all, the Japanese & Sue: The former are threatening to cut the railway, and war or other horrors may follow. Sue and I have fallen in love. . . . No, we've not been to bed together, indeed we've not go beyond kissing on the sofa physically, but emotionally it's the whole, full thing. All my worlds in some disorder—for instance I don't know what to do or say about Tony. . . . Anything may happen. The whole atmosphere is like a Russian novel. So be prepared for anything, up to and including my return with a divorcée bride and a stepchild at any moment. . . . I should of course like my friends to know all about it. But I don't think you'd better tell anyone whose discretion you don't absolutely trust. . . . Finally, there's Tony. . . . I think I must tell her. . . . I think I can manage all right—after all, if I could have 3 affairs at once in London I ought to be able to manage one each in Cambridge and Wuhan.[14]

Julian continued to live his life and became absorbed in planning the affair. He had already broached to Sue the possibility of "bed," and she was not unsympathetic, but launching an affair in Wuhan itself was fraught with problems. Simply to find a place where one could be alone, and uninterrupted, was difficult. There were always servants hovering about, and the possibility of blackmail was real. He had clear and rational discussions with her about the various obstacles to be overcome, and he continued them in letters to his friends. "It's hard to plan unconventional immorality in this strange town & country," he complained to Lettice. But the problem of a place, at least, was finally settled: they would go to Peking in January—she ostensibly to visit friends—during the long holiday between terms, and there the affair would truly begin. He was being both romantic and rather pragmatic and perhaps too calculating a planner. He wrote an extraordinarily explicit letter to his mother on December 25, his sister's seventeenth birthday, about her being prepared for a sexual life. "Well, this would have seemed a most improbable letter 50 years ago, wouldn't it? Even now, I suppose 99 out of hundred people, or more, would consider it appalling a son should write like this to a mother about a sister. I like to imagine us all becoming very famous, and then, in some new Victorian age, our letters being published. . . . Stern denunciation of the Sir Leslie's."[15] Vanessa took his letter in stride. At the time, Angelica was in Paris studying. His mother wrote to him on January 25, 1936: "As soon as she returns to London, where she'll begin to lead a grown up life, I'll get in touch with the doctor and do whatever she advises. Does that seem to you sensible? I really quite agree with all you say."[16]

His mood was jubilant but cautious. He was determined not to let romantic impulsiveness lead him further than the limits set by reason. He wrote to his mother on December 17:

> Be prepared for a cable saying "all is discovered," and a demand for money to pay my passage home, or news that I've married her and found some other job in the country. Or that she has committed suicide, as she fairly often threatens. But don't worry about it—the worst would be no worse than annoying (I don't really believe in suicide, naturally) it's all a bit unreal. I don't think I shall get permanently involved—of course I've often thought that, and then thought I should, and I've not been to bed with her yet, which always affects my judgement a lot. But after all I never have got involved yet so deeply I couldn't get out. Besides,

she really is utterly charming—I don't know anyone I've ever had an affair with I thought you'd like more.

In his next letter (a few days later) he brought up a problem to which he had not hitherto given much thought: the husband. "I dont know what his attitude may be, tho' I think he's essentially rational, and wont make a grand fuss. But I dont know if he's to be deceived or told or what." Then there was his fear of scandal, which did not inhibit his telling all his friends in England about the affair. He wrote to Eddie on December 27: "It's my oddest affair to date. She's as intense—and possessive—as your old enemy Helen, also a self-torturer and pessimist asking reassurance. And both jealous and not wanting to lose face. On the other hand, intelligent, charming, sensitive, passionate and a malicious story teller."[17] But the major problem was his feeling for her: how seriously in love was he? That he was in love with her he did not doubt, and he was willing to speculate about a future in which she played some part: perhaps they might even marry, or else live together in China, or in England. But an exclusive monogamous passion, such as she would want, was not what he wanted. He could anticipate difficulties. As he wrote to his mother on New Year's Day, "She's very jealous and I've not really forsworn polygamy." In short, he was in love with her but in his own fashion; and there was a very simple, powerful force operating behind all these doubts and hesitations: his desire to go to bed with a woman after a long period of enforced chastity.

∼

On January 10, 1936, he boarded the train for Peking. It was a long journey, Wuhan being as far from Peking as Paris is from Milan, and he was en route for two days and a night. From the train he wrote exuberantly to Eddie Playfair, "Here I am in a dust storm, in the North Chinese plain, en route for Peking and a 20 days vac with my mistress." And the next day he was there in "the most fascinating great capital I've ever seen or heard of." As he wrote to his mother on January 18, "Could you imagine anything more perfect than coming to Paris [as he had come to Peking] with a mistress who really knows the town, is devoted to one, is perfectly charming, has an impeccable taste in food—its the dream of a romantic—man-of-the-world; the sort of thing Clive ought to do. Also I am meeting Chinese intellectuals, and English, going to the theatre, skating (badly, on bad ice) and making love. . . . I suddenly feel very grown up and at ease in the world." The note of enthusiasm is sustained in letter after letter: to Virginia, "it must be the most remarkable town on earth"; to David Garnett, "the most extraordinary place . . . the right mixture of leisure and sociability and culture with squalor and disreputability"; and to Playfair, "This is undoubtedly the paradise terrest. The sense of amenity of Paris, leisure and antiquity of Cambridge and incredible beauty, frost and blue sky, and almost too much life in the streets." A greater contrast to Wuhan was hardly to be imagined: the sophistication of a great capital against the boring respectability of a provincial university town. He even had a fantasy that Vanessa might come to live there for a year. He welcomed too the opportunity of meeting the "civilized English" in Peking, so different from their counterparts in Hankow, all "punch-headed businessmen and dim missionaries." Friends in England had told him to look up Harold Acton, who was then teaching at Peking University, and he found him charming and interesting: "culture up to the hilt" was his verdict, and again, to Eddie, "very chichi and homo . . . he really understands Chinese culture." [18] Acton gave a dinner party for Julian where Robert Byron, the travel writer, was a fellow guest. On a number of occasions Acton served as a most authoritative guide. He took him to the studio of one of the leading Chinese painters, Qi Baishi, whom Julian described to his mother as "a sage with a long, twisty, thin white beard, skull-cap and spectacles and a charming smile." At length, after much conversation in Chinese between Acton and the painter, they were allowed to see some of his work: "very free, very sensitive water colours," Julian reported, "on long scrolls." The question was broached: "'Might we buy any?' Yes, we might: they cost six dollars a foot. So we picked." Acton, in his autobiography, recalls Julian in the crowded studio, examining a picture of a carp and attempting to reach a decision. "He examined it questioningly, unable to make up his mind. As he stood there, or drooped, in his shaggy clothes, he reminded me of Roger Fry. He had the same air of puzzled scrupulous refinement. One could see his qualms like porcupine quills. Was there anything in this or nothing? 'Was it merely a relic of tradition? How spontaneous was it?'"[19] Julian was extremely hesitant, but finally, when Acton threatened to buy the painting himself, his decision was precipitated, and he bought it for his mother. Acton also appreciated his poetry. The following June he thanked him for a copy of *Work for the Winter*: "It is a joy to taste October pears after the sour berries of Auden and that school . . . and [no] young comrades flushed for some futile rebellion."[20]

But the greatest pleasure, which indeed had the effect of heightening all the others, was to be there with Sue, who seemed ever more charming and fascinating and pleasing to look at, especially since she did not feel obliged to dress in the severe style of the University New Life movement, as she did in Wuhan. Although he wrote to his mother that "the mad interlude has put all else out of my head . . . we are very happy and silly," they did behave with a degree of circumspection, she staying at the house of friends, he in a German pension. They were even more circumspect than Julian would have liked: he reported disapprovingly that "alas in a Chinese restaurant you can't really flaunt a mistress, for you are all partitioned off in little rooms and cubicles." But that did not prevent them from launching their affair and becoming lovers. He was there with an enchanting mistress who adored him, and that he now discovered, just that and no more, was what he wanted. Once the affair was truly an affair, he found it easy to curb his impetuousness. At the end of their second week in Peking, when he and Sue were at their happiest together, he wrote to his mother on February 1: "Be tranquil, my dear. . . . The situation is well in hand and I am quite clear now that marriage would be a disaster. I think even if there is a scandal, it would only mean my returning this autumn instead of next." And of course one barrier to marriage was his relationship with his mother. As he wrote to her some time later, on April 13, "I'm far more devoted to you than I've ever been to a mistress, and indeed so much so that I shall find it very difficult to marry because none of my friends and mistresses can begin to compare with you." He wrote in some detail about the affair to his confidants in England. On January 20 to Lettice:

> And what's it like to have a Chinese mistress? Socially, perfect: that's why I'm enjoying Peikin so much: Sue know the town inside out. Emotionally, terrific. . . . Physically, well, queer. She's tiny. . . . I think slightly cold by nature. . . . Queerly unresponsive: I find it more than commonly hard to know if she's come. . . . I hesitate, the morning after, to send off this letter: it seems to me the sort of thing one might just say, in bed, but shouldn't write. Still, I haven't a confidant here, and indeed I cant think of any other possible confidant. So you shall have it, but I really trust you to be discreet. The situation is pretty tense. I dont see how I can last two years. Her husband is nice, but jealous. She is really desperate. . . . What can one do about a person who doesn't really want happiness, still less

pleasure: who doesnt really want intimacy. . . . I expect sometime this summer there'll be discovery and a row. Then I shall see if I can bluff her husband, or make him keep quiet. If only I can last till the end of the term I shall at least get my fare back. . . . [Yet he concluded his letter:] She's the most charming and delightful person I have ever met.

And he wrote to Eddie at the same time: "She's an admirable mistress. . . . But on the whole, I shouldn't put her very high in bed: on the other hand she's so charming out of it I don't mind. . . . I think she'll be a success in London all right. I shall certainly try and bring her back and show her round." There is a certain irony in these rather ungracious reportings of Sue's sexual character: the premise of the novel *K*, about the affair, was that by teaching Julian the Taoist art of love, she brought him to new levels of sexual ecstasy.

In the last week of the holiday he came down with flu and was confined to his bed in the German pension. Sue was in daily attendance there to nurse and distract him. Nonetheless, the romantic mood diminished further, and he fell prey to "an unreasonable depression," which he attributed to the aftereffects of flu. He wrote cynically to Eddie, who wanted to know all:

> The facts are, unfortunately, that tho' we get on well enough in bed, I'm really very cold about her that way, and she too inexperienced to be really set on me. . . . She's head-over-ears in love with me. Since she's a charming and sensitive and intelligent woman, I find this rather touching and very distressing. I've never seen such intensity of feeling in a human being. And as you can see, response is hard. It's not true that its worse to be in love unloving, than love unloved, but the passive experience is unnerving to a philosophically minded man. . . . Not that I've deceived her: I've told her the exact truth about myself, leading to several painful scenes, based on hypotheses of future unfaithfulness.[21]

Also, he was homesick, and on February 4 he turned twenty-eight.

A passionate love affair did not seem to provide the answer to the question that bothered him most: what was he to do with his life? On February 5, he wrote to his mother:

> I'm gloomy at being 28 and so little done. And at the fact that when I do come back I shall find myself again with nothing to do, tho' I rather hope I can remedy that at least with a little luck with books. . . . The odd thing is having a reputation—in China—as a poet: I feel less like the Chinese idea of a poet than words can express. Well, anyway I've got two years before I'm thirty, and

definitely middle-aged, and Stephens are allowed to begin late. Somehow or other I must get my incongruous box of tricks together.

Soon after this they returned to Wuhan, Sue full of love, Julian full of doubts. Already he had begun to regret all those letters in which he had discussed the possibility of an affair which was now in place. While still in Peking he suggested to Eddie a counter-story which would maintain his reputation as a seducer without seriously endangering his position with those he might have left behind: they were to know that he was still free. "As to the Home Front: I've been foolishly, indiscreet: one always thinks of correspondents each in a separate cell. The story I suggest is that after a short affair we found it didn't do physically, and was socially dangerous, and returned to a very pleasant, intimate friendship." It was also to be bruited about that he was getting a sing-song girl as soon as he had learned enough Chinese, and he added, "Would it were true!"

It was one thing to conduct his correspondence in the manner of *Les Liaisons dangereuses*; it was another to deal with Sue, a "charming and sensitive and intelligent woman" who was passionately in love with him. "I've never seen such intensity of feeling in a human being," he wrote. Unfortunately, he could not respond equally. In fact, he had released an emotional holocaust with which he would have to cope the rest of his time in China. This cannot have been entirely unexpected, or even unwanted: it conformed to one pattern of his affairs. These were ominous signs that his wish now was merely for a generous, untroubled "Latin-sensual" partner in bed. Yet love, desire, and the fascination of the chase drove him heedlessly on. On February 12, back in Wuhan, he was at the bottom of the wave, perhaps an aftereffect of his flu, his mood compounded of weariness, cynicism, and regret. As he wrote to Lettice:

> I've had the most romantic holiday with her in Peking—the most fascinating great capital I've ever seen or heard of. . . . It's the awful situation that usually arises when people fall in love with me. I can respond very adequately when I'm with them, but I never really lose my head. . . . Oh, my dear Lettice, if only I could find a nice, silent, moderately perverse and pox-free prostitute—or some equivalent. Better, if I could only find a couple. I am so tired of emotions—my own and other people's. I don't mean I dont have them. . . . I'm really and sincerely convinced now that I think friendship better than love. And yet one

bit of me stays ultimately involved with Tony, and another automatically makes itself agreeable to every woman it meets. And I've just had a birthday, and feel more futile and useless than words can express. I thought China would be an adventure, but I see it's going to be a period of self-inspection and meditation—perhaps a good thing, but not what I wanted.

He made no attempt to break off from Sue, however, not only because she had threatened, and continued to threaten, to kill herself if he did but because he was still, in his own fashion, in love with her. He resigned himself to the crises and rejoiced in the periods of calm. At the end of February he reassured his mother that Sue was "returning to Normalcy—i.e., not more than one threat of suicide a week, and I think she's getting on better with her husband. In between these crises—which can be moderately assuaged when I assure her at great length that I love her—she's as charming and amusing, and fascinating as ever." They saw each other almost every morning—at his house—and when they did not, she was unhappy. She resented his seeing other people, particularly other women; she forced him to refuse invitations to parties where she would not be present. As time passed, he realized that he had no intimate friends except for Sue herself, and as he complained in a letter, "a mistress isn't the same thing by long chalk." The fear of discovery made their lovemaking less rewarding than it ought to have been: in the mornings, before the arrival of Sue, he would send his servants away from the house, but there was no assurance that they would not unexpectedly return. Beyond this were the dangers of conducting a clandestine affair in an academic community that was "honeycombed with respectability and intrigue." In May he told his mother that his last letter to her had been refused at the post office—"a torn stamp . . . and when they were inquiring who to send it back to, it was opened by one of the professors—an enemy, more or less, of Sue's. However, there's not yet been any fatal result but we're nervous." The crisis passed; the affair continued, as cautiously but no less stormily than before. Julian thought of himself as being particularly adept at dealing with women of very strong emotions, but it was always with an air of resignation rather than gusto. As he wrote to Eddie on March 11: "When you've passed the years of romance—I consider I ceased to be so after my second year of Helen—and when you are at once clear headed and kindhearted—I should only be being mock-modest if I pretended I didn't know I had the qualities—at any rate in love affairs . . .

its a highly educational experience to have an affair with a chinese lady whose also a remarkable writer. . . . Sue thinks nothing of using threats of suicide." And it wasn't enough for him. As he wrote again to Eddie on April 6: "I'm bored, tired, ill at ease with myself: unless I get some excitement soon I shall get depressed and start writing poetry, I know. Perhaps its all just due to my gun having had to be repaired."[22]

Such women seemed to be for him both a necessity and a trial, and the awards and penalties were very evenly balanced. In his affair with Sue he had one commanding advantage: it was he who loved less. He was quite content to see her only in the mornings. It meant that he could busy himself with all the other things he had to do and wanted to do. He enjoyed having a mistress, but he also enjoyed teaching and writing letters, and sailing, and shooting, walking with a dog, and collecting paintings and bronzes, and wandering through the shops of Hankow, and going to dinner parties. Also, he wanted to see more of China. In May he wrote to his mother about his summer plans: "I shall go up the river to Szechuan and then to Omei Shan, a twelve-thousand foot sacred mountain on the road to Lhasa, about a thousand miles away, by river mostly—then by bus and finally on foot." He would be traveling with Yeh, his favorite and brightest pupil, and an English geologist; they would leave in June and be gone until the end of August; afterwards he would have a reunion with Sue in Peking.

∼

Absorbed in the continuing drama of his love affair and otherwise occupied in the varied activities of a provincial university town where nothing ever happened, he responded to the politics of the country with diffidence and mild irritation. Not even the recurring possibility of war between China and Japan excited him. He listened dutifully to the gossip, which he reported in letters home as "inside information," but he was part of a community that, as he said, might have inspired Chekhov or Jane Austen, not Malraux: the tiny disturbances of dons and their wives mattered as much as the movement of armies, and the political agitation of undergraduates. "Once again there's a University crisis," he reported to his mother in February, "over exams, and everyone's nerves are jumping. And again there's war talk: I'm scared over the Russian frontier trouble. . . . I've inside information that [the Japanese] are preparing a war within two months." Although he did not take this very seriously, he thought it best to reassure her that he was in no danger; in the light of later events, his choice of comparison has its prophetic irony: "However, don't get worried. . . . I'm about as far from any possible front as Cambridge is from Madrid." A month later, the possibility of crisis was still to be entertained. He wrote to a friend in the thick of European politics—which seemed real to Julian as nothing in China did—"Life here continues pretty placid—that is, there might be an unholy row or a war with Japan any day, but there's no particular reason to expect either tomorrow. The most note-worthy fact is that I have to go and read a paper to the Hankow Literary Society on Modern Poetry." But while waiting for the crisis to materialize or be dissipated, he had come round to a much stronger and more traditional pacifist position than he had held in London.

> I can't think anything worth war. . . . Even here, with everyone I know and like wanting war, and with an overwhelming case for it—and knowing too that it's not my own country to get damaged and that I should find it fascinating and wildly exciting to watch—and with intensely sympathetic people, like some of my students, being at once reasonable and patriotic—I find I can't really sympathise. . . . It is the last horror, and I can't feel sure enough of any theory to outweigh that certainty. So I'm thankful not to have to make the choice.

That was in February. Throughout the spring there were border incidents, rumors of war and civil war, accounts of Communists fighting government troops in Shensi province. Although Julian was under the impression that the Chinese authorities would not permit travel anywhere deemed dangerous, he was privately hopeful that his journey to the north that summer would take him into an area where he might actually see some fighting. In mid-June he cabled to Leonard Woolf to ask if he could help to get him accredited as a foreign correspondent, a notion more romantic than practical, as he was entirely innocent of professional experience. Nothing came of this possibility, although Leonard did try on his behalf, getting in touch with the *Herald*, the *Manchester Guardian*, and the *Telegraph*. At the same time, he wrote to his mother: "We've been having a scare over civil war, but by now it seems calmed down. . . . I wondered for a moment whether to send telegrams asking for a job as a correspondent, but decided to wait and see what happened—and now it's probably all over. There may, of course, be another crisis but it's unlikely. You're not to bother about it—they fight with paper bullets for the most part, and are terrified of foreigners—or so I've been told." In fact, he had already sent the telegram to his uncle, and when his mother heard of it she was extremely bothered. Whatever reassurance he may have intended by glossing over the truth in his letter, he had only succeeded in convincing her that he was going to put himself deliberately in danger. He apologized once, twice— "I must write again and ask you to forgive me for my telegram to Leonard," he wrote on June 27. "You see, I really felt that I had to try and do something reasonably adventurous after coming all this way—a kind of self-justification, I think. I know it seems mad to you, and so it does at times to me, but I think I can only get quite sane about adventure and danger and violence if I have some small experience of it. But for the time being there's no question of that." Vanessa was very worried about his safety given the various warlike activities going on in China. He tried to reassure her on July 1: "I'm much safer than if I were driving down to Charleston for a bank holiday." By this time the journey had begun, and he was sailing upriver to Yo-chow. (On the ship he wrote the next day, "there was no sanitation, the food (chinese) was doubtful, but we got well-boiled Yangtse water to drink. . . . The engine throbbed, the boat was pretty crowded, but one could wash in disinfectants. We slept in a line of camp beds on the top deck starboard passage way, forward.") In Yo-chow, government troops swarmed; he saw snipers with bamboo-sprigged caps practicing concealment. At a later point on the trip, on July 12, he wrote that embarking on a "Min boat" at Ichang at night, "troops flashed lights on us for red spies or deserters, and were pacified . . . with visiting cards." But encounters of this sort, and there were a few more, hardly constituted the military experience he had anticipated. Still, it was an arduous, uncomfortable, fascinating journey through long stretches of primitive country—by sampan, launch, river steamer, rickshaw, truck, and on foot.

Then, without any explanation, he concluded the diary letter of July 12 with one of the few poems he wrote while in China.

POST COITUM

Across, between, th' entangling net,
Fragile Venus, bothered Mars,
The meshes of the trap are set,
Red-rusted as the tidal stars.
Penetration Nature yet

Admits; integument debars:
Sepia crustacea can beget
As well amid their clicketing wars.

Crab-limbed lock in ocean hold
Of saline mucous foundering deep;
Escape, sea gale winged, through the cold
Red sunsets, blackbeat trees, the steep
English bird-voiced cliffs; till old,
Tangled across the bars, we sleep.

He wrote long diary-like letters to his mother, from Yo-chow, Chungking, Chengtu, and Ta-Chien-lu in Tibet, the furthest point of the itinerary. In a letter to a friend, written from Chengtu on July 23, he remarked:

> I have violent fluctuations of feeling about the country, which is often charming to look at, sometimes produces a beautiful human being and more often works of art, but is so squalid, diseased and populous it can give one the creeps. . . . One effect is to make me at odd moments violently homesick for English country. To be able to sit on the clean grass and smell clean winds, drink unboiled water, bath without disinfectants . . . walk the streets without picking one's way through ordures, and never ride fly-blown sweat stained rickshaws pulled by consumptive children. . . . We hear next to nothing of the outside world, only through the Chinese papers: the Austro-German treaty and now a *coup d'etat* in Spain. It sounds pretty gloomy.

The most remarkable, most difficult, and most rewarding stage of the journey out was the last fifty miles on foot over mountains from Yo-chow to Ta-Chien-lu. Here the sense of being tested was at its strongest, demanding a toughness and resilience Julian was relieved to discover he possessed. There was so much to tell and remember of these final days that he decided, he wrote to his mother on August 3, to "drop diarying and just impressionise. . . . Things that stand out most clearly in my mind are . . . my first corpses—just stript corpses lying beside the road, one dead of some intestinal malady—very evident—the other of typhus or opium. . . . Then there've been two 10,000 feet passes, both, alas, in rain and mist. It was a fiendish job climbing them. . . . There have been bad days—on one I got blistered—and good, as when we got here, a 20 mile stage—by 3.30."

He summed up his trip in a letter to Frances Partridge:

The summer was a most curious and amusing affair, the climax being a journey on foot into Sikong—Eastern Thibet—with an adorable Chinese student, the vice-consul from Chunking, a sensible, solid young man, and extraordinary specimen from London University, who I discovered successively to be the world's greatest bore, prig, fool and complainer. . . . Thibet and the Szechuan border are fascinating country, to which I shall return if it's ever possible. We got out with the last of the central government troops. . . . I even had the experience of hearing a shot fired in anger—tho' I suspect it was pure imbecility, or it wouldn't have come so near me as it did. Still, a feather in the cap.[23]

On August 28, he was at the Hotel du Nord in Peking, whence he had flown from Chengtu, and he wrote to his mother to reassure her that he had come through the journey with no worse aftereffects than "mere footsoreness—though this of a very superior kind. . . . Next time I get grass shoes made to fit me in advance." Then, as though he had paused to listen to her objections: "There certainly will be a next time if it seems at all practicable. . . . But who knows what next year may bring?" Then, as though answering the question, he began yet a new paragraph: "The civil war in Spain makes nasty news to return to."

"After two months' chastity, I naturally feel like a spot of infidelity," he wrote in a letter to Lettice from Chengtu. Then he flew off to Peking and disappointment. Sue was there, as they had planned, but so too was her husband; and the next week she was to go into the hospital for a minor operation. Earlier, Julian had declared that the two essential conditions for romantic love were proximity and chastity. In Peking, this held true for Sue, but not for himself. "She's," he reported to his mother, "even more in love than before, and I'm terrified, overwhelmed, and very much touched. For tho' I'm extremely fond of her, think her an extraordinary and very valuable human being . . . I cant match that sort of feeling."[24] When they returned to Wuhan in September, however, they resumed the affair, and nothing—for good or bad—had changed: he found that he was still in a position of doting and irritated dependence upon her. Her jealousy made him "feel extremely guilty and also frightfully tied and hampered: she's not really my sort of person, tho' I think she's in some ways the most interesting and important I've ever had an affair with." But he made no serious effort to break with her. "Oh these romantics," he burst out, "there's really no contenting them.... There are moments when I feel all I want is to be back where one can lie about on lawns and talk nonsense."[25] The litany of complaints was constant, but if one sets it against his equally constant affection and admiration for Sue, it becomes clear that his dissatisfaction had less to do with this affair in particular and more to do with the life of the emotions in general. "Like George II," he wrote jokingly to a friend, "I prefer the scandal of a gallantry to the fact," and the notorious kernel of truth can be glimpsed in what he said. "To tell you the honest truth, I feel rather bored with all this love business.... I should like a fairly prolonged rest from emotions." This, of course, Sue would not allow him, and his solution was to give way to her, to pretend to emotions which he did not, could not, genuinely feel. "I'm pretty well incapable of romantic love but am exceedingly attached to her. And remembering what utter hell jealousy is I give way, rather than ride roughshod." But however he might rationalize his feelings, he was still committed, as he had been since the beginning of the year, to a passionate love affair that might at any time be discovered; and when this happened, there would almost certainly be a scandal. The prospect did not put him off. "I always knew Sue was too desperate a character for me, and I still know I should have to take whatever might be the 'honourable' course." Very likely this would mean marriage, after a divorce in which he would be named correspondent. The saving thing, he told a friend,

> is that divorce in China is easy but terribly face-losing: the husband would look too ridiculous to the students to continue. This is our sheet anchor. I've an idea that quite a lot of people have guessed the essential truth, but aren't going to let themselves realize it because it would be too tiresome. I even suspect race pride will make them loath to admit anyone as remarkable as Sue would prefer a foreign devil.... If I do have to marry [her] to save her face, I can do it under Chinese law—I think—and hence could get an easy divorce later. But it would be hellish tiresome and I shall do all I can to dodge it.

This was his situation in the early autumn of 1936. Passively, but not incuriously, he waited for whatever was to happen. He wrote hundreds of letters to friends and family—eighty-two were included in the memorial volume *Julian Bell: Essays, Poems and Letters*—and they compose much the largest and perhaps the best part of his literary production during the sixteen months that he was in China. For the rest there were some poems—"little cross-correspondences on fairly trivial themes" he told his aunt, "the results being obscure but, to me, rather pleasing." He published a few short pieces in journals. He considered writing some stories but never did so. He wished to spend time revising his dissertation on the Good for publication. He was extremely busy, devoting much time to his teaching as well as to the essential pleasures of his outdoor life, shooting and sailing. He was also trying to learn Chinese. His primary writings at this time were three long essays, cast in the form of open letters. They represented his most ambitious attempt to come to terms with his heritage and with his own times. Eventually he visualized them being published together, as they eventually were, with other material in, alas, his memorial volume.[26] He himself, in a letter to a friend, referred to the essays as "my testament to our generation," and in a prefatory note written shortly before he went to Spain, he hoped that they would be "relevant and useful." The first, "On Roger Fry," was begun on the voyage out and finished in China, on January 4, 1936. The second, "The Proletariat and Poetry: An Open Letter to C. Day Lewis," was written in the latter part of the same year. The third, "War and Peace: A Letter to E. M. Forster," was begun at the very end of his stay in China, in January 1937, and finished on the ship returning to Europe. There is a significant difference between the first two essays and the third—the former are representative of conclusions he had already reached before coming out to China; the latter, however, reflects the dramatic change in his thinking that followed upon the outbreak of the Spanish Civil War.

Roger Fry had died in September 1934. In November his sister, Margery Fry, had approached Virginia to write his biography. It would be a formidable undertaking, but she hoped to start working on it by October 1935. Fry had been a great friend of Julian's, and a great influence upon him. "After you, Nessa dearest," he wrote to his mother, "I think I owe more to him than anyone, even of my contemporaries; perhaps this is hero-worshiping, but I know that my whole way of looking at life, and particularly at the arts and sciences and philosophy is very largely a result of his conversation and example. And my notion of what the arts—and what human relations—can give is very largely communicated by him." He was eager to write something about Fry and mentioned it to his aunt, who encouraged him, thinking he meant to do a brief memoir, recollections of Roger as he had known him. But in May he wrote to his mother: "As I think of it now it seems to me more a matter of my making a statement of beliefs and feelings and general attitude to life than anything at all like biography. I don't even know how much it will have to do with Roger in the end." He did not actually start writing until September, and when he finished in early January, he was not certain of what he had accomplished. At the end of his stay in Peking, he wrote to Virginia: "I'm going back [to Wuhan] to try and get my poor students to read you and Tom and all, and see what they make of it. I hope also to find typed my disquisition on Roger: perhaps seeing it all in order I shall be able to make out what it's like. I fear it hasn't really much to do with him." And he added, "I'll try and see if I can rake up any more childhood memories [for the biography]; I can't at the moment, but I know I must have lots." For some reason—perhaps his initial uncertainty—he did not send the "disquisition" to the Woolfs until the spring. (He had sent an earlier letter the previous winter with more personal memories of Roger, which Virginia quoted from briefly in her biography.) By then his doubts had been resolved; he hoped that it would be published as a pamphlet in the series of Hogarth Letters, such as Virginia's *Letter to a Young Poet*, Raymond Mortimer's *Letter on the French Pictures*, Rosamond Lehmann's *Letter to a Sister*, and Viscount Cecil's *Letter to an M.P. on Disarmament*.

She sent him a long letter on May 21, 1936, demonstrating the special place that Julian had in her mind and heart. Her beloved brother Thoby, whose first name was actually Julian and after whom, two years after Thoby's death, Julian was named (as Julian's own nephew, the artist and art critic Julian Bell, born in 1952 to Quentin and Olivier Bell, would be named after him). Virginia was also conscious of how much Julian wanted to be kept abreast of all that was happening in England, particularly to his nearest and dearest.

> It's a curse, your being so far away, and then I expect the mitigated culture of your university is rather like skimmed milk. . . . I wish I had spent three years in China at your age, with all the family deaths and extreme intensities—father, mother, Stella, Thoby, George, Jack—I felt I had lived through all emotions and only wanted peace and loneliness. All the horrors of life had been pressed in to our eyes so very crude and raw. And then came the burst of splendour, those two years at Gordon Square before Thoby died, a kind of Elizabethan renaissance, much though I disliked the airs that young Cambridge gave itself. . . . How I wish I had known you in those days. Only I should have fallen in love with you, after my fashion, and you would have loved Nessa, because I always thought her so very much more lovable than I was. . . . Yes, I am going to buy a cottage there

[she is visiting Cornwall], because Sussex is getting far too pretty and suburban. Will you share it with me? We'll live there from months at a time roaming the moors, sitting on the top of the cliffs, watching birds.

Then on June 28 she wrote again, now having read the letter on Roger:

I read your thing on Roger only very slowly. I think its full of ideas; full of sharp insights; and there are a mass of things I would like to pilfer if I write, as I hope next autumn. My criticism is: first that you've not mastered the colloquial style, which is the hardest, so that it seemed to me (but my mind was weak) to be a little discursive, loose knit, and uneasy in its familiarities and conventions. However you could easily pull it together. Prose has to be so tight, if its not to smear one with mist. L. has read it and agrees with me on the whole. As Nessa may have told you, we cant use it as a letter, because it is too long; also, the letter series has proved a failure, and we have stopped it. What L. suggests is that it should be sent to Scott James of the Mercury, who might print it in two parts. . . . I think the ideas were extremely interesting; I must go into them carefully. I wished there were more 'personality' but there's enough to give a hint of his relations with the younger generation. Thank goodness, you'll be back before Ive done anything that could be printed; so we can discuss it. Nessa relieved me greatly by saying that you mean to come home in two years—I thought it was three. . . . Leonard went to the Society dinner. . . . It seems doubtful if the Society will pull through the crisis; whether it isnt the relic of too high a civilisation to attract the young who must have politics and real life to gnaw. . . . Societies seem wrong for me, as I do nothing; and with Leonard meeting a dozen times a week and filling the drawing room with Bernal and Miss [Margaret] Gardiner and Ha [Margery Fry] and Aldous [Huxley] we do our bit for liberty. What can I do but Write? Hadnt I better go on writing—even by the light of the last combustion? . . . Never a day passes but we dont get asked either to sign a protest, telegraph a message, or join a new group. . . . How I envy them [Duncan and Nessa at Charleston]! There they sit, looking at pinks and yellows, and when Europe blazes all they do is to screw their eyes up and complain of a temporary glare in the foreground. Unfortunately, politics get between me and fiction. . . . I sometimes think that old Bloomsbury though fast dying, is still our bulwark against the tawny flood. So come back and drive your stake in, before we are overwhelmed.[27]

The Woolfs' decision not to publish, no matter how tactfully expressed, hurt Julian quite a bit. Virginia would later feel guilty about how they had handled the situation. The Woolfs must have been somewhat taken aback to discover how little his disquisition had to do really with Roger Fry, and how much with

Julian himself. Even this need not have counted against it, but the Woolfs, who were in their respective ways dedicated to their work and unrelenting in the demands they made upon themselves, were put off by what they considered the carelessness of the writing, thinking, and organization of the piece. What Julian had sent was, they considered, unfinished work: a first draft.

The following October Vanessa wrote intriguingly to him about her and David Garnett's feelings about the Woolfs. No doubt she was being supportive of Julian. "I do think there is something odd in the Woolfs attitude [toward the Fry essay], which I discussed with Bunny—I forgot if I told you his theory is that V. lives so precariously (in nerves & brain) that she cant face any other writer of any real merit. . . . Bunny thinks its not exactly jealousy—but some need to keep her own poise. . . . [Leonard] is I think curiously narrow & limited in his appreciations."[28] "The whole publishing business makes me furious," he exploded to his mother. "I do think Virginia is exceedingly tiresome. She wrote me a letter saying she thought my Roger work needed re-writing etc. I really don't believe it. I dont think I could say it any better, anyway not at present. But since they wont have it, there's an end of them."[29] Conceivably he might have profited from his aunt's suggestions, but he was too hurt or too proud to pursue the question further. Indeed, from the time he had been an undergraduate at King's, there was always a degree of ambivalence in his feeling about her: on the one hand, she was his beloved aunt; on the other, she was the older generation, a writer of great fame and achievement whom he could not help but envy. His way of dealing with the problem was to patronize her a little: "I'm sorry the novel's still on your hands: though it's still a complete mystery to me how you ever produce the things. I often think it would be great fun to sit down and invent stories." She too had mixed feelings, as she wrote after his death, on "the damned literary question."

> I was always critical of his writing, partly I suspect from the usual generation jealousy; partly from my own enviousness of anyone who can do in writing what I cant do [presumably she is referring here to Julian's poetry]. . . . I thought him very careless, not "an artist," too personal in what he wrote, & "all over the place." This is the one thing I regret in our relationship: that I might have encouraged him more as a writer. But again, thats my character; & I'm always forced, in spite of jealousy, to be honest in the end. Still this is my one regret; and I shall always have it; seeing how immensely generous he was to me about what I did—touchingly proud sometimes of my writing.[30]

But she was right about the piece itself, which was finally published in the memorial volume and proved to be very loose and discursive, "all over the place"; or as E. M. Forster remarked in a comment on the letter Julian had addressed to him, "all over the shop." It is the same complaint that can be made against all his formal efforts in prose, "The Good and All That" as well as the later essays. He would begin with one idea, appear to develop it, abandon it, launch another, follow it in its course, abandon it, launch another, suddenly return to the first idea: at times one has a sense less of argumentation and exposition than of free association. He himself was conscious that all was not proceeding as logically as it might. "So, after this endless divagation," he begins a paragraph, "I return to my theme." But the next paragraph begins, "I cannot yet get my argument clear," which is not simply a rhetorical device but a statement of fact. He is constantly commenting on his difficulties: "Now I come to the hardest part to write"; "Yet I become conscious that I am again distorting my description"; "But I am going ahead too fast again," and so forth. One can only guess at his method as a writer of prose. The evidence of the essays themselves suggests that he was a writer who thought as he wrote, his thought taking shape and reshaping itself as he went from sentence to sentence. So that very often the announced intention is not borne out by the end result, which is not to deny that the end result is very often more interesting than the announced intention. He himself was quite pleased with the Fry essay.

"On Roger Fry" is written as a letter from Julian, "a poet," to A., "a scientist." (Perhaps A. was his lover Antoinette Pirie.) The aim of the letter, announced in the first paragraph is "to give an account of one of the few men of genius who have ever made a real synthesis of the attitudes of artist and scientist. I am not trying to write a biography: what is more important is to make explicit an attitude to life; one that combines the sensuousness and sensitiveness of the artist with the clearness and hardness of mind, the resolute intellectualism of an admirable scientist." He goes on in the next paragraph to admit, "My art lacks means . . . to capture the physical and individual traits which made Roger Fry's company one of the greatest and most vivid pleasures that I have known in human intercourse," and so he will "try to deal with more simply intellectual questions, with an attitude, beliefs, opinions, lines and methods of thought." So much for prologue; we are prepared now for the entrance, so to speak, of Roger Fry. But no—"I shall find it easier to expose his attitude if I first try to define yours and mine . . . it can't be summarised by saying that we are socialists."

Having summarized, he then defines, and there is an interesting elaboration of the point, in Julian's most self-confident manner:

> Like nearly all the intellectuals of this generation, we are fundamentally political in thought and action: this more than anything else marks the difference between us and our elders. Being socialist for us means being rationalist, common-sense, empirical; means a very firm extrovert, practical, commonplace sense of exterior reality. It means turning away from mysticisms, fantasies, escapes into the inner life. We think of the world first and foremost as the place where other people live, as the scene of crisis and poverty, the probable scene of revolution and war: we think more about the practical solution of the real contradictions of the real world than possible discoveries in some other world.

It might be argued that this is an attitude that has less to do with socialism than with those eighteenth-century virtues Julian had so long idealized. And so it proves. For after admitting, "I hold the socialist attitude precariously, against both inner and outer chaos," he continues with a line of thought he had first expounded in letters to John Lehmann in the summer of 1929. "It [the socialist attitude] has been achieved [by himself] as a result of reflections on the art of poetry, and on the semi-philosophical questions that attract rationalist poets. Conscious like everyone else of the worn-out uselessness of the romantic tradition, I turned back to the classic movement that began in the seventeenth century, and found in Pope and Racine an art that used the rationalist intellect to control without denying the violent chaos of the emotions." He is now ready to take up his subject, "an exposition of Roger Fry's general attitude," and he declares, "his was a rationalism so subtle and so profound that he could cope with, and enjoy, chaos itself: that there was nothing in the universe, apparently, nor in himself, that he could not contemplate with an impartial detachment, ready to accept or reject anything on its merits."

This declaration appears on the fourth page of his forty-seven-page essay. Revealing though it might be to do so, we shall not follow him paragraph by paragraph to his final sentence: "The attempt might well baffle genius; it is not for my talents." Our particular interest is in the underlying intention of the essay as it is gradually disclosed: Julian's wish to import the ideas of Bloomsbury into the 1930s, to prove them as relevant and useful to the age of politics as to the age of art and personal relations that it had succeeded. He felt that Fry summed up in himself the ideas and ideals of Bloomsbury that he, Julian, valued most. Fry's impartiality seemed to him more sensible, for example, than the commitment of Leonard Woolf and E. M. Forster to a humanitarian liberalism, "This silly taste for democracy," as he irritatingly put it in the "Letter to Day Lewis." Why should one not approach politics, poverty, and war with the same detachment, rationality, scientific curiosity, and emotional control as Roger Fry had looked at a painting? This is the central question (or idea) of the essay, and its answer becomes a feat of extrapolation. Having offered a potted summary of "the general position of art in nineteenth century civilisation" and "the 'hardheaded' tradition of Cambridge and scientific philosophy," he arrives at Fry's "disciplined aestheticism. . . . I have talked of a 'good taste of the emotions'—it comes to very much the same thing. And the conclusion of the whole matter is to find . . . its value outside the arts, in dealing with 'life'—that is, in systematising and controlling our attitudes in the emotional situations that arise either from our dealings with individuals, or large groups of human beings, or with the brute facts of the world." He is determined to make "the jump from aesthetic to life." And the value of a "disciplined aesthetic" in "life" is that it allows one to control "violent emotions with a view to effective action." Also, it allows one "to behave rationally." In fact, this was an ideal of conduct Julian had set for himself, as we have seen, as early as 1929; and he seems to have felt, at least while writing the essay, that he had achieved it, however precariously. He had chosen a position on the Left on "impartial grounds: I am a socialist because I believe that socialism will tend to maximise human pleasure (and therefore human value) and can give us a stable society free from war in which the not uninteresting possibilities of the human race can be explored." Then, as though to prove his impartiality and detachment, he added, "If I thought fascism could do as much I should try to get over my traditional instincts and become a fascist." He was so beguiled with his notion of making Fry a kind of patron saint of the Left that he glided over an admission of some significance: the qualities of the "disciplined aesthetic" that he has singled out "are, in fact, the 'intelligence' and 'common sense' we use in life, since the pure intellect and scientific method can hardly be brought to bear upon most problems; these are presented to us with incomplete knowledge and the need for immediate action." In short, to make a revolution and to look at a painting are two very different kinds of activity; and no practising Communist would ever deny that there was something to be said for common sense and intelligence.

But there is an air of unreality about the essay that has the effect of dulling its impact: it is very much closet speculation, a recapitulation of favorite themes and notions brought into a new context—a tribute to Roger Fry—but essentially unchanged. One has no sense of engagement, that these are notions meant to be tested against the realities of politics and war. Something of the same objection must be made to the polemical letter to C. Day Lewis, "The Proletariat and Poetry." Julian's intention, as he told a friend, was "to reprove the poets for enthusiasm," and the essay does emerge as a kind of companion piece to "On Roger Fry": he sets the virtues of "disciplined aestheticism" against the vices of "hot Marxism." But for all the cleverness and justification of much of his attack it remains too restrictive a controversy, and it suffers from Julian's having been away from England. One has the sense that he has not really kept up with his rival poets, that he is refighting old wars, the hostilities and jealousies of his time in London on Taviton Street. Many of the generalizations are in a generalized way true, but the useful attack that is promised on Thirties Poetry itself, and the effect upon it of a neurotic, emotional, soft-headed attachment to the Left, is never adequately made. Meanwhile his own hardheadedness is leading him down paths of speculation that are not entirely pleasing to contemplate: "The disgraceful part of the German business is not that the Nazis kill and torture their enemies; it is that socialists and communists let themselves be made prisoners instead of first killing as many Nazis as they can." He was becoming increasingly convinced of the need to use force to achieve political aims.

The course of events of the 1930s was catching up with his essays and speculations. He felt himself under a continuing pressure to move into the role he had been straining towards (and resisting) all his life: the man of action. He had enjoyed his first year at Wuhan, but it had never been intended as a permanent arrangement, nor did he wish it to be. Almost from the time of his arrival in China he was concerned with the question of what he was to do when he returned to England. And, again, as news of European events filtered into the provincial fastness of Wuhan he was increasingly troubled as to when he should return.

In the spring of 1936, when the League of Nations was attempting to deal with Mussolini's aggression in Abyssinia and there was a possibility that Hitler might move, Julian wrote to Eddie, "I feel if it gets too threatening I shall have to try to get back before it [the war] starts. I don't fancy being stranded out here while everything at home pops."[31] This note is sounded again and again in his correspondence. But although he lived with a sense of continuing political crisis, his attitude before the outbreak of the Spanish Civil War was more resigned than determined: rueful, passive, mildly ironic. Very likely nothing would happen, and he would finish his three-year term at Wuhan and return to England most probably to some sort of political job, perhaps as secretary to someone important in the Labour Party. But nothing was definite. "You can't conceive how middle-aged I've grown," he wrote to a friend in April. "I shall return—I suppose in some months' time—thin, bald, liverish, opinionated and passé. Then a last half-hearted fling—I hope Angelica will have plenty of easygoing friends by then. And finally Hitler."

By the spring of 1936 the novelty of being in China, of teaching English literature to Chinese students, of having a fascinating and demanding Chinese mistress had quite worn off. The visit to Peking in January, where his affair with Sue was inaugurated, had been a high point. His mood then was exhilarated and self-confident: "I suddenly feel very grown up and at ease in the world." But he was never able to persuade himself for long of the reality of his Chinese present, and thoughts of his European future were only seldom absent from his mind: "I keep thinking about what will happen to me when I return," he wrote to his aunt in February. "How shall I find a steady job?, and a wife, and settle down to a contented middle age? How, indeed? However, all sorts of things will have happened by then. Or they may not. Here, in China, where they all expect the end of the world in about three months, I begin to believe it won't end. Perhaps England will just shake about a little, and then Stephens and Stracheys and all will go on as they always have done. Perhaps. But it really isn't likely." That month *Work for the Winter* was being published by the Hogarth Press. He allowed the event to pass by unnoticed in his correspondence, nor did it inspire him, then or later, to a view of himself as a full-time poet. It was part of the oddness, the unreality of things, that he should have a reputation as a poet in China but virtually none in England,

and although there had been one discerning and appreciative review, in the *Times Literary Supplement,* he knew that his second book had not established him as a poet, and felt this more keenly than he would admit. To his uncle, who wrote to him about the book in April, and as his publisher reported that sales thus far had been small and reviews sparse, he replied, "Many thanks for your letter. I didn't imagine there was much chance of anyone reading verse at the moment. But I was pleased with the Lit. Sup. review and one or two minor ones that my press cutters have sent me." And that was all; the rest of the letter was devoted to politics—it was as though he were finally closing a door. Yet if he was not to be a poet, or at least a writer of some sort, what then was he to be when he returned to England? Depressed by his "lack of achievements," he also regretted his "lack of definite specialized abilities." To be splendidly amateur in whatever one did counted for less than he had expected. That he should have written so little poetry while in China—only one minor exercise, "Post Coitum," can be surely claimed for the period—he himself explained perhaps too simply: he was not miserable enough. One might have expected that the Chinese landscape, or the romantic complications in his own life, would inspire him to poetic statement. Neither did, however. Earlier, as he was setting out for China, he had told Lettice that he must have either misery or stability to work. He seems to have found enough of the latter for prose—the three long essay-letters—but not enough of the former, despite all his agitation with his "Chinese Caroline Lamb," for poetry. In April he complained to Eddie Playfair that "the only person I can talk to intimately is hopelessly in love with me. No one to laugh and crack bawdy jokes with. I'm bored, tired, ill at ease with myself; unless I get some excitement soon I shall get depressed and start writing poetry." But already he was immersed in plans for his journey to the north that summer and its promise of new excitement, new country to explore, and even the possibility of military adventure.

On July 23, in Chengtu, he learned from a Chinese newspaper of the uprising, five days earlier, of rebellious generals against the government of Spain. In a letter written on that day he referred to it as a *"coup d'etat,"* adding, "It sounds pretty gloomy," but he had no way of knowing from the brief, rather garbled account that full-scale civil war had begun. The further he proceeded on the journey to Ta-Chien-lu, the more infrequent grew the occasions for seeing even a week-old Chinese newspaper. He was engrossed in the excitements of travel, "the buttered tea and God knows what all" in the world of the lamas. There was no news from Europe. In late August, before flying from Chengtu to Peking, he wrote to Lettice that he was waiting to "take up the papers again and face what sounds [like] bloody news of Spain. I suppose its been filling all your minds the last month?" And from Peking, five days later, after reading the English newspapers, he wrote to his mother: "The civil war in Spain makes nasty news to return to. I cant help wondering who, if any, of my friends are involved. As long as nothing of the kind starts in France." As he wrote to Frances Partridge, "I'm still expecting to hear that all the young poets have gone to Spain to fight for the proletariat."

The questions that had concerned him from the time of his arrival in China—when should he return to England, and what would he do there?—began to take on an air of urgency. From a distance of five thousand miles he followed events in Spain with the closest attention. But distance made it possible too to think a while longer in terms of familiar alternatives. Reassured by his successful year at Wuhan, he wrote, "I'm really rather a good and socratic educator. . . . The college [King's] had better give me a fellowship when I return, and let me teach their young men for them." On the other hand, "I think I shall have to see what can be done about going into politics—Labour. Can you see me as a private secretary? I'm incredibly efficient now, you know, after getting porters started at 6.0 every morning." And a month later, "I've more or less made up my mind when I come back to try and find a serious political job—but for choice one where one doesn't make speeches or argue." But in the same letter—on September 25, 1936—he preferred "the prospect of being killed in a reasonable sort of war against Fascists rather than just choking out," and concluded, "I mayn't care much about the human race, but don't like seeing our side beaten in Spain." He was always wary of "enthusiasm"—the charge he had brought against the thirties poets in his letter to Day Lewis—and he had not yet arrived at, or was not yet ready to announce, a full commitment: that he would fight in Spain, that there was where he meant to risk death against the Fascists. So he appeared to be turning over alternatives for the future in his mind; and in his letters to his mother, whom he knew would be terribly upset if he were to go to Spain, he emphasized his hopes for a political job when he returned. But he had moved the probable date of his return to the next summer—a year earlier than originally planned—and suggested he might even come back in the early spring; he would not hesitate to do so, if there proved to be a Fascist uprising in France, as Claud Cockburn's paper, *The Week* (to which he subscribed) had hinted there might be. Where France was concerned, there was an urgency, an intensity of personal feeling and attachment, that was very different from his feeling for Spain, which was not a country he knew and loved but a place where "a reasonable sort of war against Fascists" was being fought. Still, for all his determination to proceed reasonably, he must have suspected very early on what his commitment would ultimately be. Even to his mother he began—in an indirect way—to advance the possibility that he might go to Spain. On September 20 he wrote to her, "Well, you may be thankful I'm safe in China, for I know in England I should be feeling the only reasonable thing is to go and fight the Fascists in Spain—for even at this range I feel all the talking is silly." Or as he wrote more explicitly to Sue: "I've begun to believe that the fascists are going to win in Spain, which means that all the things I care about, and people, are going to be in really serious danger in a year or two. I seriously think I must go down to Shanghai some time and buy myself a revolver for future use—its not easy to get one in England. What a prospect."[32]

His political beliefs clarified. At the very time when most of his contemporaries on the Left were being caught up in a wave of idealism, he was determined to be as hardheaded and realistic as possible, and thought of himself as a convert to Machiavelli, "much more modern and to the point than Marx." Hence he dismissed the League of Nations, that favorite cause of Goldsworthy Lowes Dickinson's, as hopelessly impotent, incapable either of enforcing the peace or of putting an end to war. To Playfair, who was in Geneva to attend a session of the League, he wrote, "with luck you may hear the funeral service. An exceedingly good thing if it [the League] could be buried, for then the liberal pacifists would have to jump. . . . There just isnt a sound and decent policy visible, everything is going anyway to mean rearmament, and thats bad enough. I only hope we do it efficiently. My motto is going to be vive Machiavel, the only way to make sense of Marx."[33] He felt that the Labour Party should make a show of assenting to the government's policy of nonintervention: "It's silly to think the Tories will give any real help to the Left in Spain—so that all we can do effectively is to insist on neutrality, bring up all shady incidents, be legalistic and tiresome and give all the underhand help we can.... The only thing now is to down the Fascists with the minimum of loss and fuss."

Spain had captured his imagination more than he might have wished; the "Machiavellian" discovered himself emotionally engaged by the struggle. He wrote to a friend in late September: "I fancy being here has kept me from making a fool of myself pretty completely over the business and also salved my conscience; I know I should feel rather ashamed of myself if I'd been in England and not tried to volunteer, which would no doubt have led to some ridiculous fiasco.... Yet in a way I find it rather more inspiring to have the prospect of finishing off with a decent fight on one's own side than just going phut in a lethal chamber. As you'll see I'm moving Left in sentiment." To this he added in his next letter, "I don't know which I think sillier, Liberals or Communists—and yet I dislike being a minority of one." In his own way, at various times, he had been a theoretical Marxist and a convinced socialist and a member of the Labour Party, but he had never found a satisfactory political niche for himself in England nor a cause or movement in which he could wholeheartedly believe.

Now he was discovering one—"our side"—that aligned him with much of his generation, but still in his own way. John Lehmann has written of the outbreak of the Spanish Civil War and its impact upon young English intellectuals of the Left:

> Everything, all our fears, our confused hopes and beliefs, our half-formulated theories and imaginings, veered and converged towards its testing and opportunity, like steel filings that slide towards a magnet suddenly put near them. For, as Stephen Spender wrote in the introduction to the anthology of *Poems for Spain* which we produced together two years later, "what all felt was that the long, crushing and confused process of defeat, which the democratic process had been undergoing, has been challenged in Spain, and this challenge has aroused hope all over the world." It is almost impossible to convey the strength of this feeling to anyone who was not subjected to the pressures that preceded the summer of 1936, the mixture of relief and apocalyptic hope that flared up as the struggle began.[34]

Julian's reaction was a good deal less affirmative, and perhaps more realistic, than this. In a letter to Lehmann in September he burst out enthusiastically, "What a show, GODS what a show," although he brought himself up short almost at once with, "And if the Right wins I suppose France next, and then us. What hell." A month later he wrote to Playfair:

> Spain is getting badly on my nerves, and now *The Week* are prophesying similar horrors in France. . . . I don't see how war [presumably international] can conceivably be avoided, nor how any kind of decency, democracy, freedom or toleration can survive. In fact, Ive had to admit to myself that Ive really become by now a social fascist—in the strict meaning of the term. I don't like the idea much, but it seems preferable to being killed by common fascists. What I mean is that I no longer believe in reason, persuasion and compromise—nor in justice—which I think good things, but hopelessly out of date. And I do believe in force and treachery, which I don't really like. . . . It's a wretched business, and I can think of little else. . . . There is a temptation too to resign and come home next spring, tho I still want to stick it out if I can.[35]

At approximately the same time he told his mother, "It really makes me miserable or furious—according to my mood—to read about Spain, and think what it probably means to us." In such moods he was tempted to resign his post and return to England—at least he would be "back in the centre of things where one has a chance to get something done." By contrast, the triviality of teaching "Proust and Sidney in successive hours" was one of the minor horrors of life, "And what a fiddling while Rome burns!" In a new form, confronted by a new alternative of the utmost seriousness—Spain—it was the old problem of what he was to do with his life.

Should he remain in China for another year? Or should he return to England in the spring and make an attempt, through Leonard Woolf, to find some sort of job in the Labour Party? Then there was the third alternative, to fight in Spain. He realized that the greatest obstacle to his going to Spain to fight Fascists would not be the complication of arranging it in London, or resigning from Wuhan and terminating his affair with Sue, but its effect upon his mother. It was really a double problem. Their relationship was so extraordinarily close that to endanger it by the possibility of death in battle might seem an act of almost willful cruelty. And there was the more generalized problem that his mother and many of her friends had been conscientious objectors during the First World War, and were still dedicated pacifists. He knew that she would disagree initially with his feelings about the civil war in Spain, but he felt certain that she was capable of understanding ("even when we have perfectly different interests and desire—as mine about wars and excitements—we seem to understand each other"), and it was very important to him that she do so. They were a Bloomsbury mother and son: they would have a clear and rational discussion; he would hope that understanding would triumph over her feelings of maternal solicitude.

Early on, Vanessa sensed that he would be tempted to go to Spain given his growing antifascism and fascination with war and the military. In her letter to him on October 10 she wrote:

> I am really glad you're not in Europe now.... I understood your wanting to go & see what war was like & perhaps I should understand your wanting to go to Spain if you were here—only do think nearly all war is madness. Its destruction and not creation & its mad to destroy the best things and people in the world—if one can anyhow avoid it. You object to cutting down trees—isn't war that, a million times worse? I see one couldnt avoid joining anti-fascist if fascists started attacking as they have in Spain—But I think you & other young people, who are the only hope of the world for the next 40 or 50 years, can do much more to help by not going out of your way to be shot. Of course going as a war correspondent is different—but I *am* glad my dear that I don't have to reconcile myself to your rushing off to Spain. I think though, if it were necessary, I could find plenty of arguments against your doing so, but I wonder if they'd prevail.[36]

∼

There was tension at all levels of his life in that autumn of 1936. The two most demanding of Julian's major heterosexual relationships had been his first, with Helen, and the last, with Sue. He did have tense moments with Lettice, but on the whole the relationships with her and with Tony were on an evener keel, perhaps because these women had other lovers as well. After their difficult meetings in Peking, he and Sue had returned to Wuhan and resumed their affair. Sue was more in love than ever; Julian was restless and dissatisfied. Devoted though he still was to her, he would not have been averse to a "spot of infidelity." Possible candidates had appeared at Wuhan, the one Chinese, the other English. About both of them he wrote to his mother that they had not yet "complicated life, tho' they may do so." At the same time, Sue's marriage, not unexpectedly, was going through a period of storms. Her husband still did not know, apparently, of the nature of the relationship between his wife and Julian, but he did know that she was spending a lot of time with him, and he resented it. Julian described the situation to his mother: "Scene between Sue and her husband, followed by nerves and insomnia on her side and on his by a week of almost unbroken silence, followed by his writing in his diary—which is apparently his only means of communicating with her—that the situation had grown unbearable, and then by his telling her that she had to make up her mind what she meant to do. All this about nothing in particular, just her coming to see me, and such like. She seems to have behaved pretty hysterically."[37] The subsequent event, described in this letter and also in a letter to Eddie, was: "She—oh god how typical of her, of women, of china—started experimenting in a semi-suicidal fashion with her sleeping draught and gave herself a frightful headache."[38]

Then, almost at once, came the always feared, but never-really-expected-to-happen denouement: they were caught, in flagrante delicto, by the husband. "Well, at last there's been the great row over Sue," he wrote to his mother:

> Fortunately theres the minimum of damage done. At least, thats what I think; at the moment I feel rather appalled, and I fancy I'm in for a certain amount of misery. Well, for the facts; we were caught—a ridiculous scene reflecting credit on no one; I thought it very comic at the time—so indeed it was—but dont feel like describing it now. Then an eclaircissement, and a provisional agreement, finally decided this evening—or provisionally finally. Her husband behaved very reasonably considering what an idiotic position he was put in, and that he was pretty much bouleversee, not having got the full truth till the last moment. He offered her the obvious alternatives of a divorce by consent—an easy and private affair—a separation without a divorce or returning to him and breaking completely with me. She has chosen the last. I am going to resign—to ease the tension—on perfectly indifferent grounds; I shall say my family want me to return for undisclosed reasons, presumably disgraceful, and shall tell my friends that I want to return for political reasons, which is true. . . . From a purely selfish point of view no doubt I am well out of it, and I am at least happy to think it will relieve you. Possibly she may manage to make some sort of life for herself, though she resisted all my persuasion to separate from her husband and I think it will be very hard indeed for them to get on together. . . . I besought her to marry me, foreseeing all the storms that would mean, but reckoning that she would really thrive on them. I think I saw too what a life it would lead me. None the less, shes the only person I know who would be worth it. She rose to the occasion of a crisis, as she always does, and was very superb—its a pity furious

women attract me so much. And so completely charming. Its hard to believe I may never see her again. . . . But the temporary solution provides for everyone saving what is left of their faces, which is anyway a good thing.[39]

He sent out the news to his regular correspondents. To Eddie:

> I wont pretend to be heartbroken, but she was the most charming person I ever met, and so much so that I would marry her in cold blood and conscious of all the difficulties of her appalling temperament. . . . I shall suffer more than I thought or expected. But Nessa is a sheet anchor for me emotionally, and like previous disasters I have come out of this one harder and older and clearer. Helen cleared me of romanticism. Lettice of timidity and scrupulousness. Sue has made me feel that love affairs are really better subordinated to friendship. . . . Let me not prophesy rashly—but I will never again if I can help it get myself involved with anyone who demands more than pleasure and conversation. I shall probably tell such people as Marie [Mauron] and Phyllis [Lintott] and Lettice and Tony.[40]

To Quentin: "You've probably heard from Nessa about our catastrophe and my resignation: I expect you'll think it's the best solution; perhaps it is, but it doesn't feel like it at the moment."[41]

But the note of regret is heard most clearly in his next letter to his mother. He had wanted to be free; now that he was, he wished he were not. It was the same duality of feeling he had experienced in each of his love affairs but more intensely now than ever in the past:

> I'm finding out now what I lost, and all the little things. Having seen someone every day for more than a year, and someone so charming, it is very difficult to resign oneself. And then, the alarums and excursions. . . . She's such a devil when she cares to be, and yet completely charming. I feel reasonably certain you would have liked her a great deal—tho perhaps not as a daughter in law. . . . I try to be sensible, but Nessa, you wont be too cross with me if I do end by marrying her? Its not likely; but I can't see her suffering too much without trying what I can do. . . . I write this not to break the ice to you, but to cover a possible disaster.[42]

He had been on the verge of matrimony in the past. It had not come to that then, nor did it now. Sue would not accept his offer to marry her, perhaps because she felt it had been inspired by pity. But although she had promised not to communicate with him, in fact she continued to do so, by letters and even in person, so the crisis was not allowed to abate, and Julian's mood changed from regret to exasperation. "Sue of course can't accept the situation and writes me secret letters or contrives meetings, etc. . . . I thought I was good at standing emotion, but really I'm jumping disgracefully." Towards the end of November, he found the new turn of events intolerable. Sue was determined that they must see each other; at the same time, she refused to let Julian face it out with her husband and receive his permission for their meetings. Julian felt that everything was likely to explode in open scandal, with or without the suicide that Sue was constantly threatening. Finally, he persuaded her to go to Peking for a while, and there was calm in Wuhan. "The only pity of it all," he wrote to Eddie, "is that I find I miss her more and more as time goes on, and particularly want to go to bed with her again. But one cant have ones girl and ones peace of mind at the same time." He ran rapidly through a gamut of responses in the wake of the episode: regret, concern for Sue, then an airy cynicism. With the volcano, as he put it, safely in Peking, he could explore the possibilities of another lady: "Now that Ive found I can get women to sleep with me by having a reputation as a kind of man women sleep with I no longer bother as much as I used to over my lack of graces." He also wrote to Eddie that "[Sue] says shes going to write a history of the affair, which will be fascinating if she does it, and might possibly be an important work—and so I shall have a raison d'etre in literature after all."[43]

By the end of November he no longer regretted losing Sue; he could envision a time, perhaps in England, when he might "persuade her into moderately reasonable behaviour," and if he were able to do that, he told his mother, "I dont know anyone who would be such pleasant company." This was very different from the tone of his letters only three weeks earlier. "I begin to wonder if the tragedy isn't going to turn out comedy after all," he wrote at the end of November, and so it proved. During December and January, his final months at Wuhan, his romantic intrigues—perhaps in reaction to the long and deeply felt passion with Sue—were in the style of French farce. There were the two other ladies he was interested in, Lian Hungying and Innes Jackson; both were managed simultaneously, but neither was to know of the other, especially Lian, who belonged to the long line of "furious women." This was a particular challenge as they were sharing a house and were good friends, having met as fellow students of Margery Fry's at Somerville College, Oxford. Lian was teaching at Wuhan, and Innes was studying classical Chinese. And Sue was threatening to return from Peking.

"I seem to get far too involved, in love affairs, without being really a very emotional person—oh, rather, but not very, nor yet a Don Juan."[44] His women had their revenge upon him, for in reaction to his not caring as deeply for them as they thought he should, they became highly emotional, difficult, furious. He, who simply wanted a mistress who would share the pleasures of conversation and bed, found himself with women whom he goaded, unconsciously, into playing the virago. After the disaster of Sue, he summed up a final theory of conduct in a letter to Playfair: "An irregular polygamy and a cynical realism—as long as you realise the reality of the emotions—is about the best that can be done." Putting the theory into practice was not so simple. When he was leaving China, he had to balance seeing Sue in Hong Kong and Innes on the boat, and he was not at all sure it was worth it. "My only bother now is that I'm getting older, and finding fucking less thrilling but simply inevitable."[45] Or as he expressed it even more cynically in a letter to Eddie a month latter: "I'm getting bored with fucking, but cant possibly give it up, and that people like Innes and even S.—people who have to be taken seriously emotionally, and looked after and attended to—are ceasing to be my cup of tea. . . . Only the hell of it is, as I see with Innes, Ive got a real talent for seducing young ladies of an intellectual bent and aesthetic tastes. And how can one avoid exercising ones talent. Well, time will provide."

In April he had written to his mother: "there'll never be peace until Fascism is destroyed. I'm glad I'm not in England having to make up my mind as to what's the least bad thing to do. As you say, it doesn't really bear thinking about."[46] The news of the civil war in Spain confirmed him in his view; the last vestiges of pacifism were abandoned. "It's too late too for democracy and reason and persuasion and writing to the *New Statesman* and Virginia signing letters saying it's all a pity. The only real choices are to submit or to fight, and if we're going to fight to do so effectively." This was in a letter to his brother; a few days later he wrote to Eddie, "There's only one thing to be done with Fascists, and that's kill them."

By mid-October he felt certain that Spain would be a destination for him, either before or after his return to England. He did not think of it as an end in itself, the romantic battle for Spanish democracy. It was a preparation, even a laboratory, for the great international war against fascism he accepted as unavoidable. The earlier question of what he was to do when he returned to England still figured in his correspondence but almost at a level of fantasy (grandiloquent daydreams of political power), not as a real problem that had to be acted upon, the humdrum necessity of job hunting. But the other question—when was he to leave China—had yet to be resolved. Here the problem was real enough: he did have an obligation to the University, a contract to teach until next June. It had behaved very decently to him; walking out in midterm would create an awkward situation.

The tragicomic event when Sue's husband burst into the house and discovered all precipitated his decision. He seized upon the opportunity to conclude this chapter of his life and begin the next. Persuading himself that he had no choice but to resign, he did so at once, with no sober second thoughts or regrets. But if he had wanted to, he might as easily have stayed: there had been no public scandal; it was in the interest of the deceived husband that there be none; and it was not he but Julian who had proposed the resignation. He had already decided, weeks earlier, that as he said, he had "had" China; he was contemplating Spain; he knew that at some point in the near future, yet to be decided, he would be leaving Wuhan: it was only necessary to make the decision. Now, in effect, it had been made for him.

He offered his resignation to the University authorities, pleading "family reasons." They were dismayed, regretful, hopeful that he might yet stay; there was some question, under the terms of his contract, of who was to pay his fare back to England, if he resigned. The deceived husband found himself, as dean, in the equivocal role of having to recommend a position to the University. But by the beginning of December, everything had been worked out; the resignation had been amicably accepted, and he had received his passage home. All that was necessary was to concoct suitable public reasons for his departure, and here Julian was quite in his element, starting various stories on their rounds. In the light of his eagerness for a very bad, or rather, very good, reputation as a seducer, he was surprisingly anxious that the true story should not be known. He was almost equally anxious that it not be thought that he was leaving over a row that he had just had with a visiting English dignitary. Officially, he had resigned for "family reasons." Those to whom he felt he owed a more circumstantial explanation, if not the true one, he told that his brother had gone off to Spain, and he was returning to fetch him back. A very few people he told that he was returning in order to fight in Spain himself. This, as he wrote to Eddie, was "in intention true," but he felt constrained to add, "if its possible and if I can possibly persuade Nessa I must."[47]

In an undated letter to Sue he pointed out that it was time for him to leave, but his reasoning might well to an extent be after the fact:

> My trouble is that I've got a lot of things to say to my world. But at all events, its time I went back to London and a serious life doing real things. This place is too much make believe—at any rate for a foreigner. And I must get back to people whose motives aren't too intolerably petty. I'm all for intrigue, but I like it to be about real things—politics, power, etc—not these silly little personal gossiping intrigues. . . . Also, I resent my own powerlessness here. If I could turn round and make things difficult and unpleasant for people who gossip against me I shouldn't resent it half as much.[48]

Despite his affair being officially over, he could not let it quite go, and he and Sue continued to be in touch. On December 16, he wrote to her: "Oh, dearest Sue, its so utterly silly to have a quarrel now, when anything may be going to happen to us. Just because we at once are so different in our lives and world and yet in some ways so alike. I want more than anything to keep our friendship in existence, to have you as a person whom I can tell everything, quite freely. . . . I have never had a friend or a mistress who I could feel with so completely, who could give me so much of herself." And fulfilling this letter, two days later he wrote to her about his thinking about Spain. "I think I have made it quite clear to Nessa that you have had no slightest responsibility for my folly or what else it may be about Spain. . . . You know, I dislike the thought of dying very much indeed, and even more the notion of making people miserable. . . . I shouldn't mind being shot through the head, indeed, I'd rather die in a battle than any other way I can think of. And I've had a very good life." On December 24 he wrote to her that perhaps Franco would be defeated before he returned to Europe but in any case it was "a war that must be won, because everything we care about—in China, as much as Europe—depends on defeating fascism. . . . I find that as a result of my beliefs, and my ancestors and environment, I have a strong, unreasonable sense of honour. . . . I don't say this is reasonable—but its simply how I feel. I couldn't conceivably write, or talk to people, or make love, if I were always despising myself."[49] Despite all this turmoil, his last months in China were devoted also to fulfilling his teaching obligations for the rest of the term and enjoying the outside world; he continued to derive great pleasure from sailing the boat he had acquired.

In his letter to Vanessa, describing the end of the affair and his resignation, he had gone on to speculate about the future. "I am still undecided what I shall do." He raised a number of possibilities—travel, politics, Spain—as though all were to be given equal weight. "I'm going to ask Leonard to find me a job—unpaid, I think—in the Labour party": a notion that would be certain to reassure her. On the other hand, he persisted in his belief that once she understood how he felt, she would overcome her fears and scruples and approve of what he really wanted to do. The letter seesawed:

> Fortunately the news from Spain is better today; theres no certainty, but if the government hold Madrid I think they may win yet. . . . You know that intellectually I agree with you [about war], and emotionally too in many ways. But there is one completely irrational side of my mind which cant accept things like Fascist victories even in other countries, but wants to get out and do something. And intellectually and emotionally I have none of your horror of killing human beings as such—only when they are valuable or my friends. Still, all this wouldnt matter much if it werent my very peculiar mental kink about war as an art—or science—which I share with Quentin. I have never decided whether it is a freakish and slightly neurotic reaction to our pacifist childhood, or whether it is an even more freakish vocation. But I know that the last few days I have begun to feel about Spain not my mere desperation—which I would suppress, except about France, where Charles and Marie [Mauron] are involved, and so much of our own world—but I have been feeling what seems like a professional—no, amateur impatience—about the government defeats. I cant help believing that if I had been in England, and had gone out at the beginning, I might now be in a position to make some difference, and that if so I could have done a good deal. This may very well be a completely false judgment, but if its a true one then I am clearly not in the position of an ordinary volunteer for a good cause. It needs more careful thought than I feel inclined to give. But perhaps you had better be prepared for my wanting to go, tho' thats a very different business indeed to going. At all events, much may happen in three or four months; best of all, the left may be victorious, and there'll be no more nightmare. Its been really hideous this last week here, where I don't think anyone really understands the way it upsets me. . . . What a mercy you and I have somehow got outside age limits and can understand each other. I dont know how I should have been able

to endure my emotional life and stay sane and rather hard really if it werent for you.[50]

Julian was unwilling to recognize a simple and painful truth: that his mother might very well understand him and at the same time deeply disapprove and be hurt by what he intended to do. Or perhaps unconsciously he did recognize it, as it would account for much of the tension that is so evident in his life during his last three months in China—from the time of the confrontation scene to his eventual belated departure. Ideally, of course, he ought to have left at once, but the machinery of resignation turned at a stately pace, and he had agreed to remain until the term finished, so he was not able to get away until the end of January 1937. The frenetic, quasi-farcical aspect of his sexual intrigues represents one kind of tension; the fantasies of violence and self-conscious barbarism that erupt in his correspondence represent another. For all his faith in the power of understanding, it was not gaining him his mother's approval, and he could surmise, reading between the lines of her letters, that it was making her miserable. This too added to his guilt and anxiety. In a letter to him on November 22 she tried to anticipate by putting forth reasons against going to Spain. "It is clearly better to help by thinking, writing, speaking, planing rather than by action in the field. You would be one of many in action, no more and no less valuable, but you have a better intelligence than most people, and so it should be used, and not destroyed by a chance bullet."[51] "Dearest Nessa," he wrote to her on December 12,

> I think we must leave the whole question of Spain till I get back. For one thing, it is very painful, because the only big reason to me for not doing any rather dangerous thing is that it makes you unhappy—however good you are about being reasonable and telling me that I am not to think too much of your feelings and so on. I was horrified at even already given you such a nightmare. So lets leave it all till we can talk together. . . . And besides, the war is going so much better, I now hope the republic will have won before I can get back, and then the whole question will be academic.[52]

If he took a cheerful view of the Spanish situation, it was only in part to reassure his mother; towards the end of the year he believed it to be justified by events. Here, paradoxically, was another source of anxiety. Supposing the war in Spain to be over before he could get there—and he was genuinely fearful that he might arrive too late—then he would have to think seriously of some viable alternative for the "three years before facing War" in England: the old problem of finding a suitable niche would reassert itself. Hence the contradictions of his behavior and thinking are apparent: in his own mind he was absolutely clear that he was to go to Spain; at the same time, he was conducting a full-scale discussion with family and friends of what he was to do when he returned to England. His mother took heart when she heard that at long last he had actually written to Leonard for help in getting a political job in the Labour Party, and since that was to be nonpaying, she began to look about for something additional and lucrative for him. The solution she arrived at had just the air of the improbable that he could relish without ever taking seriously: he was to become a company director of a family business importing feathers from China. "It sounds quite wild," he wrote to Eddie. "But apparently it would produce a hundred a year which I should appreciate." From Leonard Woolf came word that he might be able to arrange something for Julian through Hugh Dalton, a fellow Kingsman of Rupert Brooke's generation who probably didn't remember meeting him. Julian did. As he wrote to Eddie: "I rather look forward to getting to know those strange animals, labour politicians. Leonard suggested Dalton as a starting point—shall I remind him that hes the only member of his majestys government I ever kissed? Do you remember that oddly mad founders feast [at King's]—with Harry [Lintott] and myself—, of all incongruous couples, holding hands under the table."[53]

Julian embarked in his correspondence upon the game of future politics, and played it as enthusiastically as the war game. Indeed, at times he seems to have confused the two—and he gloried in declaring himself at the furthest pole from "idealism, democracy, and liberalism." "Does this horrify you, by the way?" he demanded of Playfair. "It may look pretty bad by the time it gets to England." How seriously did he believe in his rather terrifying daydreams, what he was willing to call privately social fascism? It was as though, once started, he could not have enough of repudiating the civilized values of his parents: "Let's cultivate the virtues of barbarism," he crowed. Yet he knew very well, in spite of the elaborate plan-spinning in his letters, what the next stage of his life was to be: he was as little likely to settle down as anyone's political private secretary as to become an importer of feathers. With an air of absolute seriousness he was able to write to Quentin of a future coup d'état in England, to be led, presumably, by a junta of neo-Machiavellians; but in the same letter, in a single sentence, he brushed fantasy aside: "I don't really think it's much use discussing going out [to Spain] by letter: I have made up my mind to do so if it's in any way possible, and that's that."

The initial impulse to go to Spain—let us say, from mid-September, after the return to Wuhan—was an emotional one: Spain was "the right place to be." But he disapproved of doing things for emotional reasons; thereafter, he spent much of his time marshaling intellectual arguments to justify his decision. If he really fancied himself as a military man, then he was obligated to go where the fight he was interested in—against fascism—was taking place. This was very different, he would have argued, from going as a romantic volunteer in the cause of freedom. Isolated in China, he followed the progress of the war in late-arriving newspapers from England and grew increasingly impatient when events did not conform to his notions of proper strategy. "I can't help feeling there ought to be a counterstroke," he wrote to Quentin, "above all in the south, where the communications with Africa are exposed—and I should like to hear more of the guerillas. Of course if you can combine guerillas and mobile regulars and a solid defensive you ought to be safe to win—it's the peninsula formula." And a few days later he wrote to Eddie about Kléber's strategy (Kléber was one of the commanders of an International Brigade in Madrid): "I can't grasp if [he] is being too clever, or why he hasn't pulled the strings of the bag. I should have thought to bottle Franco and force a surrender wouldn't be hard, and would finish the war." He was being very much the armchair general, shocked that what to him were the obvious steps were not being taken. But the role did not satisfy him; he realized that criticism from a distance of five thousand miles is easy, and pointless. He wanted to go to Spain, and he wanted to go to Spain to fight.

In December he received an intriguing letter from I. A. Richards, who was actually in China himself, pursuing his scheme of persuading the Chinese to adopt Basic English. The letter was a wonderful dose of Cambridge rationality expressed in a rather whimsical way.

> Don't go to fight in Spain. I can't help admiring anyone who deigns to do so, enormously, as one admires certain dogs. But the outcome wouldn't justify the act and its costs, and no animal able to calculate would see it as doing so—either to you, to England or to the world & its future. Whatever scale you employ the fair estimate would not give a balance of advantage to anyone *that* way. And,

don't we agree? To say, nowadays, 'To Hell with calculation, the Heart knows!' is just *fin de siècle* Satanism and Marie Corelli. . . . I augured extremely well from the fact that you didn't seem to be in a tearing hurry & wrote of going by the slow Burma route—instead of heading for a Moscow battalion.[54]

Julian had not been able to unravel the complexities of Chinese politics and the warfare that was taking place in the country, nor had he really been interested in doing so. It seems fair enough then that his Chinese friends should not have understood why he was so exercised about Spain. When Sue heard that he might be going there, she leapt to the conclusion that it was because she had not accepted his offer to marry her; he assured her this was not the case. In Spain, by contrast, he felt the issues to be clearly defined—"if only we could beat [the Fascists] off and get breathing space"—and he realized, well before the air raids on civilian populations, that the Germans would use Spain as a testing ground for new armaments and techniques of warfare.

Throughout December he had become more and more determined in his attitude, and unshakeable in his insistence to friends and to Quentin that he would be going out to Spain, as though gathering courage for the declaration to his mother, which thus far he had not yet nerved himself to make. "Try to convince Nessa that it'll probably be over before I'm back," he wrote to Quentin, "and that anyway it's not unreasonably dangerous." Three days later, December 27, he wrote to a friend, "My ambition is to join the International Brigade." By now he had come to feel an inevitability about his going, and that he must win out against opposition to his doing so, particularly from his mother. His commitment to the civil war had become a test that he must not fail. "I foresee a fearful hullabaloo about going, and am very bothered about Nessa, who will really mind. But what else can I possibly do? Introspecting, I see that the sentiment of honour is like jealousy; outside reason or good, but ineluctable. Just as, if you're jealous, you must break, there's no cure, so I feel I must go; anything else would be inconceivable. Besides, like all would-be volunteers, I've a profound belief in my own good luck." He told Playfair, "If I dont go I shall feel too bloody to be of use anywhere—certainly none in politics and writing." In another letter, written in mid-January, he announced his plan: "I'm going by sea to Marseilles, and then by hook or crook to Spain. It seems the only rational course." Then, even more insistently: "But what else can I do? It's impossible to let other people go and fight for what one believes in and refuse the risk oneself. All right for lots of people, with real jobs worth doing, or with real dependents, or who don't like killing. But I approve of wars in principle and no one has any claim on me. And I should never recover from a sense of shame if I didn't go."

Actually, he was all too aware that his mother did have a claim on him—the claim of the extraordinary closeness of their relationship. All through the letters of this period runs the refrain of his concern for his mother and her feelings. As he wrote to Eddie, "I know I shall have a bad time of it dealing with Nessa, for I cant really go until I've got her to agree more or less. The consequence of which is some rather exhausting soul-searching and the winnowing leaves not much behind but maggots. However, my main conclusion is . . . that unless I go I shall be good for nothing."[55]

Vanessa was emotionally opposed to war and firmly opposed to her son participating in one. Her husband and closest friends had earlier resisted the state in its efforts to press them into military service; it is inconceivable that she should not have been disturbed at her son's desire to seek out military experience. These were objections on the level of principle; on the emotional level, given the intensity of their attachment, she would have responded even more strongly to the possibility of his deliberately risking his life. After their first exchange of letters on the subject, pained that he should have made her unhappy, he proposed that they "leave the whole question of Spain" until he got back. Then he changed his tack and wrote to her of the future—"I now realise that I simply must take up politics for a good many years"—not only to reassure her but also because the question genuinely concerned him. There was a slight confusion of chronology. He meant, although he did not say so, the future after Spain; she thought, and he allowed her to believe, he meant the future after China. But although he was careful to avoid mention of Spain in his letters, they reveal the state of mind in which he reached his decision to go there:

> Most of my friends are unutterably squeamish about means; they feel that it would be terrible to use force or fraud against anyone, and that they have souls to save which are the most important part of them. Even most communists seem to me to have only a hysterical and quite unrealistic notion about violent methods. . . . I cant imagine anyone of the New Statesman doing anything "unfair" to an opponent. Queer people—but dont you think I'm right? Whereas

for my own part—whether from being a Bell or from living with painters or whatever—I cant feel the slightest qualms about the notion of doing anything effective, however ungentlemanly and unchristian, nor about admitting to myself that certain actions would be very unfair indeed. . . . Well, anyway, I have written to Leonard, not in quite this style, but asking him definitely if I could find any job in the Labour Party. It would also, I think, keep me active and interested, and I cant see anything else that would do that. For I doubt if I shall ever be a whole-time writer—at any rate, not unless something changes a good deal for me.

Then, quite casually, he repudiated the summum bonum of Bloomsbury: "I dont feel, myself, as if I could ever be satisfied to do nothing but produce works of art, or even really nothing but leading a private life and producing works in the intervals."[56] Yet it seemed impossible not to touch upon the crucial subject, particularly as he wanted Vanessa to meet him in France upon his return rather than wait for him to arrive in England. In fact, he was not certain that he would go back to England at all, as it might involve him in difficulties with the Enlistment Act. The simplest solution—this was in December—seemed to be France, then Spain. Spain he was determined on "by hook or crook."

I've been trying hard *not* to write to you about what I want to do, because letters are a bad form of communication when one wants to know what one's doing. It's fiendishly difficult. I was wretched at your having nightmares over me. . . . I shant do anything unless you have seen what I'm after: I think if we talk you'll understand me. You know, I always thought one day we should find ourselves in this position, tho' I didn't expect it so soon. It's very odd indeed; here I'm a sort of Bloomsburyish recluse. In letters, all the old life goes on. And then there's this fantastic world in the newspapers. I simply cannot believe in it. . . . It's quite fantastic to think of you and me in the sort of Corneille situation that seems to be getting set for us. However, it's not going to be genuinely Corneillian if I can help it. I suppose you can remember the same sort of business in '14? I wish it were one of the situations in which you'd feel *exactly* as I do: I think we're pretty much agreed even about this. But I'm a thoroughly unreasonable creature—or so reasonable I recognize my own irrational desires, whichever you like. . . . I shall try to take a boat to Marseilles and get there about Feb. 25. Would that suit you? But I'll send you a telegram when I *do* decide. Please dont have nightmares or anxieties—how foolish of me to try and stop you when I know I cant. I can only say that when we meet we shall manage somehow to get things tangled out.[57]

Here it would appear that he was firmly determined to go to Spain. Yet he wrote in quite a different way to his mother on January 10 about his future plans. Perhaps he was trying to reassure her, raising the possibility that he wouldn't go to Spain. He was quite interested now in being an unpaid private secretary for a Labour Party figure. "Ive a notion now that if I became a private secretary it would be fun, and highly patriotic, to provide stuffy old trade unionists with an alternative to Duchesses—to wit, my sister and her friends and of course my own young women. . . . My head buzzes with plans—for fortifying England against air raids and for remodeling the British army."

He was certainly well aware that his mother would be deeply opposed to his going. She had become more politically involved, specifically with the Artists International Association, a political organization committed to help the Spanish cause, particularly its medical aspects. He remarked to his aunt that "it did suggest a really appalling situation if Nessa had noticed it."[58] But even so she would feel very differently about his actually going there. Quentin and Eddie Playfair, before the war started, had been thinking of taking a vacation in Spain, and even continued to think about the idea for a bit after war broke out. In December Eddie wrote to Julian:

> It is extraordinary how your family are blossoming out into politics; I gather that Virginia's article is definitely going to come out in the Worker, under her name. . . . I'm not surprised to hear you are thinking of going to Spain, but I hope you wont, just the same. Selfishly, because there is no one that I personally would less like to see killed; and generally, because I think you can be a great deal more useful at home. I can tell you that you wont have an easy time with Nessa. . . . I was horrified at the upheaval that our proposal created; we had never thought of running our heads into any danger, but Nessa was in a terrible state about it, and at the same time too honest not to feel guilty about interfering, and wrote me two letters to explain and apologise. . . . I'm sure she'll not stand in your way, but you can reckon on creating a good deal of misery if you do go. . . . You personally, with small private means, enthusiasm and brains, could do a whole lot in England, where we need people of that specification; its worth much more than one soldier in Spain.[59]

Julian wrote to his aunt in December. "Spain is a nightmare here, where one can do nothing at all but wait for the papers and the news, which keeps me perpetually on edge. It does look as if the most useful part of all my elaborate education was likely to be the scraps of military theory I have picked up for myself. . . . [My love life] been nerve racking and still is. But at least its a good thing that I've been pushed into doing what I thought I ought to have done at the end of the summer—resigning."[60]

Thus, with his own mind made up but aware that he had yet to convince his mother, Julian left China from Hong Kong in February 1937, after the wronged husband had been forced to preside over his farewell party in Wuhan. Julian and Sue had met once without her husband's knowledge, and he wrote Julian a stinging letter when he found out. Nevertheless, he allowed them to meet again.

> I was very much pained, but still more surprised at your conduct. . . . I thought whatever might be your moral principles in some matters, an Englishman still had to keep his word and to consider his honour. I did not know that in throwing overboard some moral principles, such as loyalty to one's friends, you threw all away. No faith, no honour, no word to keep—nothing would prevent you to seek your selfish gratification. . . . A cad would be a cad, and I had only myself to thank for believing there might be some good in him. . . . Come down at half past eight.[61]

Nevertheless, he did manage to spend four days in Hong Kong with Sue, having written to her in an undated letter, "We must see each other again in China: I'll do anything to make certain of that." He spent his twenty-ninth birthday with her, on February 4. She saw him off, and he wrote to her from the ship: "It was terrible watching you in the distance, getting further and further. . . . I feel all right about us. I think our relationship is a good one and will stand time and separation."[62] At the same time, he was not above continuing his affair with Innes Jackson, who had arranged to return to Europe on the same ship. Although he had contrived that the two ladies shouldn't glimpse one another when the ship left, he didn't hide from Sue that Innes was with him, writing to her that he was giving her advice about her forthcoming marriage! Her affair with Julian had started before he left China, as he had chronicled its progress in letters to Eddie. On December 5: "My private life is . . . almost as good as our gracious Kings, [Edward VIII] I flatter myself." On December 14: "My new affair is placid and educational, tho at times a little odd certainly. Its really getting too cold to sail, but I shoot a lot and keep fairly calm and cheerful—above all since I havent to face Sue again here." And he had written to his mother on December 7: "Innes Jackson has fallen for me. . . . Poor Innes. I'm very nice and kind and even passionate, but certainly not in love—whereas she is. . . . It's very comic, of course, but I'm bothered one of them will get hurt. The initial scene was the most comic of all, since I found myself making love to H.Y. [Lian], then to Innes, and then to both at once! And they nice, chaste virgins. Whatever is the world coming to. The Country Wife and Oscar Wilde, Edward VIII—and such goings on." On January 9 he wrote to Eddie: "Sue in Shanghai. . . . And Innes here, improving steadily under tuition—a perfect girl to talk to, because always understands and never interrupts. Ive got a horrid taste now for being educational, particularly about life. But one definite point. Innes is returning—probably with me. . . . Shes far more of a lady than any other mistress Ive ever had."[63] After his death, Innes herself wrote to Vanessa: "I had a richer happiness with him in the six months we knew each other than I believe many people possess in a life-time. More important perhaps, he helped to clear away a clutter of false romanticism and idealisms and set me in the same direction as he himself was compelled to go and that certainly seems now the only possible one for people who care at all what happens to the world. I thought you might like to know how profoundly he influenced one human being—and all for the good, and lastingly."[64] She went on to be a translator from the Chinese, particularly of poetry.

The most reasoned statement of his position—the philosophical and political assumptions that justified his progress from pacifism to Spain—is to be found in the long essay "War and Peace: A Letter to E. M. Forster," which he began to write in January and completed on the ship returning home. It was the third and last of the long essays that he intended as a testament to his generation; it is as discursive and disorganized as the Roger Fry essay and the letter to Day Lewis—Julian is still "all over the place"—but unlike them it deals with an actual rather than a theoretical predicament, one that he shared with much of his generation:

> I wish to explain why it is that I, and many more men of military age, have ceased to be pacifists. . . . I know that we have to choose war, not peace; I will not pretend this is anything but a choice of evil, not good. . . . What reasons can be given for so unnatural a choice? They are reasons of expediency, of necessity, sufficiently familiar to my contemporaries, and sufficiently obvious. Yet it is the appreciation or ignorance of this necessity that more than anything divides the generations. And it is ignorance of them, deliberate ostrich ignorance, that preserves intact the virgin cotton-wool of British public opinion.

This is a very different level of consideration from that of the earlier essays: it is one thing to prescribe a "disciplined aesthetic" for a far distant socialized future, or to reprove one's rivals for too much enthusiasm in their poetry; it is another, to evaluate a real predicament from which real consequences might ensue, not only for oneself but for much of the world. At his best in the letter to Forster, amidst all the distracting hares that are produced and pursued, he is not speculative but diagnostic, and hence relevant. We know his own solution: that he translated enthusiasm into action and chose to participate in the Spanish Civil War. He prided himself on being hardheaded and Machiavellian, but no true Machiavellian would have felt or written, "It's impossible to let other people go and fight for what one believes in and refuse the risk oneself." In fact, as Forster himself pointed out in his "Notes for a Reply," which are included with the essay in the memorial volume, there was a strong strain of idealism in Julian. And he went on affectionately to note, "he is guilty of pretty well everything he condemns except chastity and cowardice."

The letter is written to Forster as the friend and biographer of Lowes Dickinson, whose liberal ideas Julian presumes him to share, and whom he describes as "one of the greatest of the Liberals." This proves to be qualified praise: "When, in his dialogue with Plato, Lowes Dickinson discusses socialism, he does so in terms of justice and right and value. And that is still the ordinary form of discussion of socialism: the socialist is motivated by a sense of pity for human suffering, by a sense of equality or of justice, revolted at the oppressions of civilization. Consequently there is still a good deal of truth in the notion that a socialist is a man with a weak head and a capitalist a man with a bad heart." The crucial objection to liberalism, then, is that it is "political romanticism: it has no innate sense of human baseness, and can only move between illusion and disillusion." The League of Nations, Lowes Dickinson's "cause," was "made a futility by the liberal inability to think in terms of force ... it had no backing but reason and goodness, and few men are good or reasonable." And he concludes his indictment of the liberal attitude by pointing out that "nowhere is [it] so strong as it is today in England. Consequently we still think that we can protect ourselves from war and poverty by appealing to sentiment, reason, goodness."

But how is the case against liberalism to be related to the intention of the essay, "why it is that I, and many more men of military age, have ceased to be pacifists?" It is done—after some thirty-three pages of divagations and explorations, during which the point tends to disappear among a horde of other points—by merging liberalism with pacifism, so that in effect he is saying, we who were liberals and/or pacifists, believing that men are good and reasonable and that wars can be averted by appeals to sentiment, must now abandon our illusions and accept an "obvious truth": "Non-resistance means suffering the full power of fascism. And fascism means, not only violence, but slavery, and will not only kill and torture, but will destroy all chance of reasoned, or reasonable or Christian opposition [this in answer to Quaker pacifism] and will do its best, with violence and propaganda, to harry out of the world all liberal and humane ideas or men." And again, "Non-resistance to war means non-resistance to fascism and a resignation to the disappearance of most, if not all, that we value." And finally, "At this moment, to be anti-war means to submit to fascism, to be anti-fascist means to be prepared for war."

This is the central and most relevant—also the most realistic—point that Julian makes in his essay, but it is only one among a large number of other points, relevant or not, that he felt compelled to make. For example, his acceptance of force as a means to a desired end, what he called "engineering socialism"; his odd, aristocratic version of a revolution for the future, specifically, all Marxism ("the irresistible intellectual case") and no Marxists ("their lives are mainly evil"). He moves forward to an enthusiastic interpretation of what he called "the military virtues." Here he begins quite calmly: "The soldier's is not perhaps the best of lives for many people: it may not offer a very great number of highly valued states of mind. But it can be a good life. . . . It is secular and rational." Soon, however, enthusiasm catches him up, and he is setting forth the virtues that he has always admired—"common sense, an acute intuition of reality . . . practical sagacity and judgment," and so on. He might almost be writing of Roger Fry. "The essential attraction of war and of the military character lies in this submission of the intelligence to facts and of facts to the resources of the intelligence. Such is indeed the procedure of all the admirable human activities: of the engineer, the scientist, the administrator, even, in certain measure, of the artist. The soldier's form of action has certain attractions, of excitement and courage, the others lack—and the consequent evils of· death and destruction." He had been attracted by this form of action since early childhood; the political realities of the 1930s—"to be anti-fascist means to be prepared for war"—justified intellectually a commitment that on an emotional level, unconsciously, had been made a long time before. He might have said, "I want to go; therefore I must," but as Forster observed, "He had a vigorous mind, and had been brought up in Cambridge and places where they argue, so it came natural to him to pop in a bunch of reasons."[65]

When Julian left China, his decision was made: he was going to Spain to fight in the civil war on the side of the Republican government. He hoped it would not be necessary to return to England at all, partly to hasten his arrival in Madrid, partly to avoid being put in a position where he might be dissuaded from doing what he wanted to do. He would arrive in Marseilles; he would go to St. Rémy to see the Maurons; he would spend time with his mother in Cassis; then Spain: that was the tentative plan as he set sail. He had written a succession of letters to everyone but his mother, telling what he intended to do, and he had not suggested that she not be told. He underestimated her if he thought that she would not guess, read between the lines, suspect his intentions: the closeness of their relationship made it inevitable. She knew that he was planning to see the Maurons, and was fearful that afterwards he meant to go straight on to Spain. On February 20, when the ship docked at Colombo, there was a letter from her, written in great distress, asking if he had come to a decision, and if he had, to tell her, no matter what. He cabled immediately, "Undecided." Whether he was actually wavering or not is hard to tell. A week later he wrote to her from Djibouti:

> Nessa dearest
> I'm very sorry indeed about the muddle—which must have been my fault. I was thinking a great deal about the whole business, and I suppose I must have made up a letter to you in my head and never written it—a thing I often enough do. After which I thought the less I said the better. But Ive always been very clear that I should have to convince you before I could do anything, and I thought I'd said so—I certainly did to Charles when I wrote to him asking him to help me—I said that of course it would depend on my persuading you.
> Well, it wont really matter much in any event my coming back [to England]—it was really only cowardice on my part; I know it will be very much harder to leave again than if Id never come back. I shall have to see Charles on my way and possibly other people—without committing myself, of course. Id never had any idea of doing this without talking to you first, you know. But I

should like to have a chance to talk to you alone for a day or so, and I dont want much to argue with anyone else—I'm ready enough to talk practicalities and get information, of course, but I dont feel like serious argument with anyone but you, because at root the business is a personal one, not political—I mean that my decision really depends on certain judgments about what is good for me in my own life, since the world at large isn't going to be very much affected. It seems to me to be a matter between me and you. I don't think most of the consequences much matter but your feelings do.

He wrote to Sue about this situation:

> She insisted on my returning to England. . . . I am afraid of my resolution vanishing when I'm back in it all. Also I cant bear hurting Nessa. . . . I think if I were simply killed she would manage to console herself, but being frightened of what may or may not happen is much harder. Yet I don't really see how I can give in, for the instinct to go comes from the very bottom of my heart, and if I break that it will be terribly difficult to make a life of it. . . . The game of crossing a mountain range without being caught should be great fun. . . . Your photograph sits over my bed and looks very attractive indeed.[66]

Vanessa wrote to him at St. Rémy saying that she would come there if he wished, as she was unhappy that he might have thought that she was forcing him to come back to England against his will. She did prefer that he come to England and suggested that he might meet with her at Charleston; only Quentin would be there. Or to talk to others as well, in London, whichever he preferred. She wrote to him:

> It doesn't matter now about any muddles that may have been made by either of us—I daresay I wanted to be blind & perhaps you couldn't quite bring yourself to write what you knew would upset me. But I had to learn the truth sooner or later—Yes, you told Charles & you told me that you would never do anything definite without my consent—but I couldn't help all the same feeling in a way how little that might mean—I wont go into that now however. I think that you have been so terribly isolated from anyone who could talk and exchange ideas with you that you may find, as I know I often have in much shorter times of solitude, that your sense of proportion has changed—& you will look at things now from a bigger and wider point of view. . . . Oh Julian what a mixed state it is at the moment! I suppose nothing ever happens as one thinks it will. Certainly I didn't expect to feel so many different things when I was going to see you again in a few days. Only it cant help being a comfort to talk to you darling creature & I don't think anything can really come between us.[67]

On landing in Marseilles, he had gone directly to St. Rémy. Vanessa had decided against meeting him in France, as he now agreed that whatever he might ultimately do, he would first return to England; Vanessa must not be hurt. There was a corollary to the argument: if he went to Spain, Vanessa would be very deeply hurt; therefore, ought he to go, and had he the right to go? Mauron suggested alternatives for his future; Julian listened and appeared to agree—at least he agreed that he would go first to England. Mauron had written him a long letter on January 27 (which he had sent to Vanessa to be sent to Julian), in which he argued that Julian could do much more for the cause of antifascism in England than he could in Spain. At home he might be more influential rather than just one of the thousands who had come to help the Spanish republic. If he understood that Julian's driving desire was to have direct experience of war, he thought it best not to deal with that issue in his letter. As early as February 1935 Julian had written to Lettice, "I hope I shall spend at least a part of my life—even the last part—on battlefields." Nevertheless, in their discussions, the Maurons had the impression that he had decided not to go to Spain. Marie Mauron sent off the good news to a friend in London, who passed it on immediately to Duncan Grant. But what had been Julian's decision to come to England the Maurons may have misinterpreted as a decision not to go to Spain at all. Duncan telegraphed on March 12 to Vanessa that there was "no question of Spain for Julian. Thank Goodness."[68] After he was killed, Charles wrote to Vanessa. "I did what I could to prevent him from going. I used argumentation and ruse. But I knew this was useless. He had often told me that in his heart he was a soldier. It is true. . . . He certainly knew that he would go to any war. Yet I don't have any illusions: no war is worth life."[69] As he later wrote to Quentin, the death was a totally useless disaster.

Julian wrote to Sue about the state of play, which seemed to indicate that he was undecided:

> Well, its been a grim homecoming. The Maurons are clearly depressed: so am I. I have had letters from all my friends saying I'm a fool. It will be terribly hard either way. Nothing's settled yet. . . . I cant see what to do if I do stay in England, and have a feeling of really not being wanted. Dalton suggested a dull job canvassing for municipal elections in London, but it might do as a drug. . . . Its a bad place, Europe, now. They're all terribly frightened of war, and its

all pretty hopeless: I mean that there's really no way of preventing it that we can see. . . . I don't think you'll have committed suicide, tho' I've been frightened and worried all the voyage. . . . My dearest, I love you as much as I can anyone. . . . I cant live by emotion. I believe you can.[70]

He left St. Rémy on March 10, traveling across France by train, and arrived in England on the 12th. He had thought before arriving in France that he had made a good and irrevocable decision—to join the International Brigade—but already he was finding that it was easier to come to the decision than to act upon it. (One feels like crying out to him, "Don't go. Don't go.") His mother would not join him in France; therefore, he went back to England and "the strain of seeing people" whom he knew would attempt to discourage him or question the rightness of his decision. He wanted everything to be simple and clear, and it was not going to be. Even his love life, which he had hoped would subside into a state of quiescence, was proving more complicated than ever. Hungying was in a state of misery; he had spent some time with Sue in Hong Kong, and she intended to follow him in the near future to England; Innes had fallen in love with him, he thought, and to his chagrin he appeared to have thwarted her forthcoming marriage. Meanwhile, his mother was horribly upset about his future plans. Mauron had offered him work in France; his uncle had promised to help him find a political job in England; but these were not what he wanted: most of the time he thought he wanted to go to Spain as quickly as possible. He wrote to Lettice from the train returning to England:

> Life's hell at the moment. . . . No one wants me in Spain, and I don't much want myself elsewhere. . . . I can just stand the bloodiness of the world if I've something to DO, but everyone is persuaded I'm another political intellectual, and I really think that it's mere *eau de bidet* dishing about ideas and organisations and public opinion. Well, that's that. In a week's time I may have changed my mind. Or Nessa may think I'm right—about myself, I mean—and I may have got myself accepted [by the International Brigade]. I know if, like most of my friends, I didn't care about my parents, I should go unless stopped. Curious, and I suppose an atavism or something, but I really do feel horribly ashamed of myself—shall, rather, if I don't go.

CHAPTER 5

SPAIN

IN EARLY FEBRUARY Duncan wrote to Julian, expressing his view of the situation, particularly as it regarded Vanessa. It is a little hard to see what strategy he is following in the letter, perhaps trying to push Julian to reconsider the fundamental reasons for his going while appearing to say the contrary. The letter is quite calm, but the emotional subtext is that he really must not put his mother in this deeply stressful position, something she would be unwilling to say herself.

> Of course Nessa was a good deal upset at the news [that he would go to Spain] which you will know as well as I was inevitable. I am not writing to go into the question of how much her being upset must be taken into account in making up yr mind as to your plans—you must decide that. What I think you may not realize when you discuss things with her is being as reasonable as she is, she will certainly not want *you* to take it into account at all. . . . From talking things over with her today I think that what she would mind most is the possibility of not being able to agree with you about your reasons for going, quite apart from her personal fears for you. . . . It is still doubtful whether Spain is going to be the battlefield of all *our* hopes & fears. . . . I agree with Charles that you might be of far more use to the world as a free agent than a part of a machine. . . . What I really want to tell you is something of Nessa's state of mind which may be of some help when you discuss things with her.

At the end of the letter he added what might be seen as a slight reprimand. Julian's proclivity to inform many of his doings had made it plain to quite a few that he fully intended to go to Spain, while not surprisingly he was much more circumspect to his mother. Duncan wrote, "It is rather difficult for us to know from your various letters what you really plan to do, as your accounts to Nessa do not seem to tally exactly with what Charles seems to think are your plans." He then added in a postscript: "I think if by chance you have not yet definitely made up your mind what you will do, it would be the greatest relief if you could write to Nessa something like 'Not decided what to do, will discuss everything on arrival.' Or whatever you like."[1]

He returned to England on Friday, March 12, 1937. In the evening there was a family reunion at Charleston for which the Woolfs came down from London. That morning Virginia had noted in her diary, "Julian back today." He greeted them in Chinese dress, a long silk robe, lilac-colored, buttoned up to his chin. He was affectionate but cool, at times almost severe, although he laughed a great deal. His elders felt at once that he had been changed by his experience in China, was much more sure of himself than he had ever been in the past. That evening there was a determination on everyone's part to maintain the gaiety of the occasion, and a careful avoidance of the question uppermost in their thoughts: what he intended to do. He had brought back gifts for them all, and these were opened now in their bright paper wrappings: earrings and small jewels for Vanessa and Angelica; and for Virginia a glass fish. Julian explained, "I saw it in the market and I said that's my dear Aunt." It took them back to his early childhood, when Aunt Virginia would bring him toys to float in the bath, enjoying them as much as he did himself. But all that was long in the past; now they were struck by the change in him. He wore his Chinese robe like an armor, protecting himself against their love and solicitude.

The next afternoon he went over to Monk's House for tea with the Woolfs. Their first impressions were confirmed. Julian had always been a fascinating mixture of childishness and a very real seriousness; now it was the latter that dominated. Virginia did not consider the change altogether a happy one so far as the immediate future was concerned. While she admired the evident signs of a new maturity and strength, she also recognized a certain stubbornness and obstinacy which was bound to be intensified, or perhaps had even been called into existence, by his determination to go to Spain in opposition to his mother—with whom, doubtless, her sister agreed. Spain was not mentioned that afternoon, however, although there was talk of politics with Leonard. But his aunt felt that his very avoidance of the subject proved that his mind was already made up; he knew she would be critical of his going, if only because it would cause so much unhappiness to Vanessa, and therefore he chose not to discuss it with her. So again, the occasion was all cheerfulness and affection on the surface, and sadness and disquiet beneath.

Julian was in England until early June, a young man with a purpose. Now there was little doubt in his own mind that Spain was his objective, and his friends and relatives recognized this almost immediately—that was the change in him: his unwonted determination—although they continued, the older generation at least, to attempt to dissuade him from it, and as we shall see, were in one particular successful. He was extremely tense, as was clear in a letter he wrote to Sue on March 17 from London.

> Everyone is trying to stop me going. Only life seems so hopeless I cant help wanting to escape. Just possibly I might work in an ambulance or something, but I suppose not. Its all pointless: if I cant go I shall feel suicidal. Things mean nothing to me except my mother's unhappiness. I should like to go back to a quiet life in the country, doing nothing but I can't enjoy even that. . . . Sue, darling, I miss you terribly, more and more. . . . Perhaps we can make something together—I don't believe we can separately—I cant.[2]

Meanwhile, as he waited for the machinery of his future to turn, he carried on in a very "Julian" fashion his multileveled existence: art, love, and politics. He was not at all a fatalist; he did not mean to "sacrifice" himself in Spain; he intended to survive and, afterwards, when he came back, to enter upon a political career of some sort, either in party politics or as a polemicist. Leonard spoke to Hugh Dalton about Julian being involved in Labour Party activity, and in April he was canvassing for the Labour Party in Birmingham. It was "a queer business: not awfully inspiring," he wrote to his mother. "The proletariat just lumpish & dull. No real politics. A fair lot of work, and plenty of tiresome driving. I canvass and exploit my smile and Cambridge manner, not too badly." Birmingham itself he summed up as "filthy and unholy and stinking, but with compensations."[3] Two months later, on June 5, the day before he left for Spain, he wrote to Marie Mauron, "les véritables prolétariens votent solidement pour les conservateurs, comme toujours." He had not abandoned his literary activities. He had seen to it that the stories of his favorite pupil, C. C. Yeh, were translated and sent on to John Lehmann, who chose one of them for the first number of *New Writing*. He revised and arranged into a possible book the polemical essay-letters he had written in China. He wrote a hostile review (for the *New Statesman*) of *Towards Armageddon* by General Fuller, then on the extreme Right, in which Julian advanced his theory that the military establishment would be better ordered under socialism than, as the general suggested, under fascism.[4] He assembled a set of informative, albeit very compressed, notes for a memoir—prompted to this by a reading of Gibbon's *Autobiography*. But he wrote no poems. He had come to view his writing, as he viewed his life, as dedicated to a purpose. He had absolutely no interest (for himself) in Bloomsbury's belief in the sanctity of the work of art. In May he wrote to his brother that his essays were "meant to cause pain to intellectuals, thought if possible, but pain anyway. It's no use persuading woollies and softies and c.p. [Communist Party] hysterics into being honourable and common sense soldiers. But it is just worth publishing my reflections for those who are capable, but want a lead. You see, it's a matter of changing attitudes, not immediate policies. Consequently it's far more important to me to get attention than assent."[5] His writings became polemical and were intended to serve his purpose; so too were certain occasions. He revisited Cambridge to see old friends and favorite haunts but also to speak to a gathering of Apostles—the Society had been recently revived—on the military virtues. Michael Straight, John Cornford's wealthy American friend who at that time was a secret member of the Communist Party, was among the company. He described Julian as "wearing a strange cloak and a hat of black lamb's wool" brought back from China, and told how "he spoke of the soldier as his new-found ideal; beneath the outward argument lay his inward affirmation, that henceforth he would carry out the obligation of his generation as he saw it, but with the soldier's detachment, the soldier's disinterested devotion to duty. No one present, as I remember, understood all that he was saying; no one certainly grasped his point: that in a world in which no cause was above reproach, one had still to choose, and at the same time, to maintain one's own integrity."[6]

This talk was of a piece with his conviction about what writing must be: useful work intended to convince people of a certain point of view, or at least to make them aware of it, to call into question what they thought they believed. "My own proposals," he wrote to Lehmann on the day he left for Spain, "comprise one small book, polemical and likely to cause annoyance if only I can get it read." Impatient and full of ideas and "all over the place," he would not follow the example of his elders, who made writing a work of art, no matter what their subject. His aunt complained of this. Her objection centered on the seeming carelessness of his attitude towards writing, not on what he chose to write about. Polemics were not unknown in Bloomsbury. There were Virginia's *A Room of One's Own* and *Three Guineas*, the latter being in many ways a posthumous discussion with Julian; and there were works by Leonard Woolf and Keynes. The response to Clive Bell's political pamphlets had been precisely of the sort that Julian would have welcomed: most of the copies of Clive's antiwar tract of 1915, *Peace at Once*, had been seized and burnt by order of the lord mayor of London—a tribute to Clive's power to annoy. In a sense Julian was writing somewhat in his father's style, although he was never as secure in this power; he slashed out too haphazardly. He wrote to his mother in early March:

> Ive finished the thing I was writing [the "Letter to E. M. Forster"] and think it bad, but cant face doing it again. The end in particular is very weak and shabby. The worst of it is that Ive said all I had to say about as clearly as I can say it. But it wont come alive, its just one thing after another, and prose is such wretched stuff to correct in bulk because one cant see the bits of it simultaneously. I mean, I can keep a whole poem in my head and make changes accordingly. But its all I can do to remember my argument, and I know lots of the transitions are the most frightfully abrupt jerks and dont make very good sense. Altogether its a bad business.[7]

He was perhaps too severe in his final judgment, but he was as conscious of his defects as any of his critics were. Conceivably, at some point in the future he might have bettered the work, but as he wrote in the prefatory note he provided for the essays, on his last day in England, he lacked "the time and opportunity for a really minute and scrupulous revision"; nor one suspects did he feel very urgently a need to revise. He had not come back from China to further his literary career; nor to participate in a round of social activities and amorous intrigues ("une vie personelle quelque peu compliquée"); nor to lay the groundwork for a future career in politics. He had come back as far as England primarily to convince his mother of the rightness of his decision to participate in the civil war in Spain.

∼

Bloomsbury's objections to his going to Spain had to do, as one might expect, with questions of personal relations—Vanessa must not be hurt—and with questions of rationality: was it a sensible course of action that he proposed for himself? Bloomsbury was brought up short by his determination to go, his conviction that he must do this thing which he felt, whether rightly or wrongly, was necessary to do and which transcended even his great love for his mother. It was, then, a conflict of ideas, not only between the older and the younger generation of Bloomsbury but also between reason and romanticism. For there can be no question, no matter how Julian attempted to rationalize his decision, that he was spurred on at the deepest level of feeling by a romantic ideal of Honor and the Test that must not be failed, against which Bloomsbury's clearheaded appeals to reason could not hope to succeed.

David Garnett tells how he went down to Charleston "to try to persuade him that he would be far better employed in helping to prepare for the inevitable war against Hitler than in risking his life in Spain where he could take no effective or important part." But Julian was "immovably set upon going," and Garnett was so impressed by his seriousness that he only "roughly advanced" his prepared arguments. They were standing in the walled garden, "by a little marble bust of his grandmother Julia, as a young girl." Julian listened carefully, but his mind was made up: "Even if he could do nothing much in Spain, he argued that his experience might be valuable and what he saw might teach him a good deal about modern methods of warfare." Garnett did not feel he could deny this, and their discussion ended. "A few moments later we were standing by the Charleston pond, and looking at him as he eagerly watched the sticklebacks darting in and out of the weeds, I could not tell whether he was happier when he was a man or when he went back to being a child."[8]

Garnett's was the argument of reason; similarly, Virginia was persuaded that he might do more for the cause in which he believed if he remained in England and worked for it there—presumably by writing propaganda, helping to raise money, organizing petitions, doing canvassing as he had done in Birmingham, and expending his powers, as Auden put it, "on the flat ephemeral pamphlet and the boring meeting." Action of that sort, no matter how sensible or useful, had little appeal to Julian, as his time in Birmingham demonstrated. Going to Spain, as he perhaps realized, would set him apart from most of his literary contemporaries: the majority of volunteers for the International Brigade came from the working classes, not the intelligentsia, although it was not unrepresented in significant ways. Virginia, increasingly concerned for Vanessa, meanwhile cast about for spokesmen for her own position. She arranged for him to meet with Kingsley Martin, the editor of the *New Statesman*, and Stephen Spender, both of whom had been in Spain, she apparently hoping that they would convince Julian he could be as useful to the cause of the Republic in London as in Madrid.

Lettice Ramsey wrote to him, pointing out that he would be, in her view, more valuable staying in England, although she was also driven by the idea of trying to protect his life:

> Julian, because apart from *hating* you to get killed in Spain I think you can probably be more real use in England. I think that given the time & opportunity, & the right ability 100% political activity is the right thing & I'm sure its your thing. Going to Spain would of course be that & the most whole hearted & brave thing you could do. But at the same time it seems (apart from the question of being able to get there) that now they really have enough *men* & advisers & that the most important work against Fascism is at home & organising people to activity. Everyone, specially anyone who can speak as you can, is needed. . . . Guy is always asking about you. He is working for the BBC now.

But then later she wrote to him with resignation: "I wish you weren't going but I see you MUST. Don't stay too long. As for life with me here. I'm, unlike you, still wanting a stable & major affair. I go on breaking my heart over John who remains monogamously attached to Eileen [Bernal]. I have a few odd bedfellows but they fill a biological rather than an emotional need—unsatisfactory. I hope you don't leave too many broken hearts behind. . . . Come back soon. DONT get killed. We can't spare people like you, darling."

His mind did now appear to be made up: he told Spender he was "joining for the duration of the quarrel." Conviction—a belief in the rightness of his decision—made it simple to disregard appeals to reason. Appeals to sentiment, based on his lifelong and unshakeable attachment to his mother, were far more formidable and difficult to cope with, especially when it was she herself who made them. We will never know the nature or content of their talks. It seems fair to assume, though, that his mother told him of her abhorrence of war, and of her disapproval of his going to participate, on every possible ground, ranging from personal concern (her fear for his safety) to points of principle. She and Clive had never wavered in their convictions. (As far as we can tell, Julian did not have significant conversations with his father.) They would have agreed with the sentiments Julian had expressed in the letter from which we have already quoted, which he had written just one year earlier, in March 1936: "I can't think anything worth war—not even saving Russia or smashing Musso. . . . It is the last horror, and I can't feel sure enough of any theory to outweigh that certainty." In August 1938, a year after Julian's death, Clive Bell in his pamphlet *War Mongers* (published by the Peace Pledge Union) declared himself "an out-and-out pacifist" in opposition to those who "hate Fascism and Nazism more than they love peace. . . . A Nazi Europe would be, to my mind, heaven on earth compared with Europe at war . . . the worst tyranny is better than the best war. . . . War is the worst of all evils."[9] But with the outbreak of civil war in Spain, which Julian saw as a first battle in the coming international war against fascism, he had abandoned any sympathy he might have had with pacifism. He had written his "Letter to E. M. Forster" to explain why.

But on the level of personal feeling, he could not help but be affected by his mother's concern. Their private conversations—which they shared with no one, keeping no diaries, writing no letters—continued unresolved until almost the end of April. Hints of tension between them were glimpsed rarely. On the afternoon when Julian and Bunny Garnett had talked in the garden at Charleston, they had afterwards gone over to Rodmell to visit the Woolfs. When it was time to leave, Julian remarked ironically, "If I'm late, my mother will think I'm killed." The remark, trivial in itself, suggested that the strain was beginning to tell: usually she was "Vanessa" or "Nessa"; she would be "my mother" only jokingly, or as now, when her anxiety made it so painfully difficult for him to do what he wanted. Those closest to them both knew that had it not been for Vanessa, he would have gone directly to the International Brigade and not returned to England at all. He would not yield in his determination to go out to Spain, but at length, having recognized the intensity of her feeling, and indeed of his own where she was concerned, he agreed to compromise: he would go, not as a soldier in the International Brigade but as an ambulance driver for Spanish Medical Aid. This was not only a concession to her principles—to drive an ambulance was an approved activity in wartime: Garnett had done so in the First World War—but a concession also to her fears for his safety. He was intensely aware of her feelings and deeply concerned about them. As he wrote to Sue, "Its the hardest thing I've ever had to decide." And in another letter: "Its terribly difficult to talk to Vanessa, she's so upset and miserable, and so brave and sensible also. And we both care more for each other than for anything else, and are very alike. And I have to make up my mind, and cant, as to whether I can face life if I dont go." He was still not absolutely committed: "If I stay in England I shall find myself some place in the official Labour party and become a professional politician."[10] The casualty rate among drivers for Spanish Medical Aid—at least as reported—was remarkably low: only one man had been lightly wounded, as Julian told Marie Mauron in the letter in which he announced his departure for Spain, "avec la Croix Rouge, conduire un ambulance. C'est un compromis." (The total number of British medical personnel ultimately killed was twelve; strikingly, this included six others in the same battle with Julian. Contrary to his statement, one, Emmanuel Julius, had been killed before Julian went to Spain, in October 1936.[11])

Determined as he would appear to be to go to Spain, he still seemed to give the impression that he had not completely made up his mind and that he might stay in England. In her diary for March 14, 1937, Virginia remarked about a dinner she had had with Julian the previous night at Charleston: "Julian grown a man—I mean vigorous, controlled, as I guess embittered, something to me tragic in the sadness now, his mouth & fact much tenser; as if had been thinking in solitude. Nessa said he hasn't altogether given up his idea of Spain: all depends on getting a job here. I felt him changed: taut, tense, on the defensive: yet affectionate: but no longer spontaneous." And then weeks later, on May 4, he almost implied that he was going to Spain in lieu of anything else to do. "Julian was bitter at dinner at the By [Bloomsbury] habit of education. He had been taught no job; only a vague literary smattering. But I wanted you to go the Bar I said. Yes, but you didn't insist upon it to my mother, he remarked, rather forcibly. He now finds himself at 29 without any special training. . . . Julian now in favour of a settled job: even the Treasury. He is learning the mechanics of lorries. Hadn't even been taught that at Cambridge."[12] Yet in his more optimistic moments he saw going to Spain as a training for the future, as a way of learning how to deal with the coming war.

Here perhaps one must take note of a curious detail: Virginia was told by Vanessa that the crucial factor in bringing Julian round to a compromise had been some letters he was shown describing the plight of a young English Communist in the International Brigade. The young man in question, who had gone out impulsively to Spain, was appalled by the horrors of the battlefield and disillusioned by the strict military discipline that was imposed by the Communist leadership of the Brigade. These were likely to have been letters that Tony Hyndman wrote to his lover, Stephen Spender. It seems unlikely, however, that Julian was influenced to any significant degree by this correspondence, no matter what his mother chose to believe. His own decision to go out to Spain was in no sense unpremeditated; he took a hardheaded view of death and suffering as the necessary evils of war. As an admirer of the "military virtues" and a serious student of military affairs, he would have entertained no idealistic notion of a peoples' army free of rank and discipline. One can only conclude that as a kindness to his mother, he allowed her to think that he was making this compromise, not simply as a concession to her fears for his safety but for other reasons as well. Why had the discussions with his mother, to whom he would listen with more respect and love than to any other person, led only to this compromise, which fell far short of satisfying her wishes? True, he was not to bear arms, but he was still going to Spain; he would be on the battlefields; he would be exposed to danger. Chiefly, it would appear, it was because he had made a commitment to himself to go, which he refused to break. It was his obligation and a test, he felt, to prove himself to himself as a significant member of his generation who could make a contribution of example, experience, and knowledge rather than languish in a backwater, whether in London or China, as a mere second-generation and minor Bloomsburian. His determination seemed to Virginia evidence of how he had changed, but determination was not really a new aspect of Julian's character. It was simply that now, for the first time, with absolute seriousness, he had fixed on something to be determined about. As he had written to Lettice some years before, in a very different context: "I see everything in terms of struggle and victory and defeat, and get an obstinate 'no surrender' feeling. But there it is—I'm like that, and now it's too late for me to change." Clearly, his going to Spain represented a break from the domination of his elders and of Bloomsbury. It was the difference of the generations again, art (the 1920s) versus politics (the 1930s), some degree of detachment versus commitment, the swing-round, albeit unconsciously, to the principles and scruples of the Sir Leslies. And so, not surprisingly, his elders could never arrive at an entirely satisfactory explanation of Julian's going. Virginia made the point eloquently:

> I go on asking myself, without finding an answer, what did he feel about Spain? What made him feel it necessary, knowing as he did how it must torture Nessa, to go? He knew her feeling . . . and yet deliberately inflicted this fearful anxiety on her. What made him do it? I suppose it's a fever in the blood of the younger generation which we cant possibly understand. I have never known anyone of my generation have that feeling about a war. We were all C.O.'s in the Great War. And tho' I understand that this is a "cause," can be called the cause of liberty & so on, still my natural reaction is to fight intellectually: if I were any use, I should write against it: I should evolve some plan for fighting English tyranny. The moment force is used, it becomes meaningless & unreal to me. And I daresay he wd soon have lived through the active stage, & have found some other, administrative work. But that does not explain his determination. Perhaps it was restlessness, curiosity, some gift that had never been used in private life— & a conviction, part emotional, about Spain. Anyhow Q. said during one of our walks . . . "If he hadn't gone he'd have been absolutely miserable," & said it with such conviction that I believe it. My own feeling then about his going wavers: I'm sometimes angry with him; yet feel it was fine, as all very strong feelings are fine; yet they are also wrong somehow: one must control feeling with reason.

In late April, after "so many arguments," he was in touch with George Jeger, the organizing secretary of Spanish Medical Aid, and made arrangements through him to go out to Spain as an ambulance driver. Spanish Medical Aid had come into existence in early August 1936, a few weeks after the outbreak of the war. By the end of that month it had already sent a unit out, under the leadership of Kenneth Sinclair-Loutit, a contemporary of John Cornford's at Cambridge, which set up a field hospital on the Aragon front. In the months since August 1936 S.M.A. had dispatched further units to various parts of Republican Spain, where it established hospitals on the Madrid and the Córdoba fronts and at Murcia and Albacete. Spanish Medical Aid requirements were simple, and Julian easily fulfilled them. His only difficulty was in learning to drive a lorry, which he found very different from a small car, but which he mastered in his own fashion and thereafter drove with the same high-spirited disregard for the rules of the road as had terrified his friends in the past. Also there were lessons in mechanics (if one's lorry broke down, one had to be able to repair it); lessons in Spanish; lessons in first aid—how to know if someone is dead, he wrote gaily to Marie Mauron. All this demanded a good deal of his time. In May he worked on his driving and his first-aid knowledge, as well as helping out in a by-election in Birmingham.

He had been leading, as he wrote to Marie Mauron, "une vie de crises, travaux, leçons, etc." But finally the date was set for his departure: he was to leave England on June 7. He wrote to Sue in May: "I am expecting, hoping at least, to leave in June. . . . I believe myself the war will be a long one, and I shall get a chance to see plenty of it."[13] On a Sunday, June 5—a warm summerlike evening—there was an impromptu family dinner at Clive's flat in London. The Woolfs called in; it was all very casual, and deliberately so. In fact, it was the last time that they were to see Julian. Lottie, the maid, was out, and Vanessa and Virginia cooked dinner; Julian, in shirtsleeves, hovered around them, talking, joking, seeing that the toast did not burn. After dinner, the conversation turned to politics, a three-sided conversation with only the men taking part. Virginia, proud of her nephew as she always was, noticed how well Julian held his own with Clive and Leonard: he was no longer a boy to be indulged. But politics was never a subject to engross the Stephen sisters, especially Vanessa, and they went out into the square with Angelica and gossiped in the warm summer light. Presently the men joined them. At one point Virginia remarked lightly to Julian that she would leave Roger Fry's papers to him in her will. At once he replied, "Better leave them to the British Museum." They both knew what he was thinking—that he might be killed in Spain—and both quickly turned the conversation elsewhere. Later, when it was time to go, they walked across the square, Julian and his aunt to the front. She asked if he might not have time to write something in Spain and send it to them. In effect, she was making amends for the way in which she had dismissed his paper on Roger Fry. "'Yes, I'll write something about Spain. And send it you if you like.'" Then he and Vanessa drove off in her car. The others stood at the door, watching. Julian leaned out and waved, and called, "Goodbye until this time next year."[14]

∽

When he was still in China and had only the vaguest notions of how one became a volunteer, he had thought he would have to cross into Spain illegally, on foot, alone, in the guise of a hiker, eluding the guards at the frontier. Hence he had written to Quentin to get him a Swedish knapsack and maps of the Pyrenees—a request which had distressed his mother. As it turned out, it was all a good deal less romantic and more conventional than he had imagined it would be. Spanish Medical Aid was an accredited noncombatant organization: it was necessary only to sign an undertaking that one would not participate in any belligerent activity, and to pass a driving test for an ambulance; thereafter, one traveled perfectly legally with a passport into Spain. At first the S.M.A. was just in the Barcelona area, but with the new year it expanded to Madrid to work with the International Brigade in a unit of mixed nationalities, in which the number of British fluctuated from twelve to twenty.

Julian traveled with a convoy of ambulance trucks driving across France. On the third day, June 10, they reached Perpignan. "It's been a stiffish drive, but not bad fun," he wrote to his mother.

> We celebrated the sight of the Pyrenees with a smash, the man in front of me in the convoy coming off a corner and turning clear over. By miracle, he wasnt hurt at all. . . . I've spent my afternoon delivering French rhetoric to hurry camions [through the town]. In general I'm the only one of the convoy who talks fluent French—none of us talks decent Spanish! It's really rather fun—very like last year's journey to Fa-Tsien-Iu. Some of the country looks lovely, and we [that is, he and his mother] must see it again in peace. In general I'm enjoying life a lot . . . and all's boy-scoutish in the highest.

Crossing the frontier without event, the convoy proceeded down the Costa Brava: "still, to appearances, a charming, peaceful country; posters and troops a bit, but masses of leisurely civilians," as he wrote to his mother on June 13. He then went on to Valencia, since the previous November the seat of the government of Republican Spain, and now at that moment the headquarters of the British section of Spanish Medical Aid. Sir Richard Rees, when he had arrived on the same errand as Julian three months earlier, had found this command post in charge of "an English peer [Viscount Churchill], who might have come straight from Pall Mall, and an Anglo-Italian peeress, who might have come straight from the Lido."[15] One would expect Julian to report details of this kind to his mother, and no doubt he would have done so if he had had time and quiet enough—as it was, there were "too many minor events and really I'm too stupid to write good letters." He did mention that he was awaiting Churchill's return to discover where he would be posted. In the same letter from Valencia, on June 13, he remarked, "I'll try to write longer and better letters." And in the concluding paragraph, "I'll try to write more. . . . But its an unpropitious atmosphere" —which no doubt it was, for letter-writing, but he was immensely enjoying himself; his spirits were high; and he reassured her that "So far war has meant nothing worse than hard driving." Nor did he regret coming out, then or later. "I'm extremely content," he wrote. And this, without qualification, was to be his attitude throughout his short, happy life in Spain: "it's the sort of life that suits me."

Once he had reported to headquarters, he had little to do in Valencia for the next few days but hang about "waiting for orders—just like war—and China." He had been given one quasi-official task: to drive up into the mountains to buy eggs for the unit. On the return, "I broke a passengers nose on the windscreen, thanks to my infernally fierce brakes." But on the whole the tone in these first days was of a "Mediterranean Holiday," and there was time enough to picnic and bathe at a seaside villa, attend a "goodish" bullfight, and listen to gossip of the war, which was "plentiful and contradictory, and not really worth repeating." In his exhilarated mood—"it's a very good life to live"—he could even persuade himself that his "military and political education" had begun, that he was "seeing a number of things at first hand one had only read about before," which of course was an important reason for his coming to Spain. But thus far nothing of any real military significance had offered itself: he spoke only of driving through Valencia "in almost pitch darkness." And to have understood so early the politics of the Republic, even merely to have sorted out the various factions struggling for power within the government and outside it, would have required him to be an observer of superhuman acuteness and political sophistication.

At the time of his arrival in Valencia, June 13, the most extensive military activity was in the north, in the Basque provinces, a hard-fought campaign that would end with the fall of Bilbao to Franco's forces on the 19th. Politically, the chief concern of the moment was the liquidation of the P.O.U.M. (the Workers' Party of Marxist Unification), a sequel to the internecine rioting in Barcelona in May. The fighting in the north, where the Catholic Basques were firmly on the side of the Republic, and the ideological war within the war in Barcelona were complicated aspects of a struggle that was far more complex than most of the foreign volunteers who came to participate in it suspected. Julian, newly arrived in Valencia, would have been familiar only with the gossip of the cafés or the simplifications of the press, to neither of which he paid much attention. He had not come to Spain to unravel the complexities of the politics in Spain but to gain military experience. He was waiting impatiently in Valencia for the end of "this preposterous holiday" and for the beginning of his official duties as an ambulance driver. There were a number of destinations to which he might be sent, and judging from the career of Richard Rees in Spain, it is evident that members of the Medical Aid service were moved about widely and frequently. Rees, an Etonian, a socialist, a great friend of George Orwell's and John Middleton Murry's, and former editor of *Adelphi*, had come to Spain in April. In the two months since then, he had been stationed in Valencia, about fifty miles from Madrid on the Madrid-Valencia road, and also on the Córdoba front. Julian thought it likely he would be based at the convalescent hospital at Cuenca, "at first, anyway," which would have been a comparatively quiet assignment, one he hoped to avoid. He did spend some time there and met up with an old friend from Cambridge, Portia Holman, who was a medical student and was serving as a nurse. After Julian's death, she visited Vanessa in Charleston and gave her a vivid picture of Julian at this time, as conveyed in a letter from Vanessa to Eddie Playfair.

> They were together for about a fortnight at Cuenca, where there was much to do. Driving to villages to bring provisions etc. Sun bathing & a lot of waiting about. She said Julian was absolutely happy in a completely satisfied state, that it was different from anyone else's state of mind there & as if he had found just what he wanted. She gave a depressing account of the appallingly bad organisation of the Medical Aid people & of all the petty jealousies, hurt feelings etc. She said Julian simply laughed all such things away & was delighted when people told him his face was dirty or his shorts really too short etc. He evidently enjoyed being such a huge success & never seemed tired. When he came in from a long day's driving he would start digging or other jobs. He & his two friends Richard Rees & (I think) John Bolding [Boulting, later with his twin brother, Roy, a famous filmmaker] prided themselves in keeping their cars in good order. While the others (all Communists!) drove recklessly & let everything go wrong. After the fortnight it was evident that there wasn't really much need for them at Cuenca so they all moved on to Madrid.[16]

So now he was sent to Madrid—as was Rees, from the Sierra Morena—for the new offensive the government forces were about to launch, rumors of which had been bruited about in the cafés for the past two months.

It was a notable instance of how political considerations had their effect upon military decisions. As Hugh Thomas writes in his history of the war, several Republican officers of the high command proposed an attack on Extremadura in the southwest. Largo Caballero, the Socialist prime minister, supported the idea; the Communists opposed it and endorsed a proposal of the new Russian chief adviser, General Kulik, to mount a campaign at Madrid ("striking down from the Republican positions along the Corunna road towards the little town of Brunete, cutting off the Nationalists in the Casa de Campo and the University City"). "This military quarrel," Thomas points out, "merged into the larger Communist feud with Largo Caballero." In mid-May, after the rioting in Barcelona, there was a cabinet crisis. Largo Caballero resigned and was replaced as prime minister by Juan Negrín. He, a moderate socialist, "was ready to make any political sacrifice in order to win the war. This of course led him, as it had led Largo Caballero and Prieto, into close relations with Russia, since as before, Russia remained the only source of arms. Furthermore, their political moderation and ruthless realism in face of the war made the Spanish Communist party, throughout Negrin's ministry, the most useful political party in Spain."[17] What this meant, so far as the proposed offensive was concerned, was that the Extremadura scheme was abandoned and the Communist plan prevailed: an attempt was to be made to cut off the besiegers of Madrid from the west. Whatever the military value of the plan—and it was considerable—its political propaganda value was undeniable. In the eyes of the world, Madrid was Spain; it was the heart of the Republic; the effort to break the long siege would be certain to attract a maximum of sympathetic attention. This was the background, with which Julian had no way of being acquainted, of the battle of Brunete, in which Julian was soon to be involved.

By June 22 he had been sent up to Madrid. Undoubtedly, he had heard rumors of the coming offensive but "not much news now that's much use" that day he wrote to his mother; "you must have far more in London. What we do hear doesnt sound nice." But he was not prepared to write her a detailed account of what he was doing, for he knew that that would only alarm her, and as usual there was "really no time at all for writing." This, his next-to-last letter to her, was written late at night while he and his fellow drivers waited for the telephone calls that would summon them to their ambulances, in which they would drive back and forth to wherever there was fighting, on the outskirts of the besieged city or in the countryside beyond, bringing back the wounded and then driving away again. It was arduous work. "Fortunately I've partnered myself, more or less, with Rees, who's nice and competent." Between them they had "a very hard two-days' driving, about 500 miles" in a constant shuttle to and from the front. Yet his spirits were wonderfully high: "the people are often charming and almost always amusing. . . . The country is lovely—as you'll remember and singularly unmilitarised: true, one is stopped fairly often by guards, but they're all extremely friendly. Madrid is utterly fantastic in the way it keeps the war on one edge and a fairly ordinary civil life going on—you can take the metro to the front, etc. . . . Its utterly impossible to give the full fantastic effect of it all. But I find it perpetually entertaining and very satisfactory." He had only one complaint—that he had not been close enough to the actual fighting. "Tell Q. that so far I've only hearsay about technique. I'll see what I can tell him later." And so to the final paragraph: "My Spanish improves, but still has awful fade-outs into Chinese. Good-night—I'm very sleepy, and goodness knows what will happen tomorrow. But it's a better life than most I've led." This was not simply a declaration intended to reassure his mother and lessen her anxieties; it was what he truly felt, what he truly believed.

A week later, on July 1, he wrote what proved to be his last letter to his mother from Spain (or he may have written others in the next three weeks which she did not receive). It begins, "There is a sudden crisis here—at last—and rumours of an attack." In fact, the Republican army was now almost ready to launch its "long-discussed offensive." The buildup had been in progress since mid-June. There was a massive assemblage of troops and equipment in and about the town of El Escorial. Within the enormous San Lorenzo del Escorial palace itself, two hospitals were set up to receive casualties; one of the courtyards was designated a motor pool for the ambulances of the Medical Aid service. Even there he was impatient, as he felt he was too far from the front and couldn't see war as close as he might wish. The Republican army, which included the 11th, 12th, and 15th International Brigades, "numbered 50,000 in all. It was supported by 150 aircraft, 128 tanks and 136 pieces of artillery."[18]

Julian was going to take part in one of the largest and, as it proved, most costly offensives of the war. "So far"—he was writing to her five days before the battle began—"it's all an uneventful life of minor events." There had been a "furious struggle" in the best army tradition to keep the house where the Medical Aid drivers were billeted from being taken over by a transport corps, and here his fluent French again proved useful. "It's all the oddest out of the world business you can imagine." But it was not without its grim aspect: he mentioned that Richard Rees had "had his dose of horrors, evacuating badly wounded patients to a rear hospital about a hundred miles off. It was a grim story—not possible to write." What he chose not to let her know was that this was one of the occasions when he had shared the driving with Rees. And even in the course of writing to her, he had to break off for a "new crisis." When he resumed the letter the next day, he explained that he had spent the interval in a twelve-hour drive, midnight to midday, "evacuating lightly wounded some fifty miles over very bad roads. I've discovered that I can fall asleep with my eyes open—or pretty near." He was growing impatient; his military instincts were being "badly shocked, both on a large and a small scale"; he was getting "very angry over organization"; he had "the worst forebodings for anything so public as our present operation." Against this was the prospective satisfaction of seeing "something at first hand . . . it does mean, personally, excitement and events."

> One thing [he concluded]—I do think I'm being of real use as a driver, in that I'm careful and responsible and work on my car a chevrolet ambulance, small lorry size. Most of our drivers are wreckers, neglect all sorts of precautions like oiling and greasing, over speed etc. Any really good and careful drivers out here would be really valuable. The other odd element is the Charlestonian one of improvising materials—a bit of carpet to mend a stretcher, e.g.—in which I find myself at home. I don't know what will happen to this—I expect continue in a few days, after another false alarm. No, all clear and morning.

Julian and Richard Rees, with five other ambulance drivers, were stationed at a hospital at El Goloso about ten miles north of Madrid. In preparation for this battle, they drove sixty miles (rather than the thirty miles it would have been ordinarily, because of the way the front line zig-zagged) to a hospital in the great royal palace–monastery of El Escorial. The ambulance unit was then moved closer to Brunete, outside of the town of Valdemorillo.

At dawn on July 6 the offensive was begun. Republican troops moved south from El Escorial towards Brunete, some fifteen miles distant, on the road leading into Madrid from the west. If the town could be taken and held, control of the road would fall to the government, and the Nationalist forces that had been fighting on the outskirts of Madrid since the previous autumn would be cut off from supplies and reinforcements. The point was to end the encirclement of Madrid. All went with remarkable ease at first. The Nationalists apparently were surprised by the offensive—which seems odd considering the publicity that had surrounded it, which had given rise to Julian's forebodings—and Brunete was in the hands of the Republicans by noon. Ultimately, Brunete—the battle went on until the end of July—would change hands several times, and the battle would fail after a considerable number of deaths and casualties. Among the 331 British volunteers in the International Brigade, only 42 were not killed or wounded.[19] Approximately 70,000 men were involved in the battle, the Nationalists outnumbering the Republicans three to two and, in airplanes, three to one.

Two days earlier, an International Writers Congress, attended by some eighty writers from twenty-seven countries, all of them dedicated supporters of the Republic, had got under way in Valencia. On July 6 the congress was moved to Madrid—a strategic change of scene which gave the visiting writers a more vivid sense of being in the midst of the struggle; indeed, in the quieter intervals between speechmaking and applause, the sound of gunfire could be heard in the distance. During the afternoon session there was a dramatic interruption when a group of soldiers, fresh from the front, "rushed up to the platform carrying two Fascist banners taken at Brunete and the uniform of a captured Fascist colonel, and a whole handful of women's gold lockets which this same colonel had appropriated in the course of a raid on the civilian population. The soldiers announced that an advance of sixteen kilometres had been made since daybreak. Their offensive . . . was succeeding beyond expectations."

The news from the front grew progressively worse in succeeding days, but by then the delegates were caught up in a battle of their own: whether or not to vote a motion of censure against André Gide, who had written an unfavorable account of his travels in Russia in *Retour de l'U.S.S.R.* As Malcolm Cowley remarked ironically, "Sometimes the struggle was drowned out by the sound of guns." Between sessions they were driven out in limousines, like minor royalty, to raise the morale of nearby peasant villages; and in Madrid itself, "the waiters' trade union and the town council made it a point of honour to make such arrangements as to prevent their foreign guests from noticing any difference in the standard of living between Paris and Madrid."[20] Julian himself was a poet and intellectual; he might as logically have attended a congress of writers in Madrid as driven an ambulance on the Brunete front. Yet one feels quite safe in saying that if he had, he would have detested it. When he heard of it originally, in letters from London, he dismissed it in a few satirical phrases to Rees. He had chosen to be a man of action, and there is every reason to believe he was happy in his choice. The rhetoric of the congress, cast in the mold of heroic clichés—however sincerely it may in some cases have been intended—would have convinced him that he had chosen well.

On July 7, elements of the 15th International Brigade, including the British Battalion, captured the village of Villanueva de la Cañada on the Brunete–El Escorial road. But the advance, as Hugh Thomas points out, was slowed by an extraordinary confusion:

> Brigade upon brigade were sent through a small breach in the Nationalist lines, and became mixed up with each other. The known political background to the attack caused Republican officers and non-Communists in general to grumble about the direction of the battle. . . . By midnight on the first day of the attack, Varela [the Nationalist commander] reported to Franco that a front had been re-established. Twenty-four hours later, 31 battalions and 9 batteries had arrived in reinforcement of the Nationalist position. The battle, fought on the parched Castillian plain at the height of summer, assumed a most bloody character.[21]

Julian was now as much in the thick of things as he could have hoped: at last he was having his experience of war. Admittedly, he was a noncombatant, but in the Brunete campaign the ambulance driver was as exposed to danger as the soldier; the job demanded strength, endurance, resourcefulness, and courage. If Julian was denied the satisfaction of bearing arms, he was granted the satisfaction, denied to the ordinary soldier, of knowing that what he was doing was actually useful. The amateurishness, confusion, and contentiousness that seem to have marked much of the military action throughout the war were not unknown in the Medical Aid service but proved of less moment there once an action had begun. Unlike the ordinary soldier, who waits for the orders of his superior officers, who in turn wait for the orders of theirs, and so upward to the very highest political and military levels, the ambulance driver—as in the instance of the Brunete campaign—has a clear-cut idea of what he must do, and his is the responsibility for getting it done. It is an aspect of war where initiative and a talent for improvisation particularly count. In the circumstances, Julian thrived.

The medical unit established a kind of subheadquarters for ambulances among the olive trees outside Villanueva de la Cañada. From there they would drive the wounded to the hospital at El Escorial. When rebel planes flew over, strafing or dropping bombs, the drivers took shelter in the trenches the Fascist troops had dug, and had abandoned on the second day of the battle. It was there too that they would try to sleep at such odd, infrequent off-duty moments as came their way. They were continually on the move, driving out to the various first-aid stations along the front to collect the wounded, and returning with them to the hospitals at the Escorial, while day after day, night after night, the battle continued. By day, "villages, towns and fields were sprayed with steel from planes, guns and machine guns. At night whole square kilometres of earth would go up in flame." Ambulance drivers were only seldom able to take advantage of the "illusory safety of trenches and dug outs."

Much of the driving was done at night. "It was a second or third class road," Rees has recalled,

> filled with shell holes and usually thronged with military traffic; and lights were forbidden. Since I got no regular sleep during the whole three weeks I was sometimes obliged to pull up and go to sleep in order to avoid dozing off at the wheel; and I did this with complete callousness, giving no thought at all for the state of the wounded men in the ambulance. If an aeroplane flew over, the more conscious among them would begin shouting to me: "Hombre! We shall be bombed! Drive on! Do you want to kill us all?" But I was at a point of fatigue where I believe I wouldn't have stirred if I had been sitting on a bonfire which I knew someone was setting light to.[22]

This callousness, as Rees calls it, had to be adopted if one was to do one's job efficiently—after all, it would have been a doubtful service to the wounded to fall asleep at the wheel while driving; and it was entirely in accord with the attitude of hardheaded realism, the refusal to give way to sentimentality, pity, or squeamishness that Julian had advocated in his "Letter to E. M. Forster."

There he had written:

> I have always been grateful for being made, as a child, to look at a stag having its throat cut, and that I have reached the stage of contemplating a corpse in the road without a Baudelairian extravaganza of horror. This seems to me the common human experience, and I have never perceived in myself any evil consequences. It is this making a moral principle of a physical squeamishness that is the greatest weakness of all religion, and most of all pacifism. To hate war because it is wasteful of good lives and useful objects is rational; to hate war because killing is wicked is defensible; but to hate war only because a battlefield of carrion makes you sick is hardly adequate: one hates a channel crossing on the same grounds, yet is, none the less, ready to go to France.

Forster, in his "Notes for a Reply," singled this passage out: "The analysis of squeamishness helps me. By next year [1939] it is probable that some of us will be killed and all of us have to see dead people lying about. Our own deaths we must meet with equipment of longer standing, in fact, with all our civilisation, whatever that may be. But Julian's tips may come in useful over corpses."[23] Detachment (or callousness) is the recommended attitude for the battlefield; pity is a civilian luxury. One feels certain that Julian would have approved Rees's statement that his "most disagreeable experience of war so far had been its disgustingness rather than its terror. The chloroformlike-like odour of decaying corpses all through the hot breathless nights and the peculiarly loathsome sickly-sour smell of the dust in the trenches.... And the sight of dead bodies lying slumped grotesquely beside the road, like life-size wax dolls, was disgusting and sinister rather than pitiful."[24]

On July 9, the Republicans captured the village of Quijorna; on the 11th, they took two further villages. But Boadilla, beyond Brunete on the road to Madrid, although repeatedly attacked, would not yield. By July 13 offensive action was at an end. "Henceforward the Republicans would be attempting to defend the positions which they had won. On July 15, after further fierce fighting around Boadilla, orders were given for trenches to be dug. The Republic had gained a pocket of land about twelve kilometres deep by fifteen wide."[25]

When Julian had arrived at the Escorial, he had been delighted to discover that one of the medical people (who had not quite fully qualified as a doctor) assigned to the hospital there was an old friend from King's, Archie Cochrane.

Neither had known the other was in Spain. They had a brief, exultant reunion and brief but enlivening encounters thereafter. The battle raged about them day after day—there was hardly time for more than a cigarette together when Julian would drive his ambulance into the motor court. Cochrane himself had been with the medical unit since the previous September; he had seen so much of the suffering and cruelty of war that he had come to live on a kind of "grey plateau" of feeling. Julian's exuberance and vitality and unflagging spirit brightened his life immeasurably. Rees, of course, saw him much more often, and he was similarly impressed. It seemed to him that Julian was having the most wonderful time of his life. He was extremely serious about his work—down to the smallest details—determined to do whatever had to be done with a maximum of efficiency and a minimum of fuss. At the same time, he was enjoying it all: observing, making suggestions, explaining to Rees his idea of "Socialism from above" as they drove across the battlefields, and being unmistakably "upper class" in his manner—although Julian never tried to be anything other than what he was, and he felt no need or desire to pretend to be a member of the proletariat. He had come to Spain hoping to be in the midst of a major battle, and it turned out that he was in a better position as an ambulance driver to see what was going on than if he had been a soldier in the British Battalion. He wanted to learn about modern warfare; quite logically, in the sense that the totalitarians, Hitler, Mussolini, and Stalin, were using Spain as a laboratory, he was there to observe their experiments. Political subtleties and allegiances did not overly concern him. He had never thought of Spain as the incarnation of an ideal, nor had he been swept up in a rush of ideological enthusiasm; hence, he did not run the risk of being disillusioned—only of being killed.

Early in the morning of July 15, his ambulance was smashed by a bomb—he himself was unhurt. Since no other car was available for him to drive, he volunteered to go up to the front as a stretcher-bearer. It was the morning of the last fierce fighting around Boadilla. Julian was put in charge of a squad of thirty stretcher-bearers and went out to work in that very dangerous sector. Towards nightfall there was a lull in the battle. The Republican forces fell back. For the next three days there was comparative calm at the front, and the stretcher-bearers took advantage of it to bring in the dead. On the morning of the 18th, the Medical Aid unit received a new lorry: this was to be Julian's. The group was stationed in an olive orchard near the village of Valdemorillo. As

Julian and Richard Rees in Spain, July 1937. From *Julian Bell: Essays, Poems, and Letters*, Edited by Quentin Bell. The Hogarth Press, 1938.

the lull in the battle still continued, he proposed driving out to fill in the shell holes in the road, which would make the evacuation of the wounded quicker and less painful. It was a practical, concerned, and enterprising thing to have done; it showed that Julian was thinking about the situation and working to improve the efficiency of his unit. They then moved to another olive orchard near Villanueva de la Cañada. There, as Rees wrote:

> Julian was indefatigable at organizing, cleaning up, helping the cook, and scrounging for fruit and fuel and tools and rope in the ruined shops and gardens of Villanueva. As the rest of us became more and more jaded from the long night drives without lights, his energy seemed to flare up with an unearthly incandescence. In the intervals of his activity he lounged about reading Racine. "It will sound well when I come to write my memoirs," he said. With his pith sun-helmet and khaki shorts he looked eccentric, rather like a bulky Hollywood empire-builder, and it amused him to pretend that his real interest in the war was to frustrate the Germans and Italians and secure Spain as a British colony. . . . He fretted a good deal at not being in a fighting unit.[26]

On July 18, 1937, the first anniversary of the outbreak of the civil war, the battle of Brunete was renewed with a violent counterattack by the Nationalists. Their planes roared overhead, dropping bombs indiscriminately. One hit the grove where Julian was. Dr. Gerald Shirlaw, a British doctor who had chosen to be attached to the International Brigade rather than the Medical Aid group, remembered:

> There was a lorry in front of us and we jumped underneath it simultaneously and then for protection we put our arms round each other. The bombardment was pretty close and I got smothered with sand underneath the lorry. It was only gradually that I realised that Julian Bell was lying perfectly still. I got up and turned him around, and saw that a fragment of shell had cut a large hole in his chest wall, exposing his heart. We tried to give him sedatives straight away, and some dressings, and get him into an ambulance. It was clear to me that his presence beside me had saved me from injury. It was a sad day for the few of us who were there, and realised what had happened.[27]

The initial account in the *Times* on July 22 stated that Julian had been hit while driving his ambulance, and so we reported his death in the earlier book, not having seen this account. The ambiguity of the language, too, may well have led us to the wrong conclusion: the obituary stated that he was killed while driving an ambulance; the bulletin of the Spanish Medical Aid Committee stated that he had been machine-gunned from a rebel plane while driving his ambulance. Driving an ambulance was indeed his activity while in Spain, yet the phrase does not necessarily mean that he was actually driving when hit. But so, erroneously, we interpreted it. However it happened, Julian was mortally wounded.

Later in the day, a wounded ambulance driver so covered with dirt as to be unrecognizable was brought into the 35th Division Hospital at Escorial on a stretcher. Cochrane was in charge of the receiving room; he ordered the man to be cleaned. It was only after this was done that he recognized Julian. As soon as he examined him, he realized that Julian had been mortally wounded: a shell fragment had penetrated deep into his chest. All that could be done was done. Several doctors attempted to deal with the terrible situation: he received a blood transfusion and his wound was dressed. But the doctors attending him knew that the situation was hopeless.

Dr. Reginald Saxton has given the fullest account of Julian's death in a recorded interview housed in the collection of the Imperial War Museum. Saxton was particularly involved in working out ways to make blood transfusions work.

> A portion of a bomb came horizontally along the ground and hit him in the chest. It must have hit him through a wallet so quite probably it went right through his lungs taking a bit of the wallet and its contents right into his lungs. He was in pretty poor shape when I saw him and I transfused him and prepared him for the surgeon—a man whom I still know, a Spaniard, a Catalonian, a very nice guy by the name of Broggi. Well, we hadn't got facilities that are necessary for operating on a lung. . . . So all Broggi could do was really to clean off the surface. . . . Julian Bell was on the operating table and had his wound cleaned up as far as was reasonably possible and simply patched over. It was impossible to clean the wound properly owing to lack of facilities for doing lung surgery and he died within twelve hours or so. There was really nothing more we could do for him. Some of the remains of his property in fact I brought home with me . . . and gave to his relatives.[28]

He was also attended by Dr. Philip D'Arcy Hart, a member of the London Committee of Spanish Medical Aid who happened to be there on a visit. A chest specialist, he inserted a system of drainage into the lung and removed the shell splinter from his chest. Julian was still conscious, still cheerful. He murmured to Cochrane, "Well, I always wanted a mistress and a chance to go to the war, and now I've had both." Then he lapsed into French, reciting indistinctly lines of what Cochrane thought might be Baudelaire. Soon after, he fell into a coma from which he never awakened.

He was one of the estimated 35,000 men—25,000 on the side of the Republic, 10,000 on the side of the Nationalists—whose lives were lost in the battle of Brunete. The battle itself continued for another six days and ended in a stalemate. It is supposed to have provided interesting material for military theorists on the use of the tank. The Nationalists regained much of the territory taken by the Republican forces, including the town of Brunete; the attempt to gain control of the road into Madrid from the west, which had been the principal object of the offensive, had failed. The Republic had won a strip of territory five kilometers deep along fifteen kilometers of front. And together with a few other villages it continued to hold the ruins of Villanueva de la Cañada.

Julian was taken to the mortuary of the hospital in the Escorial, and there Richard Rees, who by chance was in the hospital, ill, saw him, covered except for his head and shoulders. There was no sign of any wound. He looked "very pale and clean, almost marble-like. Very calm and peaceful almost as if he had fallen asleep when very cold." [29]

Needless to say, Vanessa was totally devastated by the news; her worst fears were realized. She remarked to Virginia, "I shall be cheerful, but I shall never be happy again."[30] Virginia was anxious to protect her as much as possible and over the next weeks spent almost every day with her, not even writing in her diary from July 20 until August 6. To Leonard Julian's death was a terrible waste, and it reminded him of the death of Rupert Brooke and his brother in the First World War. Virginia's first preserved letter about Julian's death was to Vita on July 21: "I wired to you because Julian was killed yesterday in Spain. Nessa likes to have me so I'm round there more of the time. It is very terrible. You will understand." They were in London, but Virginia felt that Vanessa should go to Charleston as soon as possible. Vanessa wrote to Vita on August 16: "I cannot ever say how Virginia has helped me. Perhaps some day, not now, you will be able to tell her it's true."[31] It reminds one of the night that the sisters Margaret and Helen spent at Howards End. Personal relations had paid at the end.

On July 26 Virginia wrote to William Robson, a teacher at the London School of Economics and cofounder with Leonard of the *Political Quarterly*. "He was a great joy to us; her children were like my own. But it had become necessary for him to go; and there is a kind of grandeur in that which somehow now and then consoles one. Only—to see what she [Vanessa] has to suffer makes one doubt if anything in the world is worth it." And as she wrote to Vita, probably on the same day: "Lord, why do these things happen? I'm not clear enough in the head to feel anything but varieties of dull anger and despair. He had every sort of gift—above everything vitality and enjoyment. Why must he be set on going to Spain?—But it was useless to argue. And his feelings were so mixed. I mean, interest in war, and conviction, and a longing to be in the thick of things. He was the first of Nessa babies, and I cant describe how close and real and always alive our relation was." She made further remarks about him in a letter to Judith Stephen, her niece, on December 2, 1939, and to Vanessa on his birthday in 1940. "Julian was a magnificent creature. What would he have done, I wonder? He has such an immense store of life in him, and God knows why he went and threw it away. But I daresay it was better in Spain than in Flanders." "What a pleasure your brats are to me—I long more and more for Julian, whose birthday it is today, and cant help just saying so, though I know you know it. My own darling I do think of you and him so much."[32]

Richard Rees remains a significant witness and further testified about Julian's death. He wrote in his published account:

> Towards the evening I heard rumours of exceptional air activity and that a bomb had fallen on a car park and killed thirty drivers. I also felt that Nurse Ramshaw was keeping something from me. When I got the truth it was that Julian had been wounded at our Villanueva park. He was unconscious in the ward above and could not last out the night. My day's rest in the hospital began to look very ugly. I was up early next morning and saw Julian's body in the mortuary. I was accustomed to the sight of death, but this time it was impossible to believe. His terrific vitality and his jokes, his enthusiasm and his brains, simply *could* not have ceased and left his body so calm and unchanged. His wound was in the lung, and his face remained as if in sleep with a tranquil and slightly disdainful expression. I came away stunned. I wanted to berate the doctors and nurses for having let it happen. . . . I spent an afternoon alone under a tree; and missing Julian's company and thinking of the waste of his life, I suddenly burst into childish sobs of which I had not thought I was capable. I learnt from this the cleansing effect of an almost disinterested sorrow. I had not known Julian long enough to feel remorse for past betrayals or failures of friendship, and I was not sufficiently involved with him for his death to create any personal problems for me. It neither complicated nor simplified my own difficulties. His company had been a pure gift. Its withdrawal was a pure loss.[33]

Rees also wrote to Portia Holman on August 31, 1937, and she must have given the letter to Vanessa, as it is with her papers, alongside the letter Rees wrote to her:

> I have tried many times to write to Vanessa Bell about Julian but it is so difficult as I don't know her personally. I feel I ought to, as no one saw nearly so much of Julian out here as I did, and no one can have appreciated him more. The thing I would try to convey to her is that, however much may have lost by his death, I really do believe that he himself had reached a kind of pinnacle of living that he could hardly have surpassed however long he might have lived and however

great his achievements might have been. It was really remarkable how *perfectly* adapted he was to all the difficulties and strangeness, and how assured and serene and brilliantly competent he was. From the point of view of his friends, from the point of view of social usefulness, one may deplore his death as a wasteful loss. But from the point of view of Julian as an individual, as a unique manifestation of the human essence, I do believe he reached a perfection in life and action which is *very* seldom achieved in the longest of normal lives. You know how very difficult it is to write letters out here. I despair of ever saying all that I feel about Julian.

Rees did go to see Vanessa, as she wrote to Eddie in an undated letter in the fall. And then he wrote to Vanessa herself on October 4:

> For me personally Julian's death was by far the most terrible thing that happened in all the six months I was in Spain. He was so brilliantly vivid in my eyes that I can hardly realize it even now. But, looked at from *his* point of view (I mean from any point of view except that of personal loss), I do believe that he *was* "luckier than most of us." He was struck down suddenly and without time for morbid regrets or disillusionment, when he was at the very height and perfect fulfillment of his most unusual combination of gifts. I know that all the people who saw much of him at El Goloso and in Escorial would say the same. In saying that he was spared the pain of disillusionment I don't at all mean that he struck me as being naïve about the War. On the contrary, he seems to me to have a very mature and sane view—far more so than most of his contemporary intellectuals. But I do think that if he had lived longer he would scarcely have found any more situations in which his various gifts could all have been so perfectly expressed together; his humane and altruistic and profound and sensitive intellectualism, and his spirited and adventurous side, and his unusual practical abilities. His energy seemed inexhaustible. My own recollection of those weeks is mainly of constant and increasing and unendurable fatigue. But even in that condition of self-centred lethargy I remember distinctly that I noted how Julian's energy seemed to be renewed and increased to meet increasing demands. . . . There was something almost unnatural and super-normal about Julian's brilliance at that time—as though he were approaching a pinnacle of existence which few people ever reach and which, once reached, cannot be surpassed however many more years a person may live. But alas it still remains true that the rest of the world is the poorer for the lack of his concrete achievements that would have been his if he had lived. But to be more personal, you can imagine what a job it was during those weeks to have odd moments when one could talk about painting and Cambridge and literature. We had the New Statesman with

Virginia Woolf's essay on "Gibbon at Sheffield Place" and one of the last things Julian said to me was how much he enjoyed it. But his stoicism also enabled him to enjoy or seem to enjoy, quite other things. He persuaded me to help him to collect figs for our camp in a ruined garden where it was dangerous to be and which stank of explosives and carcasses; and as he threw the figs into the basket I held he remarked that the scene was "Baudelariean." I sometimes wonder if even you and his own family can realise what a joy his company was during those weeks.[34]

On December 9, 1937, Vanessa wrote to Sue:

I have now had a long talk with the doctor [Cochrane] who was with Julian when he died—he is nice & intelligent & he knew Julian at Cambridge & was very fond of him. . . . He made it quite clear that everything was done that could possibly be done—that he was as well or better looked after than he could have been in England & that he had no pain & did not know of his own danger. . . . I cannot myself face many people & only see a few of those I know best.[35]

Vanessa also busied herself with the making of the memorial book about him, gathering letters that might be included and deciding what else might be in the book. It would consist of a foreword from Keynes; his official short obituary from the King's College Annual Report, published on November 13, 1937; a memoir by David Garnett and his own notes for a memoir; an essay on him by Charles Mauron; selected letters and poems; as well as the three long essays on Roger Fry; on poetry, with a reply by C. Day Lewis; and on war and peace, with a reply by Forster.

Virginia had conversations as well with Cochrane and Hart about Julian's death, the first recorded in her diary on August 25.

Nothing new: only that he was conscious when they got him to hospital, & anxious to explain that the road was dangerous: then anxious to get on with the operation. He became unconscious, talked in French about military things apparently . . . [ellipsis in text] & died 4 hours later. Why do I set this down? It belongs to what is unreal now. What is left that is real? . . . Much forced talk with Hart & Cochran[e]. Cochran[e] a nice simple but rather tense (naturally) practical reddish young man giving his account stiffly kindly; Hart a Jew; neurotic, rather shiny nosed, intellectual, with a professional surgeons manner. A conflict of sympathy, tragedy, professional manner, & social politeness. Queer rather.

And then on October 13 she saw Dr. Hart again.

The facts now seem to be: Julian was brought in with a very bad wound—looked deathly white. He asked H. What chance have I? Hart told him 80 percent recover. A lie. He had only the chance of a miracle. He was very brave. After the operation, H. saw him comfortably in bed. Went back two hours later & found him dozing half conscious. And so he remained till he died that night. . . . Hart was tormented by some sense of guilt. That they had not kept J. from the front. They would have done so later. This was his first experience. Things are now much more dangerous. The Ambulance is almost as dangerous as the Army.[36]

Vanessa wrote to Keynes a quite fascinating letter triggered by what he had written in the Annual Report.

I felt that Julian had really changed more during the last 2 or 3 years than you may have realized. You saw so much of him & Quentin when they were growing up that it is probably difficult to forget them as they were then. At any rate I find that I have to be perpetually readjusting my attitude to my children & I can only do it because I'm seeing them all the time—when Julian came back from China I was aware that he had become a grown up & completely independent human being. . . . I dare say too that in many ways he would always have remained a child. . . . Still I feel he had grown up—he could make up his own mind & knew what he wanted to do & why. That is the only thing is the least reconciles me to his death. I feel he wanted, not to die—no one could have wanted that—but to run the risk he knew he would run for reasons he judged worth while. Though I cannot agree I can at moments feel that one must give in to what he chose for both himself & me. When he was on his way to China—and I think that going so far away on a real job of his own was what first made him grow up—he thought he might while there get involved in risks & be killed. He wrote to me then—I was only given the letter after his death—and explained what it was in himself which made him feel he must take certain risks even at the cost of what he knew it would mean to me. I do not think he could really know—but what he said has been a great help to me. It was an expression of his own attitude to life & death & of something very fundamental in himself which would never have changed & which I seem to myself to share. During those last three months in England, in spite of terribly difficult differences of opinion, we had an intimacy with each other greater in a way than any I have ever had with anyone else—& which could only have been possible with another grown up human being.[37]

Julian's two letters to her had been written on his way to China on September 26, 1935, before, in her opinion, he had quite made it to being "grown up."

He had entrusted them to Eddie to give to her in case of his death. In them he stated his desire to be a man of action. He also wrote, "I've had an extremely happy life, and done most of the things I wanted to do. . . . The other thing, which doesn't really need to be said between us, is that I love you more than anyone else, and always have done so, ever since I can remember."[38] She had written to him in China that year, on November 1, about how important he was to her. "Oh, Julian, I can never express what happiness you've given me in my life. I often wonder how such luck has fallen my way. Just having children seemed such incredible delight, but that they should care for me as you make me feel you do, is something beyond all dreaming of—or even wanting."[39]

His death was a terrible waste, although it is far from clear what shape his life might ultimately have taken. He might well have been one of those multitalented English men of letters. He might well have returned to poetry. He was a fine poet, and he was, as it happens, the sole Bloomsbury poet; in that area he did genuinely make his mark. He also had hopes of making a political impact and learning about war. This was the major reason for his going to Spain, as well as his desire to be a man of action and to face danger. He was both a Bell and a Stephen. Vanessa painfully captured the waste of his death, and the intensity of her relations with him, in a letter she wrote on August 27, 1937, to one of his girlfriends.

> I think there is one thing I want desperately to say to any one who will listen—if only I could—and that is simply that I am quite sure, reasonably and definitely sure, that the loss of people like Julian *is* a waste. It is not my own pain that makes me say it. In fact I am not really to be pitied—not on the whole. I never doubt for an instant that I am immensely the richer for all the feelings I have had and shall ever have about Julian. But I am old enough to know a little what he might have done and been if he had lived. I know that his life would have given infinite good and possibilities to the world which are now lost.[40]

Julian was very much part of Bloomsbury; he much enjoyed it and enjoyed benefiting from his association with it. He was part of its second generation. It is not possible to say in what ways he would have made a contribution, and how considerable it would have been. He was at the heart of Bloomsbury as one of Vanessa's children. Julian was named in memory of his uncle, Julian Thoby Stephen, always known as Thoby, who had also died young, at the age of twenty-six. Julian frequently reminded Virginia of Thoby, and now there was the terrible coincidence of their early deaths. Thoby had been the linchpin for Bloomsbury, principally through his close friends at Trinity, Cambridge—Lytton Strachey, Clive Bell, and Leonard Woolf. It was virtually in reaction to Thoby's death from typhoid in 1906 that Clive almost immediately married Vanessa and that some years later Leonard married Virginia. It was through Thoby that the young Cambridge men came to the new home of the Stephen children in Bloomsbury. Virginia conceived her first novel, *The Voyage Out,* at the time of Julian's birth. The years between the wars were the golden years of Bloomsbury when the most prominent members of that group of friends came into their eminence. It might be said that the ending of that richest period was marked by the death of Julian, deeply shadowing the lives of Vanessa and Virginia.

The blow was most devastating for Vanessa. Clive played a far less important part in Julian's life, and there is little evidence of how he reacted to his son's death. Virginia wrote about the relationship between mother and son in her diaries, on August 17:

> Julian had some queer power over her [Vanessa]—the lover as well as the son. He told her he could never love another woman as he had loved her. He was like her; yet had a vigour, a roughness, & then as a child, how much she cared for him. I mean, he needed comfort & sympathy more I think than the others, was less adapted to get on in the world—had a kind of clumsiness, of Cambridge awkwardness, together with his natural gaiety. And thats all lost for the sake of 10 minutes in an ambulance. I often argue with him on my walks; abuse his selfishness in going but mostly feel floored by the complete muddle & waste. Cant share the heroic raptures of the Medical Aid, who are holding a meeting next week to commemorate the six who were killed. "Gave their lives" as they call it.[41]

There was a memorial gathering at King's, which Vanessa felt she couldn't face, as well as one at Wuhan University, attended by about two hundred, held, perhaps deliberatively, on November 11.

It was after his death that Virginia took Julian most seriously. She noted in her diary on August 11 that he "stalks beside me, in many different shapes." There had always been a certain tension in their literary relations. He was Vanessa's beloved child, but to a degree he was also her rival as a writer. On September 8, in a letter to Vanessa, she praised his letter to Forster, feeling that it was the best thing he had written, although she still had issues with him in terms of style and content. "At last I think I understand his point of view, which I didn't—about being a soldier I mean. I dont agree: from my point of view; however that may be my fault. . . . Lord how I wish I could argue the whole thing with Julian."[42]

Julian wished to be a hard man of action, almost an antithesis of the values of Bloomsbury. The book she was writing at the time, *Three Guineas*, was to a degree an argument with Julian. As Julian was fighting fascism in his way, through action, so too was she in her new work, though in a far less militaristic fashion, taking issue with his values. She had been working on the book since 1931, but his death coincided with her greatest concentration on the question of how to prevent war. She felt a need to discuss it with him, as if he were almost with her as she was finishing it. At the end of his life, indeed beyond it, Julian found himself involved in a discussion with Virginia. He was part of Bloomsbury, but he was also apart from it. His life, though short, had been full, dramatic, and in many ways, happy.

NOTES

CHAPTER 1: A BLOOMSBURY CHILDHOOD

1. Nigel Nicolson and Joanne Trautmann, eds., *The Letters of Virginia Woolf, Volume I: 1888–1912* (New York, 1975), p. 327.
2. Paul Levy, ed., *The Letters of Lytton Strachey* (London, 1995), pp. 140–41.
3. Nicolson and Trautmann, *Letters of Virginia Woolf*, I, pp. 328–29.
4. R. F. Harrod, *The Life of John Maynard Keynes* (London, 1952), pp. 116–17.
5. Clive Bell, *Old Friends* (London, 1956), p. 28.
6. E. M. Forster, *Goldsworthy Lowes Dickinson* (London, 1947), p. 110.
7. J. M. Keynes, *Two Memoirs* (London, 1949), p. 82.
8. G. E. Moore, *Principia Ethica* (Cambridge, 1903), pp. vii, 188–89.
9. Keynes, *Two Memoirs*, pp. 82–83.
10. E. M. Forster, *Howards End* (London, 1910), p. 124.
11. Desmond MacCarthy, *Memories* (London, 1953), pp. 174–75.
12. Harrod, Life of John Maynard Keynes, p. 114.
13. Virginia Woolf, "Memoir of Julian Bell (1937)," in *The Platform of Time*, S. P. Rosenbaum, ed. (London, 2008), p. 21.
14. Ibid., p. 22.
15. "Memoir Notes by Vanessa Bell (July 1937)," ibid., pp. 39–41.
16. Nicolson and Trautmann, *Letters of Virginia Woolf*, I, p. 331.
17. Anne Olivier Bell, ed., *The Diary of Virginia Woolf, Volume I: 1915–1919* (London, 1977), Sept. 13, 1919, p. 298.

18. Quentin Bell, ed., *Julian Bell: Essays, Poems and Letters* (London, 1938), pp. 10–12.
19. Ibid., p. 3.
20. Frances Spalding, *Roger Fry: Art and Life* (Berkeley, 1980), p. 46.
21. Woolf, "Memoir of Julian Bell," pp. 29–30.
22. David Garnett, *The Flowers of the Forest* (London, 1955), p. 1.
23. Michael Holroyd, *Lytton Strachey* (New York, 1994), p. 349. A few days before, he had made his statement to an advisory committee on conscription:

> I have a conscientious objection to assisting, by any deliberate action of mine, in carrying on the war. The objection is not based on religious belief, but upon moral considerations, at which I have arrived after long and painful thought. I do not wish to assert the extremely general proposition that I should never, in any circumstances, be justified in taking part in any conceivable war, to dogmatize so absolutely upon a point so abstract would appear to me unreasonable. At the same time, my feeling is directed not simply against the present war: I am convinced that the whole system by which it is sought to settle international disputes by force is profoundly evil; and that, so far as I am concerned, I should be doing wrong to take part in it. (p. 347)

24. Garnett, *Flowers of the Forest*, p. 112.
25. Bell, *Julian Bell*, pp. 11–13, for these quotations.
26. Garnett, *Flowers of the Forest*, p. 124.
27. Nigel Nicolson and Joanne Trautmann, eds., *The Letters of Virginia Woolf, Volume II: 1912–1922* (New York, 1976), May 14, 1916, p. 95.
28. Ibid., Sept. 24, 1916, pp. 118–19.
29. Garnett, *Flowers of the Forest*, p. 161.
30. The issues are in the British Library, London, Add. Mss. 83316–83332.
31. Virginia had anticipated that she might become a figure of fun to her nephew. In a letter to Clive in 1909 she imagines him saying: "I have an Aunt who copulates in a tree, and thinks herself with child by a grasshopper—charming isn't it? She dresses in green, and my mother sends her nuts from the Stores" (Nicolson and Trautmann, *Letters of Virginia Woolf*, I, Dec. 26 [1909], p. 417).
32. Sir Percy Bates was head of the Cunard shipping line, which would commission eight years later from Vanessa and Duncan a decoration scheme for the *Queen Mary* that was subsequently cancelled. Charleston is now a place visited by the public, who are told about it in accurate ways. But as the spoof suggests, it is also a place of pilgrimage for those who are interested in the Bloomsbury group. It belongs to the Charleston Trust, having been bought from Lord Gage, and is the center of much activity. I first saw it, and the issues of *The Bulletin* still then owned by the family, in

the early 1960s. We were taken there by Quentin and Olivier Bell and had the great pleasure of meeting Grace Higgens, still in residence.

33. "Memoir Notes by Vanessa Bell (July 1937)," pp. 41–42.
34. Bell, *Julian Bell*, p. 13.
35. G. F. Jones to Peter Stansky, Oct. 9, 1963.
36. To Vanessa, Jan. 3 [1922] Charleston Papers [hereafter cited as CHA] 1/55/3/2, Archive Centre, King's College, Cambridge. Hereafter cited as KCL.
37. Bell, *Julian Bell*, pp. 13–14.
38. To Vanessa, n.d. [Spring 1923?] CHA 1/55/3/3 KCL.
39. J. Duncan Wood to Peter Stansky, Nov. 18, 1963.
40. S. W. Brown, *Leighton Park* (Reading, 1952), p. 182.
41. Vanessa Bell, "Lecture Given at Leighton Park School," in *Sketches in Pen and Ink* (London, 1997), pp. 149–65.
42. To Vanessa, Mar. 26 [1922] CHA 1/55/3/3 KCL.
43. To Vanessa, n.d. [?1924] CHA 1/55/3/4 KCL.
44. Clipping, n.d. CHA 1/55/3/6 KCL.
45. T. C. Elliott to authors, Oct. 13, 1963. Julian wrote of the staff, and Elliott in particular, in his memoir: "The staff were second-rate and tiresome, one or two tried to be kind and one, Elliott, was genuinely kind and sympathetic, and saved me from some bullying. I have always felt grateful to him" (Memoir, p. 15, part unpublished CHA 3/3 KCL).
46. John Lehmann, *The Whispering Gallery* (London, 1955), p. 141.
47. Anne Olivier Bell, ed., *The Diary of Virginia Woolf, Volume II: 1920–1924* (London, 1978), p. 308.
48. Woolf, "Memoir of Julian Bell (1937)," pp. 31–32.
49. Bell, *Julian Bell*, pp. 18–19, for this and previous quotations.
50. To Vanessa, July 1 [1927] CHA 1/55/3/8 KCL.
51. Lehmann, *Whispering Gallery*, p. 142.
52. Bell, *Julian Bell*, p. 8.

CHAPTER 2: A YOUNG APOSTLE

1. To Vanessa, Oct. 13, 14 [1927] CHA 1/55/3/9 KCL.
2. Bell, *Julian Bell*, pp. 19–20.
3. Anne Olivier Bell, ed., *The Diary of Virginia Woolf, Volume III: 1925–1930* (New York, 1980), p. 200.
4. Kate Perry to author, e-mail, Jan. 9, 2008. Virginia was intensely aware of the claustrophobia and smugness of Cambridge. Some years later, on August 30, 1936, when Julian was in China, she wrote to him vividly about the University, perhaps to console him for not having received a fellowship: "Oh Richard [Braithwaite, the

King's philosopher] was all Cambridge in one pill. How I love it and respect it and deride it! The antics, the mannerisms, the sublime remoteness from pop guns and alarms. Why should there be another war for forty years he said. I see no signs of it in the Great Court [of Trinity]" (to Julian, Aug. 30, 1936 JHB [Julian Heward Bell] 1/686/8 KCL; published in Joanne Trautmann Banks, "Some New Woolf Letters," *Modern Fiction Studies* 30 [Summer 1984], p. 193).

5. To Vanessa, Oct. 14 [1927] CHA 1/55/3/9 KCL.

6. To Julian, Oct. 16, 1927. Nigel Nicolson and Joanne Trautmann, eds., *The Letters of Virginia Woolf, Volume III: 1923–1928* (London, 1977), p. 431.

7. To Vanessa, Nov. 22 [1927] CHA 1/55/3/9 KCL.

8. To Julian, Nov. 22, 1927. Nicolson and Trautmann, *Letters of Virginia Woolf, III*, pp. 439–40.

9. JHB 1/1/ KCL.

10. To Vanessa, May 16 [1928] CHA 1/55/3/9 KCL.

11. *Cambridge Review* issues of Nov. 4, 1927; Jan. 20, May 18, Nov. 2, Nov. 16, 1928; Apr. 30, 1929.

12. Bell, *Diary of Virginia Woolf, III*, June 20, 1928, p. 187; May 12, 1929, p. 224.

13. Bell, *Julian Bell*, pp. 20–21.

14. W. C. Lubenow, *The Cambridge Apostles, 1820–1914* (Cambridge, 1998), p. 31.

15. To Julian, June 28, 1936 CHA 1/686/1 KCL. Published in Joanne Trautmann Banks, "Some New Woolf Letters," *Modern Fiction Studies* 30 (Summer 1984), p. 189.

16. JHB 3/2 KCL. "Notes for a Memoir." Respecting the semisecret nature of the Apostles, these lines were not published in *Julian Bell*.

17. To Virginia, n.d., item 11 Monk's House Papers, Sussex University Library.

18. Ray Monk, *Ludwig Wittgenstein* (New York, 1990), p. 255.

19. Miranda Carter, *Anthony Blunt: His Lives* (London, 2001), p. 68.

20. Bell, *Diary of Virginia Woolf, III*, June 16, 1929, p. 235.

21. Nigel Nicolson and Joanne Trautmann, eds., *The Letters of Virginia Woolf, Volume VI: 1936–1941* (New York, 1980), Mar. 11, 1936, p. 20.

22. Material about the meetings from the Apostles Minutes books, Vols. XVI and XVII KCL.

23. Carter, *Anthony Blunt*, p. 62.

24. Lehmann, *Whispering Gallery*, pp. 146–47.

25. See Hugh Carey, *Mansfield Forbes and His Cambridge* (Cambridge, 1984).

26. TW, "Nothing Venture," *Granta* 7 (June 1929), p. 531, quoted in Kate Price, "Finite but Unbounded: Experiment Magazine Cambridge, England, 1928–31," *Jacket* 20 (Dec. 2002).

27. To Michael Redgrave, Apr. 22 [?1930] JHB 2/44 KCL.

28. Quoted from draft letter to his mother, Aug. 11, 1938, Empson Papers,

Houghton Library, Harvard, in John Haffenden, *William Empson I* (Oxford, 2005), p. 613.

29. Julian Bell, "A Brief View of Poetic Obscurity," *The Venture* 6 (June 1930), pp. 283–88.
30. To Quentin, Feb. 6 [1930] JHB 2/5/2 KCL.
31. Lehmann, *Whispering Gallery*, p. 144.
32. To Vanessa, Apr. 24 [1929] CHA 1/55/8/10 KCL.
33. *Cambridge Review*, Mar. 7, 1930, pp. 321–22.
34. *Cambridge Review*, Nov. 7, 1930, p. 98.
35. To Quentin, Jan. 21, 1928, JHB 2/5/1/10 KCL.
36. Bell, *Julian Bell*, p. 5.
37. To Quentin, Mar. 7 [1929] JHB 2/5/2 KCL.
38. Quentin Bell, *Elders and Betters* (London, 1995), p. 203.
39. To Vanessa, postmark May 14, 1935 CHA 1/55/3/15 KCL.
40. *Cambridge Review*, May 3, 1929, p. 417.
41. To Vanessa, Apr. 24, 1929 CHA 1/55/3/10 KCL.
42. To Julian, May 6 [1929] Private Collection.
43. To Vanessa, May 14 [1929] CHA 1/55/3/10 KCL.
44. To Julian, May 17 [1929] Private Collection.
45. "Memoir Notes by Vanessa Bell (July 1937)," S. P. Rosenbaum, ed., *The Platform of Time* (London, 2008), p. 43.
46. Carter, *Anthony Blunt*, p. 71.
47. Ibid.
48. To Julian, n.d. CHA 1/377/4,11,14 KCL.
49. To Vanessa, Oct. 22 [1929] CHA 1/55/3/10 KCL.
50. To Julian, Oct. 30 [1929] Private Collection.
51. Woolf, "Memoir of Julian Bell," p. 32.
52. To Vanessa, May 22 [?1938] JHB 11/3 KCL.
53. Woolf, "Memoir of Julian Bell," p. 32; "Memoir Notes by Vanessa Bell (July 1937)," p. 41.
54. To Eddie [?Dec. 1930] JHB 82/8 2/32A KCL.
55. To Harold Barger, Dec. [1929] JHB 2/3A KCL.
56. To Vanessa, postmark Jan. 22, 1930 CHA 1/55/3/11 KCL.
57. To Julian, Jan. 23 [1930] Private Collection.
58. To Julian [?Feb. 1930] JHB 2/5 KCL.
59. To Julian, Mar. 27 [1930] Private Collection.
60. To Julian, Feb. 7 [1930] Private Collection.
61. See Tim Cribb, *Bloomsbury and British Theatre* (Cambridge, 2007), p. 69.
62. To Julian, Nov. 11 [1930] Private Collection.

63. To Helen [?Mar. 1, 1930] JHB 2/50 and X/3/1–2 KCL. All of Julian's letters to Helen are in this designation unless indicated otherwise. They were dated by Helen.

64. To Helen, MISC 81/6 KCL.

65. To Helen, MISC 81/6 KCL.

66. To Julian, Dec. 1 [1930] Private Collection.

67. To Clive, n.d. CHA 1/55/1 KCL.

68. To Quentin, May 14, 1930. Nigel Nicolson and Joanne Trautmann, eds., *The Letters of Virginia Woolf, Volume IV* (New York, 1979), p. 170.

69. To Julian [early summer 1930?] JHB 2/5/2 KCL.

70. To Eddie, Sept. 6 [1930] JHB 82/8 2/38A KCL.

71. To Vanessa [Sept. 1930] CHA 1/55/3/29 KCL.

72. To Harold Barger, Jan. 4 [?1931] JHB 2/3A KCL.

73. To Eddie, postmark, Oct. 11, 1930 JHB 82/8 2/38A KCL.

74. To Eddie, Dec. 22, 1930 JHB 82/8 2/38A KCL.

75. To Quentin, Jan. 1 [1931] JHB 2/5/2 KCL.

76. To Quentin, Feb. 8 [1931] 2/5/2 JHB KCL. Clive's brother and his brother-in-law both claimed to be the last man to leave Gallipoli.

77. Lehmann, *Whispering Gallery*, p. 143.

78. To Lehmann, June 23, 1929 Berg Collection, New York Public Library. Hereafter cited as Berg NYPL.

79. Ibid.

80. To Howarth, Feb. 22, 1976. John Constable, ed., *Selected Letters of I. A. Richards, CH* (Oxford, 1990), pp. 197–98. The Howarth book was published in 1978. For an excellent discussion of Wittgenstein, Bloomsbury, and Cambridge see S. P. Rosenbaum, "Wittgenstein in Bloomsbury," in *Aspects of Bloomsbury* (London, 1998).

81. *Cambridge Review*, Mar. 1, 1929, pp. 317–18.

82. To Lehmann, Sept. 15 [1930] Berg NYPL; in part quoted in Lehmann, *Whispering Gallery*, p. 146.

83. To Lehmann, Oct. 2 [1930] Berg NYPL.

84. JHB X/3/2 KCL.

85. To Lehmann [Autumn 1930] Berg NYPL.

86. To Julian, Nov. 4, 1930 Berg NYPL.

87. To Lehmann, Nov. 5 [1930] Berg NYPL.

88. To Lehmann, July 6, 1929 Berg NYPL.

89. Lehmann, *Whispering Gallery*, p. 165. When *A Garden Revisited* was published in 1931, Lehmann sent Julian an inscribed copy with a reference to some lines meant for him. They presage the turn to politics that was taking place for both of them at this time: "Alas, my dear, experience shows / we're not as wise as you supposed, / I, should this state of things increase / may go to war to keep the peace."

John Lehmann, *A Garden Revisited* (London, 1931) [Stanford University Library, Julian's copy].

90. To Julian, Dec. 30, 1930 Berg NYPL.
91. Lehmann, *Whispering Gallery*, pp. 172–73.
92. To Julian, Dec. 24, 1931 Berg NYPL.
93. Lehmann, *Whispering Gallery*, p. 174.
94. To Julian, Dec. 24, 1931 Berg NYPL.
95. Lehmann, *Whispering Gallery*, p. 182.
96. Michael Roberts, *New Signatures* (London, 1932), pp. 7–15.
97. Stephen Spender, *World Within World* (New York, 1951), p. 126.
98. Roberts, *New Signatures*, p. 17.
99. Forster, *Goldsworthy Lowes Dickinson*, pp. 207–8.
100. Anne Olivier Bell, ed., *The Diary of Virginia Woolf, Volume IV: 1931–1935* (London, 1982), Dec. 28, 1935, p. 360.
101. To Lehmann [?Spring 1931] Berg NYPL.

CHAPTER 3: SEARCHING

1. Charles Mauron in conversation, Aug. 11, 1961.
2. To Julian, July 11, 1930 JHB 2/27 KCL.
3. *New Statesman and Nation*, Dec. 8, 1934, p. 870.
4. To Lehmann, Aug. 9, 1930 Berg NYPL.
5. The Heretics was a discussion group at Cambridge, founded in 1909, designed to sponsor both public talks and private discussions. C. K. Ogden was a cofounder and its dominant figure. In some ways, it was a much more public version of the Apostles. It believed in questioning authority, particularly religious authority, stating as one of its "Laws" that "membership of the society shall imply the rejection of all appeal to Authority in the discussion of religious questions." Also, "the object of the society be to promote discussion problems of religion, philosophy and art." Quoted in Sargant Florence, "The Cambridge Heretics (1909–1932)," in *The Humanist Outlook*, A. J. Ayer, ed. (London, 1968), p. 228. Jane Harrison was the first speaker to the group, and it maintained a special interest in the relationship of anthropology and religion. It was unusual in having a mixed membership. Virginia Woolf gave a version of "Mr. Bennett and Mrs. Brown" to it on May 18, 1924. Florence mentions some talks Julian was likely to have heard: Wittgenstein on ethics in October 1929, and Prince Mirsky on dialectical materialism in November 1931 (ibid., p. 231). He may have suggested that his uncle Adrian speak on Freudian analysis in February 1930 (p. 236). Empson was a dominant figure in the group until he was sent down from Cambridge.
6. Bell, *Julian Bell*, p. 7.
7. To Lehmann [Oct. 6, 1931] Berg NYPL.

8. *New Statesman and Nation*, Dec. 8, 1934, p. 872.

9. To Lehmann [?Spring 1931] Berg NYPL.

10. All letters between Julian and Lettice Ramsey were in a private collection and hence will not be further footnoted. Shortly, however, they will be available at the King's College Archives Centre, Cambridge.

11. For correspondence about the publication see JHB 2/35 KCL, as well as John Dreyfus, *A History of the Nonesuch Press* (London, 1981).

12. To Julian, Mar. 21, 1932 JHB 2/27 KCL.

13. To Julian, Mar. 20 [1932] mssHM 57530 Huntington Library, San Marino, California.

14. To Lehmann [?July 21, 1932] Berg NYPL.

15. To Lehmann, Apr. 8, 1930 Berg NYPL.

16. See Frederick Grubb, "In but Not Of: A Study of Julian Bell," *Critical Quarterly* (Summer 1960), pp. 120–26.

17. JHB 1/4/3 KCL. This file contains both the dissertation and the readings.

18. To Lettice, postmark Sept. 23, 1933.

19. To Quentin [?Spring 1931] JHB 2/5/2/11 KCL.

20. To Vanessa, postmark May 2, 1931 CHA 1/55/3/12 KCL.

21. To Julian, May 5, 1931 JHB 1/4 KCL.

22. To Julian, May 5, 11, 18, 1931 Private Collection.

23. To Quentin, Apr. 24, 1931; to Vanessa, May 23 [1931]. *Letters IV*, 320, 335.

24. To Vanessa, May 16 [1931] MISC 82/12 KCL.

25. To Vanessa, May 15, 1931 CHA 1/437 KCL.

26. To Vanessa, postmark May 18, 1931 CHA 1/55/3/12 KCL.

27. To Vanessa, postmark June 2, 1931 CHA 1/55/3/12 KCL.

28. I am grateful to Gregory Lucas for his research in and translation of Charles and Marie Mauron's letters to Julian.

29. To Eddie, June 22[?] [1931] MISC 82/11 JHB 2/38A KCL.

30. To Julian, Oct. 31, 1931 Berg NYPL.

31. To F. L. Lucas, Feb. 8, 1936 JHB 2/29 KCL.

32. Lettice Ramsey, autobiographical note, Frank Ramsey Papers 3/1 KCL.

33. All quotations from Frank Ramsey papers 14/11/14 KCL.

34. The letters between Julian and Lettice were in a private collection but are now at the King's Archive Centre.

35. To Vanessa, postmark, Apr. 19, 1932 CHA 1/55/3 KCL.

36. English Association, *Poems of Today Third Series* (London, 1938), p. 18.

37. See JHB 2/20 KCL.

38. Harrod, *Life of John Maynard Keynes* pp. 450–51.

39. To Quentin [late 1933] 2/5/3/5 JHB KCL. Quentin was very sorry to miss the confrontation about the film, writing to Julian from Switzerland: "Its maddening to be here like a bloody pupa while you organize seditious exhibitions and run over undergraduates for the greater glory of peace and mankind. Do write more about it, I only had a newspaper cutting from Nessa, what weapons did you use? Next time theres a tendentious film couldn't you take a room above the cinema and throw down dead kittens and whatnot on the patriots?" (to Julian [late 1933] JHB 2/5 KCL).

40. Julian Bell and H. V. Kemp, on behalf of the Cambridge Student Anti-War Council, *The Student Anti-War Movement* (Cambridge, n.d.).

41. *New Statesman and Nation*, Dec. 9, 1933, pp. 731–32.

42. Lehmann, *Whispering Gallery*, pp. 276–77.

43. J. Cornford, "The Class Front of Modern Art," *Student Vanguard* no. 2, Dec. 3 [1933], pp. 9–10; "Julian Bell and John Cornford on Art," *Student Vanguard* no. 2, Jan. 4 [1934], pp. 16–20. They are reprinted in Jonathan Galassi, ed., *Understand the Weapon, Understand the Wound: Selected Writings of John Cornford* (Manchester, 1976), pp. 46–56.

44. To Harold Barger, Dec. 20 [?1929] JHB 1/1 KCL.

45. To Quentin [?late 1933] JHB 2/5/3 KCL.

46. *Cambridge Review*, May 19, 1933, p. 411.

47. To Julian, n.d. JHB 1/14 KCL. Translated by Gregory Lucas.

48. See JHB 11/7 KCL, and Frances Spalding, *Roger Fry: Art and Life* (Berkeley, 1980), p. 272. See Stéphane Mallarmé, *Poems*, translated by Roger Fry, with Commentary by Charles Mauron (London, 1936).

49. To Lehmann [?1934] Berg NYPL.

50. To Quentin [?early 1934] JHB 2/5/3/7 KCL.

51. To Vanessa, postmarks May 1, 14, 1935 CHA 1/55/3/15 KCL.

52. To Vanessa, Oct. 13, 16 [1935] CHA 1/55/3/15 KCL.

53. To Julian, Sept. 23, 1933 CHA 1/229 KCL.

54. Quoted as relevant to Julian Bell in Noel Annan, *Leslie Stephen* (London, 1951), p. 40.

55. Julian Bell, ed., *We Did Not Fight* (London, 1935), pp. xi–xix.

56. To Lehmann [?Jan. 1934] Berg NYPL.

57. To Quentin [?Feb. 1935] JHB 2/5/4 KCL.

58. *New Statesman and Nation*, Feb. 18, 1935, p. 224.

59. To Lehmann, Berg NYPL; part quoted Lehmann, *Whispering Gallery*, p. 277.

60. To Quentin, JHB 2/5/3 KCL.

61. *New Statesman and Nation*, May 11, 1935, p. 682.

CHAPTER 4: CHINA

1. To Quentin, 1934 JHB 2/5/3 KCL.
2. JHB 3/1 KCL.
3. Letters from Julian in this period are in chronological order in Bell, *Julian Bell*, pp. 28–187, unless otherwise indicated. The originals are in CHA 1/55/3/15–19 KCL. Minor errors in the printed versions have been corrected.
4. To Julian, Aug. 30, Sept. 3, 1935 TGA 9311/80 Tate Archives, London.
5. To Vanessa, July 27, 1937 CHA 1/462 KCL.
6. To Eddie, Mar. 20 [1936] JHB 82/9 1/38A KCL.
7. To Vanessa, Oct. 31 [1935] CHA 1/55/3/15 KCL.
8. To Eddie, Nov. 1 [1935] JHB 82/9 1/38A KCL.
9. To Virginia, item 7 Monk's House Papers, Sussex University Library.
10. To Vanessa, Nov. 22, 1935 CHA 1/55/3/15 KCL.
11. To Vanessa, Dec. 6, 1935 CHA 1/55/3/15 KCL.
12. Courtesy of Sarah Knights, David Garnett Papers, Hilton Hall, Huntington, n.d.
13. To Sue, Sept. 16 [?1938], Dec. 5, 1939, Feb. 4, 1940, Aug. 25, 1940 Berg NYPL.
14. To Vanessa, n.d. CHA 1/55/3/15 KCL.
15. To Vanessa, Dec. 25, 1935 CHA 1/55/3/15 KCL.
16. Regina Marler, ed., *Selected Letters of Vanessa Bell* (New York, 1993), p. 407.
17. To Eddie, Dec. 27 [1935] JHB 82/9 2/38A KCL.
18. To Eddie, n.d. JHB 82/9 2/38A KCL.
19. Harold Acton, *Memoirs of an Aesthete* (London, 1948), p. 378.
20. To Julian, June 7, 1936 CHA 1/3 KCL.
21. To Eddie, Feb. 3 [1936] JHB 82/9 2/38A KCL.
22. To Eddie, Mar. 11, Apr. 6 [1936] JHB 82/9 2/38A KCL.
23. To Frances Partridge, Partridge Papers, FCP 6/1/13 KCL. Transcription courtesy of Patricia MacGuire.
24. To Vanessa, Aug. 28, 1936.
25. To Vanessa, Sept. 16, 1936.
26. "On Roger Fry," in Bell, *Julian Bell*, pp. 258–305; "The Proletariat and Poetry," pp. 306–27; "War and Peace," pp. 335–90.
27. To Julian, May 21, June 28, 1936 CHA 1/686/1, 4 KCL. Not in the collected letters but published in Joanne Trautmann Banks, "New Woolf Letters," *Modern Fiction Studies* 30 (Summer 1984), pp. 184–91.
28. To Julian, Oct. 10, 1936 TGA/9311/63 Tate Archives, London.
29. To Vanessa, Sept. 20, 1936.

30. Woolf, "Memoir of Julian Bell," p. 22.
31. To Eddie, Apr. 13 [1936] JHB 82/9 2/38A KCL.
32. To Sue [?Sept. 1937] Berg NYPL.
33. To Eddie, Sept. 25 [1936] JHB 82/9 2/38A KCL.
34. Lehmann, *Whispering Gallery*, pp. 273–74.
35. To Eddie, Oct. 21 [1936] JHB 82/9 2/38A KCL.
36. To Julian, Oct. 10, 1936 9311/63 Tate Archives, London. Published in Marler, *Selected Letters of Vanessa Bell*, p. 423.
37. To Vanessa, Oct. 20, 1936.
38. To Eddie, Oct. 21, 1936 JHB 82/9 2/38A KCL.
39. To Vanessa, Oct. 31/Nov. 1, 1936 [one letter with two dates].
40. To Eddie, Nov. 1 [1936] JHB 82/9 2/38A KCL.
41. To Quentin, Nov. 1. 1936 JHB 100/2/5/4/17 KCL.
42. To Vanessa, Nov. 8, 1936.
43. To Eddie, Nov. 27 [1936] JHB 82/9 2/38A KCL.
44. To Vanessa, Nov. 29, 1936.
45. To Eddie, Dec. 5 [1936], Jan. 4 [1937] JHB 82/9 2/38A KCL.
46. To Vanessa, Apr. 3, 1936.
47. To Eddie, Nov. 12 [1936] JHB 82/9 2/38A KCL.
48. To Sue, n.d. Berg NYPL.
49. To Sue, Dec. 24 [1936] Berg NYPL.
50. To Vanessa, Oct. 31/Nov. 1, 1936 [one letter with two dates].
51. Marler, Selected Letters of Vanessa Bell, p. 428.
52. To Vanessa, Dec. 12, 1936.
53. To Eddie, Jan. 4 [1937] JHB 82/9 2/38A KCL.
54. To Julian, Dec. 3, 1936 CHA 1/519 KCL. Published in Constable, *Selected Letters of I. A. Richards,* pp. 98–99.
55. To Eddie, Dec. 16 [1936], Jan. 4 [1937] JHB 82/9 2/38A KCL.
56. To Vanessa, Nov. 29, 1936.
57. To Vanessa, Dec. 24, 1936.
58. To Virginia, n.d. item 6 Monk's House Papers, University of Sussex.
59. To Julian, Dec. 5, 1936 JHA 1/4/6/100 KCL. Virginia's piece in December in the *Daily Worker* had discussed that art had to deal with politics at the present moment but that nevertheless the crude antifascist pamphlet needed to be avoided.
60. To Virginia, Dec. 5, 1936 item 10 Monk's House Papers, University of Sussex.
61. To Julian, dated Mar. 16, 1937, but this is an error as the letter was written while Julian was still in Wuhan. CHA 1/124 KCL.
62. To Sue, Feb. 7, 1937, Berg NYPL.

63. To Eddie, Dec. 5, 14 [1936], Jan. 9 [1937] JHB 82/9 2/38A KCL.
64. To Vanessa, July 24, 1937, CHA 1/322 KCL.
65. E. M. Forster, "Notes for a Reply," in Bell, *Julian Bell*, pp. 391–92.
66. To Sue, Feb. 26 [1937] Berg NYPL.
67. To Julian, Mar. 7 [1937] TGA/9311/80 Tate Archives, London.
68. To Vanessa, Mar. 12, 1937 CHA 1/55/3/18 KCL.
69. To Vanessa, n.d. CHA 1/415 KCL. Translation by Gregory Lucas.
70. To Sue, Mar. 9 [1937] Berg NYPL.

CHAPTER 5: SPAIN

1. To Julian, Feb. 2, 1937 JHB 2/23 KCL.
2. To Sue, Mar. 17 [1937] Berg NYPL.
3. To Vanessa, Apr. 23, 27, 1937.
4. *New Statesman and Nation*, June 3, 1937, pp. 934–35.
5. To Quentin, May 3, 1937.
6. Michael Straight to authors, Dec. 3, 1962. See also Michael Straight, *After Long Silence* (New York, 1983), p. 108.
7. To Vanessa, postmark Mar. 3, 1937.
8. David Garnett, *The Familiar Faces* (London, 1962), p. 166; Bell, *Julian Bell*, p. 8.
9. Clive Bell, *War Mongers* (London, 1938), pp. 2–12.
10. To Sue, Mar. 23, 30 [1937] Berg NYPL.
11. Jim Fyrth, *The Signal Was Spain* (London, 1986), p. 6.
12. Anne Olivier Bell, ed., *The Diary of Virginia Woolf, Volume V: 1936–1941* (London, 1984), pp. 68, 86.
13. To Sue, May 5 [1937] Berg NYPL.
14. Woolf, "Memoir of Julian Bell," pp. 28–29, 20, for this and previous quotations.
15. Richard Rees, *A Theory of My Time* (London, 1963), p. 95. These were Viscount Churchill, a distant cousin of Winston's; and Cristina, Lady Hastings, the daughter-in-law of the Earl of Huntington.
16. To Eddie, Sept. 9 [1937] JHB/1/4/17 KCL.
17. Hugh Thomas, *The Spanish Civil War* (London, 1961), pp. 430–34.
18. Thomas, *Spanish Civil War*, p. 460.
19. Richard Baxell, *British Volunteers in the Spanish Civil War* (London, 2004), p. 85.
20. Malcolm Cowley, "To Madrid III," *New Republic*, Sept. 15, 1937, p. 154; Jef Last, *The Spanish Tragedy* (London, 1939), p. 199.
21. Thomas, *Spanish Civil War*, p. 462.

22. Rees, *Theory of My Time*, p. 100.
23. Bell, *Julian Bell*, p. 364.
24. Rees, *Theory of My Time*, p. 101.
25. Thomas, *Spanish Civil War*, p. 462.
26. C. 1823 [Richard Rees], "Close-Up of a Battle," Part I, Supplement to *Adelphi* 16 (Feb. 1940), pp. 11–12.
27. Dr. Gerald Shirlaw, "The Spanish Civil War" Manuscript 1/5/00 Imperial War Museum, London.
28. Dr. Reginald Saxton, Sound Archive, 13778/2, recorded 1983, 8735/09, transcribed Nov. 1984, pp. 52–53, Imperial War Museum, London.
29. The account here of Julian's death is based on: Keynes, "Foreword," in Bell, *Julian Bell*, pp. v–vi; Dr. Leonard Crome, "Letter," *New Statesman and Nation*, Aug. 28, 1937, p. 308; conversations with Professor A. C. Cochrane and Dr. Philip D'Arcy Hart; Jim Fyrth, *The Signal Was Spain* (London, 1986), pp. 91–94; and Rees, *Theory of My Time*, as well as a conversation with and a letter from him, from which the quotation is taken.
30. Bell, Diary of Virginia Woolf, V, p. 106.
31. Marler, Selected Letters of Vanessa Bell, p. 439.
32. Nicolson and Trautmann, *Letters of Virginia Woolf*, VI, pp. 146, 150–51, 372, 381.
33. [Rees], "Close-Up of a Battle," pp. 18–19.
34. To Portia Holman, Aug. 31, 1937; to Vanessa Bell, Oct. 4, 1937 CHA 1/510 KCL.
35. To Sue, Dec. 9 [1937] Berg NYPL.
36. Bell, *Diary of Virginia Woolf*, V, pp. 109, 113–14.
37. To Keynes, Keynes Papers PP 45/27/7/9 KCL.
38. Bell, *Julian Bell*, p. 195.
39. Marler, Selected Letters of Vanessa Bell, p. 401.
40. Ibid., p. 440, recipient unidentified.
41. Bell, Diary of Virginia Woolf, V, p. 108.
42. Nicolson and Trautmann, *Letters of Virginia Woolf*, VI, pp. 167–68.

ACKNOWLEDGMENTS AND CREDITS

As with the earlier book, many have displayed great kindness and helpfulness in the present work. My greatest debt is to William Abrahams, my collaborator and companion from 1961 until his death in 1998. Quentin and Olivier Bell's help was crucial for the earlier book as was that of Julian's sister, Angelica Garnett. My greatest present debt is to Olivier for her extraordinary kindnesses, and I am grateful again to Angelica Bell as well. The passage of time has meant that I have also benefited from the interest, support, and help of the next generation, particularly Julian Bell, his uncle's namesake, as well as his sister Virginia. I should state again gratitude to those who provided help for the earlier book: Sir Harold Acton, Lord Annan, A. C. Cochrane, Richard Eberhart, T. C. Elliott, E. M. Forster, David Garnett, Grace Higgins, John Lehmann, Charles Mauron, Christopher and Helen Morris, Sir Edward Playfair, Lettice Ramsey, Sir Richard Rees, G.W.H. Rylands, Ivor and Dorothea Richards, J. Duncan Wood, and Leonard Woolf. In the writing of this book I have incurred new and considerable debts of gratitude, particularly to the wise readers of the manuscript, Peter Mandler, S. P. Rosenbaum, and Patricia Laurence. Others too have been very helpful, such as Richard Baxell, William Beekman, Susan Bell, Ying Chinnery, Peter Davis, Wendy

Hitchmough, Glen Leonard, Isabelle Lescent-Giles, and the splendid staff of the History Department at Stanford University. For help in moving forward the publication of the book, I am indebted to Thomas Wallace and Christopher Sinclair-Stevenson. I've much enjoyed working with that excellent editor Norris Pope of Stanford University Press as well as his extremely helpful colleagues, John Feneron and Sarah Crane Newman, and particularly the meticulous and encouraging copyediting of Jeff Wyneken. An immense thanks for the endless guidance and help of Patricia MacGuire of the Archive Centre at King's College, Cambridge, where the vast majority of Bloomsbury manuscript material is to be found. I also enjoyed the hospitality of my old College, King's, during my visits, and particularly of its librarian, Peter Jones.

I am grateful to the holders of copyright who have given permission for quotations. (I have followed the convention of not requesting permission for less than four hundred words and apologize to copyright owners who may feel I have erred in that course of action. I also apologize to the copyright holders of some of the illustrations, whom I have not been able to locate.) For longer quotations I am grateful to the Society of Authors, as the literary representative of the estate of Virginia Woolf, for permission to quote from her writings other than her published diaries and letters. For the latter, I am grateful for permission to quote from the diaries and letters of Virginia Woolf, in the United Kingdom from the Random House Group Ltd. as published by the Hogarth Press, and in the United States from as follows: Nigel Nicolson and Joanne Trautmann, eds., *The Letters of Virginia Woolf,* Vols. I (1975), II (1978), III (1977), IV (1978), V (1979), and VI (1980); Anne Olivier Bell, ed., *The Diary of Virginia Woolf,* Vols. I (1979), II (1978), III (1980), IV (1982), and V (1984). I also acknowledge the following: letters of Vanessa Bell, © The Estate of Vanessa Bell, courtesy of Henrietta Garnett; extracts from unpublished works of Julian Bell, © 2011 The Estate of Julian Bell, as well as for permission to quote his previously published works; extracts from unpublished works of Quentin Bell, © 2011 The Estate of Quentin Bell; and the Society of Authors as the literary representative of the Julian Bell and Quentin Bell estates. I extend special thanks to Jeremy Crow, its head of Literary Estates, for his gracious aid in administering the permissions for Virginia Woolf and Vanessa, Julian, and Quentin Bell. I am also grateful to Lettice Ramsey's daughter, Jane Burch, for her permission to quote her mother's letters and reproduce her photographs. And I am grateful to Ann Morris Dizikes for permission to print two photographs taken by her mother. The images *Virginia and Julian at Blean* and *Lettice Ramsey*, © 2010 Tate, London, are courtesy of Tate Britain. Quotations from John Lehmann, *The Whispering Gallery* (Longmans, Green), are by permission of the publisher.

I apologize if the citation of quotations appears to be erratic. This became a problem because in the earlier study, most often for concerns of privacy, some quotations were not cited. Now, forty-five years on, it is no longer possible to recover the sources for some of those quotations. Also, quotations from letters that are or were in private collections are generally cited only the first time they are quoted. Some quotations are not cited when their source is clear from the text.

Peter Stansky

Stanford, California
December 2010

INDEX

Ackerley, J. R., 63
Acton, Harold, 206–207
Adelphi, 110, 268
À la recherche du temps perdu, Marcel Proust, 193
Ancient Melodies, Ling Shuhua Chen, 202
Angell, Sir Norman, 169
Anrep, Helen, 83
Apostles, the, 6–7, 11, 49, 53, 72–73, 119, 121, 123, 126, 131, 142, 154, 193, 257
Art, Clive Bell, 13
Artists International Association, 245
Asheham, Sussex, 23
Aspects of the Novel, E. M. Forster, 56
Auden, W. H., 59, 60, 108, 110, 113, 124, 196, 207, 259

Baishi, Qi, 206
Barger, Harold, 90, 162,
"Le Bateau," Rimbaud, 164
Beerbohm, Max, 1

Bell, Angelica, 4, 5, 15, 20, 24, 26, 30, 82, 102, 104, 133, 203, 204, 225, 255, 265
Bell, Clive, 2, 4, 5, 6, 8, 11, 13, 14, 20–21, 25, 30, 38, 65, 82, 128, 131, 193, 261, 265, 286; belonged to two different communities in Cambridge, 11; did not fit into the Stephen inheritance, 14; influence of G. E. Moore on, 8; influence on Julian, 25; marries Vanessa Stephen, 2, 6; pacifism of, 21
Bell, Julian Heward: affair with Anthony Blunt, 70–6; affair with Antoinette Pirie, 165–167, 177–178; affair with Helen Souter (Morris), 77–78, 80–81, 83–84, 87–92, 99, 100, 101, 133–140; affair with Lettice Ramsey, 140–149; affair with Ling Shuhua (Sue) Chen, 198, 200–205, 207–211, 215–216, 225, 230, 231, 232–237, 242, 246, 253; becoming a poet, 41; birth of, 2, 15; as concealed romantic, 132; connection between his poetry and the paintings

of Vanessa Bell and Duncan Grant, 44, 46, 96; connection to mother, 15–18, 20, 131, 185, 258; active in Cambridge Union, 51–52; courses and authors taught at Wuhan University, 192–193; death of, 278–279, 285–286; decides to go to Spain to fight fascism, 241–245, 247–248, 250–253; deprecates Goldsworthy Lowes Dickinson, 195; early poems, 42, 45–46, 49, 59, 63; elected to, and participation in, Apostles, 53–54, 55, 58; exposure to Bloomsbury rationality as child, 18; happiness in Spain, 267; importance of Bloomsbury Group on, 2–3; intention of his essays, 257; interest in war and military strategy, 23, 263, 285; at King's College, Cambridge, 45–46, 49, 50, 117; at Leighton Park School, 32–38, 51, 71; love of Charleston, 24, 27; love of countryside, 19–20; love of discussing his affairs, 197; love of home, 38; life of mind versus life of action, 19; at Owen's School, 30–32; parodying Virginia Woolf's writing style, 38; passion for astronomy and history, 18; as poet, 92–109; on political career, 256; political involvements, 149–162, 168–169; political pragmatism of, 228, 224, 235; psychological reasons for going to China, 185–186; rationalist view of life and art, 66; rebels against Bloomsbury, 64–65, 259; as reviewer, 68–69; resolves to go to Spain, 255–256, 258, 262–264; responsibilities as professor at Wuhan University, 189–190, 192, 193; romantic life, 69–70, 79, 80; social life at Wuhan, 197–198; "theory of conduct" in his affairs, 235; tries for Fellowship at King's College, 117, 120, 122, 125, 128, 130, 184; views on Chinese youth, 194–195; views on religion, 18; views on scholarly endeavors, 118–119; views on Spanish Civil War, 226–230, 235, 237, 238, 239; views on war, pacifism, and war resistance, 169–170, 171–175, 212, 261; at Wissett, 22; writes dissertation on philosophy and ethics, 123, 126, 127; writes dissertation on Pope, 119–120, 121–122; year in Paris as youth, 39–41
—Works of: "Arms and the Man," 112–115, 153, 176; "Autobiography," 12, 178–180; "Ballad of the Dancing Shadows," 66–67; "A Brief View of Poetic Obscurity," 65; "Brumaire," 95; "Cambridge Revisited," 164–165; "Epistle to Braithwaite," 176; "An Epistle on the Subject of the Ethical and Aesthetic Beliefs of Herr Ludwig Wittgenstein," 64, 94; "Frimaire," 95; "The Goldfinch in the Orchard," 96; *The Good and All That (Some general considerations on ethical theory, with their application to aesthetics and politics)*, 124–127, 192, 221; "The Hedge," 67, 95; *Julian Bell: Essays, Poems and Letters*, 216; "The Labour Party and War," 170; "Marsh Birds Pass over London," 97–99; "Military Considerations of Socialist Policy," 172; "The Moths," 63, 95, 96; "To My Bourgeois Friends in the Communist Party," 160, 169; "To My Friends in the Communist Party," 169; "Nivôse," 63; "Nonsense," 151; "Notes for a Memoir," 69; "Post Coitum," 213–214, 226; "The Progress of Poetry," 68; "The Proletariat and Poetry: An Open Letter to C. Day Lewis," 217, 223, 224; "Song from a Masque," 102; "Still Life," 96, 112; "Tranquility Recollected," 112; "Vendémaire," 95; "Vienna," 173–174; "War and Peace: A Letter

to E. M. Forster," 217, 247, 248, 249, 258, 261, 274–275; *We Did Not Fight*, introduction, 169; *Winter Movement*, 88, 102, 106, 109, 112, 175, 191; "Winter Movement: A Formal Ode," 63, 67, 68; *Work for the Winter*, 176–178, 182, 206, 225
Bell, Julian (son of Quentin and Olivier Bell), 29, 218, 285
Bell, Olivier, 71, 218
Bell, Quentin, 3, 4, 5, 15, 20, 22, 24, 25, 27, 35, 70, 71, 75, 77, 82, 92, 131, 133, 136, 137, 156, 163, 165, 172, 181, 203, 218, 233, 240, 242, 251, 252, 257, 266, 270, 284; as biographer of Virginia Woolf, 3
Bell, Vanessa (neé Stephen), 2, 5, 12, 13, 20, 22, 23, 24, 25, 35, 38, 65, 73–80, 82, 84, 92, 96, 102, 122, 128, 131, 133–136, 140, 163, 178, 182, 183–184, 191, 194, 197, 200, 201, 202, 204, 205, 207, 208, 212, 217, 220, 227, 228, 230, 231, 232, 233, 235, 238, 239, 243, 244, 245, 247, 250–256, 258, 260, 262–263, 266, 268–270, 280–286; as emotional heart of Bloomsbury, 4; intensity of relationship with Julian, 20, 207, 230–231; on Julian as a baby, 15; views on Julian's affair with Anthony Blunt, 74, 75; views on Julian's affair with Helen Souter, 76–77, 133–136; tries to persuade Julian not to go to Spanish Civil War, 231, 239; writes to Ling Shuhua Chen after Julian's death, 203
Berg Collection, New York Public Library, 198
Bernal, Eileen, 165
Bernal, J. D., 165
Bernal, Martin, 165
Beves, Donald, 82
Birrell, Francis, 48
Bloomsbury Group, 2, 3, 4, 20, 21, 127
Blunden, Edmund, 103

Blunt, Anthony, 47, 54, 56, 57, 58, 62, 63, 70–76, 154, 175
Boyle, Andrew, 73
Bradbrook, Muriel, 48
Braithwaite, Richard, 54, 141, 142, 144
Bridges, Robert, 193
British Anti-War Council, 155
Broad, C. D., critiques Julian's dissertation, 128–130
Bronowski, Jacob, 61
Brooke, Rupert, 4, 68, 193, 280; described by Lytton Strachey, 4
Burgess, Guy, 54, 72, 73, 154, 156, 175
Byron, Robert, 206

Caballero, Largo, 269
Cambridge Poetry 1929, 95, 106
Cambridge Review, 66, 68, 73, 95, 11, 164
The Cambridge Spies, TV serial, 73
Cambridge Union, 49, 50–51
Cambridge University Press, 164
Carpenter, Edward, 19
Carter, Miranda, 73, 75
Chadwick, H. M., 60
Chang, Professor, 190
Charleston, Sussex, 23–24, 38, 47, 74, 82, 83, 87, 96, 100, 137, 143, 144, 149, 152, 168, 178, 185, 213, 251, 255, 259, 261, 262, 268, 280
Chatto & Windus, 95, 100, 121, 164
Chen, Ling Shuhua (Sue), 198, 200–205, 207–210, 215–216, 225, 228, 230, 231–233, 234, 235, 236–237, 242, 246, 251, 252–253, 256, 262, 265, 283
Chen, Yuan, Professor, dean of the School of Letters, Wuhan University, 189, 231, 232, 234, 236, 246
Chih-tung, Chang, 186
A Chinese Painter's Choice, Ling Shuhua Chen, 202
Civilization, Clive Bell, 13

Clapham, John, 49
Clapham Sect, 6, 7, 12, 13
The Climate of Treason, Andrew Boyle, 73
Cobden-Sanderson, T. J. 169
Cochrane, Archie, 275–276, 279, 283
Cockburn, Claud, 228
Cohen, Andrew, 54
Collins, Michael, 172, 173, 189
Communist Party, 154, 160, 182, 257
"A Communist to Others," W. H. Auden, 169
Cornford, John, 72, 77, 154, 155, 161, 162, 257, 264
Cowley, Malcolm, 272–273
Crescent Moon Society, 201
Cresset Press, 164
The Criterion, 110
Cornhill Magazine, 2, 4

Dalton, Hugh, 240, 256
Dane, Clemence, 63
Das Kapital, Karl Marx, 159
Davenport, John, 62
Day Lewis, Cecil, 59, 60, 108, 109
Delane, John, 4
Dickinson, Goldsworthy Lowes, 7, 115, 116, 193, 194–195, 228, 248
Dickinson, Violet, 15
Dictionary of National Biography, 2
Dizikes, Ann, 78
Dizikes, John, 78
Duckworth, Julia Jackson, 1, 259
Duncan Wood, J., 35
Duncan-Jones, Elsie (neé Phare), 48

Eberhart, Richard, 61, 63, 95, 108, 169
Edward VII, 10–11
Eliot, T. S., 41, 62, 64, 68–69, 105
Elliott, Sir John, 71
Elliott, T. C., 37
Empson, William, 60, 61, 63, 90, 91, 95, 108, 110, 113, 116, 169

Enlistment Act, 244
Evans, Charles, 33
Experiment, 61–3

Faber & Faber, 164
Fedden, H. Romilly, 62
Forbes, Mansfield, 60
Forster, E. M., 4, 7, 10, 12, 46, 49, 56–57, 104, 221, 223, 248, 250, 275, 286
Freud, Sigmund, 55, 193
Fry, Margery, 164, 182, 187, 217, 234
Fry, Roger, 4, 12, 13, 14, 15, 19, 20, 25, 30, 32, 38, 46, 65, 83, 118, 127, 128, 130, 137, 163, 164, 178, 193, 195, 206, 217, 218, 219, 265, 283
Fuller, General, 175
Fushimi, Marui, 186, 187

Gage, Lord, 152, 153
A Garden Revisited, John Lehmann, 106, 107
Gardiner, Margaret, 165
Garnett, David, 18–19, 22–23, 38, 43–44, 70, 78, 79, 104, 117, 119, 122, 168, 169, 176, 202, 206, 259, 261, 262, 283; on Julian as poet, 43–44
Gielgud, Sir John, 72
"Gibbon at Sheffield Place," Virginia Woolf, 283
Gide, André, 272
Gilbert, Stuart, 62
Girton College, Cambridge, 47, 48, 88
Glynde, Sussex, 152, 153
Gordon Square, Bloomsbury, 12
Grant, Duncan, 4, 12, 20, 21–2, 23, 24, 38, 65, 92, 96, 133, 252, 254–255; tries to dissuade Julian from going to Spain, 254–255
Granta, 62
Graves, Robert, 146

Hallam, Arthur, 6, 54
Harding, Gilbert, 52
Hare, William, 61
Hart, Dr. D'Arcy Philip, 279, 283
Heretics, 119
Higgins, Grace, 26
History of England from Henry VIII to the Corn Laws, Gardiner, 22
Hitler, Adolf, 153, 155, 169, 225, 276
Hogarth Letters Series, 218
Hogarth Press, 47, 106, 100, 138, 163, 164, 202, 206
Holman, Portia, 268, 281
Howards End, E. M. Forster, 10, 280
Howarth, T. E. B., 94
Hulme, T. E., 193
Hungying, Lian, 234, 247, 253
Hutchinson, Mary St. John, 25
Huxley, Aldous, 64, 105
Hyndman, Tony, 263

International Brigade, 253, 260, 261, 263, 266, 272, 278
International Writers Congress, 272
Isherwood, Christopher, 60, 196

Jackson, Innes, 234, 235, 246–247
Jackson, Laura Riding, 146
Jeffries, Richard, 63
Jeger, George, 264
Jennings, Humphrey, 61, 63
Journey to a War, W. H. Auden and Christopher Isherwood, 196
Joyce, James, 193–194
Julia, 71, 75, 76, 90

K: The Art of Love: Based on a True Story, Hong Ying, 198, 208
Kemp, Harry, 146, 157
Keynes, John Maynard, 4, 7, 8–9, 11, 12, 21, 23, 24, 27, 28, 54, 56, 57, 87, 118, 128, 138, 154, 182, 193, 258, 283, 284
Keynes, Lydia (née Lopokova), 24, 27, 29, 46, 47, 57, 76
King's College, Cambridge, 32, 45, 46, 117, 120, 121, 122, 123, 124, 128, 138, 142, 143, 193
Kléber, General, 241
Kulik, General, 269

Labour Party, 151–153, 157, 170, 171, 173, 225, 227, 228, 230, 238, 244, 245, 256, 262
Lawrence, D. H., 193–194
League of Nations, 162, 225, 228, 248
"Leave for Cape Wrath," W. H. Auden, 173
Leavis, F. R., 60, 95
Lee, Hermione, 3
Left Review, 172
Lehmann, John, 43, 58, 59, 60, 62, 64, 66, 92, 94, 99, 100, 101, 103, 106, 107, 108, 109, 118, 119, 120, 122, 138, 143, 149, 151–152, 160, 163, 173, 174, 175, 176, 184, 190, 191, 195, 222, 257, 258; on impact of Spanish Civil War upon English intellectuals of the Left, 229; on Julian's poetry, 43, 66, 99
Lehmann, Rosamond, 107
Leighton Park School, 32–38, 51, 71, 184
"Letter to the Intelligentsia," Charles Madge, 169
"Letter to a Wound," W. H. Auden, 169
"Letter to a Young Poet," Virginia Woolf, 59
"Letter to a Young Revolutionary," C. Day Lewis, 169
Letters from John Chinaman, Goldsworthy Lowes Dickinson, 195
Lewis, Wyndham, 64, 193
Liddell Hart, Captain, 175

Lily Briscoe's Chinese Eyes: Bloomsbury, Modernism and China, Patricia Laurence, 198
Limited Editions Club, 122
Lintott, Phyllis, 233, 253
The Listener, 110
Llewellyn-Davies, Richard, 54
The London Mercury, 202
London School of Economics, 161
Lowry, Malcolm, 62, 63
Lucas, F. L. (Peter), 82, 87, 138, 193
Lucas, Topsy, 76, 142

MacCarthy, Desmond, 7, 11, 12
MacCarthy, Molly, 8, 25
MacCarthy, Rachel, 25
MacDonald, Ramsay, 113, 152
Maclean, Donald, 72, 175
MacNeice, Louis, 59, 60
Macy, George, 122
Mallarmé, Stéphane, 163, 164, 182
Mansfield, Katherine, 201
Martin, Kingsley, 168, 260
Martin's Farm, Elsworth, 119, 123, 132, 143
Masefield, John, 62
Maurice, E. M. Forster, 73
Mauron, Charles, 117, 137, 163, 164, 250, 252, 253, 283
Mauron, Marie, 137, 233, 250, 252, 256, 262, 265
Maxton, James, 169
The Meaning of Meaning, I. A. Richards, 60
Meynell, Francis, 121
Midnight Society, 6
Montagu, Lord, 72
Moore, G. E., 4, 7, 8–9, 11, 54, 55, 126, 140, 193. See also *Principia Ethica*
Morrell, Ottoline, 21, 22
Morrell, Philip, 21
Morris, Christopher, 77–78, 138

Murry, John Middleton, 268
"Music and the People," Edward J. Dent, 63
Muspratt, Helen, 143
Mussolini, Benito, 225, 276

National University of Wuhan, China, 182, 186, 187, 190, 192, 286
Nineteen Eighty-Four, George Orwell, 1
Negrín, Juan, 269
New Bulletin (*The Bulletin, Charleston Bulletin*), 27–29, 191
New Country, 169, 175
New Fabian Research Bureau, 168
Newnham College, Cambridge, 47, 48
New Signatures, 124, 153, 169, 175
New Signatures Group, 109–112, 116
New Statesman and Nation, 120, 158–159, 163, 168, 172, 257, 260
New Writing, 196, 257
Nonesuch Press, 121, 164
"Notes for a Reply," E. M. Forster, 248, 250, 275

O'Flaherty, Liam, 141
The Orators, 169
Orlando, Virginia Woolf, 20, 29
Orwell, George, 1, 77, 268
Osborn, George, 194
Our Fighting Navy, film, 156
Owen's School, 30–32
Oxford Union, 154

Partridge, Frances, 214–215, 227
Peace Ballot, 169
Peace at Once, Clive Bell, 258
Peace Pledge Union, 169, 261
Peking, China, 205–206
Peking University, China, 206
Perry, Kate, 48
Philby, Kim, 72

INDEX

Pinault, 39–40, 130
Pirie, Antoinette (Tony), 140, 147, 165–166, 177, 191, 218, 231, 233
Pirie, Norman "Bill," 165
Playfair, Eddie, 46–7, 58, 71, 75–76, 88, 90–91, 130, 131, 132, 133, 136–137, 138, 163, 189, 191, 193, 196, 205, 206, 208, 209, 210, 225, 226, 228, 230, 232, 233, 234, 235, 237, 240, 242, 242, 242, 245, 268, 282, 285
Plomer, William, 108, 109
Political Quarterly, 280
Pollitt, Harry, 169
Pope, Alexander, 118, 119, 120, 121, 122, 130, 163
Popular Front, 155
Practical Criticism, I. A. Richards, 60, 193
Principia Ethica, G. E. Moore, 8–9, 55, 126
Principles of Literary Criticism, I. A. Richards and C. K. Ogden, 60
Proctor, Dennis, 54
Proust, Marcel, 193

Quiller-Couch, Arthur, 60

Raine, Kathleen, 61
Ramsey & Muspratt, 143
Ramsey, Frank, 56, 140–142, 193
Ramsey, Lettice (née Baker), 121, 124, 130, 138, 140–149, 153, 155, 159, 163, 165, 166, 167, 168, 175, 182, 185, 204, 207, 209, 215, 226, 227, 231, 233, 252, 253, 260, 263
Ramsey, Michael, 140–141
Redgrave, Michael, 62, 63, 75, 82
Rees, Sir Richard, 266, 268, 269, 270, 271, 273, 274, 275–277, 280, 281, 282
Retour de l'U.S.S.R., André Gide, 272
Robertson, A. J., 6
Roberts, Michael, 104, 105, 107, 109, 110, 111, 112

Richards, I. A., 55, 60, 61, 62, 64, 94–95, 241–242
Robson, William, 280
A Room of One's Own, Virginia Woolf, 47, 258
Russell, Bertrand, 7, 21, 169, 193
Rylands, George ("Dadie"), 47, 62, 63, 82, 123

Sackville-West, Vita, 20, 47, 48, 202, 280
Sassoon, Siegfried, 169
Saxton, Dr. Reginald, 278–279
Sheppard, Canon Dick, 169
Sheppard, John, 47, 56, 182
Shirlaw, Dr. Gerald, 278
Sidgwick, Henry, 8
Significant Form, 13
Sinclair-Loutit, Kenneth, 264
Sitwell, Edith, 120
Socialist Society, 156
Souter (Morris), Helen, 77–78, 80, 81, 82, 83, 84, 87–92, 99–100, 101, 102, 132, 133–138, 142, 144, 210, 231, 233
Spanish Civil War, 153, 215, 217, 225, 226–231, 235, 236–239, 241–243, 261
Spanish Communist Party, 269
Spanish Medical Aid, 261, 262, 264, 266, 270, 271, 273, 278
Spanish Medical Aid Committee, 278, 279
Spender, Stephen, 59, 60, 77, 105, 106, 107, 108, 109, 111, 113, 124, 260, 263
Stalin, Joseph, 276
Stephen, Adrian, 2, 5, 12, 20, 169
Stephen, Judith, 280
Stephen, Sir Leslie, 1, 7, 13, 168
Stephen, Thoby, 2, 5–6, 12, 14, 82, 285–286
Stephen, Vanessa (*see* Bell, Vanessa)
Stephen, Virginia (*see* Woolf, Virginia)
Strachey, Lytton, 2, 4, 5, 6, 7, 11, 12, 13, 14, 20, 35, 47, 54, 93, 118, 120, 136, 286
Strachey, Pernal, 47

Strachey, Oliver, 22
Strachey, Sir Richard, 5, 21
Straight, Michael, 72, 257
Student Christian Movement, 156, 157
Student Vanguard, 161
Sydney-Turner, Saxon, 6, 22
Sykes Davies, Hugh, 54, 61

Tagore, Rabindranath, 201
Tennyson, Alfred, Lord, 6, 54
Tessimond, A. S. J., 108, 109
Thatcher, Margaret, 73
"This Last Pain," William Empson, 116
This Quarter, 110
Thomas, Hugh, 269, 273
Thomas, Margaret Ellen, 48
Thornely, Thomas, 69
A Thousand Miles of Dreams: The Journey of Two Chinese Sisters, Sasha Su-Ling Welland, 198
Three Guineas, Virginia Woolf, 258, 287
T'ien Hsia Monthly, 202
Tillyard, E. M. W., 60
Tilton, Sussex, 27
The Times, 278
Times Literary Supplement, 226
Trevelyan, G. M., 54
Trevelyan, R. C., 4
Trinity College, Cambridge, 2, 12, 21, 32, 46, 56, 140, 286
Turnell, Martin, 63
Twenty Poems, Stephen Spender, 109

The Venture, 61–63, 66, 73
The Voyage Out, Virginia Woolf, 59, 286

War Mongers, Clive Bell, 261
Warner, Rex, 59, 60, 63
Waterlow, Sidney, 46
Watson, Alister, 53, 56, 63, 124
We Did Not Fight, 169

Webb, Sidney, 36
"The Widow and the Parrot," Virginia Woolf, 29
Whims and Moods, Thomas Thornely, 69
The Whispering Gallery, John Lehmann, 43
White, T. H., 61
Whitehead, Alfred North, 7
Wiskermann, Elizabeth, 90
Wittgenstein, Ludwig, 57, 140, 142
Woolf, Leonard, 2, 4, 5, 6, 10, 12, 20, 21, 23, 24, 38, 42, 47, 48, 82, 127, 168, 171, 188, 202, 212, 213, 219–220, 223, 226, 230, 238, 240, 244, 253, 255, 256, 258, 265, 280, 286
Woolf, Virginia (neé Stephen), 2, 4, 12, 13, 14, 15, 20, 23, 24, 25, 29, 38–9, 42, 44, 47, 48, 49, 53, 56, 57, 65, 79, 82, 116, 136, 187, 193, 194, 200, 201, 202, 206, 217, 218, 219, 220–221, 225, 245–246, 255, 259, 260, 262, 263, 264, 265, 280, 283, 286, 287; comments on Julian in diary, 38–9; compares Julian to Thoby Stephens, 14; could not find a satisfactory explanation for Julian's decision to go to the Spanish Civil War, 264; as emotional heart of Bloomsbury, 4, 12, 13; on Julian as a baby, 15; on Julian's affair with Helen Souter, 79, 136; marries Leonard Woolf, 2; rivalry with Julian as poet, 44, 220–221; on special place Julian had in her mind and heart, 218–219
"Work in Progress," James Joyce, 62
Workers' Party of Marxist Unification, 267
World Within World, Stephen Spender, 111–112
Wright, Basil, 61, 63
Wuhan, China, 186, 189, 190, 191, 202, 206, 209, 227

Yeh, C. C., 195–196, 211